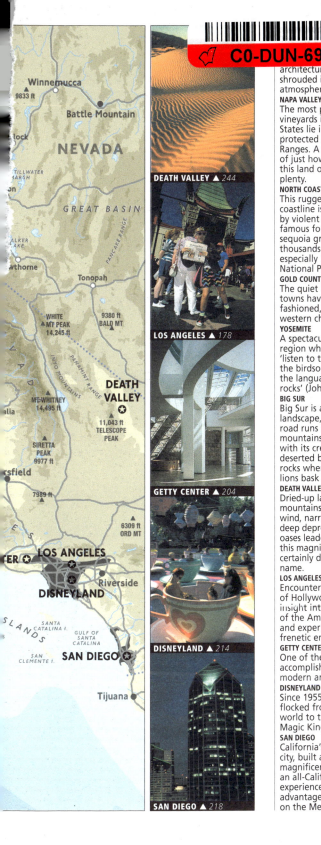

NEVADA

Winnemucca
9833 ft

Battle Mountain

lock

TILLWATER
MARSH

on

GREAT BASIN

ALKER
LAKE

wthorne

Tonopah

WHITE
MT PEAK
14,245 ft

9380 ft
BALD MT

MT WHITNEY
14,495 ft

**DEATH
VALLEY**

SIRETTA
PEAK
9977 ft

11,043 ft
TELESCOPE
PEAK

alia

sfield

7989 ft

6309 ft
ORD MT

LOS ANGELES

ER

Riverside

DISNEYLAND

SANTA
CATALINA I.

GULF OF
SANTA
CATALINA

SAN
CLEMENTE I.

SAN DIEGO

Tijuana

DEATH VALLEY ▲ 244

LOS ANGELES ▲ *178*

GETTY CENTER ▲ 204

DISNEYLAND ▲ 214

SAN DIEGO ▲ 218

architecture, is often
shrouded in an
atmospheric drifting fog.

NAPA VALLEY
The most prestigious
vineyards in the United
States lie in a valley
protected by the Coast
Ranges. A fine example
of just how good it is in
this land of wine and
plenty.

NORTH COAST
This ruggedly beautiful
coastline is often swept
by violent storms. It is
famous for its giant
sequoia groves with trees
thousands of years old,
especially in Redwood
National Park.

GOLD COUNTRY
The quiet little Gold Rush
towns have an old
fashioned, typically
western charm.

YOSEMITE
A spectacular mountain
region where you can
'listen to the waterfalls,
the birdsong and learn
the language of the
rocks' (John Muir).

BIG SUR
Big Sur is an unspoiled
landscape, where the
road runs between the
mountains and the shore
with its creeks and
deserted beaches, and
rocks where seals and sea
lions bask in the sun.

DEATH VALLEY
Dried-up lakes, dunes and
mountains shaped by the
wind, narrow canyons,
deep depressions and
oases leaden with heat –
this magnificent valley
certainly deserves its
name.

LOS ANGELES
Encounter the legend
of Hollywood, gain an
insight into the mysteries
of the American dream
and experience its
frenetic energy.

GETTY CENTER
One of the most
accomplished works of
modern architecture.

DISNEYLAND
Since 1955, people have
flocked from all over the
world to the famous
Magic Kingdom.

SAN DIEGO
California's second largest
city, built around a
magnificent bay, offers
an all-Californian
experience. It also has the
advantage of being right
on the Mexican border.

CALIFORNIA

KNOPF GUIDES

● Encyclopedia section

■ **NATURE** Geomorphology and the San Andreas fault, biogeography and the Californian climate (the flora and fauna of the region's habitats are covered in the itineraries).

HISTORY The history of California, from the arrival of the first inhabitants to modern days, with key dates appearing in a timeline alongside the text.

ARTS AND TRADITIONS Cultural diversity, the Californian way of life, the performing arts and their industries (music, cinema), food, and their continuing role in contemporary life.

ARCHITECTURE The architectural heritage, from the Hispanic period to modern times, focusing on style and topology; a look at rural and urban buildings, as well as major civil, religious and military monuments.

AS SEEN BY PAINTERS A thematic selection of paintings by different artists and schools from California and around the world, from the 19th century to today.

AS SEEN BY WRITERS An anthology of texts, taken from works of writers from California and around the world, arranged thematically.

▲ Itineraries

Each itinerary begins with a map of the area to be explored.

✪ **NOT TO BE MISSED** These sites should be seen at all cost. They are highlighted in gray in the margins.

★ **EDITOR'S CHOICE** Sites singled out by the editor for special attention.

INSETS On richly illustrated double pages, these insets turn the spotlight on subjects deserving more in-depth treatment.

◆ Practical information

All the travel information you will need before you go and when you get there.

USEFUL ADDRESSES A selection of hotels, restaurants, cafés, etc.

PLACES TO VISIT A handy table of addresses and opening times.

APPENDICES Bibliography, list of illustrations and index.

MAP SECTION Maps of areas covered by the guide, preceded by an index; these maps are marked out with letters and figures, making it easy for the reader to pinpoint a site.

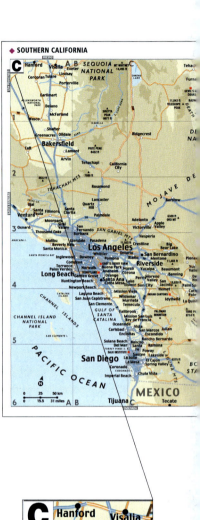

◆ SOUTHERN CALIFORNIA

Each map in the map section is designated by a letter. In the itineraries, all the sites of interest are given a grid reference (for example: ◆ **C** B2).

The mini-map pinpoints the itinerary within the wider area covered by the guide.

The itinerary map shows the main sites.

● ■ ▲ ◆ The above symbols within the text provides cross-references to a place or a theme discussed elsewhere in the guide.

▲ SACRAMENTO AND THE GOLD COUNTRY

1. Sacramento ▲ 156
2. The southern Gold Country ▲ 158
3. The northern Gold Country ▲ 160
4. Lake Tahoe ▲ 162

JOHANN A SUTTER
In 1839, the Swiss-born immigrant Johann Sutter (1803–80) was granted land concession of several hundred thousand acres. He named it Nueva Helvetia (New Switzerland) and built Sutter's Fort, which served as a staging post for the first immigrants. He could not have imagined the catastrophe that would befall him one January morning in 1848. The tragedy of the Swiss general, ruined by an event that made California's fortune, was described by the Swiss writer Blaise Cendrars in *L'Or* (Gold).

THE BIG FOUR AND THE RAILROAD ADVENTURE
Collis Huntington, Mark Hopkins, Leland Stanford and Charles Crocker, all from Sacramento, became famous when they financed the construction of the Transcontinental Railroad ▲ 26. They stopped at nothing, not even the Rocky Mountains, the misappropriation of funds and the exploitation of Chinese laborers during the laying of the 1765 miles of track. The railroad made a fortune for the Big Four ▲ 122.

SACRAMENTO ◆ A D6, CAPITAL OF CALIFORNIA

The history of Sacramento is inseparable from that of Johann Sutter, who settled there in 1839. All that remains of his reign as a prosperous landowner is the building known as Sutter's Fort, his main residence. For a long time several towns fought to have the honor of becoming the capital of the new state of California, each claiming economic supremacy during the turbulent period of the Gold Rush. Sacramento was finally chosen in preference to Auburn, Sonora and Nevada City, since it seemed better organized and less dominated by the violent law of the West which held sway in the mining towns.
STATE CAPITOL. Part of the building has been converted into a state history museum. The Capitol is open to the public and a public gallery offers an opportunity to see the Californian Parliament in session.
CROCKER ART MUSEUM ★. The museum, situated behind the Capitol, on 2nd and O Streets, was named after its generous founder, Judge Edward Bryant Crocker, brother of Charles Crocker, the railroad magnate. He acquired this beautiful building in 1870 to house the rich collection of paintings (especially German Romantics) brought back from a lengthy trip to Europe. The collection was enlarged by commissions placed with such artists as Charles Nahl, to provide heroic illustrations of the greatest hours of the Gold Rush.

156

'In the days of old, in the days of gold, How oftentimes I repine,
For the days of old when we dug up the gold,
In the days of '49.'
Old Put's Golden Songster

CALIFORNIA STATE RAILROAD MUSEUM. This vast museum, to the north and only a few minutes' walk from the Crocker Art Museum, houses what all Western fans really ought to go and see: the famous locomotives, complete with 'cowcatcher' grilles, that conquered the West. In summer, some even take to the tracks once again.
OLD SACRAMENTO. The OLD SACRAMENTO HISTORIC DISTRICT, on the banks of the Sacramento River, has been restored to its former glory and given a DISCOVERY MUSEUM. The district's wooden houses, old schoolhouse, stores and saloons are a reminder that this was originally a town of pioneers and gold prospectors. This is also reflected in SUTTER'S FORT STATE HISTORIC BUILDING, on the corner of L and 26th Streets, on the east side of town. The restoration work carried out in recent years has tried to give this beautiful museum complex an air of authenticity, which is highlighted each spring during the Living History festival, when local volunteers dress up and reenact life in the fort in the 1850s. Visitors can see the blacksmith, home distiller and apothecary going about their business in their reconstructed stores. On K Street, behind Sutter's Fort, is the CALIFORNIA STATE INDIAN MUSEUM, remarkable for its presentation of the state's history from the point of view of its early inhabitants.

THE GOLD COUNTRY ● 34

The small towns of the Gold Country, forgotten for almost 100 years, are being revived by a tourist industry in search of nostalgia. Modern tourists, sitting at the wheel of their air-conditioned 4 x 4 or snuggling under the duvet in a hotel, like to think of the thousands of men who spilled their sweat and blood to tear a few ounces of precious metal from the mountains in the hope of a better life. They came from the East Coast, Europe and China. Many died on the way, burned by the searing desert sun, perishing of exposure in the high Rocky Mountain passes, or victims of snake bite, poison oak or Indian arrows. In 1848, news of the discovery of a gold nugget on the land of a Swiss general named Sutter traveled round the world. In the space of a few years, thousands of men (more than 90 percent of California's immigrants) and a few women and children completely changed the face of what had been a rural landscape. Towns sprang up overnight and sometimes disappeared as quickly, leaving the disjointed wooden ghost towns that are visited so reverently today. Tunnels were dug through mountains, rivers were diverted, forests uprooted and peoples exterminated. All this so that every last ounce of precious metal could be extracted from the deposit known as the Mother Lode. The history of the Gold Rush is also the history of California, and the whole of America, with its moments of glory and heroism, its cruelty and its bloody appetite for conquest, and its obsessive desire always to push back the last frontier, in the largest intermingling of races ever known to humanity.

A MONUMENTAL STATE CAPITOL. ❂
The neoclassical building of the State Capitol was designed by the architect Miner Butler. Its 125-foot dome, completed in 1874, was inspired by the dome in Washington. The Californians placed the building under the protection of Minerva, Roman goddess of the professions and the arts, who appears on the bas-relief of the pediment, as well as on the state seal.

THE GOLD COUNTRY ❂
The small town along highway 49 are among the prettiest and quaintest in the state of California. Most of the gold prospectors have left (though not all?) making way for more peaceful tourists, artists, poets, singers and travelers. However, the memory of that heroic age is still very much alive, scored out of the mountainsides and reflected in the Western-style streets.

157

★ The star symbol signifies sites singled out by the editor for special attention.

◆ A D6 This reference pinpoints the place's location on one of the maps at the back of the book.

❂ This symbol indicates a place not to be missed.

● <u>Encyclopedia section</u>

▲ Itineraries in California

◆ Practical information

SAN FRANCISCO AND NORTHERN CALIFORNIA ▲ 113
Discover the dazzling city of San Francisco, its hills adorned with Victorian 'painted ladies' and its sea shimmering in a subtle interplay of light. San Francisco Bay stretches from the gently rolling landscapes of Marin County to the university towns of Berkley, Palo Alto (Stanford) and other urban centers. These centers, largely devoted to the new technology industries, are known collectively throughout the world as Silicon Valley. To the north, the coastline becomes more rugged and darkened by sequoia groves as it nears the Oregon border.

THE GOLD COUNTRY ▲ 155
The region has become much quieter since prospectors exhausted the gold deposits. Even Sacramento, the state capital, seems to doze in the shade of its Capitol. Beyond the city, visitors can discover the equally peaceful surrounding area with its rolling hills and valleys. Here, the small towns all look alike, with western-style wooden buildings lining the straight streets. They have an outdated charm, reminiscent of a movie set, that is totally irresistible.

SAN FRANCISCO OVERLAND TO LOS ANGELES ▲ 163
To travel between these two cities, you have to chose between the Central Valley route or the coastal route (Highway 1). The first takes you through an agricultural valley which, although apparently monotonous, has been unspoiled by tourist development. And there is no shortage of beautiful architecture and unusual features. Visitors who choose Highway 1 will be amazed by the famous sites along the way, including such architectural and natural treasures as Monterey, Big Sur and San Simeon with its massive Hearst Castle.

LOS ANGELES AND ORANGE COUNTY ▲ 177
An incredibly multifaceted urban complex where you can visit the wealthy districts of Beverly Hills and Pasadena, or the legendary – if slightly run-down – Hollywood and Sunset boulevards. Relax on the long beaches of Malibu, Venice and Santa Monica; take advantage of some truly wonderful museums, including the Getty Center and the LACMA; or reminisce about classic movies in the studios that produced them. Visitors can also rediscover their childhood in Orange County's theme parks, including the legendary Disneyland.

SAN DIEGO ▲ 217
Although less well known than San Francisco and LA, California's second largest town is well worth a visit. Attractions include a magnificent bay, a downtown area whose towers are illuminated at night, and Balboa Park with its dozens of museums and world-famous zoo. To the south, less than half-an-hour's drive from the city center, is the Mexican border. To the north, the coast is punctuated by resorts and bordered by long, sandy beaches. To the northeast, impressive expanses of desert separate San Diego from the amazing oasis of Palm Springs.

NATIONAL PARKS OF CALIFORNIA ▲ 231
Parks and nature reserves reflect the infinite variety of California's natural sites: the marine environment and the seacoast where marine mammals can be seen in winter; the harsh desert environment of Death Valley and the Mojave Desert with its twisted Joshua trees; the grandiose mountains of the Sierra Nevada and the dense groves of giant sequoias with trees thousands of years old; high volcanic plateaus and depressions, with their scoria cones and lava flows forming long, winding ridges and extinct volcanoes such as Mount Shasta.

→ ALL INFORMATION CONTAINED IN THIS GUIDE HAS BEEN APPROVED BY THE MANY SPECIALISTS WHO HAVE CONTRIBUTED TO ITS PRODUCTION.

ANDREW BENDER
Journalist living in Los Angeles. Among other activities, he writes a weekly food column in the *Los Angeles Times*. Author of the 'Hotels and Restaurants' section.

JEFFREY CARMEL
Journalist, editor and photographer living in San Diego. Author of 'San Diego'.

FRANCE CARP
Reporter for the women's press (*Elle*, *Marie-Claire*, *Marie-France*) who has lived in Los Angeles since 1994. Specialist subject: social trends and phenomena specific to the West Coast of the United States. Author of 'Entertainment'.

ALAIN DISTER
Journalist, writer and photographer. In the 1960s, he made some extended visits to the United States, especially New York and California. He has published a number of works on contemporary Anglo-Saxon culture – from Rock to the poetry of the Beat Generation – and his photographs have been exhibited in museums on both sides of the Atlantic. Author of 'The cult of self', 'The cult of the automobile', 'Music: the style industry', 'Photography', 'California as seen by painters', 'San Francisco and Northern California',

'Gold Country', 'San Francisco to Los Angeles'.

ANNICK FOUCRIER
Assistant professor at the University of Paris-XIII. Field of research: the North-American West, the world of the Pacific and population migration. Author of the 'History' section.

JACQUES GAUCHEY
Former West Coast correspondent for the French publications La Tribune and Le Point. Now living in the San Francisco region, he advises US Internet companies that want to move into Europe and writes travel articles on California and the Pacific. He has published a book on Silicon Valley. Author of 'Silicon Valley'.

CATHERINE GERBER
Traveler and writer based in Los Angeles. Author of travel guides and articles published in the Los Angeles Times, the San Francisco Chronicle and the Denver Post. Author of 'Los Angeles and Orange County'.

CYNTHIA GHORRA-GOBIN
Geographer and town planner. Director of research at the CNRS (French National Center for Scientific Research) and lecturer at the IEP (Institute of Political Studies) in Paris. Field of

research: the American city. Author of 'Cultural diversity', 'The Californian way of life' and the introduction to 'Los Angeles'.

ISABELLE GOURNAY
Associate professor in the School of Architecture at Maryland University. Field of research: the relationship between France and the United States in the field of architecture. Author of the 'Architecture' section.

SUZAN KEEVIL
Journalist for London's *Decanter Magazine*, who regularly visits the wine-growing regions of California to research her articles. Author of 'Californian wines' and 'Wine Country'.

KEITH MCKEOWN
Vice-president of the Department of Communications and Marketing at the LACMA. Author of 'LACMA'.

JACQUES PORTES
Lecturer in North American history at the University of Paris-VIII-Vincennes-Saint-Denis, specializing in American popular culture. Field of research: the relationship between American cinema and history. Author of 'California in the movies' and 'Hollywood movies'.

ADA SAVIN
Lecturer in American civilization at the University of Versailles-Saint-Quentin. Field of research: inter-cultural history within the ethnic minority groups of North America, with a special interest in the language and literature of the Chicanos (young Mexican-Americans) of California. Author of 'Language'.

JIM VAN BUSKIRK
Director of the James C. Hormel Gay & Lesbian Center of the San Francisco Public Library. Among other things, he has published a history of the gay community in San Francisco. Author of 'The gay scene'.

ALICE WATERS
One of California's best-known chefs. Her restaurant, Chez Panisse, is situated in Berkley. Author of the recipe in the 'Food' section.

DORRIS WELCH
A field biologist who travels widely in California observing its plant and wildlife. Conservator for the Department of Natural Sciences of the Oakland Museum of California. Fields of study include aquatic life in Monterey Bay. Author of 'Nature' and 'National Parks of California'.

→ ADVISOR: JACQUES GAUCHEY

THIS IS A BORZOI BOOK
PUBLISHED BY
ALFRED A. KNOPF

**Copyright © 2002
Alfred A. Knopf, New York**

Library of Congress
Cataloging-in-Publication Data
Californie. English
California.
p. cm. — (Knopf guides)
Originally published: Californie.
Paris: Éditions Nouveux-Loisirs, ©2001
Includes bibliographical references
(p.) and index.
ISBN 0-375-70959-2 (pbk.)
1. California — Guidebooks.
I. Alfred A. Knopf, Inc.
II. Title   III. Series
F859.3.C23 2002
917.9404'54 — dc21
2001038565

First American Edition

Originally published in France by
Nouveaux-Loisirs, a subsidiary of
Gallimard, Paris, 2001.
Copyright © 2001 by
Editions Nouveaux-Loisirs

CALIFORNIA

■ **EDITORS**
Florence Lagrange-Leader,
assisted by Céline Metge
and by Vincent Grandferry
for the practical information
■ **GRAPHICS**
Brigitte Célérier
assisted by Céline Metge
■ **LAYOUT**
Valentina Lepore, Laure Massin
■ **ILLUSTRATIONS**
NATURE
François Desbordes, Claire Felloni
ARCHITECTURE
Denis Brumaud, Philippe Candé,
Jean-Marie Guillou, Serge Langlois,
Bruno Le Normand, Jean-François Péneau,
Claude Quiec
■ **MAPS**
Édigraphie, Patrick Mérienne (nature)

TRANSLATED BY
Wendy Allatson

EDITED AND TYPESET BY
Book Creation Services Ltd, London

Printed in Italy by Editoriale Lloyd

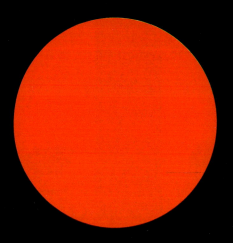

Encyclopedia section

Cable car on the steeply sloping streets of San Francisco, in 1947.

The Olympic Drive-in Theater in Hollywood, in the 1950s.

Fredric March and Elissa Landi on the set of Cecil B. DeMille's *The Sign of the Cross* (1932).

Nature

GEOMORPHOLOGY

DESERTS
Volcanic and tectonic activity have molded the stark, dramatic desert basins in southeast California. Mountains created along fault lines rise above the deserts – the flat basins dropped as the surrounding mountains rose. California's deserts have been mined for gold, silver, copper, borax, dolomite and more.

California's dramatic and varied topography is the result of major earth forces acting upon the landscape over millions of years. California has both the highest peak and the lowest valley in the mainland United States. Within the state, the traveler can visit ancient volcanos, striking granitic alpine terrain, lush valleys, jagged deserts, underground caverns and dramatic coastlines. Some of the forces creating this geological display include tectonic uplift, seismic activity, volcanism, glaciers and erosion, and many of these forces are still at work today, slowly changing the landscape.

COAST RANGES

Klam
M

2

4

San Francisco

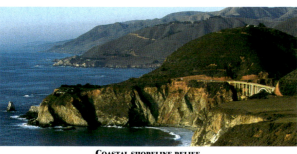

COASTAL SHORELINE RELIEF

The 1100 miles of coastline offer a wide variety. You can walk for miles on sandy beaches, explore rocky shelves for marine life at low tide, view dramatic cliffs and rock formations and discover secluded cove beaches. Offshore, the continental shelf is intersected by submarine canyons, one over a mile deep.

Most of the coastline has a sedimentary origin, but some sections host dramatic granite outcrops. The areas which match rock formations 350 miles to the southeast are proof that the coastline is moving slowly north and west.

CENTRAL VALLEY

The Central Valley is a vast lowland running between the Sierra Nevada and the Coast Range, and is the largest valley in the western United States. It formed as runoff from the Sierra Nevada poured sediments down into the basin, creating vast marshes, wetland habitats and fertile soils.

Much of the valley has been converted to agriculture and the water diverted to Southern California. Two main rivers flow through the valley, the Sacramento and the San Joaquin, meeting in the delta to flow together into the San Francisco Bay.

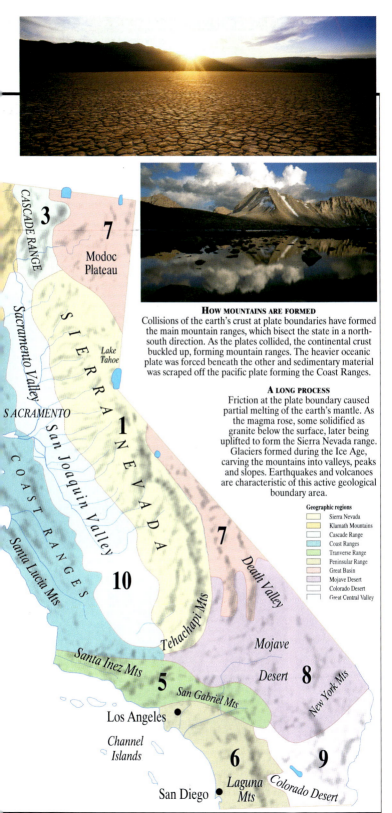

HOW MOUNTAINS ARE FORMED

Collisions of the earth's crust at plate boundaries have formed the main mountain ranges, which bisect the state in a north-south direction. As the plates collided, the continental crust buckled up, forming mountain ranges. The heavier oceanic plate was forced beneath the other and sedimentary material was scraped off the pacific plate forming the Coast Ranges.

A LONG PROCESS

Friction at the plate boundary caused partial melting of the earth's mantle. As the magma rose, some solidified as granite below the surface, later being uplifted to form the Sierra Nevada range. Glaciers formed during the Ice Age, carving the mountains into valleys, peaks and slopes. Earthquakes and volcanoes are characteristic of this active geological boundary area.

Geographic regions

- Sierra Nevada
- Klamath Mountains
- Cascade Range
- Coast Ranges
- Tranverse Range
- Peninsular Range
- Great Basin
- Mojave Desert
- Colorado Desert
- Great Central Valley

Map labels:

CASCADE RANGE

3

7

Modoc Plateau

Lake Tahoe

S I E R R A   N E V A D A

Sacramento Valley

S ACRAMENTO

San Joaquin Valley

1

C O A S T   R A N G E S

Santa Lucia Mts

10

Death Valley

7

Tehachapi Mts

Mojave Desert

8

New York Mts

Santa Inez Mts

5

San Gabriel Mts

Los Angeles

Channel Islands

6

Laguna Mts

Colorado Desert

9

San Diego

● SAN ANDREAS FAULT ZONE

The San Andreas Fault zone is a network of faults, 600 miles long, that extends northwest from the Gulf of California, passes through San Francisco Bay and veers offshore near Cape Mendocino. The transform fault was created about 30 million years ago when two tectonic plates collided. Today, the Pacific Plate is moving north relative to the North American plate at a rate of 2½ inches per year. This movement causes about 10,000 small earthquakes each year. In the 20th century there were two major earthquakes in San Francisco, in 1906 and 1989. The 1906 earthquake measured 8.25 on the Richter scale and largely destroyed the city. The next large earthquake is expected to occur along the Hayward Fault, directly east of the San Andreas Fault, in the highly populated area east of San Francisco Bay.

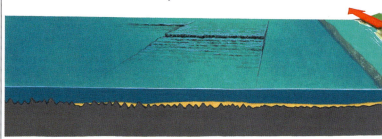

CALIFORNIA BADLY HIT ● 28
Several earthquakes occurred in the 20th century: in 1906 and 1989 in San Francisco, and 1994 in LA. It is difficult to predict earthquakes, but studies are looking at how to minimize the effects.

SECONDARY EFFECTS
It is the secondary effects of the earthquake that tend to cause deaths and injuries, not the shock itself: tidal waves, ruptured pipes, landslides and fires can cause a great deal of damage.

WHAT CAUSES EARTHQUAKES?

Seismic disturbances occur as great slabs of the earth's crust override or grind past each other. The crust is made up of a dozen segments, or plates, that constantly move over the planet's molten interior. Along the San Andreas Fault, two plates are sliding past each other. This is not a steady movement. As pressure builds up over the years, large slips occur, creating earthquakes.

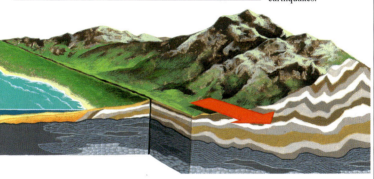

MOUNT SHASTA, AN ANCIENT VOLCANO

The phenomenon of subduction goes hand in hand with volcanic activity: this is how the Cascade Range was formed. The extinct volcano of Mount Shasta ▲ 261, 268 is part of it.

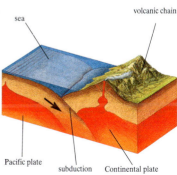

sea

volcanic chain

Pacific plate

subduction

Continental plate

SUBDUCTION

The San Andreas fault is on a transform boundary, where plates slide past each other horizontally, the friction creating seismic waves, or earthquakes.

● BIOGEOGRAPHY

The hot, dry slopes of the inland foothills and southern mountains support dense scrubby brush known as chaparral. These drought-resistant shrubs grow up to fifteen feet high. They offer good cover for birds, small mammals and deer.

The dramatic topography, diverse geology and varied climates of California determine the wide range of plant communities found. These communities are influenced by precipitation and water availability, shape and contour of the land, elevation, soil and underlying rock types, temperature, wind and slope exposure. Illustrated here are seven characteristic California communities. Within each grouping there is wide variation due to local geological, topographic and climatic conditions.

Vegetation
1
2
3
4
5
6
7

OAK WOODLANDS

At the base of California's mountain ranges rise sweeping golden foothills dotted with broad canopied oak trees, the oak woodlands. The largest expanse is found along the western slope of the Sierra Nevada from 1000–3500 feet. There are twenty species of oak in California. Most are drought-tolerant, with small evergreen leaves. Acorns provide food for acorn woodpeckers, gray squirrel and deer.

ACORN WOODPECKER
You can hear the noise of its pecking from far away, as well as its distinctive cry.

RAIN SHADOW EFFECT
As the west winds collide with the mountains, the moist air is forced up until it is cooled to the point of precipitation, dropping most of its moisture on the western slopes.

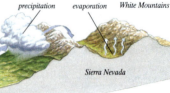

precipitation   evaporation   White Mountains

fog

Sierra Nevada

Coast Ranges

upwelling

As the winds descend the eastern slopes, they warm and dry, which results in desert climates in eastern and southern California.

During the spring months northwest winds along the coast, along with the Coriolis effect, push the warmer coastal water offshore. Upwelling of cold, nutrient-rich water from the ocean's depths supports rich plankton blooms.

SPRING WILDFLOWER BLOOM
Seasonal wildflower blooms are often spectacular, beginning in early spring after the first rains in the lowlands and peaking at the higher elevations in mid summer.

CALIFORNIAN POPPY ● 60
The fire poppy, emblematic of California, gets its name from the fact that it blooms after fires.

SAGE PRAIRIE
This is found in the Modoc Plateau and on the east side of the central Sierra in the Mono Basin. These vast open spaces are dry, about 3000 feet in height, and are covered with sagebrush, a low growing aromatic shrub.

WETLANDS
The Central Valley once supported vast wetlands, before the arrival of European settlers and the conversion of wetlands to farmlands. Currently the only remaining wetland areas are protected by the government as wildlife refuges. They are found scattered along the Central Valley, in the Modoc plateau and along the coast, and support the remaining populations of migrating and breeding waterfowl.

DESERT ▲ 242
The two major deserts are the Colorado and the Mojave, along with the desert region of the Mono Basin. The warmer latitude and drying winds, along with low rainfall due to the rain shadow effect, create hot, dry deserts with cactus and shrub vegetation and animals adapted to the hot, dry environment.

● CLIMATE

FOG
Coastal fog is common in summer months, as the warmer inland air masses draw the moist colder coastal air eastward, creating a natural air conditioning effect.

California has a Mediterranean climate with warm, dry summers and mild rainy winter seasons. The long coastline provides a significant maritime influence. The climate is strongly affected by large air masses from the Pacific Ocean and from the North American Continent east of the Sierra. Within California can be found many climatic extremes, from hot, dry deserts in the southeast to cold, windy alpine mountains in the Sierra and wet temperate rain forests in the northwest.

SNOW IN SIERRAS
Elevations above 5000 feet receive more than 100 inches of snow each winter. In the High Sierra, snow levels can reach an average of 450 inches each year, closing mountain passes for the entire season.

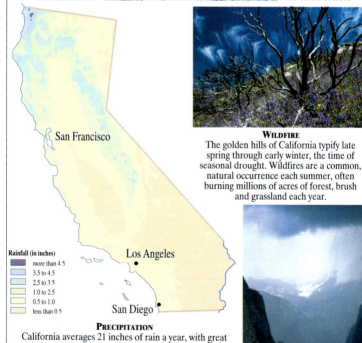

WILDFIRE
The golden hills of California typify late spring through early winter, the time of seasonal drought. Wildfires are a common, natural occurrence each summer, often burning millions of acres of forest, brush and grassland each year.

San Francisco

Los Angeles

San Diego

Rainfall (in inches)
more than 4.5
3.5 to 4.5
2.5 to 3.5
1.0 to 2.5
0.5 to 1.0
less than 0.5

PRECIPITATION
California averages 21 inches of rain a year, with great variation between locales. Death Valley gets less than 2 inches, and the northern mountains can have up to 109 inches a year. Winter rains are brought by storms over the Pacific and carried east by the westerly winds. Storms alternate with periods of fine weather. The Sierra Nevada sometimes has thundershowers in the spring and summer.

History

1602 Sebastián Vizcaíno names a number of towns along the coast.

1770 Foundation of Monterey.
1776 Foundation of San Francisco.
1786 La Pérouse lands at Monterey.

1550   1600   1650   1700   1750   1800

1521 The writer Garcí Ordóñez de Montalvo describes Amazons living on an island named California.

1579 The English sailor Francis Drake lands on the coast north of San Francisco.

1701 The Jesuit priest Eusebio Francisco Kino proves that California is not an island.

1769 Portolá leads an expedition to found missions and discovers San Francisco Bay.

EARLY INHABITANTS

Until recently, it was believed that the early inhabitants of the American continent, the Amerindians, crossed the Bering Strait 35,000–20,000 BC and that California has been inhabited for between 8000 and 12,000 years. However, recent archeological discoveries could lead to the revision of these theories. A human skull thought to be around 48,000 years old has been excavated near Del Mar in Southern California, while a number of stones carved some 200,000 years ago were found near Calico in the Mojave Desert.

1542–1848: HISPANIC CALIFORNIA

THE 'ISLAND' OF CALIFORNIA

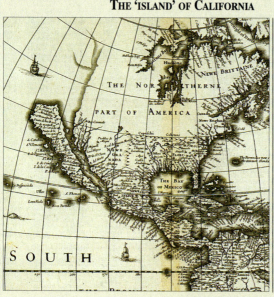

California was explored relatively late, because the northwest winds made access from the sea difficult. The Spanish were more interested in the rich trade between Manila and Acapulco and simply sailed along the coast. At first California was thought to be an island, but in 1701 a Jesuit priest, Eusebio Kino, proved the contrary. Near the Gila River (Arizona), Native Americans ● *30* offered him blue shells (ormers) like those found on the Pacific Coast, proof of trading links between coastal and inland regions.

THE FIRST MISSIONS ● *32, 62*

In the 18th century the Spaniards were alarmed when Russians came south to hunt sea otters, so in 1769 the Spanish envoy, José de Gálvez, organized an expedition to colonize California. Under the leadership of Gaspar de Portolá, governor of Lower California, and Junípero Serra, a Franciscan missionary, several groups set out by land and sea to meet up in San Diego. Serra founded nine missions. His successors completed the chain of 21 missions stretching from San Diego (1769) ▲ *219* in the south to Sonoma (1823) ▲ *149* in the north. Four *presidios* (garrisons) were founded in San Diego, Monterey, San Francisco and Santa Barbara to provide protection against sea attack. The customs building, governor's house and prison were built at Monterey. Colonization began slowly. The indigenous people, who had no immunity against such diseases as smallpox, died by the thousands, while soldiers' attacks on indigenous women provoked uprisings.

JUNÍPERO SERRA (1713–84)

Serra was born in Mallorca, Spain. He entered the Franciscan order at the age of 16 and soon established a reputation as a preacher. During the journey to California he walked from San Blas to San Diego, in spite of a leg injury. He devoted all his energies to his missions, even clashing with the military governor.

Serra's cell at Mission Carmel (right).

1812	1833–34	1846–48
Foundation of Fort Ross by the Russian-American [fur] Company.	Law secularizing the missions.	War between the United States and Mexico.

1810	1820	1830	1840	1850	1860

1818 Hippolyte Bouchard, a French sailor in the service Argentina, attacks of Monterey and Santa Barbara. | **1821** Mexico gains independence. Spain does not recognize the new government until 1822. | **1836** Juan Bautista Alvarado, the first Californian-born governor, is recognized by the Mexican government. | **1846** Commodore J D Sloat takes possession of California in the name of the United States.

THE AGE OF SPANISH RULE

The Spanish authorities tried to encourage families to leave Mexico and settle in California. Three *pueblos* (towns) – San José (1777), Los Angeles (1781) and Branciforte (1797) near Santa Cruz – were founded using the traditional Spanish layout of a central *plaza* bounded by a church, houses and plots of land. Towns were founded along the coast due to the sparse settlement of the inland regions. In 1821, Mexico gained independence. To attract settlers to California, the government granted land concessions which could not legally exceed 48,850 acres. From 1833 to 1834, the missions were secularized and reduced to the status of parish churches. Cattle farms known as *ranchos* ● *32* sprang up throughout the territory. Trade in leather and tallow developed with the Pacific and New England ports, and powerful families vied for power. Gradually, foreign settlers came to California from the United States, England and France, including merchants, deserters from the whaling ships and trappers from the Rockies. Some became naturalized, married Californian women and acquired land. However, increasing numbers of settlers came from the United States with the intention of fomenting rebellion against the Mexican government, gaining independence and demanding annexation in the same way that Texas had done. An initial attempt, in 1836, failed. The people of California then drove out the Mexican governor and replaced him with a local, Californian-born governor, Juan Bautista Alvarado, who was more sympathetic to their interests. In the 1840s, California, whose ports were the envy of the United States, Great Britain and France, became the focus of rivalries between these countries. Mexico, weakened by civil strife, could do little to protect the territory, which thus became an easy prey.

1846–70: CONQUEST AND AMERICANIZATION

In 1835 and again in 1837 the President of the United States, Andrew Jackson, had tried to buy California. His successors pursued the project, which would enable the United States to extend its territory from the Atlantic to the Pacific coasts. Many Americans were convinced that this was their 'true destiny' and the will of divine Providence. Texas, which had been rebelling against Mexican rule since 1836, provided the ideal opportunity. In 1845, when Mexico refused to allow its former province to be annexed by the United States, incidents broke out along the disputed border, and in May 1846 the United States declared war on Mexico. The US navy lost no time in taking possession of California. On July 7, 1846, the American flag was hoisted over the customs building in Monterey. Meanwhile on June 14, a small group of trappers, concerned by the Mexican government's order to expel all 'unauthorized' foreigners, seized the commander of the northern border, Mariano Guadalupe Vallejo ▲ *149*, in the village of Sonoma. Ironically, he was one of the Californians most sympathetic to the American cause. The trappers hoisted a flag on which they had depicted a bear and a red band and star, and proclaimed the 'Republic of California', even if it meant calling upon the United States for protection. The republic was short-lived but the 'bear flag' is still the emblem of the modern State of California.

CHRONOLOGY

1849 The voters approve the Constitution of California.

1850 California becomes the 31st State of the United States. Foreign miners are taxed.

1845	1850	1855	1860	1865

1847 California's capitulation is accepted at Cahuenga.

1848 January 24: gold is discovered on the land of the Swiss settler J A Sutter.

1848 Treaty of Guadalupe Hidalgo. Mexico is defeated and sells half its territory, including California, to the US.

1854 Sacramento is chosen as the capital.

1856 First railroad between Folsom and Sacramento.

CALIFORNIA IN THE UNITED STATES

Without weapons, California could not resist the United States, but harassment by the military authorities provoked an uprising in Los Angeles in 1846. The Californians were excellent horsemen. Armed only with spears, they successfully defeated the American military reinforcements at San Pascual, near San Diego. However, they were outnumbered and therefore surrendered in January 1847. For the last time, California's fate was decided by Mexico. Defeated in the war, Mexico was forced to sell half its territory to the United States. The Treaty of Guadalupe Hidalgo, signed on February 2, 1848, made provision for Mexican nationals who wanted to remain on what was now American territory. It gave them the same rights as American citizens, made Spanish and English the official languages, and respected their property rights. However, a week earlier, gold ● *34* had been discovered on the land of Johann A Sutter, a Swiss settler in California since 1839. He tried in vain to keep the discovery secret, but in December 1848 the President of the United States, James Polk, officially confirmed the news. Gold prospectors flocked to California from all over the world. In the space of a few months the population had exceeded the number required (60,000) for it to become a State. In 1849, the inhabitants were called upon to elect 48 delegates to draw up a Constitution. On September 9, 1850, California became the 31st state of the United States of America. At a time when Congress was making every effort to maintain the balance between the number of free and slave states, California rejected slavery. The massive influx of immigrants totally submerged the Mexican society in the North, though it managed to hold out longer in the South, where there was less demand for land. The newcomers wanted gold and land, and settled wherever it suited them, with scant regard for the existing occupants. An act of Congress in 1851 made the occupants responsible for proving their right of ownership, which was not only difficult, but involved legal costs that often led to financial ruin. The result was a massive transfer of property to the new settlers, the main beneficiaries being the lawyers and speculators.

THE TRANSCONTINENTAL RAILROAD

The long journey – either by sea, or overland by stagecoach – between the Pacific and the Atlantic coasts greatly increased the cost of merchandise. The people of California called for the construction of a transcontinental railroad which would reduce prices and enable them to receive news more rapidly. The engineer Theodore Judah (1826–63) found a suitable crossing through the Rocky Mountains and presented the project to Congress. It was in 1862, during the American Civil War, that the federal government, fearing that California would not secede, decided to build the railroad, 2000 miles long, linking the East and West coasts. The work was entrusted to two railroad companies, which began building at the same time from opposite ends of the line: Omaha in Nebraska and Sacramento in California. The contract for the Western section was given to four Sacramento merchants, Collis Huntington, Mark Hopkins, Charles Crocker and Leland Stanford ▲ *156*, who had made their money selling supplies to the gold miners. Each company tried to make better progress than the other, since

1871 Anti-Chinese riots in Los Angeles.

1872–73 War against the Modoc Indians.

1882 A federal law prohibits Chinese immigration.

1892 Oil is discovered in Los Angeles.

1870   1875   1880   1885   1890

1869 The two sections of the Transcontinental Railroad meet at Promontory Point, Utah.

1873 The navel orange is introduced to Riverside.

1876 The railroad reaches Los Angeles.

1886 Price war between the railroad companies.

the US government was offering financial rewards and land along the railroad. The railway laborers lived in tents in mobile camps, and worked between 12 and 15 hours a day in difficult and dangerous conditions. They had to construct

bridges up to 1000 feet long, blast out tunnels with dynamite and be constantly on their guard against snowstorms and avalanches. The Union Pacific company in the East employed Irish immigrants, while the Central Pacific

company in the West brought in 15,000 Chinese laborers. On May 10, 1869, the two lines met at Promontory Point in Utah. A nail made of Californian gold was used to join the two sections symbolically. The telegraph

line that ran the length of the railroad was immediately used to transmit the good news throughout the country. In the official photo of the joining ceremony (below), the Chinese laborers are conspicuously absent.

MIGRANTS IN THEIR THOUSANDS ● *38*

During the American Civil War, the supply of produce from the East was interrupted, thereby favoring the development of the local Californian economy. With the completion of the transcontinental railroad, many of the migrant laborers decided to settle in California, and in the 1870s the

population increased by 54 percent. However, produce from the East began to compete with local produce, while land prices soared to levels far beyond the means of ordinary farmers and immigrants. A period of prosperity was followed by economic crisis. The Chinese who had worked on the

railroad flooded onto an already saturated labor market. They became an easy target for such demagogues as Dennis Kearney, who formed the Californian Labor Party in 1877. They were often victims of violence and were forced to live in ghettoes known as 'Chinatowns'. In 1882, Californian

politicians succeeded in having a federal law passed to prohibit further Chinese immigration. In 1924, these measures were extended to the Japanese and all other Asiatic peoples by a law prohibiting their immigration to the United States and reserving American citizenship for 'white men'.

1915 International Exhibition in San Francisco to mark the opening of the Panama Canal and the reconstruction of the city.

1938 Hewlett Packard founded in a garage in Palo Alto.

1900	1910	1920	1930	1940	1950

1906 San Francisco earthquake.

1911 The Nestor Film Company opens a studio in Hollywood.

1924 A federal law prohibits Asian immigration into the United States.

1934 General strike in San Francisco.

1941–45 Pacific War. Over 100,000 Japanese living in the United States are deported to internment camps.

THE CALIFORNIAN DREAM

The construction of new railroad lines ● *26* greatly reduced the journey time between the East and West coasts. Competition brought prices down, and many people living in the East left for California, whose award-winning fruits embodied the image of a land of plenty. Between 1870 and 1920, new images were added to those associated with the Gold Rush – images illustrating the dreams and aspirations used by promoters and land agents to attract tourists and investors to California. Their advertisements combined spectacular sunsets over the beaches, the magnificent landscapes of the Sierra Nevada and the golden fruit of the orange production to impart to California a Mediterranean stylishness evoking a healthy, open-air

lifestyle. The restoration of the missions and architecture in Spanish Colonial style ● *64* were part of a trend that reevaluated the state's Spanish history and invested it with a local identity. However, behind the idyllic descriptions was a major trend towards the concentration of wealth. With the help of politicians, the railroads were dominating the economy. There was also an ever-present natural danger ● *18*. In 1906, an earthquake measuring 8.3 on the Richter Scale destroyed a

large part of San Francisco and caused fires that burned for several days. Although the city was rebuilt in record time, the disaster increased the tendency for new arrivals to settle in the southern part of the state, which developed rapidly. Los Angeles, which had more available space, reaped greater benefits from the opening of the Suez Canal (1914) than San Francisco. The discovery of oil in Los Angeles in 1892 led to the establishment of a chemical industry, and later favored the development of the automobile. In the

1910s, when movie studios began to take advantage of California's climate and year-round sunshine, Hollywood became the center of the film industry ▲ *180*. The landscapes of Southern California were made famous by the movies, while the Californian way of life became the ideal to which many Americans aspired, and gave the region a prosperous, avant-garde reputation. In the 1930s, the small farmers of Oklahoma (Okies) and Arkansas (Arkies) bankrupted by the Great Depression ● *39* and the dust bowl came to California to make a new start. To their disappointment, they found a land occupied by vast properties worked by harshly treated agricultural workers.

The 1906 San Francisco earthquake (below).

| 1947–53 Witch hunt in Hollywood. | 1964 The Free Speech Movement is founded at Berkeley University. | 1966 Foundation of the militant Black Panther Party. | 1994 Vote for Proposition 187, which barred illegal immigrants from social security, education and medical care. |

| 1960 | 1970 | 1980 | 1990 | 2000 | 2010 |

| 1955 Disneyland opens. | 1965 Riots in the Watts section of Los Angeles. | 1967 *Summer of Love* in San Francisco. | 1989, 1994 Earthquakes in San Francisco and Los Angeles. | 1992 Riots in the South Central section of Los Angeles. |

WAR IN THE PACIFIC

When war broke out in Europe in 1939, the United States decided to remain neutral. However, the Japanese bombardment of the US naval base in Pearl Harbor (Hawaii) on December 7, 1941 brought the Americans into the war. On February 23, 1942, a Japanese submarine attacked an oil refinery north of Santa Barbara. It didn't cause any damage, but it did cause widespread alarm. On February 19, 1942, President Roosevelt signed a decree sanctioning the deportation of all US inhabitants of Japanese origin (over two-thirds were born in the United States and were American citizens) to camps in neighboring states where they were placed under military guard. Japenese residents of California were allowed to return in 1945, but by then had lost their property and possessions and received insufficient compensation. The war kick-started the Californian economy.

Aircraft factories and shipyards were built in Los Angeles, San Diego and around San Francisco Bay to meet miltary needs. The population increased by almost two million between 1940 and 1945. Thousands of Black and Mexican workers came to fill the vacant jobs in the factories and on the land.

WITCH HUNT

California became a strategic zone for the wars fought in the Pacific (Korea, Vietnam), while federal military funding maintained the dynamism of its economy. However, the Cold War was also a period of intense anti-Communist feeling, which Senator Joseph R McCarthy of Wisconsin turned into a witch hunt. In California, a Republican candidate for the Senate, Richard Nixon, used the 'Red Scare' as an electoral weapon against his less conservative rivals. Even Hollywood came under suspicion, since during World War Two the movie industry had been asked to make propaganda films, at a time when the USSR was an ally of the United States. The Un-American Activities Committee called upon actors, screenwriters, directors and producers to swear on oath that they were not Communists and to denounce those who were. Ronald Reagan, president of the Screen Actors' Guild, agreed to cooperate. Those who refused were imprisoned, like the 'Hollywood Ten' in 1947, while hundreds more were placed on a blacklist and their careers destroyed. Others, like Charlie Chaplin, preferred to leave the United States. Teachers, too, had to pledge an oath of allegiance. As a reaction to this 'silent generation', the 1960s witnessed an increasing number of nonconformist protest movements ● *36*.

A LABORATORY

The electronic 'adventure' of the Santa Clara Valley, renamed Silicon Valley (Apple headquarters, right) ▲ *146*, was greatly influenced by the dean of electrical engineering at Stanford University ▲ *145*, Frederick Terman, who encouraged his students to start up their own businesses. Existing connections with the government guaranteed contracts for the US army and space research. In 1981, the former governor of California, Ronald Reagan, became President of the United States and surrounded himself

with Californian advisors. As a result, California's businesses continued to enjoy the benefits of government connections. In spite of periods of recession, California's booming economy made it even more attractive. During the 1960s, the population increased by around 600,000 inhabitants per year, and by 1964, California was the most densely populated state in the US. Since then, it has become one of the key states in elections to the Presidency and the House of Representatives. In 2001, California had more than 34 million inhabitants.

For centuries, the early inhabitants of California, a region surrounded by mountains and deserts, remained relatively isolated. Before Europeans arrived in the 18th century the population, which probably barely exceeded 130,000, was divided into a large number of small units (villages). These early inhabitants spoke around 135 different dialects which can be linked to several North American language groups: Hokan, Penutian, Shoshonean, Athabascan and Algonkian. Their customs, traditions and way of life were extremely varied, but generally speaking, they were peaceable hunter-gatherers who migrated between the coast and the inland regions depending on the season. Only the Mojave, in the southwest, were farmers, who used the floods of the Colorado River to irrigate their crops.

BASIC CLOTHING AND HOUSING
Because of the temperate climate, clothing was reduced to a minimum, while the use of face and body paint, tattoos, shells and necklaces (possibly a symbol of strength or the identity assumed on the attainment of adulthood) was widespread. The shape of the houses varied according to region. Some were conical, others dome-shaped, but most were covered with branches, bark and earth. In the north, they were made of wooden planks.

Cave paintings.

SKILLED HUNTERS
To hunt deer, the early American Indians disguised themselves by wearing animal skins, or simply covered their heads with skins. This camouflage enabled them to get close enough to the herd to fire their arrows. Those who lived on the coast caught fish with nets or spears, and also gathered and ate mollusks. The Chumash, skilled sailors from the Santa Barbara region, put to sea in wooden-plank canoes which were caulked with bitumen.

ENTERTAINMENT
The early Indians loved music and dance. They also enjoyed games which they played in teams or individually, with a preference for those involving wagers.

DECORATED BASKETS
The baskets made in California were among the most beautiful in North America. The ceremonial baskets made by the Pomo, for example, were decorated with feathers and shells. They were woven by the women from dried grasses, and were sometimes dyed to create motifs. Some baskets were so tightly woven that they could be used to carry water, and even for cooking. A coating of bitumen ensured that the baskets were watertight.

ACORNS
Acorns constituted an important part of the diet. The women extracted the tannic acid by crushing the acorns to a powder which they then washed until the water was clear, a sign that the toxins had been removed.

BODY CARE
The *temescal,* or sweat lodge, was used to treat certain illnesses, such as rheumatism, and for ritual purification. It was also used as a meeting house for the menfolk. After spending time in the heated atmosphere of the lodge, they would dive into the icy waters of a nearby lake or river.

BELIEFS
The Indians believed that there are spiritual forces present in nature which must be pacified. The shaman (medicine man), in particular, communicated with animals and trees and acted as an intermediary with the spirits. He also treated illnesses and officiated at the initiation ceremonies of young boys and girls who had reached adulthood.

The missions were part of Spanish expansionism. Their aim was to convert the American Indians, make them loyal subjects of the Spanish crown and pave the way for civilian populations. From 1769, the Franciscans founded 21 missions in California, linked by *El Camino Reàl* (the Royal Road). They developed agriculture (wheat, vegetables, vines, fruit trees) and cattle ranching. In 1834, the missions were secularized by order of the Mexican government and their lands given to private owners, who formed vast cattle ranches known as ranchos. In the villages, agricultural activities were more diversified.

CONVERTING THE NATIVE AMERICANS
According to the writer Malcolm Margolin, the American Indians were not, as has been sometimes suggested, rounded up by soldiers and herded into the missions like prisoners of war. Initially at least, they seem to have come to the missions of their own accord, even eagerly, attracted by the promise of gifts and food. Soldiers were relatively few in number and would not have been able to quell a determined rebellion.

LAYOUT OF A MISSION
● *62*
(Mission San Gabriel in 1832, above). A mission consisted of a church, stores, dormitories and workshops built around a central *plaza* or square. In 1786,

La Pérouse gave a detailed description of the Mission San Carlos Borroméo del Río Carmelo, founded on Monterey Bay in 1770 by Junípero Serra. He noted that the church was large enough to

hold between 500 and 600 people, but that there were no benches. In front of the church, a square courtyard was surrounded by buildings where agricultural produce and implements were

stored. The mission was built by the American Indians, using construction techniques learned from the missionaries, from making beams and adobes (sun-dried clay bricks) to painting frescos.

American Indian dances at
the Mission Dolores ▲ *138.*

RANCHOS
Ranchos were vast
cattle ranches on
which the herds
roamed in complete
freedom. Each year,
a proportion of these
animals was killed
during the rodeos,
which offered an
opportunity for the
vaqueros – the first
cowboys of American
Indian and mixed
race (below) – to
demonstrate their
skill and courage.
The hides and tallow
were traded for
manufactured goods
brought by ship from
the northeastern
United States via
Cape Horn. This
trade was described
by Richard Henry
Dana ● *94,* a student
at Harvard University
who had been forced
to take a break from
his studies because
of an eye ailment.
In 1834 he signed on
for two years as a
seaman on one of
these ships. Foreign
immigrants to the
region gradually
established
themselves as
merchants or
carpenters, while
some planted
vines.

● THE GOLD RUSH

Advertisement for a clipper ship (below).
A wooden sieve or cradle-rocker (bottom,
left) used by gold prospectors.

A NEW AND MAGNIFICENT CLIPPER FOR SAN FRANCISCO.
MERCHANTS' EXPRESS LINE OF CLIPPER SHIPS!

CALIFORNIA

The discovery of gold gave new
heart to those experiencing
economic difficulties or
bankruptcy following the social
and political upheavals of
1848. The newspapers hyped
the discovery and prospectors
came from Asia and Europe as well as America. Contrary to the
legend perpetuated by Bret Harte and Mark Twain, the gold
prospectors were neither mystics nor outlaws, but ordinary men
hoping to make their fortune and return home. Prostitutes and
adventurers were a high-profile minority. The worst violence
did not take place in the saloons but during encounters with
Native Americans, Hispanics and Chinese.

GOLD IN THE RIVER!
On January 24, 1848,
gold nuggets were
discovered in a dried-
up river bed on the
land of Johann A
Sutter (1803–80),
near Sacramento
▲ 156, by Sutter's
employee, James
Marshall.

A few months later,
Samuel Brannan, a
Mormon, caused a
sensation in San
Francisco when
he went around
brandishing a vial of
gold dust, shouting:
'Gold! Gold on the
American

River!' He had first
bought up
all the equipment
used by the gold
prospectors.
He resold the
equipment and so
became one
of the first
millionaires.

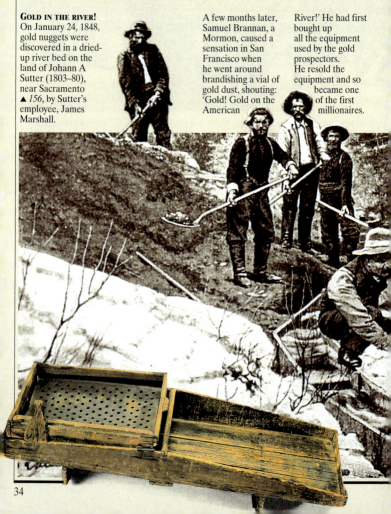

Gold nugget.

THOUSANDS OF PROSPECTORS IN SEARCH OF ADVENTURE

Prospectors flocked to California from all over the world: the East Coast, Europe Mexico, Chile, the Pacific Islands and China. There were three ways of reaching California from New York. The sea voyage via Cape Horn took between four and eight months. This could be shortened by taking a ship to Panama, crossing the isthmus on foot and by canoe, and taking another ship to San Francisco. The overland pioneers' route crossed 2,175 miles of prairies and mountains and took six months.

DEPOSITS SOON EXHAUSTED

The first prospectors found a great deal of gold, but the best claims were soon occupied. Miners formed groups to work their concession (bottom). Mining towns often disappeared as quickly as they had sprung up.

A MAN'S WORLD

There were not many women in California: 8 percent of the population according to the 1850 census (but only 2 percent in the mines), and 30 percent in 1860. The gold miners did not like being separated from their families. Alongside the stereotyped image of actresses, singers and prostitutes, it was wives and mothers, schoolmistresses and missionaries who joined their menfolk and recreated a society based on the East Coast model. The exceptional mixture of population, cultures and religions (a saloon, below), in fact gave rise to an atmosphere of greater tolerance.

THE OTHER SIDE OF THE COIN

As the more easily mined surface deposits were exhausted, hatred of foreigners increased. In 1850, a heavy tax, primarily targeting the Chinese and Mexicans ● *38*, was levied on 'foreign' miners in order to discourage them. The American Indians were the main victims of the Gold Rush. Their lands were invaded by prospectors who destroyed their food supplies and had no scruples about massacring entire villages if they offered any resistance. Those who did not live in villages were literally enslaved on the pretext of vagrancy.

After World War Two the United States was the richest country in the world, but its population was divided by deep-seated social inequalities and racial discrimination. After the literary rebellion of the Beatniks, the 1960s witnessed student protests against a conformist, money-led society. At the same time, America faced the social demands of the casualties of prosperity: Blacks living in ghettos, dispossessed American Indians and harshly exploited immigrant agricultural workers.

EARLY PROTESTERS
In the 1950s, young writers like Jack Kerouac (below) and Allen Ginsberg rejected the social constraints of the East Coast and left for California, which had a reputation for greater tolerance. They used to meet in the City Lights Book Store in San Francisco ▲ *120* or in Big Sur ▲ *171*, near Monterey. The 'Beat Generation' attached great importance to spontaneity and living for the moment. A journalist named Herb Caen called them the 'Beatniks'.

STUDENT PROTESTS
Like other American universities, the University of California owed its prosperity to its links with US economic and military interests. In September 1964, the president of the University of Berkeley ▲ *143* banned all political activities on or around the university campus. On October 1, the expulsion of eight students provoked a spontaneous sit-in (above). Two days later, the Free Speech Movement was founded, a reference to the First Amendment of the Constitution. After 1965, student protests became more extreme with the growing opposition to the Vietnam War.

THE BLACK PANTHERS

Some Blacks in the Civil Rights Movement became increasingly extreme in the face of the slow implementation of reforms. On August 11, 1965, the arrest of a Black youth for drunken driving provoked riots in the Watts section of Los Angeles. The Black Panthers, founded in Oakland in the fall of 1966, advocated armed protest against white racist society.

THE PROTEST SPREADS TO OTHER ETHNIC GROUPS

In 1965, Mexican agricultural workers in the National Farm Workers' Association, led by César Chavez, joined forces with Filipino agricultural workers to organize a long-term strike and a national boycott of grapes. In July 1970, the grape producers finally agreed to their demands of better pay and improved working conditions.

Meanwhile, young militant Mexican-Americans (*Chicanos* ● *39*) proudly proclaimed their *raza*: their Indian, Mexican and Spanish heritage. Influenced by the Black Civil Rights Movement, between 1969 and 1971 Native American militants occupied the island of Alcatraz ▲ *126*, a disused federal prison in San Francisco Bay, which they wanted transformed into a cultural center.

City Lights Publications
1967

'LOVE, PEACE AND DRUGS'

Among the children of the 'baby boom' there developed an alternative culture which rejected conformist society in favor of a community lifestyle, brightly colored clothes, psychedelic art, drugs and free love. Information and announcements were circulated by such underground press publications as the

Berkeley Barb, founded in 1965. The movement reached its height in the summer of 1967, when 100,000 young people from all over the United States converged on San Francisco. After that it gradually disappeared, eroded by drugs and repression, but it had certainly contributed to the liberation of morals and strengthened the tradition of tolerance.

HAIGHT ASHBURY
MUSIC
ARTS
CRAFTS
FOOD
STREET FAIR

In 1999, according to census estimates, California became the first US state to have a European-American population in the minority. This phenomenon can be explained by the proximity of the main immigration zones, both in the past and today. It also reflects contradictions in the American population, between those who stress the importance of European (Anglo-Saxon) origins and the historical reality of a country that has witnessed the influx of immigrants from all over the world. Although tensions are eased in periods of prosperity, they can quickly resurface in an economic crisis as an upsurge of violence against recent immigrants.

SELECTIVE IMMIGRATION

During the Gold Rush (1849–56) ● *34*, immigrants came from all over the world in the hope of making their fortune overnight. But even then, there was a noticeable tendency to favor Americans, or English-speaking Europeans likely to become US citizens. On the other hand, steps were taken to limit the immigration of Blacks (even those who were free), Mexicans and especially Chinese (mainly from the Canton region).

LABORERS FROM ASIA

The first Chinese came to California at the time of the Gold Rush. Many were also employed on the construction of the Transcontinental Railroad. But between 1882 and 1943 a law prohibited further Chinese immigration, and employers brought in Japanese workers instead. In 1942, the immigration law was extended to the Japanese, and during World War Two they were deported to internment camps outside California ● *29*. The laws against Chinese and Japanese immigration were abandoned after 1945, and by 1999 Asians constituted 11.4 percent of California's population.

MEXICO

It used to be easy to cross the US-Mexican border, and large numbers of Mexicans crossed into California looking for work or to escape the 1910 revolution. Mainly employed as agricultural workers, they were expelled during the economic crisis of the 1930s and then encouraged to return when there was a labor shortage during World War Two. In 1942 and 1962, the US and Mexican governments signed an agreement that made provision for the entry of *braceros* (day laborers) into the US until 1964.

MEXICANS BY ANY OTHER NAME
The term *Californio* is applied to the Mexican population of California, which was annexed by the United States in 1848. Mexican-Americans are US citizens of Mexican origin. The term *Chicano*, often heard as a synonym for Mexican, was first used in the late 1960s to refer to the Mexican militants protesting against discrimination and fighting for their civil rights ● *37*.

THE GREAT DEPRESSION ● *28*
During the Great Depression of the 1930s, California witnessed the arrival of immigrants fleeing from the ecological disasters of Oklahoma and Arkansas. Their hopes and disappointments were described by the writer John Steinbeck ▲ *166* in *The Grapes of Wrath*.

THE CREATION OF GHETTOS
In 1850, California was incorporated into the United States as a free (non-slave) state. Blacks represented a very small part of the population until World War Two, when many came to California in response to the labor shortage. However, they found themselves confined to separate districts known as ghettos. The racial discrimination to which they were subjected led to violent riots, especially in Los Angeles in 1965 (Watts) ● *37* and 1992 (South Central, below) ● *43*.

WAVES OF IMMIGRANTS
The most recent wave of immigration followed the law (1965) which abolished quotas and imposed a maximum number of entries per nation. The Asiatic nations have benefited the most, while Mexicans account for the largest number of illegal immigrants (the border, below). The continuous influx of immigrants creates problems of over-population, with population growth and urban expansion placing increasing pressure on the environment and on water and energy resources, especially in the semi-arid climate of the South. Relations between the different ethnic groups are strained, as evidenced by the vote for Proposition 187 ● *29*.

LAID-BACK ENGLISH

Travelers planning to visit California can relax. They do speak English there, although it is a more relaxed, or as the Californians would say 'laid-back', form of English than on the East Coast. Accents and turns of phrase evoke the desire for freedom and simplicity felt by the pioneers of the Far West, who didn't want to burden themselves with the rigid standards and constraints of New England. Californians feel far removed from the political preoccupations of Washington DC. Their language reflects a way of life that gives pride of place to a close relationship and communion with nature ● 44.

ENGLISH, SPANISH OR *SPANGLISH*?

Until it was annexed by the United States, California was a Mexican province whose inhabitants spoke Spanish. Most place names, such as San Francisco, San Juan Bautista, San Luis Obispo and Los Angeles, are a legacy of the Spanish conquest ● 24. Around 1847, Anglo-Americans streamed into California, established their institutions and imposed their language ● 26. Spanish, which was on the verge of disappearing in the late 19th century, has made a comeback, due to the massive influx of Mexican migrants after the 1910 revolution ● 38. These immigrants usually live in *barrios* (Hispanic districts) where they cultivate their language and culture. Although English was imposed as the official language of California, Spanish

continues to be the spoken language of a great many Mexican- and Spanish-speaking Americans. The inhabitants of East Los Angeles, the city's Spanish district, can live their entire life from cradle to grave without speaking English. Many radio stations and TV channels statewide are also aimed at the Spanish-speaking population. English and Spanish speakers in the border cities of San Diego and Tijuana often speak 'Spanglish', a colorful dialect which uses both languages within a single sentence. In the streets of East Los Angeles, you may well hear expressions such as: *'Bueno, I'll see!'*, *'Me dieron un check-up!'* or *'What a day, hombre!'* Originally a spoken language, Spanglish has also begun to make inroads into Mexican-American literature. The gradual 'tropicalization' of the United States, described by the Mexican writer Carlos Fuentes, is already a reality in California where the Mexican language, music and cuisine are firmly established. But Californian English is also enriched by expressions borrowed from Spanish. Most English speakers know a basic number of Spanish words, if only to satisfy their desire for a *margarita* or *quesadilla* in the Taco Bell on the corner.

CALIFORNIA, A MODERN TOWER OF BABEL

California, the epitome of a multicultural and multilingual state ● 38, reflects the future profile of the American identity. During the 20th century, Los Angeles became the center of attraction for most Hispanic and Asiatic immigrants. No less than one hundred languages are spoken in this linguistic metropolis, a modern Tower of Babel, from Spanish to Persian, and Russian to Japanese. The Chinatowns, Japantowns and Koreatowns of San Francisco and Los Angeles are cultural microcosms where Asiatic immigrants rediscover and reestablish their ancestral traditions. Today, Hispanics and Asiatics are more numerous than the state's white population. Will English continue to be the linguistic bond in the California society of the future? Who knows? *¿Quién sabe?*

Arts and traditions

Young Mexican salesgirl
in Los Angeles.

Cultural diversity was an intrinsic part of the foundation of Los Angeles and San Francisco, since the inhabitants were composed of Whites (Spanish) and people of mixed race (Negro-Spanish and Indian-Spanish). For more than half a century, this diversity was somewhat overshadowed by the arrival of Americans from the East Coast and Midwest, an influx that gave these two cities and the surrounding area a predominantly WASP (White Anglo-Saxon Protestant) profile. However, things began to change in the late 1960s, when greater prominence was given to civil rights issues and the federal law of immigration, which rejected the principle of quotas in favor of family unity. This led to an increase in the number of immigrants arriving from Latin America and Asia.

INDEPENDENT COMMUNITIES

In California, ethnic groups live side by side in independent communities that avoid mixing or meeting in public places other than shopping malls and leisure parks. Districts such as Chinatown, Little Tokyo, Little San Salvador and Koreatown, mainly located near the city's downtown area, cater to a specific ethnic community, although the entire population goes there to buy food and eat in the restaurants. Store signs are in different languages and English is seldom seen.

RELIGIOUS PRACTICES

There is a wide variety of different places of worship, with Christian churches, Buddhist temples, mosques and synagogues among the most prominent. They tend to be located near the communities they serve.

INTER-COMMUNITY DIVERSITY

There are differences between new and established residents within the same ethnic community. For example, in the South Central district of LA, apartment blocks and houses that used to be inhabited by Black families (who have now moved into the suburbs) are gradually being occupied by new immigrants from Central America, who are not accepted in the more established Mexican districts such as East Los Angeles.

ETHNIC TENSIONS

Ethnic tensions tend to have socio-economic and racial rather than religious origins. They can quickly erupt into revolt, as in San Francisco in 1871, and in Watts and Oakland in 1965–66. The riots that broke out in South Central LA in 1992 (left) following the acquittal of the white policemen charged with beating up a black citizen, Rodney King, expressed the anger of the Black and Latino community. They also highlighted the diversity of a population of African-Americans, Hispanics and Koreans competing in the job and housing markets.

● THE CALIFORNIAN WAY OF LIFE

The Californian way of life is indissolubly linked to the automobile, the vital link between town and country ● 48.

A beautiful landscape, sunshine and a land filled with promise soon made California the ideal place to combine an open-air life with a spirit of enterprise. Thus the Californian way of life became the model for the American way of life. California is in fact two very different regions. The North is often described as restrained, intellectual and alternative. In the South, which is more dynamic, and arguably more transitory in character, the distinction between the real and the imaginary becomes blurred. But all Californians share the same values: openness to progress, passion for work, desire for personal success and a love of entertainment – the state's main industry.

BoBos
Living in a natural environment that favors outdoor activities, Californians often tend to dress very casually. In a book published in 2000, an American journalist describes the BoBos, the young executives and entrepreneurs of Silicon Valley ▲ 146, and their lifestyle, a subtle blend of the bohemian and bourgeois cultures. BoBos hate suits and ties and much prefer shorts or sweat pants, tee-shirts and running shoes.

FEAR OF THE BIG ONE
The ever-present threat of the Big One – the earthquake that will separate California from the rest of North America or cause it to be engulfed by the Pacific Ocean – is reflected in everyday patterns of behavior. Most Californians keep a flashlight on their bedside table, a permanent stock of drinks in their car trunk, and sometimes enough food reserves in the house to last for a week. All organizations and businesses have an emergency action plan to be implemented in the event of an emergency.

THE OPEN-AIR LIFE

Of all the sporting activities enjoyed by Californians, from jogging to body building, skiing and windsurfing (there are any number of marinas), one has become popular worldwide: surfing ▲ 210 (below). The English critic Reyner Banham went so far as to invent the term 'surfurb' to describe the middle-class residential areas which, like Malibu ▲ 208 in LA, are near the ocean and where many of the residents are keen surfers.

INDOOR PUBLIC SPACES

Apart from a few committed joggers, residential areas appear to be deserted. In fact, most urban activities take place indoors. Since 1920, shopping malls have become increasingly popular. Disneyland ▲ 214 represents the prototype for these reassuring public spaces that simulate the urban environment and are, in fact, one vast consumer area.

PRIVATE HOUSES

Since the 19th century, the private house has been considered the ideal setting for family life and social living. In the last twenty years, 'gated communities' have appeared, groups of houses surrounded by a secure perimeter fence or wall and run by owner-occupiers who share similar lifestyles.

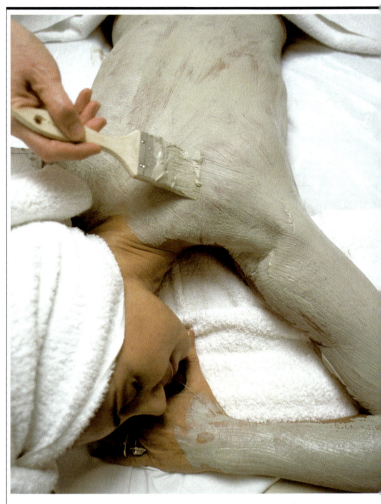

Visitors sometimes smile at the proverbial Californian preoccupation with self. But are they right to make fun of it? In California, more than anywhere else, speaking about self is as commonplace in the field of art as it is in medicine and show-business. It was already established in the glorious age of the immigrant refugees from the Midwest. During the depression of 1929, Woody Guthrie knew better than anyone how to express his melancholy in his songs. Before him, the 'bluesmen' only sang of their own lives and personal sufferings. In the mid-1950s, the poets and writers of the Beat Generation continued in the same autobiographical vein, and turned this way of talking about personal experiences into a 'principle of faith'.

Mud treatment in a beauty salon (left).

SELF ... AND OTHERS Today, egotism has almost become a form of etiquette.

However, there are still Californians who are able to transcend the self.

OCCULT SCIENCES FOR COMPLETE WELL-BEING

Those involved in the San Francisco hippie scene were constantly striving to gain better self-knowledge. Parapsychology and alternative medicine boomed, and traces still exist today, as shown by the city's many clairvoyants and acupuncturists. In California, genuine institutes such as the Esalen Institute ▲ 171 in Big Sur exist alongside charlatans. Introspection holds no fears for Californians who indulge in special regimes and extreme yogic practices such as daily internal cleansing, ascetic retreats and so on.

ANALYSTS OR GURUS?
From around 1960, Hindu ashrams and centers for yoga and meditation began to spring up. Gurus such as Jiddu Krishnamurti ▲ 176 have been made famous by their followers from the world of entertainment. For example, the singer Leonard Cohen (above) chose to withdraw to a Zen Buddhist monastery for long retreats. California's fascination with the East is still very much alive.

BEATNIKS AND ZENS

The Beat Generation ● 36 were largely responsible for the establishment of Eastern philosophers on the coast of California. Before them, Henry Miller ▲ 170 had shown a marked interest in Zen. The first Zen Buddhist center was built on the cliffs of the magnificent northern coast at the instigation of Suzuki Roshi, while the philosopher Alan Watts disseminates Zen teachings from his Sausalito retreat. People no longer refer to the 'cult of self' but rather the search for spirituality.

THE BEAUTIFUL PEOPLE

Is 'beauty at any price' one of the vagaries of Hollywood? Many people want to create a new, ideal body, or at least seriously reshape the one they have. Los Angeles has large numbers of orthodontists and cosmetic surgeons offering dentures, breast implants, face lifts, liposuction and other cosmetic operations which seem to hold the promise of eternal youth for people who are terrified of growing old. The myth of the perfect body is constantly reinforced by the reality on the beaches of Southern California, inhabited by beautifully formed nymphs and 'body-built' surfers, all perfectly blond and sun-tanned.

Female lifeguards from the television series *Baywatch* (below).

Many Californians are very reliant on their 'wheels'. Long distances lead them to depend on cars for doing their shopping, getting to and from work and visiting theaters, clubs, and so on. Towns such as Los Angeles, whose freeway loops were the forerunners of their European counterparts, would have a completely different layout without the automobile. Automobiles appear in the early Hollywood movies, starring alongside the likes of Buster Keaton and Laurel and Hardy – a tradition that has been perpetuated to the present day in films such as *Bullitt*, *Bonnie and Clyde*, *The Blues Brothers* and *Rebel Without a Cause*. Among the famous automobiles owned by the stars are Clark Gable's Jaguar XK 120 and James Dean's Porsche RSK 550, which he died in on the road to Salinas in September 1955.

WHERE THE AUTOMOBILE RULES From the early 1950s, the urban environment began to be almost exclusively designed for the automobile. The drive-in system gave access to a number of services: banks, fast-food restaurants, movie theaters (above) and even churches, where you can get married without getting out of your car! At the same time the mall culture ● 77 developed. The architecture of these malls was designed for the automobile, with much space given over to parking.

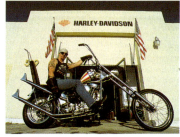

THE MOTORCYCLE California contributed to the creation of the legend of the motorcycle with the unforgettable performance of Marlon Brando in *The Wild One*, and the early history of the Hell's Angels, iconic figures to motorcycle gangs throughout the world (above).

James Dean with his Porsche spyder (right) just before his fatal accident.

AUTOMOBILES AND ATTITUDES

In the 1950s, the convertible was the embodiment of sunshine, light and the pursuit of pleasure in a carefree California. In the late 1960s, the Volkswagen Beetle and Minibus reflected the aspirations of the Beatniks ● *36*: a nomadic lifestyle, community spirit and free inspiration in art. Witness the patched-up school buses of the Merry Pranksters ▲ *114*. Japanese cars became popular after the first oil crisis (1973), when economy became the order of the day. The 4 x 4 boom of the 1980s and 90s reflects a sporty, casual attitude and a passion for the outdoors. The open convertible has been replaced by tinted windows. But the weekend procession along Sunset Strip ▲ *198* still creates traffic jams!

Since the early 1920s Hollywood, the center of movie production in the United States, has presented the most legendary aspect of Southern California to the world. The advent of digital technology, special effects and ultra-elaborate multimedia techniques has done much to revolutionize the movie industry in the past couple of decades. Situated outside the vast city of Los Angeles, it plays a major role in the economic growth of California by spawning new but related leisure markets. From music to theme restaurants, amusement parks and the production of consumer items and video games, California has become the world center of entertainment.

HOLLYWOOD, DISCOVERED BY ACCIDENT
In December 1913, Cecil B DeMille, captivated by the climate and beauty of the little village of Hollywood ▲ 197, persuaded his New York producers to lease a farm for the shooting of one of his films. The event marked a spectacular development in movie production ▲ 180. Short periods of economic recession were always overcome by the development of new techniques: for example, in 1950, Cinemascope (wide-screen cinema).

Storage of MGM's reels c. 1930 (above).

MOVIES TAKE OVER FROM AEROSPACE
The end of the Cold War marked the decline of the aerospace industry, until then the flagship of the Californian economy. However, it was also responsible for a technical explosion in the movie industry which reemployed skilled aeronautics workers and took over the construction hangars. Between 1990 and 1998, the number of people employed in the field of movie-making leapt from 143,000 to 262,000 (an increase of 83 percent), not including those employed in associated fields – agents, lawyers, physical trainers, trailer-hire agents – who accounted for at least another 50,000.

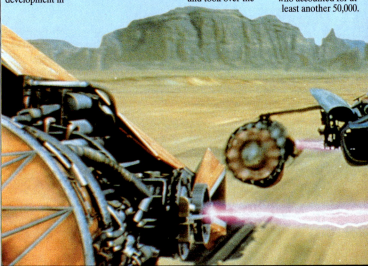

FOOD AND FASHION

'Star culture' and the 'entertainment dollar' have changed the Californian way of life. Many stars now have interests in the luxury restaurant business: Robert DeNiro owns the *Ago* restaurant on Melrose Avenue and Francis Ford Coppola is the proprietor of the *Coppola Vineyard* in Napa Valley. Similarly, fashion designers such as Randolph Duke, Calvin Klein and Vera Wang use stars to promote their clothes by creating special designs for them, particularly for such media events as the Academy Awards.

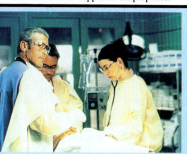

TELEVISION AT THE SERVICE OF CINEMA

Since the 1950s, television has become part of our daily lives, and the television industry has expanded, basing itself in Burbank. Apart from national and cable TV, the major film studios create their own TV departments which produce talk shows, soaps, sitcoms and films such as the *ER* drama series (left). With the introduction of the video cassette, television made billions of dollars for the movie industry. Satellite TV has meant an explosion in demand for videos.

HOLLYWOOD: THE ENTERTAINMENT BUSINESS

When Disneyland ▲ *214* was opened by Disney in 1955, it attracted some 3,600,000 visitors per year. Universal Studios ▲ *194* followed suit by opening a theme park in its studios, while Warner amalgamated with Magic Mountain. In the same vein, the studios of the major film companies make their films pay by marketing consumer items sold in their 'studio stores', often located in the theme parks.

HOLLYWOOD AND BEYOND

New industries, such as the games industry in Santa Monica, began to colonize the towns and cities around Los Angeles. Further afield, the special effects guru George Lucas (*The Phantom Menace*, below) set up shop in Marin County. Hollywood was soon using the services and technology of Silicon Valley ▲ *146*. In 1995, *Toy Story* was the first film to be produced entirely on computer.

MUSIC AND VIDEO CLIPS

In 1981, Warner Amex Cable Communications created its MTV channel, which revolutionized the music world. Advertising was taken a step further by the use of the video clip. In the wake of Michael Jackson's *Thriller* (1984), MTV was responsible for a huge growth in video production.

Rock and movie star Madonna (right).

● MUSIC:
THE STYLE INDUSTRY

Janis Joplin (right).

California soon became a major music production center. In the early 1930s, the advent of the 'talkies' provided work for performers and composers alike. The most famous of these was Miklós Rosza, who produced the original tapes for numerous action films and epics in the 1950s and 60s. In the late 1930s, artists flocked to Southern California to take advantage of the recording studios that were springing up there. Twenty years later, Hollywood had become one of the world's leading record production centers, with jazz and rock musicians among the first to benefit from the boom.

JAZZ

Around 1950, a musical trend emerged known as West Coast Jazz – a name that was geographical rather than stylistic. Musicians met at the Lighthouse, a club on Hermosa Beach. Drummer Shelly Manne and clarinetist Jimmy Giuffre were the driving forces of West Coast Jazz, but its symbolic figures were saxophonist Gerry Mulligan and his fellow musician, singer/trumpet player Chet Baker. Mulligan and Baker were heroes of the Beat Generation and prophets of the 'cool jazz' invented by Miles Davis. The pianist Dave Brubeck composed themes that became classics of a more commercial type.

SHOW BUSINESS IN LOS ANGELES

In the 1950s, records opened up the youth market while radio broadcast 'easy listening' music. Whereas artists had previously performed live in the studio, black 'rhythm 'n blues' and 'doo-wop' groups (Coasters, Rivingtons) were among the first to take advantage of 45s to produce hits in the style of light-hearted swing. The studios developed specific sounds, such as the 'wall of sound' created by the record producer Phil Spector, who promoted female groups such as the Ronettes.

BEACH, SUN AND FUN

In the early 1960s a new style made its debut, based on vocal harmonies and more sophisticated arrangements. This was the 'surf sound' primarily associated with the duo Jan and Dean and the quintessential Californian group, the Beach Boys (below). Their songs painted an idyllic picture that featured beautiful nymphs (*California Girls*), young, bronzed Adonis-like swimmers surfing the waves (*Surfin' USA*), pure enjoyment (*Fun, Fun, Fun*) and a feeling of well-being (*Good Vibrations*).

ROCK AND FOLK

Around 1965, a folk-rock trend emerged in LA with, among others, the Byrds (who performed Bob Dylan songs using electric guitars), Sonny and Cher, the Turtles and later, The Mamas & The Papas (*California Dreamin'*). The Mamas & The Papas were also the coorganizers of the legendary Monterey Festival in June 1967, which marked the beginning of media coverage of the hippie phenomenon. The folk-rock wave reached its peak around 1970, with Crosby, Stills, Nash and Young. Pure folk also enjoyed great popularity during the same period with the voices of Joan Baez (above) and Judy Collins.

SAN FRANCISCO COMPETING WITH LA

In 1967, a song by Scott McKenzie entreated those going to San Francisco to wear flowers in their hair, while local groups performed in Golden Gate Park. The Grateful Dead (above), Jefferson Airplane and Janis Joplin (top left) are forever linked to the hippie saga. Their music was backed up by concerts at the Fillmore Auditorium and Avalon Ballroom, and on the new FM radio stations. San Francisco, with its more psychedelic style of rock seemed determined to distinguish itself from the more commercial LA sound. However, the music of LA-based artistes like the Doors and Frank Zappa seem to have better stood the test of time.

RETURN TO LA

Today, a large proportion of US musical production is located in Los Angeles, where the local legend has been perpetuated by such hits as *Hotel California* by the Eagles, a perfect example of a West Coast group. LA has produced a diverse mixture of musical talents, including punks like Henry Rollins (also a publisher) and Jello Biafra (a regular candidate for the office of mayor of San Francisco); rappers like Snoop Doggy Dog; apostles of cross cultural music like Carlos Santana; and women who have broken into the very macho world of rock 'n' roll: yesterday it was the Runaways, today it is Courtney Love (top right).

Mount Whitney (1940) by Ansel Adams (below) and *Agave* (1920) by Imogen Cunningham (bottom).

Photography has always occupied an important place among Californian art forms; perhaps the exceptional light and magnificent landscapes have something to do with it. Local photographers were not content to produce beautiful pictures, which would have been enough to establish their reputation in Europe. They also established influential movements, revolutionized the accepted ways of looking at things and inspired other would-be photographers throughout the world.

ANSEL ADAMS (1902–84)

Ansel Adams was 14 years old when he photographed the Yosemite region for the first time. He often returned, bequeathing such legendary images as that of the sheer rock face of El Capitan. To perfect the quality of the image, he invented an elaborate system for measuring light known as the 'zone system', which made it possible to reproduce all the nuances of a subject exposed to different light intensities. He also gave California a photographic gallery: the Friends of Photography gallery in San Francisco.

CARLETON WATKINS (1829–1916)

Carleton Watkins was an early immigrant to San Francisco. He specialized in architectural photography, but it was his landscapes that established his reputation. From 1861 he traveled in the Yosemite region, where he discovered natural landscapes that had escaped the ravages of the gold prospectors. The publication of his albums so impressed the state authorities that Yosemite ▲ *254* was designated a national park.

GROUP F.64

Although Watkins influenced later photographers such as Ansel Adams, in 1932 Adams became one of the founder members of Group *f*.64, whose clearly stated aim was to break with the soft-focused pictorial traditions of the past. Inspired by Preston Holder and Willard Van Dyke, the group took its name from the smallest aperture of the lens which produced good resolution and maximum depth of field.

Self Portrait (1932) by Alma Lavenson (above).

IMOGEN CUNNINGHAM (1883–1976)

Discovered by Group *f*.64, this portraitist produced sharply focused images which influenced colleagues such as Judy Dater. It was due to her that the collection of Group *f*.64 now belongs to the SFMoMA ▲ *116*.

Photography arrived in the American West by courtesy of the railroads. The first trains had mobile photographic laboratories to the rear, providing developing facilities for early photo-journalists, whose work recorded the beauty of the new territories. During the Gold Rush, there was a huge demand for daguerreotype portraits, and each town along the Mother Lode River had its own portrait studio.

EDWARD WESTON (1886–1958)

The work of the leading light of Group *f*.64 consists of still lifes and nude studies. The emphasis is on the perfect quality of the image rather than the object represented. Many of his images verge on abstraction, such as *Shells* (1937) (left). His sons Brett and Cole carry on his work, perpetuating the tradition of this great photographer.

POST-1960

The 1960s reinstated the pictorial techniques rejected by Group *f*.64. Jim Marshall and Baron Wolman, who covered the *Summer of Love* in 1967, published portraits of the rock stars. Michelle Vignes, who preferred blues images, embodied a new generation of artists reviving the commitment of Walker Evans and Dorothea Lange. Their photographs of the rural resettlement program reflected an attitude opposed to that of such leading lights of Californian photography as Herb Ritts (*Tatjana Veiled Head*, above) and Bruce Weber, who preferred to slip into the mold of the 'star system'.

● Californian Wines

California wine arrived with the Spanish missions in the 1700s, following them north from Mexico across the state. The grapes used then for sacramental wine bore little resemblance to the varieties we know today, but were so important to the missionaries that their spread marked the first stages of an unparalleled infiltration into the local culture. When California was annexed to the United States in 1847 it became known as the 'Wine State'. Today it still produces 90 percent of the country's wine, its vineyards covering 600 miles from north to south.

What's made Californian wine big?

Over the last 30 years California has developed one of the most powerful wine cultures in the world. A strong research ethic, built up by institutes such as Fresno and the University of California, Davis, has ensured that the industry is a leader in wine development. The founding of 'single-varietal' wines with easily-recognized grape names has done much to popularize wine. And in the last 10 years, California has developed a range of expensive, small-production wines with their own distinctive character. These are taking the state to a new level of quality, dispensing with the need to emulate the Old World classics.

CABERNET SAUVIGNON
California's premium grape, producing deep-colored wine. Distinctively blackcurrant in flavor and aroma.

SAUVIGNON BLANC
Known as Fumé Blanc when matured in oak barrels. The unoaked wines have fresher, crisper green fruit aromas.

ZINFANDEL
California's own grape. Highly versatile, ranging from sweetish rosés to intense, deeply colored blockbusters.

CHARDONNAY
Popular white grape producing toasty, buttery, full-flavored wine, characterized by tropical fruit and vanilla.

MERLOT
Second in line to
Cabernet Sauvignon,
with equally dark fruit,
but giving a softer,
rounder, more
approachable wine.

REGIONS
Napa and Sonoma, the most
important, were established by
the 1890s, but other regions grew
in importance too, not least the
Central San Joaquin Valley.
Other regions springing up
included the Livermore Valley to
the east and Monterey, San Luis
Obispo and Santa Barbara to the
south. Today, it's the regions of
cooler climate that are arousing
interest: Santa Barbara,
Carneros and the sprawling
Sonoma Coast region. Cooler
climates are important for
tempering the high-alcohol,
fruity wines typical of the state.

FOOD: MIXED SALAD WITH BEANS, PEPPERS AND ANCHOVIES

California doesn't have its own cuisine as such but, like the state, its food is a melting-pot of cultural influences. Here, even the fast food invented in North America has a Chinese or Mexican flavor. In the case of more sophisticated cuisine, particular attention is paid to the freshness of the ingredients and the nutritional value of the food. In the 1980s, Alice Waters, chef of the Chez Panisse restaurant in Berkeley, redefined the parameters of a gastronomy, inspired by French cuisine, which gives pride of place to fresh, seasonal, local produce. For example, her entrees may combine Californian vegetables and fish or shellfish from the Pacific, like this mixed salad with beans, peppers and anchovies which can also be served as a main course.

INGREDIENTS
1 cup each dried flageolet beans, red kidney beans and black beans
2 bay leaves
6 sprigs fresh thyme
1 teaspoon finely chopped thyme
8 anchovy fillets in brine
½ cup virgin olive oil
1 red onion
2 tablespoons red wine vinegar
2 cloves garlic
1 bunch flat-leaved parsley
1 red and 1 yellow pepper
salt and pepper

3. Chop the onion into small pieces.

Crush the garlic with a pinch of salt. Chop

the parsley finely to give the equivalent of 2 tablespoons. Cut the peppers into fine strips.

1. Soak the beans separately for 12 hours.

2. Simmer each type of bean separately, with a bay leaf and 2 sprigs fresh thyme, for between 5 and 30 minutes, until tender. Season with a pinch of salt and leave to cool for 1 hour.

Kidney beans are a key ingredient in Mexican cuisine, which is extremely popular in California – especially Southern California.

CHEZ PANISSE
28TH
BIRTHDAY

4. Rinse the anchovies in cold water and taste a small piece to make sure they are tender. If not, soak the fillets in cold water for between 15 and 60 minutes to soften them. Drain and cover with 2 tablespoons olive oil. Marinate the onion in 2 tablespoons vinegar with a pinch of salt for 15 minutes.

5. Mix the crushed garlic, parsley, finely chopped thyme, peppers and onion with the rest of the olive oil.

6. Drain the cold beans through a sieve and remove the herbs.

7. Add the beans to the above mixture (5) and season with salt, pepper and a little vinegar.

8. Place the salad in a serving dish, remove the anchovies from the oil and arrange on top of the salad.

ALMONDS
Almonds, especially roasted, are produced in the Central Valley and Sacramento region. They have made the fortune of the Blue Diamond label.

CALIFORNIAN SEEDS
Californian wildflower seeds – including the famous poppies ● *21*, the symbol of California – can be found in the nurseries of San Francisco. They should be sown in late autumn or early spring.

RAISINS
Fresno is the home of California sun-dried raisins. You can't miss them in their red box with its 'Sun-Maid' logo.

BEEF JERKY
The American Indians used to dry bison meat to preserve it. Today, beef jerky is found in the candy section of supermarkets and gas stations.

A DESIGNER LABEL
Levi's were first produced in San Francisco in the second half of the 19th century, and were an immediate success ▲ *121*. Initially worn by cowboys and miners, in the 1940s they benefited from the American fascination with the Far West. In the 50s, they became very popular since they enabled young people to identify with their denim-clad Hollywood heroes. Levis became a classic that crossed the fashion boundaries and were worn throughout the world. They are more expensive in Europe than in their home town of San Francisco and elsewhere in the United States.

CALIFORNIAN WINES
California is ideal wine-producing country, and vines have been grown here since they were imported by missionaries in the 18th century ● *56*. There are growers in the north (especially the Napa and Sonoma valleys) and south (around Santa Barbara) of the state. The labels on the bottles give the grape variety (the main criterion of choice), the region and the producer.

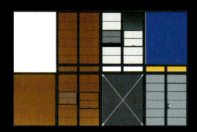

Architecture

California's earliest architectural heritage dates from the time of the Franciscan missions scattered along the Pacific Coast. To convert the indigenous peoples and cultivate their land, the *padres* established agricultural communities dominated by a church. Since they had no architects or stonemasons at their disposal, they drew up the plans, inspired by medieval monasteries and Spanish and Mexican churches, and supervised their construction by the indigenous workforce. They had to use local materials, mainly sun-dried bricks (*adobe*) or fired bricks for the whitewashed walls and curved tiles for the roof.

RETABLE OF THE HIGH ALTAR
(Mission Dolores ▲ *138* above)
This internal façade is made of painted wood with columns and statue niches. Its lavish Churrigueresque (late baroque) decor offers a striking contrast to the bare walls.

A RUSTIC MISSION: SAN DIEGO DE ALCALÁ ▲ *219*
The *espanadaña* (**1**), the festooned gable higher than the nave (whose modest height reflects the ever-present fear of earthquakes), is flanked by the *campanario* (**2**), a wall belfry pierced with arcades. Although the façade has lost part of the lower section of its decor, it has retained the delightfully fluid curves of the outline characteristic of the more rustic missions. The Franciscan building, the oldest in California (1808–1913), was restored in 1930.

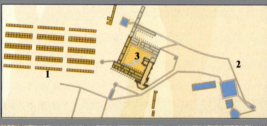

TYPICAL LAYOUT OF A MISSION
(Santa Barbara ▲ *175*)
A mission included an Indian village (**1**) and had its own irrigation system (**2**). The church and *convento* (monastery) (**3**) had an enclosed courtyard to guard against possible attack, with living accommodation, workshops, storehouses and an infirmary, forming a compact complex.

Reconstruction of the house in its original state (1851).   Casa Guajame, San Diego.

PLAN OF THE CASA GUAJAME

1. Enclosure wall
2. Stable
3. Forge
4. Storeroom
5. Indians' dining room
6. Kitchen
7. Family dining room
8. Family bedrooms
9. Living room, study
10. Store
11. Storerooms
12. Bedrooms
13. Bathroom

A TRADITIONAL HISPANIC HOUSE

This beautiful ranchero house (1851) ● *33* – the distant ancestor of the sprawling suburbs – had a single story and low-pitched roof covered with curved tiles. The bedrooms and living rooms opened onto a central patio (**A**), surrounded by an arcaded gallery, which was reminiscent of the cloisters of Franciscan monasteries. Behind this lay an enclosed service courtyard (**B**) with a forge. The foundations were made from local stone and the walls roughcast in the same clay from which the sun-dried bricks (*adobes*) were made.

THE MONTEREY STYLE: THE FIRST CALIFORNIAN STYLE (Larkin House ▲ *169*)

The Monterey house (1835–37) was built by a prosperous and highly respected merchant. Apart from the whitewashed *adobe* walls, everything in it contrasts with the traditional *casa* and acts as a reminder of the Bostonian origins of its owner: the upper story supported by a sequoia-wood framework, the four-paneled roof covered with wooden shingles, the overhang protecting an exterior gallery, the sash windows, the large central hall, the type of chimneys and even the wallpaper. The two-story house with its double gallery initiated the Monterey style that enjoyed a revival in the 1930s.

A BAROQUE MISSION: SANTA BARBARA, THE 'QUEEN OF MISSIONS' ▲ *174*

Echoing the symmetrical design of baroque churches with their central pediment and tall lateral towers, the lack of spontaneity in the church's façade is offset by its studied elegance. Its Ionic columns were copied from a Spanish edition of *De architectura*, a treatise on architecture in ten books by the Roman architect and theorist Vitruvius.

Unusually for a mission, the walls and towers were made not of *adobe,* but of local sandstone. Following a major earthquake in 1925, the towers were reinforced with concrete.

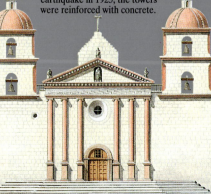

HISPANIC HERITAGE

Azulejos (glazed tiles), which originated in Spain and Portugal, are one of the decorative elements of the Hispanic style.

The Mission Revival style, a reaction against the aesthetic dominance of the East Coast, cultivated the myth of a paradise lost, and set the honesty and kindness of the Franciscan priests against the greed of the Anglo-Saxon settlers. The mission style, which expressed a need for historical legitimacy and a desire to adapt to the climate and natural environment, enjoyed a revival between 1905 and 1915, when it spread throughout the United States. It was superseded by a neo-Mediterranean style combining Spanish, Mexican, Italian and Moorish influences. Spanish Colonial Revival, a product of eclecticism and the picturesque, has been perpetuated – by building regulations as much as personal preference – up to the present day.

EXOTIC TOURISM (Burlingame station, 1894)
To offer businessmen escaping the blizzards of New York and Chicago a welcome change of scenery, railroad companies used the mission style for their stations and hotels. It is purely the external architectural elements – gently sloping red-tiled roofs, festooned gables and semicircular arched bays – that classify a building as Mission Revival style. Apart from the presence of patios, the interior layout and decor can equally well be in the Queen Anne or Arts and Crafts styles ● 68.

MEDITERRANEAN DREAMS
(house by Wallace Neff, San Marino, 1928, above) Wallace Neff was best known for his buildings in neo-Hispanic style. However, he was an eclectic architect who willingly designed Norman farms or Tudor manors to order. Here, picturesque details, including elements imported from Spain and Morocco, stand out against the balanced proportions of the building. The façade (above) was inspired by the farms of Lombardy, especially the loggia above the main entrance. The rear patio (**1**), with its covered gallery (**2**) and exterior staircase, gives the building a more intimate feel.

The layout of the San Juan Capistrano library (left) is based round a central patio, bounded by galleries reminiscent of mission cloisters.

BAROQUE REVISITED: A SYMBOL OF CALIFORNIA
(California Building ▲ *223*, 1915)
In 1915, an international trade fair was held in Balboa
Park in San Diego to mark the completion of the
Panama Canal. The chief architect, Bertram Goodhue,
designed the California Building whose slender tower
acts as a landmark for visitors. The lavish
Churrigueresque (late baroque) decor
of the pavilion entrance, with its
historic scenes, was inspired – as were
the top of the tower and the interior
layout – by the plans for Mexican
churches which Goodhue copied
from a work entitled *Spanish
Colonial Architecture in Mexico*
(1901).

The Mission
Revival style, was
criticized as
unsuitable for
non-religious
buildings. It was
replaced by a
Spanish Colonial
Revival, which
was both
charming and
authentic in the
hands of
architects and
landscape
designers with
an in-depth
knowledge of
their local and
international
sources.

A CIVIC SYMBOL (County Courthouse, Santa Barbara ▲ *174*, 1927)
Critics and historians regard
this as the most beautiful
public building in the
Spanish Colonial Revival
style, the quasi-official style
of Santa Barbara. Built by
William Mooser & Co. and J Wilmer Hersey, the
courthouse comprises a series of wings, with
different façades punctuated by towers and porches,
arranged around a huge landscaped courtyard.
There is nothing institutional or forbidding about it.

A POSTMODERN ADAPTATION (San Juan Capistrano library, 1983)
Local building regulations stipulating a 'Mediterranean style' have stimulated rather than
hindered architectural design. With materials characteristic of the Mission Revival style and a
personal vocabulary of massive structures and muted tones, Michael Graves,
the postmodern architect, built a library next to one of California's most
beautiful Franciscan missions ▲ *216*.

● VICTORIAN ARCHITECTURE

Detail of a bow window.

During the economic boom of 1850–1915, some 50,000 wooden houses were built in San Francisco. Many survived the fires caused by the 1906 earthquake and today constitute an exceptional part of the heritage of the United States. They are simply designed – usually with a flat roof – and have a standard layout, but the Victorian influence is reflected in a wide range of variously inspired details made possible by the use of bow saws. The most characteristic motif is the bay or bow window (*above*), usually surmounted by an Italianate cornice.

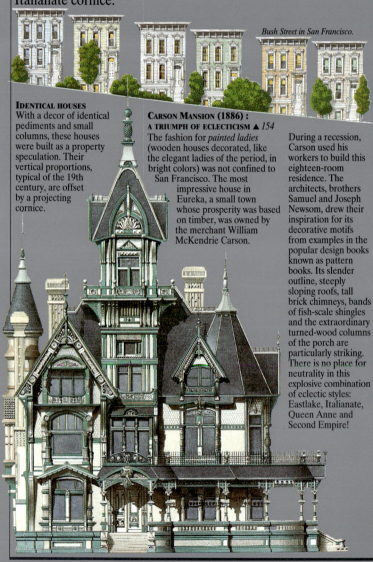

Bush Street in San Francisco.

IDENTICAL HOUSES
With a decor of identical pediments and small columns, these houses were built as a property speculation. Their vertical proportions, typical of the 19th century, are offset by a projecting cornice.

CARSON MANSION (1886) :
A TRIUMPH OF ECLECTICISM ▲ *154*
The fashion for *painted ladies* (wooden houses decorated, like the elegant ladies of the period, in bright colors) was not confined to San Francisco. The most impressive house in Eureka, a small town whose prosperity was based on timber, was owned by the merchant William McKendrie Carson.

During a recession, Carson used his workers to build this eighteen-room residence. The architects, brothers Samuel and Joseph Newsom, drew their inspiration for its decorative motifs from examples in the popular design books known as pattern books. Its slender outline, steeply sloping roofs, tall brick chimneys, bands of fish-scale shingles and the extraordinary turned-wood columns of the porch are particularly striking. There is no place for neutrality in this explosive combination of eclectic styles: Eastlake, Italianate, Queen Anne and Second Empire!

WOOD: AN ARCHITECTURAL MAINSTAY

Since the early 17th century, Americans have developed ingenious methods for treating wood. However, forests are rare in Southern California, and to build the Hotel del Coronado, pine for the framework had to be imported from Oregon, and timber for the cladding from the north of the state.

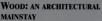

Cross section of the original ballroom.

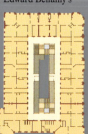

General plan of the first floor of the Hotel del Coronado.

THE WESTERN STYLE OF THE GOLD COUNTRY ▲ *157*

A great many of these natural wood buildings still symbolize the pioneering spirit of California. At the time of the Gold Rush, the region to the east of Sacramento became filled with buildings whose balconies usually overhung shops, Western-style saloons or even small churches bordering both sides of the main street.

A VACATION RESORT: HOTEL DEL CORONADO (1888) ▲ *221*

The hotel, situated in San Diego, was designed by James and Merritt Reid and is the last testimony to the great resort tradition of the coast. Apart from the red-painted roofs and whitewashed walls – a concession to the Mission style ● *64* – this 400-room hotel, whose dining room can seat 1000 guests, could equally well be situated on the Atlantic Coast. Its dynamic, picturesque outline is dominated by the conical roof of the great ballroom. The rooms are reached via walkways surrounding a huge landscaped courtyard.

The common areas of the hotel are in ocher: the lobby (**1**), ballroom (**2**), dining room (**3**) walkway around the central patio (**4**). Bedrooms and apartments are shown in gray.

BRADBURY BUILDING (1893):
TECHNICAL PROGRESS AND MODERNITY ▲ *186*

Behind the rather anonymous brick façades lies a glass-roofed atrium said to have been inspired by Edward Bellamy's Utopian novel *Looking Backward*. Visitors are delighted by the attention to detail, for example the openwork cast-iron mesh used for the cages of the elevator, a new piece of equipment at the time. The interior patio, widely used in office buildings from the end of the 19th century, has remained a popular architectural feature in the United States.

Several generations of Californian architects have been particularly receptive to the ideas of the British designer William Morris. Morris advocated a return to simplicity after the profusion of the Victorian age, a design that was integrated into the site, and the use of local construction techniques and materials. The abundance of wood in Northern California gave rise to the Bay Area tradition around the turn of the 20th century. However, its scarcity in the Los Angeles region did not affect the fashion for bungalows, built with consummate skill by the Greene brothers. In the 1930s, the key players of the second Bay Area tradition, mainly based in San Francisco, were seeking a progressive and human response to international style. They developed a regional style based more on geography than history and heritage.

GAMBLE HOUSE (1907) ▲ *191* AND THE ARTS AND CRAFTS STYLE ▲ *182*

The house was designed by the Greene brothers who learned practical skills before they studied architecture. Although situated in Pasadena, it nevertheless reflects the ideal of a return to the simple life. The design for the open-plan hall incorporating the upper story and living area is based on East Coast *Shingle Style* houses. The simple yet sophisticated staircase is typical of the Greene brothers' work. The framework (in which each construction detail gives rise to an original solution), ceiling and interior space are influenced by Japanese architecture and the pavilions of international trade fairs. Beams are rounded and hand-polished. As in the more modest middle-class bungalows, the exterior is characterized by low-pitched overhanging roofs and covered terraces. Before the invention of air conditioning, bedrooms were extended by 'sleeping porches' – covered terraces with a bed for hot summer nights.

Cross-section of the staircase in the main hall.

1. Entrance porch
2. Main hall
3. Staircase
4. Living area
5. Dining room
6. Study
7. Guest room
8. Kitchen
9. Terrace

FIRST CHURCH OF CHRIST SCIENTIST (1911): THE PERSONAL STYLE OF BERNARD MAYBECK

Although he trained at the École des Beaux-Arts in Paris, Maybeck did not belong to a particular school. According to the influential critic Esther McCoy, only Maybeck has been able to portray the weight of the past with such lightness. In spite of a limited budget, he turned this essentially square assembly hall in Berkeley into a jewel of decorative eclecticism and structural rationalism. The framework is supported by four hollow concrete pillars surmounted by neo-Byzantine capitals which rise to the main intersecting beams. The gilt wood paneling is inspired by the Flamboyant Gothic style.

Inside the church, each detail is treated with great care, as evidenced by the molded concrete desks and openwork chandeliers made of hammered steel.

JENSEN HOUSE (1937) AND THE MODERNISM OF THE 1930s

William Wurster, dean of the influential Berkeley school of architecture, developed a style similar to the Finnish architect Alvar Aalto. Simplicity and the maximum use of space characterize this flat-roofed house built on a narrow plot of land. Wurster made the rooms seem more spacious by the use of large bay windows and offset the façade to create a terrace and balcony. The white window frames, set flush with the horizontal planking of the walls, are reminiscent of Scandinavian architecture.

SEA RANCH CONDOMINIUM (1965) AND THE SECOND BAY AREA TRADITION

In this condominium of second homes, the team of architect Charles Moore and landscape designer Lawrence Halprin have tried to preserve the rugged aspect of the coastline north of San Francisco. The houses form compact groups and access roads have been kept to a minimum. The need for protection against the prevailing winds dictated the position of the terraces and the pitch of the roofs. Within these simple exteriors, the use of internal space is unexpectedly elaborate.

The natural wood architecture, using vertical wooden planks in the style of the site's original barns and buildings, reflects the ecological and libertarian ideals of 1960s California.

MODERNISM:
MACHINES FOR LIVING

The Chair, *designed by Charles and Ray Eames (1948).*

The private house has served as a laboratory for three generations of architects. Using industrial materials and the latest techniques, they have met the challenge of narrow sites and steep slopes. The pioneer was Irving Gill, who came to San Diego in 1893 and made concrete a fashionable material. Between the wars he was succeeded by Rudolf Schindler and Richard Neutra, who both trained in Vienna and then with Frank Lloyd Wright. Between 1945 and 1962 the Case Study Houses program, organized by John Entenza, editor of *Arts and Architecture*, democratized innovation.

CONCRETE AND MECHANIZATION (La Jolla Women's Club, 1913) The club attests to the important contribution made by Irving Gill to the Modern Movement. He condemned the excessive decoration of the Mission Revival ● *64* style but adopted its arcades, patios and bare walls. The concrete walls with their integrated metal framework were poured *in situ* – on the ground – and raised into position by jacks, using the 'tilt slab' process developed by the engineer Robert Aiken in 1908.

A HOUSE BUILT ON PILES (Lovell Beach House, LA, 1924, right) Rudolf Schindler erected five reinforced concrete portico-piles – which he described as an organic skeleton – into which the wooden floors and ceilings were embedded. The first storey is designed as an extension of the beach, with showers, a barbecue and children's games. The visible parts of the structure – parapets of the staircases, balconies and sleeping porches – create a dynamic sculptural effect.

AN UP-MARKET 'PREFAB' (Lovell House ▲ *183*, LA, 1929) Contemporary with Le Corbusier's Villa Savoye, this asymmetrical house by Richard Neutra symbolizes the industrial aesthetics of the 1920s. The technique used is the same as for skyscrapers. The prefabricated elements of the metal framework and door and window fittings were erected in record time: 48 hours! Nicknamed the 'Health House', it reflects the ideal of health through sport and a healthy lifestyle advocated by Dr Lovell in his articles in the *Los Angeles Times*. It was much admired by avant-garde circles for its technical innovations and elegance.

The parapets and balconies – made from concrete projected by a cement gun – are suspended rather than overhanging.

METAL AND GLASS (Case Study House # 9, LA, 1949)
This Case Study House, built in Pacific Palisades, belongs to Charles Eames. The house and studio are arranged around a patio. Transparent, translucent and opaque glass panels set in a metal framework (left) – a trellis of girders, ceilings in sheet metal, metal door and window fittings – create a sophisticated interplay of colors reminiscent of a Mondrian canvas. The overall effect is softened by the curved lines of the furniture, for example *The Chair* (top left, opposite) designed by Charles and Ray Eames in 1948.

TRANSPARENCY (Case Study House # 22, LA, 1960)
A metal framework creates the ultimate in transparency and open-plan living in this house in Hollywood Hills (above). As if defying gravity, Pierre Koenig designed an L-shaped plan around a pool (right). The two walls overlooking the street are blind, while the glass walls on the other sides are protected from the summer sun by broad roof projections.

1. Entrance/garage
2. Pool
3. Living room
4. Dining room
5. Kitchen
6. Pantry
7. Bathroom
8. Dressing room
9. Bedrooms

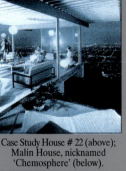

Case Study House # 22 (above); Malin House, nicknamed 'Chemosphere' (below).

BASED ON SCIENCE FICTION
(Malin House, LA, 1961)
John Lautner, who studied with Frank Lloyd Wright, branched out on his own, specializing in 'science-fiction' houses. On a site in Hollywood Hills considered impossible to build on – access is by funicular **(1)** – he perched an octagonal platform on a concrete column, covered it with a wooden shell and held it steady using steel struts **(2)**.

● Art Deco and Frank Lloyd Wright

'Textile blocks' on the façade and interior walls. Frank Lloyd Wright alternates plain and stamped blocks, creating an original design for each house by subdividing the basic square of the layout.

In California, as in the rest of the United States, the commercial architecture of the Roaring Twenties was influenced by modern jazz. Lavish, geometric decors were not only inspired by the Paris International Exhibition of Decorative Arts in 1925, but also by the Viennese Sezessionen and the German Expressionists. Eclecticism and exoticism were also still extremely popular, especially for places of public entertainment. In the 1930s, the Depression favored the development of the streamlining design style, which was simpler and more aerodynamic, not unlike the aesthetics of the avant-garde movement in Europe.

In the 1920s, most of Wright's designs were for Los Angeles.

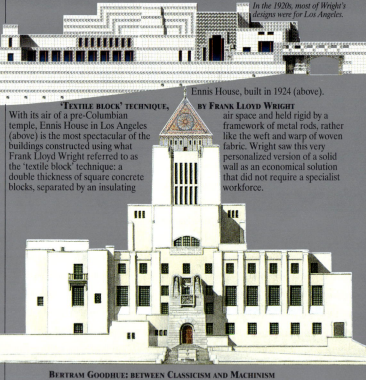

Ennis House, built in 1924 (above).

'Textile block' technique, by Frank Lloyd Wright

With its air of a pre-Columbian temple, Ennis House in Los Angeles (above) is the most spectacular of the buildings constructed using what Frank Lloyd Wright referred to as the 'textile block' technique: a double thickness of square concrete blocks, separated by an insulating air space and held rigid by a framework of metal rods, rather like the weft and warp of woven fabric. Wright saw this very personalized version of a solid wall as an economical solution that did not require a specialist workforce.

Bertram Goodhue: between Classicism and Machinism
(Los Angeles Central Library ▲ 187, 1926)

The concrete façades of the building, with their slight backward tilt, are not particularly academic. The corner pillars of the tower contrast with the polychrome tiles of the roof. The sculpted and painted decor, which illustrates the theme of the 'Light of Learning', is inspired by Egyptian, Islamic, Byzantine and Roman art. Interestingly, the human figures, by the sculptor Lee Lawrie, blend with the architectonic order.

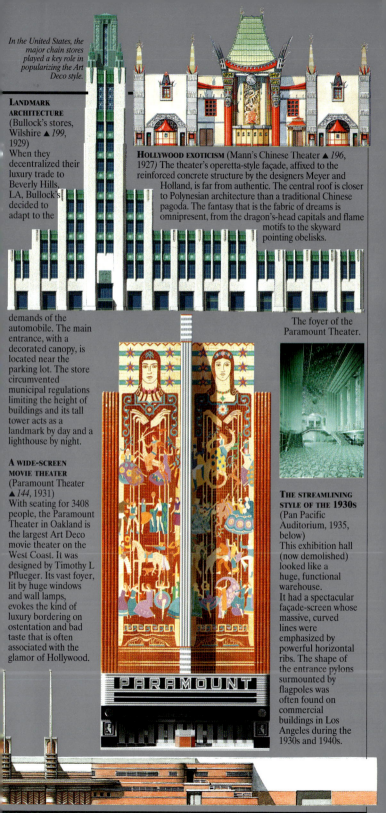

In the United States, the major chain stores played a key role in popularizing the Art Deco style.

LANDMARK ARCHITECTURE (Bullock's stores, Wilshire ▲ *199*, 1929) When they decentralized their luxury trade to Beverly Hills, LA, Bullock's decided to adapt to the demands of the automobile. The main entrance, with a decorated canopy, is located near the parking lot. The store circumvented municipal regulations limiting the height of buildings and its tall tower acts as a landmark by day and a lighthouse by night.

HOLLYWOOD EXOTICISM (Mann's Chinese Theater ▲ *196*, 1927) The theater's operetta-style façade, affixed to the reinforced concrete structure by the designers Meyer and Holland, is far from authentic. The central roof is closer to Polynesian architecture than a traditional Chinese pagoda. The fantasy that is the fabric of dreams is omnipresent, from the dragon's-head capitals and flame motifs to the skyward pointing obelisks.

The foyer of the Paramount Theater.

A WIDE-SCREEN MOVIE THEATER (Paramount Theater ▲ *144*, 1931) With seating for 3408 people, the Paramount Theater in Oakland is the largest Art Deco movie theater on the West Coast. It was designed by Timothy L Pflueger. Its vast foyer, lit by huge windows and wall lamps, evokes the kind of luxury bordering on ostentation and bad taste that is often associated with the glamor of Hollywood.

THE STREAMLINING STYLE OF THE 1930s (Pan Pacific Auditorium, 1935, below) This exhibition hall (now demolished) looked like a huge, functional warehouse. It had a spectacular façade-screen whose massive, curved lines were emphasized by powerful horizontal ribs. The shape of the entrance pylons surmounted by flagpoles was often found on commercial buildings in Los Angeles during the 1930s and 1940s.

73

● Postmodernism

Frank O Gehry and the sculptor Claes Oldenburg framed the main entrance to the parking lot of the publicity agency Chiat/Day in Venice with a huge pair of binoculars ▲ 183.

In Los Angeles, the abstract minimalism of the 1950s and 1960s was abandoned in favour of more complex forms and less noble materials, which better reflected social tensions and the disjunction of the urban fabric. Frank O Gehry had a large following, popularizing the concepts of collage and DIY. The postmodern architecture produced in Southern California was entertaining and had widespread appeal, with more than a touch of irony and eclecticism. It has retained its experimental character and continues to occupy an avant-garde position on the world stage.

A NEW REGIONAL SENSITIVITY
(Kresge College, Santa Cruz, 1974) Charles Moore and William Turnbull were the precursors rather than the leaders of the Californian Postmodern Movement. Their plans for a convivial university residence involved the students in the design stage. They wanted to recreate the urban feel and atmosphere of Italian towns, with their narrow streets and tiny squares, while avoiding the neo-Mediterranean pastiche widely found in the region.

Elevation of the Lindblade Tower (above).

THE FRANK O GEHRY MANIFESTO
(The architect's residence ▲ 183, Los Angeles, 1978)
The deconstruction process to which Gehry subjected his own house in Santa Monica made it a symbol of American Postmodernism.

This modest residence in a quiet, middle-class district lost its anonymity due to an outer wrapping on three sides that made it possible to redesign the interior. The most shocking aspect was the use of inexpensive materials – chain-link fencing, plywood and corrugated steel – which totally contradicted traditional domestic ideals and created a deliberately unfinished effect.

INDUSTRIAL RESTORATION
(The Lindblade Tower and the Paramount Laundry, Los Angeles, 1989, above)
Owen Moss renovated these two warehouses, built in 1940 as movie production studios, typical of the Culver City environment. For the central part of the Paramount Laundry, which today houses a graphics agency, he designed a vaulted foyer lit by a large semicircular window. He also added the canopy, which is visible from the street. It is supported by a series of ordinary glazed terracotta sewage pipes filled with concrete, the last at an angle, in defiance of the traditional notions of balance.

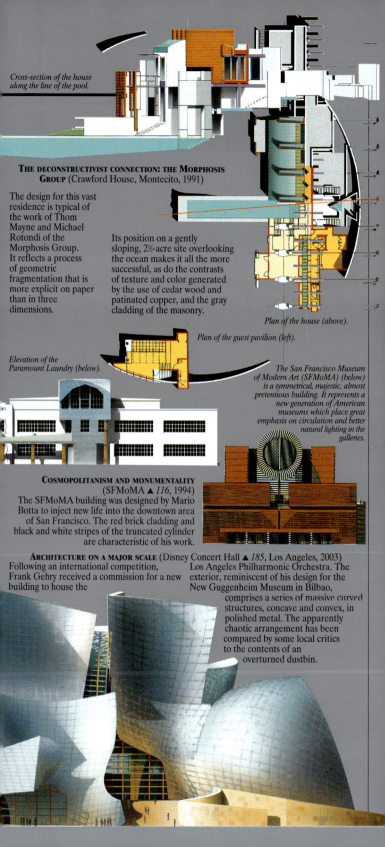

Cross-section of the house along the line of the pool.

THE DECONSTRUCTIVIST CONNECTION: THE MORPHOSIS GROUP (Crawford House, Montecito, 1991)

The design for this vast residence is typical of the work of Thom Mayne and Michael Rotondi of the Morphosis Group. It reflects a process of geometric fragmentation that is more explicit on paper than in three dimensions.

Its position on a gently sloping, 2½-acre site overlooking the ocean makes it all the more successful, as do the contrasts of texture and color generated by the use of cedar wood and patinated copper, and the gray cladding of the masonry.

Plan of the house (above).

Plan of the guest pavilion (left).

Elevation of the Paramount Laundry (below).

The San Francisco Museum of Modern Art (SFMoMA) (below) is a symmetrical, majestic, almost pretentious building. It represents a new generation of American museums which place great emphasis on circulation and better natural lighting in the galleries.

COSMOPOLITANISM AND MONUMENTALITY
(SFMoMA ▲ 116, 1994)
The SFMoMA building was designed by Mario Botta to inject new life into the downtown area of San Francisco. The red brick cladding and black and white stripes of the truncated cylinder are characteristic of his work.

ARCHITECTURE ON A MAJOR SCALE (Disney Concert Hall ▲ 185, Los Angeles, 2003)
Following an international competition, Frank Gehry received a commission for a new building to house the Los Angeles Philharmonic Orchestra. The exterior, reminiscent of his design for the New Guggenheim Museum in Bilbao, comprises a series of massive curved structures, concave and convex, in polished metal. The apparently chaotic arrangement has been compared by some local critics to the contents of an overturned dustbin.

DESCRIPTIVE ARCHITECTURE: THE CULT OF THE AUTOMOBILE

The automobile way of life.

More than any other city in the United States, Los Angeles' spectacular development has been closely linked to that of the automobile.

In the 1930s, it began to bring about major changes in the American way of life. Because commercial buildings were seen at a speed of 40 mph in a fairly uniform urban setting, they had to develop an immediately identifiable form of architecture, and provide parking spaces. This outlook, which introduced a kitsch element into the architecture of the time, was responsible for the development of buildings, based on the mass consumption and leisure industries, which became increasingly colossal and at variance with their environment.

ROUTES WITH A HIGH TRAFFIC FLOW (traffic plan for the central district of Los Angeles, 1949)
Automobile-led architecture was a spontaneous response by traders and entrepreneurs taking advantage of the land resources of LA. At the time, the city stretched along endless boulevards and it was not until 1945 that an attempt was made to create a coherent freeway network – landscaped parkways and then highways.

PARKING A PRIORITY (plan for off-street parking, LA, 1941)
Plots bordering the commercial streets began to change shape in order to provide the maximum number of parking spaces. The Regional Planning Commission designed functional and aesthetic plans.

SUPERMARKETS (Ralphs Supermarket, Inglewood, LA, 1940)
Supermarkets, which developed from on-street warehouses, began to cover increasingly vast sales and parking areas. This chain with its distinctive logo adopted the self-service formula and relied on quality façades. During the 1930s and 1940s, its brand image in the modern streamlining style was orchestrated by the architect Stiles O Clements. This building, formerly on Crenshaw Boulevard, is no longer standing.

MIMETIC ARCHITECTURE

These buildings, mainly 24-hour snack bars, are designed so that their function is immediately obvious to drivers. They use decorative motifs representing a particular consumer product, hugely magnified for publicity purposes. The idea is more important than its execution in these modestly sized structures, typical of Southern California, and their future is usually precarious.

THE 'DRIVE-IN' CULTURE

The population of Los Angeles more than doubled during the 1920s. In 1930, there were 806,264 automobiles for 1,238,048 inhabitants, mostly owned by private householders. The increase favored the almost chaotic development of fast-food establishments (for example the Carpenters chain, which

DESCRIPTIVE DECORS

Although still very much in evidence, the publicity value and architectural quality of façade decors are tending to be overshadowed by freestanding signposts of impressive dimensions and increasingly original and spectacular design. Competition between signs on the main commercial routes merely accentuates the phenomenon.

was fastidious about its architectural image), and then banks and movie theaters where drivers could complete transactions or see a film without getting out of their cars. Richard Hollingshead, who designed the first drive-in movie theater in New Jersey (1933), established himself in 1934 on the corner of Pico and Westwood boulevards. However, it was not until 1945 that the drive-in theater became a real cultural institution.

Carpenters Drive-in, Hollywood, 1935 (above), and the El Rancho Drive-in, Sacramento, 1933 (below).

Principles of a drive-in theater.

THE MALL, RETAIL AND LEISURE CENTER
(City Walk Universal City, Los Angeles)

This pedestrian precinct, in association with Universal Studios ▲ *194*, is located in a cul-de-sac surrounded by vast parking lots and is only accessible from the freeway. It was devised by John Jerde, who specializes in the huge shopping centers known as 'mega-malls'. He has incorporated a touch of the bad taste which he considers

typical of LA. Restaurants and boutiques, designed by various architects, border a single 'street' and circular 'squares'. The extravagant and deliberately disparate accumulation of signs and billboards was inspired by Sunset Strip ▲ *198*.

During the 20th century the county of Los Angeles experienced a development unique in urban history. Although similar examples of expansion can be found on the East Coast and in the Midwest, it has reached its peak in Los Angeles. The political policies that promoted individual family dwellings and private transport early in the century have led to an urbanization which is not, as has often been said, 'unplanned', but rather planned as a 'non-city', where automobile, horizontal growth and decentralization are the key words.

THE POPULATION EXPLOSION

In the late 19th century, Southern California was regarded as a vast Garden of Eden. In 1900, Los Angeles was a small town whose population of 100,000 was about to explode, increasing to 576,673 by 1920 and 1,238,048 by 1930. During the same period, the region's population more than doubled in size, from 936,000 to 2,208,000. In 1904, various 'zoning' measures were taken to organize the urban expansion of residential, commercial and industrial districts.

HORIZONTALITY

Three conditions are required for urban expansion: an urban transport network, strong economic potential and autonomous supplies of water and energy.

THE AUTOMOBILE

The powerful Pacific Electric railroad company, which had run a major intercity railroad network since the 1900s, could not compete with the automobile. Los Angeles had 160,500 vehicles in 1920, 860,000 in 1930 and 1,093,000 in 1940.

The Los Angeles County Regional Planning Commission (1941) outlined the political policies that would irrevocably affect the urban development of LA via a non-convergent freeway system.
• A decentralized city (except for the administrative center downtown) where the automobile is the principal means of transport.
• A city in which (as was already the case in 1940) 25 percent of the surface area was devoted to roads, including highways and parking lots.
• A city with a low population density per square mile, dominated by private houses set in an idealized environment.

ECONOMIC POTENTIAL
From 1900 onwards, the vacation industry and land and property speculation were the major economic factors that contributed to expansion. Although the area was subject to earthquakes, there were no restrictions on building. The oil, movie, automobile and aeronautics industries were the other driving forces of the region's economy ▲ 178.

ESSENTIAL RESOURCES
Water and electricity were a constant problem, and so the city authorities try to ensure quantity rather than quality. This was achieved in 1931 by the construction of the Hoover Dam on the Colorado River. Today, LA relies on this inherited system, which is fast reaching the point of overload. But whatever measures are taken, now or in the future, to remedy the situation, they will not significantly alter an urban landscape that is the product of the American dream.

● GROUPED HOUSING

Apartment building in Amancio Ergina Village in San Francisco.

The pressure of an increasing population and rising land prices have inspired architects to find space-saving, collective or semi-collective solutions which are also aesthetically pleasing. In spite of bureaucratic obstacles, solutions are emerging that will enable the middle classes and the underprivileged to be housed in original and well-designed apartment blocks.

COOPERATIVE HOUSING
While using a hint of abstraction to avoid a cheap pastiche, Solomon echoes the traditional features of San Francisco's row houses. Shingles, balconies and pergolas are reminiscent of the Arts and Crafts style ● *68*.

THE COURT (West Horatio, Santa Monica)
The climate and Hispanic influence of LA is ideally suited to the mini-condominiums that group maisonettes around a central walkway or courtyard. Arcaded porches, integrated windowboxes and chimney stacks offset the cubic design. The living room has windows on three sides to take advantage of the view of the Pacific.

The absence of moldings and recesses reflects an obsession with clean lines.

1. Street
2. Garages
3. Accommodation units
4. Private courtyards
5. Apartments
6. Private central walkway

Plan of level 4.

Plan of levels 2, 3, 5.

SINGLE ROOM OCCUPANCY (Simone Hotel, LA, 1993)
Highly acclaimed for his luxury houses, Koning Eizenberg also designs non-profit-making accommodation. This 'apartment building' provides accommodation for people who would otherwise be on the streets. The inexpensive façade is skillfully designed.

First storey.

1. Street
2. Private parking lot
3. Reception
4. Reception accommodation
5. Room with kitchen and bathroom
GRAY: Bedrooms
ORANGE: Bathrooms
YELLOW: Common areas (living room and kitchen)

80

California
as seen by painters

The discovery and settlement of California attracted the first generation of artists in the mid 19th century. Before that, the missions ● *32* had employed painters to decorate the interiors of their religious buildings. Later, the houses of the railroad and mining magnates were decorated with paintings illustrating the conquest of the territory and the magnificence of its landscapes, as in Thomas Hill's *Bridal Veil Falls, Yosemite* (**1**) (1870–84). For artists such as Alfred Bierstadt and George Brewerton, these landscapes represented a paradise as yet unspoiled by industrialization. But it was not long before there was a demand for more realistic images, especially from magazines. The development of the country, its living and working conditions, replaced landscapes as the key themes in Californian pictorial art, which had become a medium for information rather than decoration. Thus one of the events leading to the settlement of California – the Great Depression of the 1930s ● *39* – inspired William Gropper to paint *Migration* (**2**) (1932), in the same politically committed vein as many other (literary and photographic) works on the subject. This tradition of militant painting has survived to the present day, mainly influenced by such masters of the Mexican art of fresco painting as Orozco, Siqueiros and Rivera. While Europe explored cubism and abstract art, a number of Californian

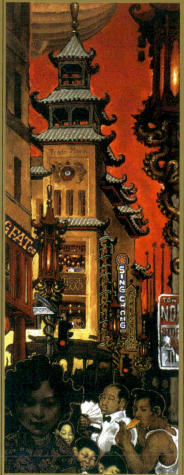

generation of painters who express themselves in terms of the language and traditional forms of representation of their community. Unlike their New York counterparts, they do not compete on the international art market, preferring to express their solidarity with a constantly changing local reality.

The realism of Martin Wong's Chinatown – *Grant Avenue, San Francisco* (**3**) (1992) – was undoubtedly inspired by the techniques of strip cartoons rather than Mandarin art. At the other side of the city, the Blacks and Chicanos ● *39* use similar techniques, in a blend, not without irony, of militant themes, scenes of local life and the key figures of their respective movements.

1	
	3
2	
	4

painters were moving in the opposite direction. Their compositions, characterized by realism, depicted the world of work (Barse Miller, Otis Oldfield, Paul Sample) or, as in *Tenement Flats* (**4**) (1934) by Millard Sheets, living conditions in the working-class districts. The accurate portrayal of reality was a permanent feature of the work of these artists who lived in close contact with their models. The decor is intensified by the use of warm colors that reflect a dearly won happiness. For all these people, California was a promised land.

The melting-pot of San Francisco has produced a

If there is a recurrent theme dear to the Californian imagination, it is that of the road, or at least everything associated with the cult of the automobile ● *48*. The landscape has been affected by this cult to the point of becoming a cliché of modernity, with its motel, restaurant and gas-station signs ● *77*. The combined influences of pop art and photography have produced the hyper-realist style of painting that captures these landscapes in wide-angle 'shots', as in *Denny's Arco* (**1**) (1987) by Stephen Hopkins, or in close-ups of a façade, a detail of a store window or a particular piece of bodywork. The style, which is at times reminiscent of

trompe-l'oeil technique, doesn't balk at the use of effect: an accumulation of signs, reflected scenes lit by a sunset, idealized colors, and so on. It has also progressed from painting on canvas to the decoration of customized vehicles, from bikers' Harley Davidsons to hippies' VW vans and the low riders driven by the Chicanos. This has become a myth within a myth, difficult to imagine in any other context. Another characteristic of this art form is its dehumanization. It is in fact a realistic representation of a landscape in which the human presence has been replaced by man-made machines and the decor that develops around them. It has therefore

passed beyond the stage of the populated urban melancholy so accurately portrayed by artists such as Edward Hopper, and achieved the concrete representation of an abstract idea that can be experienced by anyone driving through Los Angeles or San Bernadino. The most surprising thing is that, in spite of its impersonal functionalism, this universe continues to exert a certain fascination for which painting, like other mythicizing art forms, is undoubtedly responsible.

1

2

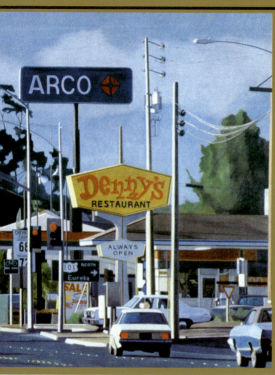

For the painter David Hockney, as for many European artists before him, California was the country of his choice. He settled in Los Angeles, attracted by the vast landscapes of the American West and the pleasure-seeking lifestyle of Hollywood. There he painted certain characteristic features: a love of the sun, latent homosexuality and the omnipresent pool, as in *Pool with Two Figures* (**2**) (1972). Other pop artists have endeavored to portray a less static Californian reality while making a critical point: for example, Edward Kienholz and his automobile installations or Bruce Connor and his amazing collages made from decomposed fabrics and newspaper.

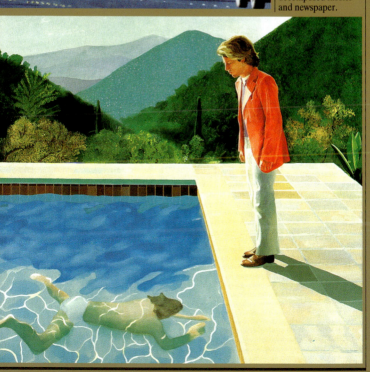

VERTICAL CITIES

Wayne Thiebaud is one of California's leading figurative artists. Although he was born in Arizona (in 1920), the majority of his landscapes represent the city and environs of San Francisco. The realistic style of his compositions during the 1960s (cakes, yo-yos, candy machines, slot machines) could have linked him to the pop art movement, if he had not decided to live on the West Coast, far from the New York galleries that promoted his early work. His paintings of urban landscapes, developed in the 1980s and 90s, are characterized by the use of multiple perspectives and unusual close-ups. In *Apartment View* (1933) (above), these features are combined, in an apparent aberration, to emphasize the characteristic switchback effect of San Francisco, and at the same time highlight the phantasmagorical aspect of the rows of houses bordering the steeply sloping streets. Thiebaud rarely paints his subject at first hand, preferring to rely on his memory to recreate it in his studio perched high on Potrero Hill. He sometimes even uses a telescope, which has the effect of foreshortening the perspective. This is just one more way of distorting reality, a technique that has become a recurring theme in his work.

California
in the movies

From 1910 onwards, the climate and landscapes of California began to attract moviemakers ▲ 180, and Hollywood movies continually 'rediscovered' the splendor of the desert or the ocean, the magnificence of a sequoia forest ● 91, or the amazing perspectives of the long, straight boulevards of Los Angeles and the steeply sloping streets of San Francisco ● 92. Although most movies have, for a long time, been shot in studios, this natural movie set still continues to be part of the American movie industry. For example, Michelangelo Antonioni's *Zabriskie Point* (**1**) (1970) is mainly set in Death Valley ▲ 244. In the western United States, these desert landscapes of pale hills and rocky peaks leaden with heat are not particularly unusual. The beautiful 'American' in the movie did not have the advantage of air-conditioning, as evidenced by the flimsy attire of the heroine, played by Daria Halprin. In the early years of Hollywood, westerns were frequently set in these impressive landscapes, where a lone horseman or stagecoach could be seen approaching from a long way off, in the clear, dry air. Against such as backdrop, strong feelings and emotions can be expressed openly, as if magnified by the natural harshness of the landscape. In Dennis Hopper's *Easy Rider* (**2**) (1969), Billy and Wyatt (Peter Fonda and Dennis Hopper) ride the strange 'easy

rider' bikes to travel from Los Angeles to New Orleans, through west California and the neighboring states. The Los Angeles they have left behind has nothing in common with the city of palm trees and beautiful villas so often depicted in the movies. They sold drugs in the seediest, most sordid parts of the city, in a derelict industrial district dominated by the pillars of a freeway. Their journey through the desert represents a rite of purification, as if they have left behind the dark side of their existence. Here, the desert gives way to the characteristic and monotonous brush which borders the straight roads heavy with heat. The gleaming motorbikes provide a striking contrast with the monotonous landscape of this 'road movie', which celebrates the freedom of riding in the sun and wind. *Safety Last* (**3**) (1923), a silent movie by Fred Newmeyer and Sam Taylor, was shot in Los Ángeles in a real setting. In this extraordinary scene, Harold (Lloyd) was not replaced by a stunt man. The downtown area is ill-defined, as it was in a number of movies and series shot subsequently in Los Angeles, since the city was already beginning to develop around a number of different centers ▲ *178*.

	3
1	
	2

One of the movie sets used for *Citizen Kane* (**1**) (1941), the off-beat and inspired biography of William Randolph Hearst, was Hearst Castle ▲ *172,* whose vastly proportioned, eclectic decor reflects the megalomania of the newspaper magnate. Without ever having set foot inside the castle, Orson Welles reconstructed a replica of this vast residence which he called Xanadu. The huge fireplace was imported from Europe, as were the statues on either side and most of the furniture for the castle's many rooms. Like some of the luxury villas owned by the stars in Beverly Hills and Malibu, the flagships of Californian heritage, this type of residence provides the setting for a great many movies. They are sometimes also used as a foil, as for example in *Annie Hall* (1977), when Woody Allen shows the Los Angeles he hates by driving along one of these elegant boulevards and commenting on the styles, as varied as they are tasteless, of the luxury residences. Conversely, these villas can also feature as symbols of Hollywood success, as in Curtis Hanson's *LA Confidential* (1997) or, in a more ironic vein,

Robert Altman's *The Player* (1991). Billy Wilder's *Some Like it Hot* (**2**) (1959), starring Marilyn Monroe and Tony Curtis, is a wonderful comedy in which two musicians dress up as women to escape their would-be killers. Although the story is set in Florida, the studios chose a backdrop much nearer home, in San Diego: the magnificent Hotel Del Coronado ▲ *221,* located on a peninsula of the same name. The palm-fringed beaches of fine sand to the south of Los Angeles are particularly photogenic, even if the luxury hotels are by and large the only monuments of any note. Some of the beaches are open to the public, others are more select. Those of San Diego provided an ideal setting for the amorous adventures of the characters.

The pure, clean lines of the Golden Gate Bridge have made it the unmistakable symbol of San Francisco. Its outline often appears in the movies, more often than not in car chases. In John Huston's *The Maltese Falcon* (1941), the bridge can be seen through the window of the office of detective Sam Spade, played by Humphrey Bogart. It is also used to symbolize freedom for the hero of Don Siegel's *Escape from Alcatraz* (1979).

Vertigo (**3**) (1958) is one of the great movies by Alfred Hitchcock, the British director who emigrated to the United States. The extremely complicated plot, involving memory games and double identities, unfolds in San Francisco and the surrounding area. This provided

Hitchcock with an ideal opportunity to feature the region's most remarkable sites and monuments: the streets and hills of the city, its Victorian houses, sequoia forests, its beach pounded by the waves and, above all, the Mission San Juan Bautista ▲ *167*, the key to the mystery and its denouement.

Of course, Hitchcock did not forget the Golden Gate Bridge ▲ *128*. Here, the hero, John Ferguson (James Stewart), carries the apparently lifeless body of Madeleine (Kim Novak) against the backdrop of the huge piers of San Francisco's symbolic bridge.

1

2   3

Hollywood has produced a whole series of police movies which frequently end with car chases interspersed with spectacular stunts and crashes. It all started with the early Charlie Chaplin movies, where characters were often pushed through wooden walls. In later productions, cars exploded in a ball of flame, for example in the *Starsky and Hutch* series, the Clint Eastwood *Dirty Harry* movies and Michael Bay's *The Rock* (1996, above) to name but a few. During the classic Hollywood period ▲ *180*, these special effects were produced in the studio by technicians who didn't always have a great deal of equipment but managed to put the scenes together with whatever resources they had. More recently, increasingly spectacular special effects are produced by small companies, which have the specialist equipment demanded by digitized production methods and experience of making video-clips for television ● *51*. Although car chases are shot everywhere in California, the switchbacks of San Francisco are particularly well suited to the exercise. Moviemakers soon realized the potential of a street layout in which the cars almost take off at the intersections and are liable to veer out of control at any moment.

In Peter Yates's *Bullitt* (1968, below), the police lieutenant, played by Steve McQueen, pursues a drug dealer trying to reach the airport. He soon abandons his motorbike, which is too vulnerable, for a Ford Mustang. The ensuing car chase through the steeply sloping streets (seen in the background) well and truly marks the climax of the movie. The same setting is used in Michael Bay's *The Rock*, which also takes advantage of the city's characteristic cable cars and Victorian houses. Here again, the movie set imposes itself, like a subliminal image, on the minds of the audience.

Hal Chase   Jack Kerouac   Allen Ginsberg   William Burroughs

California
as seen by writers

Jack London (1876–1916) was born and brought up in Oakland, California. He had an impoverished childhood, and ran away to sea at the age of fifteen. In 1897 he took part in the Klondyke gold rush. His adventures were the inspiration for his many successful books, such as Call of the Wild *and* The Sea Wolf. Martin Eden *is a semi-autobiographical novel which describes the struggles of a sailor from a poor background who tries to educate himself and become a writer.*

'As Martin Eden went down the steps, his hand dropped into his coat pocket. It came out with a brown rice paper and a pinch of Mexican tobacco, which were deftly rolled together into a cigarette. He drew the first whiff of smoke deep into his lungs and expelled it in a long and lingering exhalation. "By God!" he said aloud, in a voice of awe and wonder. "By God!" he repeated. And yet again he murmured, "By God!" Then his hand went to his collar, which he ripped out of the shirt and stuffed into his pocket. A cold drizzle was falling, but he bared his head to it and unbuttoned his vest, swinging along in splendid unconcern. He was only dimly aware that it was raining. He was in an ecstasy, dreaming dreams and reconstructing the scenes just past...

He staggered along like a drunken man, murmuring fervently aloud: "By God! By God!"

A policeman on a street corner eyed him suspiciously, then noted his sailor roll.

"Where did you get it?" the policeman demanded.

Martin Eden came back to earth. His was a fluid organism, swiftly adjustable, capable of flowing into and filling all sorts of nooks and crannies. With the policeman's hail he was immediately his ordinary self, grasping the situation clearly.

"It's a beaut, ain't it?" he laughed back. "I didn't know I was talkin' out loud."

"You'll be singing next," was the policeman's diagnosis.

"No, I won't. Gimme a match an' I'll catch the next car home."

He lighted his cigarette, said good night, and went on. "Now wouldn't that rattle you?" he ejaculated under his breath. "That copper thought I was drunk." He smiled to himself and meditated. "I guess I was," he added; "but I didn't think a woman's face'd do it."

He caught a Telegraph Avenue car that was going to Berkeley. It was crowded with youths and young men who were singing songs and ever and again barking out college yells... He noticed one with narrow-slitted eyes and a loose-lipped mouth. That fellow was vicious, he decided. On shipboard he would be a sneak, a whiner, a tattler. He, Martin Eden, was a better man than that fellow. The thought cheered him. It seemed to draw him nearer to Her. He began comparing himself with the students. He grew conscious of the muscled mechanism of his body and felt confident that he was physically their master. But their heads were filled with knowledge that enabled them to talk her talk, – the thought depressed him. But what was a brain for? he demanded passionately. What they had done, he could do. They had been studying about life from the books while he had been busy living life. His brain was just as full of knowledge as theirs, though it was a different kind of knowledge. How many of them could tie a lanyard knot, or take a wheel or a lookout? His life spread out before him in a series of pictures of danger and daring, hardship and toil. He remembered his failures and scrapes in the process of learning. He was that much to the good, anyway. Later on they would have to begin living life and going through the mill as he had gone. Very well. While they were busy with that, he could be learning the other side of life from the books.'

JACK LONDON,
MARTIN EDEN,
1909

SAN FRANCISCO

John Steinbeck (1902–68), American novelist who won the Nobel Prize for literature, was born in Salinas. He is noted for his moving, realist stories about the poverty and hardships of those who worked on the land, particularly the Dust Bowl emigrants to California, whom he describes in The Grapes of Wrath. Travels with Charley, *his description of a journey across America with his dog, shows the writer's attachment to his origins.*

'Once I knew the City very well, spent my attic days there, while others were being a lost generation in Paris. I fledged in San Francisco, climbed its hills, slept in its parks, worked on its docks, marched and shouted in its revolts.

San Francisco put on a show for me. I saw her across the bay, from the great road that bypasses Sausalito and enters the Golden Gate Bridge. The afternoon sun painted her white and gold – rising on her hills like a noble city in a happy dream. A city on hills has it over the flat-land places. New York makes its own hills with craning buildings. But this gold and white acropolis rising wave on wave against the blue of the Pacific sky was a stunning thing, a painted thing like a picture of a medieval Italian city which can never have existed. I stopped in a parking place to look at her and the necklace bridge over the entrance from the sea that led to her. Over the green higher hills to the south, the evening fog rolled like herds of sheep come to cote in the golden city. I've never seen her more lovely. When I was a child and we were going to the City, I couldn't sleep for several nights before, out of bursting excitement. She leaves a mark.'

JOHN STEINBECK,
TRAVELS WITH CHARLEY,
1962

Oscar Wilde (1854–1900), who early made his mark as a writer and esthete, went on a lecture tour of the United States in 1882. His tour took him to California, where he was fascinated by the exotic atmosphere of San Francisco, particularly Chinatown.

'San Francisco is a really beautiful city. China Town, peopled by Chinese labourers, is the most artistic town I have ever come across. The people – strange, melancholy Orientals, whom many people would call common, and they are certainly very poor – have determined that they will have nothing about them that is not beautiful. In the Chinese restaurant, where these navvies meet to have supper in the evening, I found them drinking tea out of china cups as delicate as the petals of a rose-leaf, whereas at the gaudy hotels I was supplied with a delf cup an inch and a half thick. When the Chinese bill was presented was made out on rice paper, the account being done in Indian ink as fantastically as if an artist had been etching little birds on a fan.'

OSCAR WILDE,
IMPRESSIONS OF AMERICA,
1882

EARTHQUAKE

Mark Twain (1835–1910), the famous author of Tom Sawyer, *was born in Missouri. He traveled widely in America, working as a newspaper correspondent, particularly in Nevada and California. We are indebted to him for this first-hand account of an earthquake in California.*

'A month afterward I enjoyed my first earthquake. It was one which was long called the "great" earthquake, and is doubtless so distinguished till this day. It was just after noon, on a bright October day. I was coming down Third Street. The only objects in motion anywhere in sight in that thickly built and populous quarter, were a man in a buggy behind me, and a street car wending slowly up the cross street. Otherwise, all was solitude and a Sabbath stillness. As I turned the corner, around a frame house, there was a great rattle and jar, and it occurred to me that here was an item! – no doubt a fight in that house. Before I could turn and seek the door, there came a really terrific shock; the ground seemed to roll under me in waves, interrupted by a violent joggling up and down, and there was a heavy grinding noise as of brick houses rubbing together. I fell up against the frame house and hurt my elbow. I knew what it was, now, and from mere reportorial instinct, nothing else, took out my watch and noted the time of day; at that moment a third and still severer shock came, and as I reeled about on the pavement trying to keep my footing, I saw a sight! The entire front of a tall four-story brick building in Third Street sprung outward like a door and fell sprawling across the street, raising a dust like a great volume of smoke! And here came the buggy – overboard went the man, and in less time than I can tell it the vehicle was distributed in small fragments along three hundred yards of street.

One could have fancied that somebody had fired a charge of chair-rounds and rags down the thoroughfare. The street car had stopped, the horses were rearing and plunging, the passengers were pouring out at both ends, and one fat man had crashed half way through a glass window on one side of the car, got wedged fast and was squirming and screaming like an impaled madman. Every door, of every house, as far as the eye could reach, was vomiting a stream of human beings; and almost before one could execute a wink and begin another, there was a massed multitude of people stretching in endless procession down every street my position commanded. Never was solemn solitude turned into teeming life quicker . . .

The "curiosities" of the earthquake were simply endless. Gentlemen and ladies who were sick, or were taking a siesta, or had dissipated till a late hour and were making up lost sleep, thronged into the public streets in all sorts of queer apparel, and some without any at all. One woman who had been washing a naked child, ran down the street holding it by the ankles as if it were a dressed turkey. Prominent citizens who were supposed to keep the Sabbath strictly, rushed out of saloons in their shirt-sleeves, with billiard cues in their hands. Dozens of men with necks swathed in napkins, rushed from barber-shops, lathered to the eyes or with one cheek clean shaved and the other still bearing a hairy stubble. Horses broke from stables, and a frightened dog rushed up a short attic ladder and out on to a roof, and when his scare was over had not the nerve to go down again the same way he had gone up.'

MARK TWAIN,
ROUGHING IT,
1872

Jack London the writer (1876–1916) and his wife were at their ranch in nearby Glen Ellen at the time of the San Frncisco earthquake and fire in 1906. Collier's *magazine asked him to write an eye-witness account, which was published in London two weeks after the disaster.*

'San Francisco is gone. Nothing remains of it but memories and a fringe of dwelling-houses on its outskirts. Its industrial section is wiped out. Its business section is wiped out. Its social and residential section is wiped out. The factories and warehouses, the great stores and newspaper buildings, the hotels and the palaces of the nabobs, are all gone. Remains only the fringe of dwelling houses on the outskirts of what was once San Francisco…

Within an hour after the earthquake shock the smoke of San Francisco's burning was a lurid tower visible a hundred miles away. And for three days and nights this lurid tower swayed in the sky, reddening the sun, darkening the day, and filling the land with smoke…

There was no opposing the flames. There was no organization, no communication. All the cunning adjustments of a twentieth century city had been smashed by the earthquake. The streets were humped into ridges and depressions, and piled with the debris of fallen walls. The steel rails were twisted into perpendicular and horizontal angles. The telephone and telegraph systems were disrupted. And the great water-mains had burst. All the shrewd contrivances and safeguards of man had been thrown out of gear by thirty seconds' twitching of the earth-crust…

On Thursday morning at a quarter past five, just twenty-four hours after the earthquake, I sat on the steps of a small residence on Nob Hill. With me sat Japanese, Italians, Chinese, and negroes – a bit of the cosmopolitan flotsam of the wreck of the city. All about were the palaces of the nabob pioneers of Forty-nine. To the east and south at right angles, were advancing two mighty walls of flame

The Dawn of the Second Day

I passed out of the house. Day was trying to dawn through the smoke-pall. A sickly light was creeping over the face of things. Once only the sun broke through the smoke-pall, blood-red, and showing quarter its usual size. The smoke-pall itself, viewed from beneath, was a rose color that pulsed and fluttered with lavender shades Then it turned to mauve and yellow and dun. There was no sun. And so dawned the second day on stricken San Francisco.

An hour later I was creeping past the shattered dome of the City Hall. Than it there was no better exhibit of the destructive force of the earthquake. Most of the stone had been shaken from the great dome, leaving standing the naked framework of steel. Market Street was piled high with the wreckage, and across the wreckage lay the overthrown pillars of the City Hall shattered into short crosswise sections.

This section of the city with the exception of the Mint and the Post-Office, was already a waste of smoking ruins. Here and there through the smoke, creeping warily under the shadows of tottering walls, emerged occasional men and women. It was like the meeting of the handful of survivors after the day of the end of the world.

San Francisco, at the present time, is like the crater of a volcano, around which are camped tens of thousands of refugees At the Presidio alone are at least twenty thousand. All the surrounding cities and towns are jammed with the homeless ones, where they are being cared for by the relief committees. The refugees were carried free by the railroads to any point they wished to go, and it is estimated that over one hundred thousand people have left the peninsula on which San Francisco stood.'

JACK LONDON,
COLLIER'S,
MAY 6, 1906

John Muir (1838–1914) is famous as a naturalist, conservationist and founder of the Sierra Club. Born in Scotland, he emigrated to America with his family in 1849. He went to California in 1868 and spent six years there studying and exploring Yosemite and the High Sierras on his own. He is noted for his writings on nature and for his work in helping to set up the Yosemite and Sequoia National Parks.

The Earthquake

'In Yosemite Valley, one morning at about two o'clock I was aroused by an earthquake; and although I had never before enjoyed a storm of this sort, the strange, wild thrilling motion and rumbling could not be mistaken, and I ran out of my cabin, near the Sentinel Rock, both glad and frightened, shouting, "A noble earthquake!" feeling sure I was going to learn something. The shocks were so violent and varied, and succeeded one another so closely, one had to balance in walking as if on the deck of a ship among the waves, and it seemed impossible the high cliffs should escape being shattered. In particular, I feared that the sheer-fronted Sentinel Rock, which rises to a height of three thousand feet, would be shaken down, and I took shelter back of a big Pine, hoping I might be protected from outbounding boulders, should any come so far. I was now convinced that an earthquake had been the maker of the taluses and positive proof soon came. It was a calm moonlight night, and no sound was heard for the first minute or two save a low muffled underground rumbling and a slight rustling of the agitated trees, as if, in wrestling with the mountains, Nature were holding her breath. Then, suddenly, out of the strange silence and strange motion there came a tremendous roar. The Eagle Rock, a short distance up the valley, had given way, and I saw it falling in thousands of the great boulders I had been studying so long, pouring to the valley floor in a free curve luminous from friction, making a terribly sublime and beautiful spectacle – an arc of fire fifteen hundred feet span, as true in form and as steady as a rainbow, in the midst of the stupendous roaring rock-storm. The sound was inconceivably deep and broad and earnest, as if the whole earth, like a

living creature, had at last found a voice and were calling to her sister planets. It seemed to me that if all the thunder I ever hear were condensed into one roar it would not equal this rock roar at the birth of a mountain talus. Think, then, of the roar that arose to heaven when all the thousands of ancient canon taluses throughout the length and breadth of the range were simultaneously given birth.

JOHN MUIR,
OUR NATIONAL PARKS,
1901

HOLLYWOOD

Charles Bukowski (1920–1994) lived all his life in Los Angeles. His writing, whether it is poetry, fiction or autobiography, describes life at the edge, those who live on the margins of society in California. Sex, drugs and violence are always part of his world.

'It was still splinter-group time. Even in that broken-down backyard there were ghetto areas and Malibu areas and Beverly Hills areas. For example, the best-dressed ones with designer clothes hung together. Each type recognized its counterpart and showed no inclination to mix. I was surprised that some of them had been willing to come to a black ghetto like Venice. Chic, they thought, maybe. Of course, what made the whole thing smell was that many of the rich and the famous were actually dumb cunts and bastards. They had simply fallen into a big pay-off somewhere. Or they were enriched by the stupidity of the general public. They usually were talentless, eyeless, soulless, they were walking pieces of dung, but to the public they were god-like, beautiful and revered. Bad taste created many more millionaires than good taste. It finally boiled down to a matter of who got the most votes. In the land of the moles a mole was king.'

CHARLES BUKOWSKI,
HOLLYWOOD,
1989

Nathaniel West (1903–40) was born in New York and had already published Miss Lonelyhearts, *a satire on journalism, when he left for Hollywood in 1933 to work as a scriptwriter.* The Day of the Locust *is a comic, sometimes grotesque, picture of the excesses, neuroses and violence of Hollywood*

'When he saw a red glare in the sky and heard the rumble of cannon, he knew it must be Waterloo. From around a bend in the road trotted several cavalry regiments. They wore casques and chest armour of black cardboard and carried long horse pistols in their saddle holsters. They were Victor Hugo's soldiers. He had worked on some of the drawings for their uniforms himself, following carefully the descriptions in Les Misérables.

He went in the direction they took. Before long he was passed by the men of Lefebre-Desnouttes, followed by a regiment of gendarmes d'élite, several companies of chasseurs of the guard and a flying detachment of Rimbaud's lancers.

They must be moving up for the disastrous attack on La Haite Santée. He hadn't read the scenario and wondered if it had rained yesterday. Would Grouchy or Blucher arrive? Grotenstein, the producer, might have changed it. . .

Tod stood near a eucalyptus tree to watch, concealing himself behind a sign that read, "Waterloo – A Charles H. Grotenstein Production". Near by a youth in a carefully torn horse guard's uniform was being rehearsed in his lines by one of the assistant directors.

"Vive l'Empereur!" the young man shouted, then clutched his breast and fell forward dead. The assistant director was a hard man to please and made him do it over and over again…

For the French, a man in a checked cap ordered Milhaud's cuirassiers to carry Mont St Jean. With their sabres in their teeth and their pistols in their hands, they charged. It was a fearful sight.

The man in the checked cap was making a fatal error. Mont St Jean was unfinished. The paint was not yet dry and all the struts were not in place. Because of the thickness of the cannon smoke, he had failed to see that the hill was still being worked on by property men, grips and carpenters.

It was a classic mistake, Tod realized, the same one Napoleon had made … for a different reason.

This time, the same mistake had a different outcome. Waterloo, instead of being the end of the Grand Army, resulted in a draw. Neither side won, and it would have to be fought over again the next day.'

NATHANIEL WEST,
THE DAY OF THE LOCUST,
1939

MINING AND ITS IMPACT

Robert Louis Stevenson (1850–94), best known as the author of Treasure Island, *was a great Scottish writer and traveler. In 1879 he travelled to California by immigrant ship in pursuit of his future wife, Fanny Osborne. He was greatly struck by California, and constantly contrasted it with France, where he had also lived for some time. The* Silverado Squatters *is an account of his stay at Calistoga.*

'The whole canyon was so entirely blocked, as if by some rude guerilla fortification, that we could only mount by lengths of wooden ladder, fixed in the hill-side. These led us round the further corner of the dump; and when they were at an end we still persevered over loose rubble and wading deep in poison-oak, till we struck a triangular platform, filling up the whole glen, and shut in on either hand by bold projections of the mountain. Only in front the place was open like the proscenium of a theatre, and we looked forth into a great realm of air, and down upon tree-tops and hill-tops and far and near on wild and varied country. The place still stood as on the day it was deserted; a line of iron rails with a bifurcation; a truck in working order; a world of lumber, old wood, old iron; a blacksmith's forge on one side, half buried in the leaves of dwarf madronas; and on the other, an old brown wooden house.

Fanny and I dashed at the house. It consisted of three rooms, and was so plastered against the hill that one room was right atop of another, that the upper floor was more than twice as large as the lower, and that all three apartments must be entered from a different side and level. Not a window-sash remained. The door of the lower room was smashed, and one panel hung in splinters. We entered that, and found a fair amount of rubbish; sand and gravel that had been sifted in there by the mountain winds, straw, sticks and stones; a table, a barrel; a plate-rack on the wall; two home-made bootjacks, signs of miners and their boots; and a pair of papers, pinned on the boarding, headed respectively "Funnel No. 1" and "Funnel No. 2," but with the tails torn away. The window, sashless of course, was choked with the green and sweetly smelling foliage of a bay; and through a chink in the floor a spray of poison-oak had shot up and was handsomely prospering in the interior. It was my first care to cut away that poison-oak, Fanny standing by at a respectful distance.

That was our first improvement by which we took possession.

The room immediately above could only be entered by a plank propped against the threshold, along which the intruder must foot it gingerly, clutching for support to sprays of poison-oak the proper product of the country. Herein was, on either hand, a triple tier of beds, where miners had once lain; and the other gable was pierced by a sashless window and a doorless door-way opening on the air of heaven five feet above the ground. As for the third room, which entered squarely from the ground level, but higher up the hill and further up the canyon, it contained only rubbish and the uprights for another triple tier of beds...

Following back into the canyon, among the mass of rotting plant and through the flowering bushes, we came to a great crazy staging, with a wry windlass on the top; and clambering up, we could look into an open shaft, leading edgeways down into the bowels of the mountain, trickling with water and lighted by some stray sungleams, whence I know not…

Such was our first prospect of Juan Silverado. I own I looked for something different: a clique of neighborly houses on a village green, we shall say, all empty to be sure, but swept and varnished; a trout stream brawling by; great elms or chestnuts, humming with bees and nested in by song birds; and the mountains standing round about, as at Jerusalem. Here, mountain and house and the old tools of industry were all alike rusty and downfalling. The hill was here wedged up, and there poured forth its bowels in a spout of broken mineral; man with his picks and powder, and nature with her own great blasting tools of sun and rain, laboring together at the ruin of that proud mountain. The view up the canyon was a glimpse of devastation; dry red minerals sliding together, here and there a crag, here and there dwarf thicket clinging in the general glissade, and over all a broken outline trenching on the blue of heaven. Downward indeed, from our rock eyrie, we beheld the greener side of nature; and the bearing of the pines and the sweet smell of bays and nutmegs commended themselves gratefully to our senses. One way and another, now the die was cast. Silverado be it!

ROBERT LOUIS STEVENSON,
SILVERADO SQUATTERS,
1883

Bret Harte (1836–1902), who was originally from New York, made his career as a writer and journalist in California, publishing the short stories for which he became famous. Many of his stories, such as The Luck of Roaring Camp, *are full of the popular imagery of the Gold Rush.*

'There was commotion in Roaring Camp. It could not have been a fight, for in 1850 that was not novel enough to have called together the entire settlement … The whole camp was collected before a rude cabin on the outer edge of the clearing. Conversation was carried on in a low tone, but the name of a woman was frequently repeated. It was a name familiar enough in the camp, – "Cherokee Sal."

Perhaps the less said of her the better. She was a coarse and, it is to be feared, a very sinful woman. But at that time she was the only woman in Roaring Camp, and was just then lying in sore extremity … Deaths were by no means uncommon in Roaring Camp, but a birth was a new thing.

The assemblage numbered about a hundred men. One or two of these were actual fugitives from justice, some were criminal, and all were reckless. Physically they exhibited no indication of their past lives and character. The greatest scamp had a Raphael face, with a profusion of blonde hair; Oakhurst, a gambler, had the melancholy air and intellectual abstraction of a Hamlet; the coolest and most courageous man was scarcely over five feet in height, with a soft voice and an embarrassed, timid manner. The term "roughs" applied to them was a distinction rather than a definition. Perhaps in the minor details of fingers, toes, ears, etc., the camp may have been deficient, but these slight omissions did not detract from their aggregate force. The strongest man had but three fingers on his right hand; the best shot had but one eye.

Such was the physical aspect of the men that were dispersed around the cabin. The camp lay in a triangular valley between two hills and a river. The only outlet was a steep trail over the

'She wanted to hire a nice clean private detective who wouldn't drop cigar ashes on the floor and ever carried more than one gun.'

Raymond Chandler

summit of a hill that faced the cabin, now illuminated by the rising moon. The suffering woman might have seen it from the rude bunk whereon she lay,--seen it winding like a silver thread until it was lost in the stars above.

A fire of withered pine boughs added sociability to the gathering. By degrees the natural levity of Roaring Camp returned. Bets were freely offered and taken regarding the result. Three to five that "Sal would get through with it;" even that the child would survive; side bets as to the sex and complexion of the coming stranger. In the midst of an excited discussion an exclamation came from those nearest the door, and the camp stopped to listen. Above the swaying and moaning of the pines, the swift rush of the river, and the crackling of the fire rose a sharp, querulous cry, – a cry unlike anything heard before in the camp. The pines stopped moaning, the river ceased to rush, and the fire to crackle. It seemed as if Nature had stopped to listen too.'

BRET HARTE,
THE LUCK OF ROARING CAMP AND OTHER SKETCHES,
1870

THE CRIME SCENE

Raymond Chandler (1888–1959) was educated in Europe but then returned to America, settling in California. His famous series of thrillers started with The Big Sleep *in 1939, which introduced his tough guy private detective Philip Marlowe. Almost all his books were set in Los Angeles in the 1940s.*

'Bunker Hill is old town, lost town, shabby town, crook town. Once, very long ago, it was the choice residential district of the city, and there are still standing a few of the jigsaw Gothic mansions with wide porches and walls covered with round-end shingles and full corner bay windows with spindle turrets. They are all rooming houses now, their parquetry floors are scratched and worn through the once glossy finish and the wide sweeping staircases are dark with time and with cheap varnish laid on over generations of dirt. In the tall rooms haggard landladies bicker with shifty tenants. On the wide cool front porches, reaching their cracked shoes into the sun and staring at nothing, sit the old men with faces like lost battles.

Out of the apartment houses come women who should be young but have faces like stale beer; men with pulled-down hats and quick eyes that look the street over behind the cupped hand that shields the match flame; worn intellectuals with cigarette coughs and no money in the bank; fly cops with granite faces and unwavering eyes; cokies and coke peddlers; people who look like nothing in particular and know it, and once in a while even men that actually go to work. But they come out early, when the wide cracked sidewalks are empty and still have dew on them.'

RAYMOND CHANDLER,
THE HIGH WINDOW,
1943

James Ellroy (b.1948) as a young man was a troubled personality whose life was marked by drugs, alcohol and even prison. He saved himself through his writing, exorcising his angst in composing thrillers. LA Confidential *became a screen hit in 1997.*

'21 FEBRUARY 1950
An abandoned auto court in the San Berdoo foothills; Buzz Meeks checked in with ninety-four thousand dollars, eighteen pounds of high-grade heroin, a 10-gauge pump, a .38 special, a .45 automatic and a switchblade bought off a pachuco at the border – right before he spotted the car parked across the line: Mickey Cohen goons in an LAPD unmarked, Tijuana cops standing by to bootjack a piece of his goodies, dump his body in the San Ysidro River

He'd been running a week; he'd spent fifty-six grand staying alive: cars, hideouts at four and five thousand a night – risk rates – the innkeepers knew Mickey C. was after him for heisting his dope summit and his woman, the L.A. Police wanted him for killing one of their own. The Cohen contract kiboshed an outright dope sale – nobody could move the shit for fear of reprisals; the best he could do was lay it off with Doc Englekling's sons – Doc would freeze it, package it, sell it later and get him his percentage. Doc used to work with Mickey and had the smarts to be afraid of the prick; the brothers, charging fifteen grand, sent him to the El Serrano Motel and were setting up his escape.'

JAMES ELLROY,
LA CONFIDENTIAL,
1990

CALIFORNIAN SPLENDORS

Walt Whitman (1819–92) is considered to be one of America's greatest poets. Born in New York, he traveled widely all over the United States, Considered daring at the time, his poems celebrate the freedom of the individual and also the brotherhood of man. Leaves of Grass, *one of his earliest and best-known works, is noted for its unconventional content and technique, as well as for its expression of a deep-seated love of nature, and particularly the northern coast of California.*

SONG OF THE REDWOOD-TREE
'Along the northern coast,
Just back from the rock-bound shore and the caves,
In the saline air from the sea in the Mendocino country,
With the surge for base and accompaniment low and hoarse,
With crackling blows of axes sounding musically driven by strong arms,
Riven deep by the sharp tongues of the axes, there in the redwood forest dense,
I heard the mighty tree its death-chant chanting.
The choppers heard not, the camp shanties echoed not,
The quick-ear'd teamsters and chain and jack-screw men heard not,
As the wood-spirits came from their haunts of a thousand years to join the refrain,
But in my soul I plainly heard.

Murmuring out of its myriad leaves,
Down from its lofty top rising two hundred feet high,
Out of its stalwart trunk and limbs, out of its foot-thick bark
That chant of the seasons and time, chant not of the past only but the future.
***
The flashing and golden pageant of California,
The sudden and gorgeous drama, the sunny and ample lands,
The long and varied stretch from Puget sound to Colorado south,
Lands bathed in sweeter, rarer, healthier air, valleys and mountain cliffs,
The fields of Nature long prepared and fallow, the silent, cyclic chemistry,
The slow and steady ages plodding, the unoccupied surface ripening, the rich ores forming beneath.'

WALT WHITMAN,
LEAVES OF GRASS,
1855

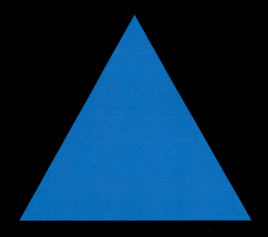

Itineraries in California

Joshua Tree National Park ▲ 246

Death Valley National Park ▲ 244

Bodie State Historic Park ▼ 263

Golden Gate Bridge, San Francisco ▲ *128*

Surfers on the California coast

72ND ANNUAL ACADEMY AWARDS

Preparations for the Academy Awards ceremony, Los Angeles ▲ 181

Harvesting peppers in the Central Valley ▲ 164

San Francisco and Northern California

▲ SAN FRANCISCO
AND NORTHERN CALIFORNIA

1. San Francisco ▲ *115*
2. Marin County ▲ *140*
3. East San Francisco Bay ▲ *143*
4. South San Francisco Bay ▲ *145*
5. Wine Country: Sonoma Valley ▲ *148*
6. Wine Country: Napa Valley ▲ *150*
7. Northern Coast ▲ *152*

SAN FRANCISCO ✪
A city where you can relax is rare in this part of the world! San Francisco is popular for its human dimension and cultural diversity – Chinese, Hispanic, Italian, beatnik, hippie and gay communities live in harmony on hills bathed in the light of the Pacific Ocean.

SAN FRANCISCO, A TOLERANT CITY
In the 1950s, San Francisco began to embrace new philosophies of life. In 1957, Alan Ginsberg's *Howl* marked the presence of the Beat Generation in the Bay Area. In 1964, author Ken Kesey's Merry Pranksters began to travel through California in an old bus, spreading the psychedelic word and advocating the use of LSD. They heralded the arrival of the hippie era, remembered for the first Human Be-In, in Golden Gate Park in 1967. Since 1972, the year of the first Gay Pride ▲ *136*, San Francisco has been the gay capital of the world.

FROM YERBA BUENA TO SAN FRANCISCO. In 1776, the Spanish founded a mission on the site of Yerba Buena. To protect their mission, the Franciscans built a garrison, the Presidio ▲ *129*, which stayed on good terms with the local American Indians and the Russians who had settled in Bodega Bay ▲ *152* to hunt sea otters. In 1834, Yerba Buena became San Francisco and, in 1846, English-speaking Mormon settlers began to arrive in the town. Two years later, the Treaty of Gudalupe Hidalgo forced Mexico to surrender California where, a week later, James Marshall discovered a gold nugget. The ensuing Gold Rush passed through San Francisco ● *34*.

CALIFORNIA'S LARGEST CITY. San Francisco expanded rapidly. In 1850, its wooden houses were burned to the ground only to be replaced by more durable ones. With the advent of the railroad ● *26*, completed in 1869, it was opened up to the entire continent. Magnificent houses were built by men who had made their fortune mining gold, or by providing services required by the rapidly expanding population. In 1860, the Chinese who had worked on the railroad and in the mines began to settle in their own district, as did the Irish, French, Italians and Mexicans. Although many dreams went up in smoke during the earthquake ● *28* of 1906, the city was magnificently rebuilt, with a layout of absolutely straight streets with no regard for the hills. To negotiate these, the cable car was invented.

A CENTURY OF EXPANSION. Since San Francisco became a banking center during the Gold Rush it has pursued economic expansion, helped by the construction of bridges across the bay in 1933. The city also entered the political arena when the UN was created in 1945. However, San Francisco, the home of the beat, hippie and gay communities, above all enjoys a reputation for tolerance. The city has recently experienced a new economic boom owing to the Internet and its connections with the famous Silicon Valley ▲ *146*.

A HAVEN FOR BOBOS ● *44*. Today, San Francisco is wealthy, well beyond the means of the artists and poets who established its reputation. Cultural areas were the first victims of the new Internet economy. However, a city that has withstood earthquakes and gold rushes will certainly not allow anything to detract from its charm and gentle way of life.

THE HEART OF THE CITY

Union Square, with its nearby banks and department stores and Market Street, the main thoroughfare, lies at the heart of this peaceful city. The square is bordered by such busy streets as Powell, Geary, Post and Stockton.

UNION SQUARE ◆ **E** C4
The granite column with *Victory* (1903) commemorates the victory of Manila Bay (1898) in the Spanish-American War. Today the square sees a wide cross section of people: vagrants from the Tenderloin district, business-men snacking on hot dogs and wealthy clients from such luxury hotels as the Westin Saint Francis. Many crowned heads and world leaders, from Queen Elizabeth II to the Dalai Lama, have

passed through this 19th-century square. In striking contrast to the department stores (Macy's, Neiman-Marcus, Saks Fifth Avenue), is the high-tech Levi's store which sells vintage jeans for $250 per pair! The square is also the center of the theater district.

CABLE-CAR RIDE ✪
The cable-car station is on the corner of Market and Powell Streets. There is always a small crowd of people waiting patiently to board one of these ancient machines, lovingly maintained by the city. Don't miss the opportunity to take a cable-car ride over the vertiginous switchback of streets between Market Street and Fisherman's Wharf, and enjoy the most spectacular view of the bay from the top of Russian Hill.

SFMoMA ● 75
◆ E D5
The San Francisco Museum of Modern Art, opened in 1995, was designed by the Swiss architect Mario Botta. It juxtaposes blocks of brick surmounted by a sloping glass roof that diffuses natural light into the building. The museum, founded in the Civic Center district in 1935, specializes in contemporary American art and exhibits the work of some of its key exponents: Sam Francis, Richard Diebenkorn and Clyfford Still. With some 7000 images, photography has a prominent place in the museum's collection.

THE COMMERCIAL CENTER

MARKET STREET, SAN FRANCISCO'S MAIN THOROUGHFARE ◆ E E3-B6. Since the mid 19th century, Market Street has cut diagonally across the checkerboard layout of the city's streets. It runs from the ferry terminal, Ferry Building (1898), to the hills of Diamond Heights, where it is continued by Portola Drive. Between the quays and the Castro district, Market is mainly a commercial street and parking is impossible. It is better to take one of the trams which the city authorities have bought from cities such as Boston and Newark, with the oldest and most attractive from Milan in Italy. A single ticket will take you down and back up Market, round the Embarcadero, ending up at Fisherman's Wharf ▲ 127.

SoMA ◆ E D5-E5. In recent years, the streets south of Market have been developed, pushing back the boundaries of the rather shady district known as Skid Row. The bars, seedy hotels and moneylenders that once occupied this area have been gradually replaced by the high-tech cafés and restaurants of this fast-developing district known as SoMA (South of Market). The rents are now so high that museums such as the AMERICAN INDIAN CONTEMPORARY ARTS GALLERY have had to give way to more profitable companies.

YERBA BUENA CENTER ◆ E D5. The center occupies the quadrilateral formed by 4th Street, Mission Street, 3rd Street and Folsom Street. It comprises gardens dotted with contemporary sculptures and an open-air auditorium that gives free daily concerts. On the corner of Mission and 4th Streets, the METREON or Sony Entertainment Center, is a vast ultramodern complex devoted to the fad for electronic games. The SFMoMA stands on the far side of 3rd Street.

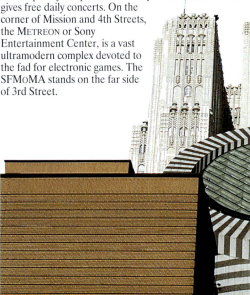

ANSEL ADAMS CENTER ◆ E D5. This museum of photography, which has opened in new premises on Mission Street, presents classic works by its founder ● *54* and works by young designers. It also organizes workshops under the guidance of master photographers. The 'airport architecture' of the nearby MOSCONE CONVENTION CENTER is particularly striking.

FINANCIAL DISTRICT ◆ E D4-E4

With the Gold Rush, San Francisco became the financial stronghold of the West. The beautiful old buildings that have survived are today dwarfed by the skyscrapers of the major banks. The district's oldest building, the BANK OF CALIFORNIA, is situated on California Street, at the intersection of California and Sansome. On the first floor is an exhibition of gold coins and nuggets. Opposite the bank is the MERCHANT EXCHANGE, a stock exchange that was once as active as Wall Street. It is worth taking time out to visit the 52nd floor of the head office of the BANK OF AMERICA to enjoy a magnificent view of the bay. On Montgomery Street (just after California Street), the WELLS FARGO HISTORY MUSEUM evokes the age of the stagecoach. On the corner of Montgomery and Clay, the spectacular TRANSAMERICA PYRAMID appears to look down on the occasional sequoia from its 850 feet. Back on Market Street, the FEDERAL RESERVE BANK at No 101 is also worth a visit.

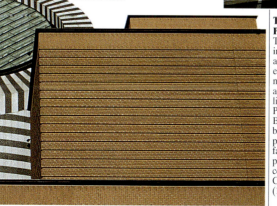

TRANSAMERICA PYRAMID (1972)
The city's older inhabitants, though accustomed to eccentricities, did not immediately appreciate the slender lines of William Pereira's design. But over the years the building has become part of the city's familiar skyline and provides a striking contrast with the Columbus Tower (1907) (right).

CHINATOWN ◆ **E** D3-D4

Chinatown continues to be one of the main attractions of San Francisco. For decades, it occupied only a few blocks but, over the past twenty years, it has gradually expanded to the point that it is now encroaching on the Italian district of North Beach ▲ *120*. Once a very closed, secretive community, Chinatown has learned to open up to the outside world without losing any of its original character and popular activity. It dates from the mid 19th century, when tens of thousands of Chinese ● *38*, fleeing from famine and revolution, went to work in the mines of the Gold Country ▲ *157*, or were employed on the construction of the railroad. Most eventually settled in California, in the small towns on the Fresno plain ▲ *165*, and above all in San Francisco, where they specialize in a number of small trades such as laundry, a business that is still largely run by the Chinese community. The Chinese brought their culinary and medicinal traditions with them, as well as their family and religious values, and their presence has led to the development of Buddhism in the region.

A TOURIST DISTRICT. Visitors enter this state within a state through the Chinatown Gate, erected in 1969 on Grant Avenue, on the corner of Bush Street. Like many of the city's streets, Grant is named after a US president. This part of Chinatown has been largely overtaken by tourism, and is mainly filled with knick-knacks of little interest.

MARKETS. The real life of Chinatown is found in its markets, like the one on the street running parallel to Stockton, near North Beach. They have all the frenetic activity of an Asian town, exploding in a blaze of color in the heart of the American metropolis. Here you can breathe in the aromas as you buy spices, fresh fish (it arrives by the truckload), fruit and vegetables imported from China, and medicinal herbs. Chinese housewives rub shoulders with trendy Americans who come here to buy their ginseng roots.

CHURCHES AND TEMPLES. The first major building that visitors encounter is OLD ST MARY'S CHURCH, in the center of a square. This Catholic church, built in 1853, looks rather

MAKING THE MOST OF CHINATOWN ✪
Visiting this corner of Asia in the heart of America is a truly amazing experience. The best way to see Chinatown is on foot. This makes it easier to slip into the alleys, steeped in secrecy, or immerse yourself in the lively street life that escapes most tourists, who don't get beyond the souvenir stands on Grant Avenue. Eating in one of the district's many restaurants is also an absolute must. Choose one used by the local inhabitants, who go there to enjoy the traditional steamed dishes. The R & G Lounge (631 Kearny Street), between Clay and Sacramento Streets, is highly recommended. Ignore the decor and concentrate on the crab and fresh fish.

out of place, even though a large section of the Chinese community has converted to Christianity. However, there is no shortage of temples devoted to various Oriental spiritual beliefs. The KONG CHOW TEMPLE (855 Stockton) is decorated with exotic wood. A little further on, the TIN HOU TEMPLE (125 Waverly Place), dedicated to the Queen of the Heavens and Goddess of the Seven Seas, was the first Chinese temple to be built in the United States. While a visit to the temples provides a good introduction to an age-old culture, this should be followed up by a visit to the district's museums.

MUSEUMS OF CHINATOWN. The best-known is the CHINESE HISTORICAL SOCIETY MUSEUM (965 Clay Street), with its huge library tracing the history of the peoples of Southern China. A visit to this museum is complemented by visits to the PACIFIC HERITAGE MUSEUM, at 108 Commercial Street, near the Transamerica Pyramid, and the CHINESE CULTURE CENTER two blocks away at 750 Kearny Street, which has exhibitions on the way of life and commercial organization of this large community of almost 100,000 people.

PORTSMOUTH SQUARE.
The square is one of the last havens of peace in Chinatown and the preserve of the district's older inhabitants where, indifferent to the hustle and bustle of tourism, they can indulge their passion for dominoes and mahjong. Many of the local residents no doubt attend the Buddha's Universal Church, with its delightful little roof garden, in the northwest corner of the square. On Washington Street, the former telephone centre of the Pacific Telephone and Telegraph Company was San Francisco's first Chinese-style building (1909).

The façade of the Vesuvio and the
streets of North Beach (below).

**A LITTLE TASTE
OF ITALY**
Here the population
is of predominately
Italian origin, in spite
of the rapid
expansion of nearby
Chinatown.
Consequently, the
district not only has
the city's best
pizzerias, but also
some elegant
restaurants on
Columbus, where
long limousines park
out front. The more
friendly cafés dotted
along Grant Avenue
still attract a clientele
loyal to the
enlightened
reputation of North
Beach. The most
popular is the Café
Trieste, on the corner
of Vallejo, where
musicians sometimes
extemporize.

THE BOHEMIAN DISTRICT ◆ E B3-C3

North Beach is still one of the most popular districts in
San Francisco, in spite of the meteoric rise in the cost of
housing and the gradual disappearance of the writers and
artists who once lived there. North Beach proclaims this
bohemian heritage loud and clear, on the signs of its bistros,
hotels and elegant restaurants. You can still enjoy a stroll
along the sidewalks of Columbus, Broadway and Grant,
where you can hunt for bargains in second-hand stores and
stores selling 1950s memorabilia, and around WASHINGTON
SQUARE, dominated by the impressive CHURCH OF SAINTS
PETER AND PAUL (1922).

CAFÉS AND INTELLECTUALS. The cafés serve real Italian
espresso, and sometimes have a terrace where you can still
see the odd writer or poet scribbling away in a notebook or, in
the case of the CAFÉ GRECO on Columbus, working on a
laptop. They are a reminder that the Beat Generation ● *36*
set up its headquarters in the smoky rooms of these cafés, as
close as possible to the City Lights Book Store. The most
famous is still the VESUVIO, next door to the book store, on
Jack Kerouac Street.

CITY LIGHTS BOOK STORE. Visitors come to 261 Columbus
Avenue to immerse themselves in the atmosphere of the
myth. This was where Lawrence Ferlinghetti, the founder

of the City Lights Book Store,
used to read poetry with Allen
Ginsberg, Neal Cassady, William
Burroughs, Gregory Corso and
others. Their works are on sale in
the store.

CLUBS AND NIGHT CLUBS. Many
visitors spurn the poetry readings
of the City Lights Book Store in
favor of the strip-tease shows
in the district's night clubs, an
old local tradition. According
to another local tradition, West
Coast Jazz ● *52* originated on
the hill of North Beach, in clubs
wedged between the strip joints.
Today, these jazz clubs have
disappeared, along with what
constituted the charm, or danger,
of what was known 100 years
ago as the 'Barbary Coast' – a
series of busy streets where
prostitution, gambling and all
sorts of criminal activities
flourished.

TELEGRAPH HILL ◆ E D2

Beyond North Beach, Telegraph
Hill is dominated by the famous
Coit Tower. The streets leading
up the hill from Broadway are so
steep that they can be difficult to
climb, even on foot.

COIT TOWER. An elevator takes you to the top of the tower. At the bottom, a series of murals depicts the life of the ordinary people of California during the depression of 1929. Some thirty or so artists painted the murals in the realist-socialist style of the great Mexican painter Diego Rivera. The 285-foot tower was built by the architect Arthur Brown Jr at the request of Lillie Hitchcock Coit. This exhuberent and wealthy widow was rescued from a fire at the age of eight, during the earthquake of 1906, and liked to wear a fire-fighter's uniform as a symbol of her regard for the profession. She donated a substantial sum, inherited from her late husband, so that the city could build a monument in the form of a fire hose to pay homage to these brave men.

FILBERT STEPS. Near Coit Tower, flights of wooden steps wind down to the Embarcadero for the equivalent of twenty stories, through gardens fragrant with the scent of rare flowers. The magnificent 1930s building on the corner of Filbert and Montgomery was used as the setting for the movie *Dark Passage* (1947), starring Humphrey Bogart and Lauren Bacall. Most of the streets on Telegraph Hill are cul-de-sacs which end near delightful wooden houses with spectacular views of the bay. Formerly occupied by poets and artists, today these much sought-after residences are bought for a small fortune by people who have made their money in the computing and software industries.

LEVI PLAZA. Levi Plaza, at the foot of the Filbert Steps, is named after the parent company of the famous jeans manufacturer which stands on the square. It is surrounded by a series of red-brick industrial buildings which incorporate a harmonious blend of old and contemporary structures. The plaza was built when the shore (hence the name North Beach) was covered over in the late 19th century, leaving several boats buried beneath the streets and buildings.

TELEGRAPH HILL ★
The top of the hill offers a sweeping view across the bay and beyond. It is also the quietest place in the city, since the steeply sloping streets are unsuitable for automobiles. This is ideal for the people living in the delightful flower-covered houses suspended above the void.

LEVI STRAUSS & CO.
In 1853, a German immigrant named Levi Strauss landed in San Francisco at the height of the Gold Rush, and had the idea of manufacturing durable work pants for the miners. He initially used tarpaulin and tent canvas, reinforcing the points of stress with copper rivets, and then the equally durable blue *serge de Nîmes* (denim). The famous 'blue jeans' ● *60* were widely worn by Western cowboys before becoming a popular item of leisurewear worldwide.

LOMBARD STREET ★
It would be a pity to just drive down Lombard Street, since walking is the best way to admire this beautifully landscaped block and breathe in the fragrance of the densely planted flowers. The panoramic view as you leave Hyde Street is spectacular, especially the views of Coit Tower and North Beach.

THE FASHIONABLE HILLS OF SAN FRANCISCO

Russian Hill, Nob Hill and Pacific Heights are, by tradition and inheritance, wealthy residential districts. This did not, however, prevent their magnificent wooden Victorian houses from being ravaged by fire in the 1906 earthquake. They were subsequently rebuilt in stone, with a display of luxury and extravagance unrivaled on the West Coast.
RUSSIAN HILL ◆ E B2-C2. The district was so called because it was formerly occupied by immigrants from Central Europe. The most pleasant and spectacular way to approach it is via the delightful hairpin bends of Lombard Street (below), between Hyde and Leavenworth. At the foot of the hill, on Francisco

FLOWER-FILLED BENDS OF LOMBARD STREET
When the city authorities built the hairpin bends of Lombard Street for motor traffic, c. 1920, it was a two-way street! The residents planted shrubs and flowers in the bends, with a marked preference for hydrangeas.

Street, are several narrow, sun-drenched café terraces. A block away, on the corner of Chestnut and Leavenworth, the SAN FRANCISCO ART INSTITUTE – a strange building inspired by an Italian priory and decorated with a mural by Diego Rivera – houses the California School of Design, and offers visitors an opportunity to admire the work of its students. Between Broadway and Filbert, POLK STREET, the heart of the gay scene before the emergence of the Castro, has become extremely trendy, with its bistros, exotic restaurants and antique stores. All that remains of the earlier Slavonic residents is the HOLY TRINITY ORTHODOX CATHEDRAL with its blue roof, on the corner of Van Ness and Green.
NOB HILL ◆ E B4. Nob Hill, to the south of Russian Hill, is much more luxurious. It is said to have been named for the wealthy 'nabobs' of the Gold Rush ● *34*. It was the fortunes amassed through the gold mines, the construction of the railroad – especially by the Big Four ▲ *156* whose names have been given to streets, hotels and parks – and the fitting-out of ships that financed the palatial mansions, most of them now converted into luxury hotels. For example, visitors can enjoy a drink and a magnificent panoramic view of the city in the Top of the Mark bar of the MARK HOPKINS

INTERCONTINENTAL. Although these luxury mansions were destroyed in the fires of 1906 most, like the Fairmount Hotel with its *trompe l'oeil* decor, were magnificently rebuilt in the years that followed. The only one to remain unscathed is now the PACIFIC UNION CLUB (1000 California Street), one of the city's most select clubs and a fine example of the type of stone and wood construction used on Nob Hill. However, the hill's most monumental building is undoubtedly GRACE CATHEDRAL, built in neo-Gothic style. It has a rose window, a copy of the one in Chartres Cathedral, but the stained-glass windows of the nave depict very modern heroes: scientists and astronauts. In front of the cathedral, the lawns of Huntingdon Park are popular with picnickers and people relaxing. On the

GRACE CATHEDRAL
The cathedral was built on a plot of land bequeathed to the Episcopalian Church by the heirs of Charles Crocker ▲ *156*. Do not be misled by its medieval appearance: it was built between 1924 and 1925 using concrete and steel to better withstand earthquakes!

Cable car climbing Nob Hill.

far side of California Street, the Masonic Temple and Museum, built in modern post-war style, has an auditorium, one of the city's best-known concert halls. No visit to the district would be complete without seeing the CABLE CAR BARN, on the corner of Mason and Washington Streets. An underground area in this delightful little museum enables visitors to see the huge cable wheels that pull the cars to the top of the city's hills.

PACIFIC HEIGHTS ◆ **E** A3-A4. The richest of the city's fashionable hills is Pacific Heights, where some of the streets are bordered by mansions that look more like royal palaces. Some have since changed hands, for example SPRECKELS MANSION (2080 Washington Street), built by the industrialist Adolph Spreckels ▲ *131* in the early 20th century and now owned by the popular novelist Danielle Steel. Others have remained the property of legendary dynasties, such as the Getty family mansion, on the corner of Broadway and Baker. Still others are open to the public, for example FLOOD MANSION with its exotic-wood decor, built by the wealthy part-owner of the silver deposit known as the Comstock Lode, or the Victorian-style HAAS LILIENTHAL HOUSE at 2007 Franklin Street.

WESTERN ADDITION
◆ **E** A4
The small unprepossessing district of Western Addition lies at the foot of the wealthy hill of Pacific Heights. Its old alleys bordered by wooden houses were demolished during renovation work. However, not all its former magic has been destroyed, as evidenced by the church dedicated to St John Coltrane! A bust of this greatly revered jazz saxophonist stands at the entrance (351 Divisadero).

ALAMO SQUARE ★
South of Western Addition and west of the Civic Center lies one of the city's favorite places for indulging in the popular art of relaxation. What could be better than to lie on the square's sloping lawns, opposite the rows of brightly colored Victorian houses on Steiner. Beyond the houses are the skyscrapers of the Financial District, the heart of a much more hectic lifestyle.

HOMAGE TO BILL GRAHAM
San Francisco wanted to pay homage to the memory of Bill Graham, who died in a helicopter crash in 1991 on his way back from a Grateful Dead concert. Graham did much for the city's reputation by placing it on the map of the cultural capitals of the world. His name continues to be associated with the extraordinary rise of pop music here in the late 1960s, and the great concert hall of the Civic Center has been named in his honor: the Bill Graham Civic Auditorium (99 Grove Street).

THE JAPANESE DISTRICT ◆ E A5-B5

If you've explored the busy streets of Chinatown, the tiny enclave of Japantown seems very peaceful by comparison. It is like entering another world on the edge of Geary Boulevard, between Fillmore and Octavia Streets. Its five-roofed pagoda, a gift from the Japanese government, is an easily recognizable landmark. Visitors are particularly attracted by the district's bazaars and restaurants in NIHONMACHI MALL. For a few hours you can imagine you are in a real Japanese city, taste sashimi and drink green tea, enjoy the very latest in electronic games and buy wonderful gadgets whose designs range from the infantile to the avant-garde. Traditional Japan is also much in evidence at the KONKO KYO TEMPLE, dedicated to one of the many branches of the Shinto religion. In spring, during the Cherry Blossom Festival, the members of San Francisco's Japanese community make it a point of honor to wear the traditional costume of kimonos and rice-straw sandals. Visitors can also take advantage of the fish market, the SUPER KOYAMA on Sutter, between Webster and Laguna, to buy the ingredients for sushi and sashimi.

FILLMORE ◆ E A5 AND THE MEMORY OF ROCK

Only a stone's throw from Japantown, this district has become rather classy, especially between Geary and California, with its exotic restaurants, galleries and fashion boutiques.
JOHN LEE HOOKER'S BOOM BOOM ROOM. The district's main attraction is located on the corner of Fillmore Street and Geary Boulevard. This bar-cum-concert hall is a blues club, formerly presided over by the 'boogie man' himself, who was a resident of Frisco for many years. It presents classic programs in a violently colored decor. On certain evenings, the extremely animated atmosphere acts as a reminder that the 'good old blues' was one of the sources of rock 'n' roll.
FILLMORE AUDITORIUM. Directly opposite John Lee Hooker's Boom Boom Room, on the other side of Geary, is the legendary Fillmore Auditorium. San Francisco lovingly promotes its nostalgia, and it is not unusual to see legendary

figures from the golden age of the 1960s performing there. Former members of Jefferson Airplane and the Grateful Dead ● 53 play the songs that inspired the parents of their ecstatic audience, when it's not the parents themselves who have come to take a trip down memory lane. The illusion is perfect: the walls of the bar are covered with psychedelic posters of that golden era, the dazzling 'light show' still plays on the wall behind the musicians, and people dance as if nothing had changed in the last thirty years. Bill Graham, who founded this first Fillmore Auditorium in 1965, is sadly no longer there to introduce the bands who perform on its stage.

THE ADMINISTRATIVE DISTRICT ◆ E B5-C5

The International Exposition of 1893 in Chicago sanctioned the return to classical architecture. San Francisco was captivated by this 'city beautiful' movement, particularly as it wanted to gain an international reputation, and so built a Civic Center adjacent to Market Street, between Hayes, Franklin, Turk and Hyde.

CITY HALL. This neo-classical structure is the point of convergence of a number of views, the most beautiful of which looks across to the heights of Alamo Square. Whichever entrance you use, you cross a vast, bare hall before reaching the four-story rotunda surmounted by its majestic dome.

ASIAN ART MUSEUM. In 2002, the Asian Art Museum will be relocated opposite the City Hall, to house the collections rarely seen at the M H de Young Memorial Museum ▲ 132.

UNITED NATIONS PLAZA. The plaza is adjacent to Market Street, near the exit to the BART Civic Center station. It acts as a reminder that the UN was founded in a nearby building, the War Memorial Opera House, on the corner of Grove and Van Ness. The plaza is decorated with the declarations contained in the Charter of the United Nations and houses a market of traditional crafts from all over the world.

MONUMENTAL ARCHITECTURE. The other buildings that form the Civic Center – the OLD CALIFORNIA STATE BUILDING (Polk and McAllister), the FEDERAL BUILDING (Polk Street), the VETERANS BUILDING (Franklin and McAllister) – provide some impressive examples of early 20th-century official architecture. The only concessions to Modernism are the STATE BUILDING (Van Ness and McAllister), the LOUISE M DAVIES SYMPHONY HALL (Van Ness and Hayes) and the PUBLIC LIBRARY (Grove and Larkin), which is well worth a visit if only to admire its refined architectural style (1999).

CITY HALL
The dome, inspired by St Peter's, is 3 feet taller than the one in Washington.

ASIAN ART MUSEUM
San Francisco owes this museum – the largest in the United States dedicated to Asian art – to the billionaire Avery Brundage. There are no less than 12,000 works covering 6000 years of history from places as diverse as India, Japan, Tibet, Nepal and Southeast Asia. In 2002 it will be rehoused in the former Public Library.

▲ SAN FRANCISCO
FISHERMAN'S WHARF

View of Alcatraz from
Hyde Street Pier.

ALCATRAZ

Popular imagery has long identified the island as a penitentiary reserved for the most hardened criminals. Al Capone was in fact one of its inmates between 1934 (when the present prison system was implemented) and 1939. But the history of Alcatraz – Isla de los Alcatraces (Island of Pelicans) – did not end with the closure of the prison. American Indians settled there in 1969, in accordance with a treaty that granted them the territory, and occupied it until 1971, when they founded one of the bases of the American Indian Movement, which fights for the recognition of their rights. Today, numerous boat trips from Pier 43 land at the rock, allowing visitors time to see not only the cells, but also the older buildings built by the Spanish in 1857.

THE CITY'S NORTHERN WATERFRONT ◆ E A1-C1

The northern shores of San Francisco Bay, between Fort Mason in the west and the Embarcadero in the east, are a center of attraction for often dense crowds of tourists. The general atmosphere is friendly, and a number of stores and restaurants have some quality offers.

NATIONAL MARITIME MUSEUM. The museum, whose white Art Deco shell looks like a steamer, houses some beautiful model boats and all kinds of marine exhibits that trace the maritime history of the bay.

GHIRARDELLI SQUARE. The square is famous for the chocolate made here in the mid 19th century by Domenico Ghirardelli. The factory was relocated in 1960, but the rich, dark chocolate can still be bought in the former factory. The buildings have been converted into a charming shopping mall, a wonderful blend of old and new, whose stylish stores sell all kinds of antiques, books and other luxury goods. The clock tower above the mall was inspired by the Château de Blois, in France. Opposite Ghirardelli Square, the jetties offer fine views of the bay and Alcatraz Island. The Municipal Pier is a favorite venue for anglers, joggers and intrepid swimmers who plunge into the icy waters of the bay. Visitors can also admire at first hand the magnificent sailing ships moored along Hyde Street Pier, superb survivors from the 19th century.

Tram on the Market Street–Fisherman's Wharf line.

THE CANNERY. This former fruit and vegetable cannery, in patinated red brick, occupies an entire block between Jefferson and Beach Streets. Today it houses cafés, shopping malls and, near the Beach Street entrance, the MUSEUM OF THE CITY OF SAN FRANCISCO, devoted to the city's history. Opposite the cannery and its architectural counterpart, the ANCHORAGE, FISH ALLEY suddenly takes a more authentic turn with its lobster pots, the heady odor of fish and courtyards reminiscent of Elia Kazan's *On the Waterfront* (1954).

THE 'FUN' MUSEUMS OF FISHERMAN'S WHARF. Several 'museums' attract customers with publicity more worthy of a fairground than a cultural institution. THE GUINNESS BOOK OF WORLD RECORDS MUSEUM attempts to illustrate the sporting and eccentric records listed in the book of the same name. Next door, the WAX MUSEUM regularly updates its collection of the usual waxwork figures to keep pace with current events. The last and most popular is RIPLEY'S BELIEVE IT OR NOT. The exhibition of drawings by the famous illustrator will delight children but leave parents perplexed, soon feeling they've had more than enough of this profusion of grotesque and often controversial effects.

PIERS. The panoramic view from Pier 45 offers a striking, and peaceful, contrast to the museums opposite. The quays become more animated during the arrival and departure of the fishing boats. A World War Two submarine, the *Pampanito*, is open to the public while, further east, Pier 39 is another vast shopping and restaurant complex and amusement arcade. Some visitors may prefer to sit and contemplate the noisy colony of sea lions that has taken up residence near the quays to take advantage of the rich pickings from Fisherman's Wharf. Alternatively they can visit the spectacular UNDERWATER WORLD, on the corner of the Embarcadero, and move between aquariums filled with formidable sharks.

FAST SEAFOOD ★ Fisherman's Wharf, midway along Jefferson Street, at the foot of Taylor Street, is a favorite place for seafood aficionados. Here you can taste some excellent shellfish and other seafood specialties, cooked right on the quayside.

WILLIAM RIPLEY
William Ripley, a native of Santa Rosa, published his first drawing in 1918. It depicted an athlete breaking the 100 meters record – backwards! The illustrator signed a contract with William Randolph Hearst ▲ 172 to travel the world and publish extravagant stories, based on a format of drawings and a short text.

GOLDEN GATE BRIDGE ✪

During 1936, the anglers on Baker Beach were able to watch a truly amazing sight as intrepid construction workers braved dizzying heights to build the world's most famous suspension bridge between the promontories of Fort Point and Marin Headlands ▲ *140*. The bridge, constructed under the direction of project manager Joseph B Strauss and engineer Charles A Ellis, was completed in 1937. With its 745-foot high piers and 1⅔-mile roadway, it is still as impressive today, and has become one of the emblems of San Francisco. A walk across the bridge is unforgettable, both from the visual point of view and for the delicious vertiginous thrill when it begins to vibrate.

A PROMENADE BETWEEN LAND AND SEA

A beautiful promenade runs along the bay between Fort Mason and the Golden Gate Bridge. Most of the promenade is accessible only on foot, or possibly on roller blades or a bicycle (both can be hired from the Aquatic Park end).

FORT MASON ◆ D D2. This was the former embarkation point for the marines who went to fight in the Pacific during World War Two. Today, the disused military buildings house such peaceful institutions as the CRAFT AND FOLK ART MUSEUM (Building A), devoted to arts and crafts from around the world with a special section for contemporary Amerindian art. Next to it, the MEXICAN MUSEUM (Building D) is divided into three sections, pre-Columbian, Hispanic colonial and contemporary art, with some fascinating exhibitions of Chicano ● *39* art. In Building C, two areas pay homage to other important local communities. The MUSEO ITALO-AMERICANO presents works by both immigrant and native Italian artists, while the AFRICAN AMERICAN HISTORICAL AND CULTURAL SOCIETY presents temporary exhibitions on the part played by Black Americans in the major events of US history. Fort Mason is also the home of the famous Mime Troupe, managed by Bill Graham ▲ *124*, which gave rise to the Diggers movement, the legendary 'Robin Hoods' of the 1960s. In fine weather, the lawns are an ideal place to relax or fly kites. Mini music festivals are sometimes held here, and there is a market of organic products at weekends.

PALACE OF FINE ARTS
(east of the Presidio)
This strange
neoclassical
monument (detail
left) was built by
Bernard Maybeck
● *69*, in 1915, for the
Panama-Pacific

MARINA DISTRICT ◆ D C2. To the west of Fort Mason, this elegant and expensive district, with its Italian- and Spanish-style houses is inhabited by an almost exclusively white, English-speaking population. Although partially destroyed during the 1989 earthquake, it was rebuilt without relinquishing a certain tasteful extravagance. Beyond Marina, Chestnut Street is particularly busy in the evenings with its cafés, restaurants and Presidio movie theater with a 1930s façade. Unsurprisingly, the Marina district also has an attractive marina, the Yacht Harbor, from where you can see the dome of the Palace of Fine Arts, about a block away on Lyon Street.

PRESIDIO ◆ D B2-C2. The garrison was built by the Spanish in 1776 to stem the rising tide of Russian immigration from the north. The various waves of military occupation, from the American Civil War to the Vietnam War, have each left their mark, in particular a vast cemetery and the impressive WEST COAST MEMORIAL. The fairly simple buildings are now occupied by ecological organizations and are also preparing to house the Digital Arts Center, one of the branches of the George Lucas (*Star Wars*) empire. In 1967, the Presidio was

Exposition held to celebrate the completion of the Panama Canal. It is surmounted, among other things, by caryatids turning inwards in a posture of apparent grief. The building, which has the charming air of an ancient Roman ruin, is reflected in a lake frequented by large numbers of birds.

also the scene of a rebellion by soldiers refusing to leave for Vietnam. The now peaceful city within a city is a national park where the roads wind between trees and offer some beautiful views of the Golden Gate Bridge and San Francisco Bay.

AND FINALLY…GOLDEN GATE BRIDGE. The promenade continues below the Presidio, following the bay from the marina to the suspension bridge. Anglers, daydreamers, young lovers and sometimes swimmers come here to breathe in the sea air and admire the spectacular view. You can even walk out a little further into the bay along the short jetty at Fort Point, part of a defense system built by the American army to protect the city, especially during the Civil War. There is also a minor road suitable for vehicles which winds its way from the Presidio to Fort Point. Visitors can actually go under the pier of the bridge, which enables them to appreciate the scale of this impressive structure.

EXPLORATORIUM
(behind the Palace of Fine Arts)
In the 1920s, this semicircular pavilion housed exhibitions of sculpture and painting. Since 1969, these have been replaced by the EXPLORATORIUM, a discovery center designed by Frank Oppenheimer, brother of J Robert Oppenheimer, one of the inventors of the atomic bomb. Everything in the center is designed to make even the most obscure branches of science accessible to children, with a vast array of educational exhibits and electronic simulations.

THE CITY'S
WESTERN WATERFRONT

Over the years, San Francisco has expanded and encroached upon the last remaining natural sites in the western part of the city. The Presidio escaped urban development since it was classified as a national park after the departure of the military. Golden Gate Park and Lincoln Park are also sacrosanct, but the dunes that once stretched between the two parks were given over to property development, especially after World War Two. One of these developments was the Richmond district.

RICHMOND ◆ D A3. Richmond, which lies along the northern edge of Golden Gate Park, has been colonized in turn by the Russians, Irish and, more recently, Asiatics (Chinese, Thais and Vietnamese) to the point that these blocks are beginning to be regarded as a new Chinatown. Clement and Geary are the district's busiest streets with their inexpensive boutiques and restaurants. These exotic places are as yet undiscovered by tourism, and so have kept their authenticity. On the edge of Richmond, a beautiful synagogue stands on the corner of Arguello Boulevard and Lake Street. Another religious building, the ST THOMAS MISSION, on the corner of Balboa Street and 39th Avenue, is a typical example of a Catholic church based on the style of the early missions.

SEA CLIFF ◆ D A3. To the north of Richmond lies the small enclave of Sea Cliff, an elegant residential complex of Italianate mansions, at the northern end of 25th Avenue. From here you can reach the long stretch of sand known as Baker Beach which extends beneath Golden Gate Bridge. In fine weather, this is a nudist beach.

SUTRO AND THE SUTRO BATHS
In the 1880s, Adoph Sutro, who made his fortune from the invention of a tunnel for draining mines, became one of San Francisco's benefactors. Not content with giving the city the then luxuriant Lands End park, he also built the world's largest public swimming baths. The tickets included the hire of a swimming cap, costume and towel and admission to the seven heated pools equipped with trapezes and chutes. Today the ruins (the baths were destroyed by fire in 1966) can be seen at the foot of Lands End.

HONNEUR ET PATRIE

LINCOLN PARK ◆ **D** A2. Lincoln Park, on the northwestern edge of the city, covers several acres of dunes planted with conifers. In this area, known as LANDS END, nature has been allowed to take its course, much more than in the city's other parks. The CALIFORNIA PALACE OF THE LEGION OF HONOR (below), founded in 1924, is devoted to French art. Its founder, Alma de Bretteville Spreckels, was born into a modest family of Norman origin and married the sugar magnate Adolph Spreckels ▲ *223*, whose luxurious mansion ▲ *123* can be admired in the district of Pacific Heights.

SUTRO HEIGHTS ◆ **D** A3 (off the map). This is the name given to the small green area that extends Lincoln Park and overlooks the long expanse of OCEAN BEACH to the south and SEAL ROCKS to the west. These rocks are the haunt of seals, seagulls, cormorants and pelicans. CLIFF HOUSE, the huge early-20th-century residence built by the then mayor of San Francisco, Adolph Sutro, today houses a restaurant. Below it, the MECHANICAL MUSEUM presents an array of fairground automatons from all over the world. Most are still in excellent working order and visitors would be well advised to take a supply of quarters and nickels to take full advantage of their antique charm. The nearby CAMERA OBSCURA, built in 1949, gives a large-scale explanation of the principles of photography: simply step inside this huge camera to see the surrounding view projected onto a screen.

OCEAN BEACH ◆ **D** A4 (off the map). The rollers of the Pacific Ocean break on this interminable beach of white sand which is popular with families of picnickers, and surfers rigged out to combat the cold currents.

CALIFORNIA PALACE OF THE LEGION OF HONOR
This majestic building, dedicated to Californians killed in World War One, was mainly inspired by the Palais de la Légion d'Honneur in Paris. It houses a number of masterpieces by El Greco, Rembrandt, Rubens, Turner, Cézanne, Monet, Matisse and Picasso, as well as a series of bronzes by Rodin (*The Thinker*, left, in the center of the courtyard) which are as fine as those in the Stanford Art Museum. Two haunting monuments are situated nearby. One is a sober memorial to California's Japanese emigrants, evoking the sufferings endured by these Japanese nationals interned throughout World War Two. The other, the Jewish Holocaust Memorial, is a striking collection of sculptures dedicated to the victims of the Holocaust, many of whom belonged to families which later settled in California.

CONSERVATORY OF FLOWERS

Crossing the park from west to east, the Conservatory of Flowers (below), inspired by the famous Kew Gardens in London, marks the first stage of your visit. The huge glasshouse contains an amazing collection of tropical plants, including several species of palms.

SAN FRANCISCO'S LARGEST PARK ◆ D A4-B4

In the 1860s, San Francisco's mayor, Frank McCoppin, decided to create a park on what was then nothing but sand dunes. Two landscape designers, William Hammond Hall and especially John MacLaren, who worked there for 53 years, took up the challenge and succeeded in growing hundreds of different varieties of plants from all over the world. San Franciscans were soon flocking to the park. In 1893, it hosted the Midwinter Fair, California's first world fair, at the instigation of Michael Harry de Young, co-founder of the *San Francisco Chronicle*. The Japanese Tea Garden, the M H de Young Memorial Museum and the Music Concourse have survived from this early period. Visitors approaching from the direction of the Panhandle, the green driveway planted with

GOLDEN GATE PARK
★

The long rectangular park occupies a slightly undulating site that covers an area of almost 1000 acres. It is planted with attractive groups of trees and shrubs, and populated by cyclists, skaters and lovers, as well as appealing animals such as chipmunks and deer. Take full advantage of this beautiful park by hiring a bicycle in one of the stores on Stanyan Street. Most of the paths are closed to automobiles, especially at weekends.

eucalyptus between Oak and Fell Streets, can drive along the winding John F Kennedy Drive leading to the ocean. Begin by visiting the amazing Conservatory of Flowers.

MUSIC CONCOURSE. Free concerts are held here, ranging from good old local folk-rock, through various blends of Hispanic-American music, to the classical repertoire.

M H DE YOUNG MEMORIAL MUSEUM. This is associated with the California Palace of the Legion of Honor and is devoted to the arts of Africa, the South Sea Islands and the Americas. Its collections include North American paintings dating from the 18th to the 20th centuries, by such artists as George Caleb Bingham, Mary Cassat, Winslow Homer, Thomas Eakins and John Singer Sargent. Currently closed, it will reopen in spectacular new buildings in spring 2005. Meanwhile, the De Young Art Center, near Golden Gate Park (2501 Irving Street), is open to the public.

CALIFORNIA ACADEMY OF SCIENCES. This is both a discovery center and a natural history museum, the exhibits including the reconstruction of a dinosaur. The nearby MORRISON PLANETARIUM and spectacular STEINHART AQUARIUM, with its 200 tanks, finish this long visit.

JAPANESE TEA GARDEN. Visitors can stroll in the garden, which covers an area of five acres, among bonsais, a miniature waterfall and a Zen raked-sand garden, under the watchful eye of a bronze Buddha.

STRYBING ARBORETUM. In an area of some 74 acres the arboretum and botanical gardens contain no fewer than 6000 species of trees and plants from all over the world. The sympathetically designed Garden of Fragrances was planned with sight-impaired people in mind.

SHAKESPEARE GARDEN. The garden is dedicated to lovers of Elizabethan literature in particular. Each variety of flower grown here is mentioned in the works of the Bard.

STOW LAKE. The lake and surrounding pathways are a paradise for sports enthusiasts who practice all kinds of activities, from the more energetic to the less demanding. You can skate on the pathways or row on the lake. In the center of the vast, circular expanse of water, STRAWBERRY HILL offers some spectacular views of the mountains encircling the bay.

Further west are more lakes, ELK GLEN LAKE, MALLARD LAKE, METSON LAKE, whose surroundings have been left as natural as possible.

BUFFALO PADDOCK. This meadow situated to the north of Middle Lake has some rare examples of the buffalo that once roamed the Great Plains in their millions.

QUEEN WILHELMINA TULIP GARDEN. The garden lies at the most westerly end of the park. In spring, its flower beds are filled with a wonderful display of multicolored tulips, set against the backdrop of a greenhouse and a picture-postcard windmill. On the edge of the road running along the beach, the BEACH CHALET has murals recounting the history of California.

JAPANESE TEA GARDEN
In this charming little garden visitors can drink excellent green tea, served in traditional Japanese style by young women in kimonos. It was here, before World War Two, that a certain Mr Hagiwara invented the custom of the Fortune Cookie, the biscuit containing a prophetic text served at the end of (Chinese) meals. Newlyweds come to have their photographs taken in this delightful garden, with its pagoda, little bridge and bonsais, as a guarantee of future happiness.

HIPPIE MEMORIES
The park provided the setting for the first Human Be-In, held on the Polo Field in January 1967. Subsequently, many free concerts were held here, in the hippie tradition of the Haight-Ashbury district, on the eastern edge of the park. Hippie Hill, near the Children's Playground, was the grassy slope where hippies from the sidewalks of Haight Street would come to listen to music and smoke marijuana. The hill, still a place of pilgrimage for some, is now mainly the preserve of frisbee players.

The stone lions at the entrance to the park are relics of the Midwinter Fair (1893).

A HIPPIE PILGRIMAGE
The real hippies left
the district at least 30
years ago, retreating
to such north coast
villages as Bolinas
▲ *141* and Petrolia.
However, the myth is
still exploited, with
the help of T-shirts
and psychedelic
bracelet charms made
'somewhere in Asia'.
But that's no reason
for not visiting the
hippie district and
maybe even staying in
the Red Victorian
Inn (1665 Haight),
whose charming
rooms are decorated
in Flower Power style.
And if you fancy, you
can still make a
pilgrimage to the
places where the
stars of the hippie
movement once lived:
the Grateful Dead at
710 Ashbury Street,
Jefferson Airplane at
2400 Fulton Street
and Big Brother and
Janis Joplin at 1090
Page Street ● *52*.

THE HIPPIE DISTRICT ◆ **D** C4

Former hippies wouldn't recognize the modern Haight-
Ashbury, which has become a lot more expensive than it
was during the 'Summer of Love' of 1967, when many services
were free of charge. The only survivor of this generous period
is the Free Clinic, on the corner of Clayton and Haight, which
still offers free treatment, although the funds needed to
maintain it are in increasingly short supply.

HAIGHT STREET. Today, high-profile businesses take pride of
place: bars, restaurants and such excellent record stores
as the vast Amoeba store at the top of Haight Street. The
Booksmith book store (1644 Haight) organizes meetings
with well-known writers in the store or in nearby All Saints
Church (1350 Waller). The famous Haight and Ashbury
intersection, after which this legendary district is named,
is now the preserve of clothing and ice-cream chains.
In spite of its social and cultural revolutions, the district has
managed to preserve the charm of its elegant Victorian
houses, on the upper part of Ashbury Street and Ashbury
Terrace, as well as on Waller Street and at the upper end of
Clayton Street. Away from the retail businesses of Haight
Street, the café terraces and restaurants of the small district
of Cole Valley, two blocks away, are frequented by a
moderate clientele of bohemian intellectuals. Nowadays,
you have to go to the bottom of Haight, between Fillmore
and Gough, to find a younger, more relaxed atmosphere in
the rock, reggae and techno bars.

THE GAY DISTRICT ◆ **D** D4

San Francisco has always traditionally been a center for social
innovation. However, it was after World War Two that its
reputation began to attract gays and lesbians ▲ *136* and a
number of homosexual districts were established. Originally,
the Castro was known as 'Eureka Valley' and inhabited by the
families of Irish Catholic workers. In the late 1960s, these

Mural in Castro.

families gradually moved away, the stores closed and rents plummeted. Large numbers of hippies and other social and sexual 'marginals' settled there and breathed new life into the district. Its reputation spread by word of mouth and increasing numbers of white homosexuals moved into the Castro until, by the mid-1970s, it had become the most famous gay ghetto in the world. In spite of its unalluring appearance, HARVEY MILK PLAZA, at the intersection of Castro and Market Streets, is the vibrant heart of this constantly changing district, which stretches along Castro to 19th Street on the one hand, and along Market to Church Street on the other.

CASTRO THEATER. The movie theater at 429 Castro Street is one of the best known in San Francisco. This is only partly due to the fact that its canopy and sophisticated neon signs are the symbol of the district and that it hosts the annual San Francisco International Lesbian & Gay Film Festival. The theater, built in 1922 in Spanish Colonial Revival style by T Pfleuger, has been classified as an historic monument and contains a magnificent chandelier, Art Deco murals and a Wurlitzer organ. It has hosted a number of world premieres, including Peter Adair's *Word Is Out* and Rob Epstein's *The Celluloid Closet*. This last movie, which deals with the image of homosexuality in Hollywood cinema, was based on a novel by the late Vito Russo whose ashes, according to Epstein, were placed in one of the walls of the theater.

CAFÉ FLORE. This cosy and intimate gay café, situated at the busy intersection of Market and Noe Streets, is primarily a see-and-be-seen venue. The small front courtyard is usually crowded with an extremely colorful set of people.

A DIFFERENT LIGHT. This book store at 489 Castro Street is also a community center. It stocks thousands of titles and a wide variety of newspapers and magazines (from the international press to less widely read fanzines), as well as videos, discs and posters. Lectures are organized on a regular basis.

THE GAY FLAG
The huge rainbow-colored flag was designed by Gilbert Baker for San Francisco's Gay Freedom Parade in 1978. It still hangs above Harvey Milk Plaza, at the intersection of Castro and Market, and marks the entrance to the city's gay district. Each of its colors was carefully chosen to symbolize a particular concept or idea: bright red (sex), red (life), orange (healing), yellow (the sun), green (peace with nature), turquoise (art), indigo (harmony) and purple (the mind). Previously reduced to six stripes to make production easier, the flag has today been restored to its original glory, at least in the Castro.

QUEER CULTURAL CENTER. The center is a kind of gay HQ, which publicizes the activities of gay organizations and has a café, meeting and conference rooms and exhibition galleries. It also publishes a program of events and organizes its own events for newcomers to the district. It is an ideal place to go for information on the gay community.

OTHER PLACES OF INTEREST
The Names Project Visitor Center (284 Sanchez Street), where the panels of the Names Project AIDS Memorial Quilt ▲ *136* are on display.

The San Francisco region, renowned for its tolerance since the 19th century, has always been at the forefront of artistic, political, social, cultural and sexual activism. In the 20th century, this tradition was perpetuated by the Beat and hippie movements, the 'Summer of Love' and the Free Speech Movement. San Francisco's reputation as the world capital of the gay community stems from the publication in 1964 of an article in *Life* magazine, 'Homosexuality in America', which included photographs of the city's gay bars. The article appeared five years before the Stonewall riot in New York in 1969, which drew attention to the problem of gay rights. Since then, San Francisco has attracted increasing numbers of men and women who regard it as a city where they can be completely open about their homosexuality, bisexuality or transsexuality.

AIDS MEMORIAL QUILT
The first known cases of AIDS occurred in San Francisco in January 1981. The city would pay a heavy toll to the epidemic. In 1982, the gay community began to hold candlelit vigils in memory of the AIDS victims. The Names Project AIDS Memorial Quilt was launched in 1986 when Cleve Jones, a militant homosexual activist, created the first panel in memory of his partner.

THE ASSASSINATIONS OF MOSCONE AND MILK
The progressive mayor George Moscone and Harvey Milk (above), San Francisco's first homosexual city councilor, both played a key role in involving the gay communities in the city's administration. On November 21, 1978 they were shot dead by Dan White, a retired police officer and former city councilor. Tens of thousands of San Franciscans held a spontaneous candlelit vigil on the steps of the city hall to pay their respects.

AN UNJUST VERDICT
On May 21, 1979 White was judged guilty of manslaughter but not of premeditated homicide, which meant that his sentence was much lighter than anticipated. The news provoked riots during which 5000 homosexuals caused over one million dollars' worth of damage, followed by a violent police raid on the Elephant Walk bar, at the intersection of 18th and Castro.

TRANSSEXUALISM

San Francisco has always played a key role in acknowledging the transsexual community. Organizations such as FTM International and Transgender Nation work tirelessly in the pursuit of their fight for civil rights.

THE GAY OLYMPICS

The first Gay Olympic Games, held at Kezar Stadium in 1982, brought together 1300 gay athletes. The aim was to counter their stereotyped image and combat the divisions that threatened the community. The games are held each time in a different country.

GAY PRIDE

The Lesbian Gay Bisexual and Transgender Pride Parade and Celebration is held each year on the last weekend in June to commemorate the Stonewall riot. Today it is the largest Gay Pride event in the United States.

A member of the Sisters of Perpetual Indulgence (left).

Sensationalism, feathers, frills and flounces during the Gay Pride celebrations.

◆ SAN FRANCISCO
MISSION

The Mission Dolores is California's sixth largest mission. Inside, the richly decorated altar dates from the 18th century.

MISSION ★
Mission is one of the city's liveliest districts. Although it attracts young middle-class San Franciscans, it has lost none of its Hispanic warmth and passion. This is borne out by its many *taquerías* and magnificent murals which are real masterpieces of Chicano art.

THE HISPANIC DISTRICT

MISSION DISTRICT ◆ D D5 is the city's Mexican district par excellence. In fact, it would be more correct to describe it as Latino, since the numbers of migrants from the south have been vastly increased by refugees from the totalitarian regimes of Spanish-speaking America. Their presence is reflected on the walls: Mission is well known for its murals, which are predominately social and political. The district is crossed by several broad avenues, the most beautiful of which is Dolores, named after the mission on the corner of 16th Street.

MISSION DOLORES. The mission was built in 1776 and extended until 1791. It was damaged in the 1989 earthquake and restored in 1994. Although officially dedicated to St Francis of Assisi, it has always been know locally as Dolores, previously the name of a nearby river. The impressive building is more richly decorated than the other Californian missions ● *62*, with a curious blend of baroque elements and geometric motifs. Its tiny garden is a reminder of the Alcázar in Granada. The mission was the first official building to be built in the city and its cemetery contains the remains of the first governor of Alta California, Don Luis Antonio Arguello and the first *alcalde* (mayor) of Yerba Buena ▲ *115* (the future San Francisco), Don Francisco de Haro.

DOLORES AVENUE. This palm-lined avenue provides a striking contrast with the adjacent, parallel streets: Guerrero, Valencia and Mission. The last is one of the city's main working-class districts, with its inexpensive stores, rather seedy hotels, South-American transvestite clubs, and open-air stalls selling fruit, vegetables, clothes, cassettes and religious artifacts. Visitors come to slum in Mission and rub shoulders with the gangs of dangerous-looking (and possibly dangerous) Chicanos ● *39*.

VALENCIA STREET. For some time, the most northern part of Mission has witnessed the expansion of the gay scene ▲ *136*, as the main thoroughfare of Valencia Street has gradually become a lesbian preserve, with its own bars, restaurants and book stores. Valencia has also become the center of intense nocturnal activity, where smart bohemians come to rub shoulders with a more marginal population, lining up on the

People visit Mission to eat in the excellent and very affordable *taquerías* which serve Mexican specialties.

sidewalk to get a table in the latest fashionable bistro. The intersection of Valencia and 16th is now as fashionable as Haight-Ashbury and North Beach during other eras. As you make your way back to Dolores, the attractions of 16th Street include its movie theater, The Roxie (at 3117), which shows rare movies. The outlandish Taquería Pancho Villa, near the corner of Valencia, is frequented by the district's disparate population. A little further south, 24th Street offers a totally different experience depending on whether you turn west to the intersection with Church Street, or east to the hills of Potrero.

TWIN PEAKS, A PANORAMIC VIEW
◆ **D** C5
(west of Mission, beyond the Castro) These twin hills rise to a height of 985 feet in the geographical center of San Francisco. Their rounded contours earned them the Spanish nickname *Los Pechos de la Chola* (the breasts of the young Indian). The hills have been spared development and remain a small area of natural beauty in the heart of the city. They also offer one of its most beautiful panoramic views, from beyond Golden Gate Bridge ▲ *128*, in the west, to Bay Bridge ▲ *143*, in the east.

BEYOND MISSION

EAST TO POTRERO ◆ **D** E4. This district is currently being renovated to house the entrepreneurs of the new economy ▲ *146*. The result is an interesting cultural mix of WASPs and Chicanos, rich and poor. Today, the fruit and vegetable market, on the corner of Mission Street, is next to web cafés, and the cheapest clothes stores in town sit side by side with designer stores. The murals of Balmy Street reflect the extent of Mexican migration, while a small museum, the GALERIA DE LA RAZA, exhibits works of Chicano art (2857 24th Street). A little further on is a mural of the great guitarist, Carlos Santana, who was born in the district.

WEST TO NOE VALLEY ◆ **D** D5 **AND DIAMOND HEIGHTS** ◆ **D** C5. Beyond Dolores Street lies a more middle-class world. The district of Noe Valley stretches from Dolores to Twin Peaks, with its attractive late Victorian houses, and between Church and Diamond Streets, with their Italian restaurants, book stores and fashion boutiques. Two blocks further on, Clipper Street leads to the hills of Diamond Heights, where a small parking lot on Portola offers a panoramic view of the entire city which is truly magical at night.

Highway 1 runs along the edge of Bolinas Lagoon (right), a favorite haunt of many different species of birds.

HOUSEBOATS AT SAUSALITO

The floating village, established in the 1960s, consists of houseboats linked by pontoons. These are mostly constructed from odds and ends of materials salvaged from old ships.

NORTH OF SAN FRANCISCO BAY

More and more San Franciscans now live in one of the towns scattered between the northern end of the bay and the ocean, resulting in interminable rush-hour traffic jams. Visitors would therefore be well advised to leave Highway 101 on the far side of Golden Gate Bridge and head for MARIN HEADLANDS ◆ A B6. In summer, you can enjoy spectacular views of San Francisco to the sound of foghorns as the fog sweeps in at a truly amazing speed, swirling around the piers of the bridge and retreating as quickly as it came.

MARIN COUNTY ✪

According to legend, Marin was the name of a very popular American Indian who operated the ferry between San Francisco and Sausalito Bay in the 19th century. These old ferries are now ending their days in the county's floating villages. Today, Marin County is attracting increasing numbers of visitors. Some like to walk around its original wooden houses and drink in the scents and sounds of nature. Others prefer to devote themselves to one of the New Age philosophies that abound in the county.

The surrounding hills, formerly an army range, have retained all their wild splendor. Unless you continue along a footpath such as the Miwok Trail, you have to retrace your steps to continue northward.

SAUSALITO ◆ A F1. Today, very little remains of the floating village which was one of the main alternative communities of the 1960s: Alan Watts ● 47 lived here. The bohemian lifestyle has given way to mass tourism and a new, wealthy middle-class population with a marina filled with hundreds of yachts. Steeply sloping streets bordered by beautiful late-19th-century Victorian houses lead off the main shopping street, BRIDGEWAY BOULEVARD. At 2001, a former army depot houses the BAY MODEL VISITORS CENTER, where a huge model of San Francisco Bay even reproduces the tidal system.

ALONG THE COAST TO BOLINAS ◆ A F1. When it reaches Mill Valley, Highway 1 starts to twist and turn as it winds its way round the contours of the coast. Sheer cliffs plunge into the sea where they break up into isolated black rocks. You may like to leave the coast for a while to walk through MUIR WOODS and climb MOUNT TAMALPAIS.

The little beach known as MUIR BEACH marks the true point of departure of the North Coast. A little to the east, on a bend in the road, is the sign for the GREEN GULCH FARM AND ZEN CENTER, an organic farm and Buddhist retreat. Visitors are welcome to take tea (it has a Japanese tea-house), meditate in the prayer hall and possibly even meet the *roshi*. A little further north, MUIR BEACH OVERLOOK offers a unique view of the rugged coastline from a wooden walkway on a rocky outcrop. The vertiginous road winds its way northward for about 9 miles to STINSON BEACH with its cafés, book store and three-mile stretch of sand – an ideal place to indulge in the Californian art of relaxation. Beyond the beach, BOLINAS LAGOON stretches for several miles. This bird-watchers' paradise is frequented by hundreds of pelicans, herons, seagulls, albatross, moorhens, sandpipers and ducks under the watchful eye of the local branch of the Audubon Society. A minor road skirts round the edge of the lagoon to the 'green' village of Bolinas at the far end before rejoining Highway 1 via an archway of eucalyptus.

POINT REYES AND TOMALES BAY ◆ A B6 **▲** *236*. Point Reyes Station is a small, typically West Coast town. With its cafés and antique stores, it makes a pleasant place to break your journey. It lies at the southern end of TOMALES BAY, whose resemblance to a loch must have inspired Scottish settlers to found the fishing village of INVERNESS. The bottom of the bay is carpeted with oyster beds which provide the local specialty, eaten raw, boiled or grilled. In TOMALES is the Church of the Assumption and its colonial-style presbytery (1897), while a few of the strangely shaped houses, built by inventive carpenters, have survived from the imaginative hippie culture that flourished in the region.

MOUNT TAMALPAIS
Mount Tamalpais, known locally as 'Mount Tam', is covered with flower-filled pastures and sequoia and cork-oak forests. In spite of the steep slopes, this makes for a pleasant climb to the summit at 2600 feet, which offers an unrivaled view of the surrounding region. As the home of the mountain bike, 'Mount Tam' is well equipped with cycle tracks.

MUIR WOODS NATIONAL MONUMENT
This evergreen sequoia forest was saved from the ax by a businessman in 1906. In 1908, it was declared a national monument by President Theodore Roosevelt. It is an ideal alternative for those who don't have time to go as far as the Redwood National and State Parks **▲** *258*.

BOLINAS, IN SEARCH OF OBLIVION
Signposts to Bolinas are constantly being removed by the local residents, who want to preserve the peace and quiet of their village. Most experienced the golden age of the hippie movement in the 1960s ● *37*, and are resolutely keeping to its customs. The village has an organic produce cooperative (a field of pumpkins, left), amazingly decorated wooden houses and, unusually, dogs running free on the beach.

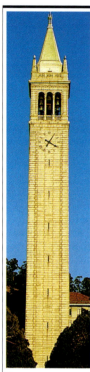

As you head back inland, the little road to Santa Rosa passes through the town of SEBASTOPOL ◆ A B6, whose name attests to the former presence of Russian immigrants in the region. However, the Orthodox church is built in the Spanish Mission style. SANTA ROSA ◆ A B6 is a fairly large town whose main attraction is its cellars where visitors can taste the local wines ▲ 148.

PETALUMA ◆ A B6. Petaluma may be smaller than Santa Rosa, but it is far more attractive and has one of the widest choices of antique dealers in California. It seems that every disused building in this formerly industrial town has been given over to the trend for bargain hunting. Former mills and ex-banks offer reasonably priced items, from 1950s bric-a-brac, through all kinds of attractive late-19th- and early-20th-century furniture and jewelry, to pre-war cars. Petaluma also has some fine examples of Gold Rush architecture, for example ST VINCENT DE PAULS' CHURCH, the porch of ST JOHN'S EPISCOPAL CHURCH, industrial canal-side buildings and some attractive Victorian houses.

NOVATO ◆ A F1. About 12 miles south of Petaluma, the town of Novato is well worth a visit for its MARIN MUSEUM OF THE AMERICAN INDIAN which gives pride of place to the Miwok and Olompali cultures.

SAN RAFAEL ◆ A F1. About 9 miles south of Novato, San Rafael is an attractive, relaxed, academic town. It is passionate about the New Age and has the largest New Age store in California – Open Secrets, on C Street. The only evidence of an earlier culture is the MISSION SAN RAFAEL, built in 1817 and rebuilt in 1949. Just before you turn back across the bay via Richmond Bridge, you can see San Quentin

BERKELEY CAMPUS
Most of the buildings were constructed using funds collected by William Randolph Hearst ▲ 172. His favorite architect, Julia Morgan, designed only part of the complex. In fact, most of the buildings were designed by her rival, John Galen Howard, whose European taste is very much in evidence, particularly in the extremely tall bell-tower, inspired by the Campanile of St Mark's Basilica in Venice. Visitors can climb to the top of the tower, which offers a magnificent view of the campus and San Francisco Bay. Don't leave Berkeley without hunting for a few bargains in one of the well-stocked book stores on Telegraph Avenue.

State Prison which is famous for 'accommodating' such famous inmates as Neal Cassady, the hero of the Beat Generation ● *36*, and Johnny Cash, who recorded one of his best albums there, in front of a prison audience.

EAST OF SAN FRANCISCO BAY

BERKELEY ◆ A B6. The very name of Berkeley evokes a monument of American culture, better known for its protest movements during the 1960s than the subjects taught there. Today, the campus reflects the attitudes of a new generation, determined to obtain their diplomas, and the smell of tear gas is a thing of the past. How many in fact remember the great rebellions of the Free Speech Movement ● *36*, on the steps of Sproul Hall in 1963, or the People's Park in 1969? Their respective legacies are a freedom of expression on the campus that no one would dare challenge, and a green space that is sacrosanct, since it is heavily imbued with symbolic value. Today, a visit to the campus and its buildings is a peaceful affair. Of the buildings open the public, the PHOEBE HEARST MUSEUM OF ANTHROPOLOGY houses the strange mementos of an American Indian named Ishi, the last survivor of the Yahi, a Stone Age tribe that lived in Northern California. The unfortunate Ishi was the subject of 'scientific' studies and died in semi-captivity on the campus, shortly after he was captured in 1911. The BERKELEY ART MUSEUM, built in 1963, acts as a reminder that this essentially scientific campus has always attracted artists. It houses a great many of the works of its founder, the abstract artist Hans Hoffmann.

BAY BRIDGE
Bay Bridge, which links San Francisco and Oakland ▲ *144* near Berkeley, was built (1933–36) by engineer Charles Purcell. Its completion brought the monopoly of the ferries to an end. The structure is more than 8 miles long, over 4 miles over the water. It consists of an earlier bridge built between San Francisco and Yerba Buena Island, extended by a second between the island and the far shore. The lower roadway is used by traffic traveling in the direction of Berkeley, and the upper roadway by traffic traveling in the opposite direction. Treasure Island, reached from Yerba Buena Island, offers an unrivaled view of the bay.

JACK LONDON

Jack London (1876–1916) was brought up by his mother, a skilled story-teller, and step-father whose name he used. The wharves of Oakland provided the setting for his poverty-stricken childhood up to the age of fifteen, when he ran away to sea. In 1897, he set out for Alaska in search of gold. However, it was not gold that would make him rich but the adventures that inspired his writing. *The Son of the Wolf* (1900), *Call of the*

Wild (1903), *The Sea Wolf* (1904), *White Fang* (1907) and *Martin Eden* (1909) were all hugely successful. But although he became rich, he never abandoned his fight against social injustice, the theme of his life and writing. In 1916, he took his own life on his Glen Ellen ranch ▲ *149*.

OAKLAND ◆ B A1. The town is virtually an extension of Berkeley and the names of the avenues are often duplicated, as in the case of Telegraph Avenue, although it loses its student image as it enters Oakland. Once a famous stronghold of the Black Panther movement, founded there in 1965 ● *37*, Oakland is today one of the new high-tech centers with a growing Asian population. However, African-American culture is still very much in evidence, and several of its blues clubs are among the best on the West Coast. In the Chinese district, the old

IRIS & B. GERALD CANTOR
CENTER *for* VISUAL ARTS
STANFORD UNIVERSITY

buildings, including the Paramount Theater ● *73* (2025 Broadway) with its Art Deco mosaics, are a reminder that this was an extremely lively town in the 1930s.

JACK LONDON SQUARE. Oakland has honored the memory of its most famous son by dedicating a village to him, built in the style of the early pioneers, near the old docks (left). The image of Jack London is in fact an appropriate choice for a local population of blue-collar workers employed on the port or in the surrounding industrial towns.

OAKLAND MUSEUM OF CALIFORNIA. It is worth visiting Oakland, if only for this museum which summarizes every aspect of California's history – historical, geographical, natural and artistic. It includes 19th-century landscape painting (Yosemite region, sequoia forests), the figurative expressionism of the Group of Six formed by local artists in the 1920s, and the Bay Area Figurative Art of the 1950s. This last movement brought together such artists as David Park and Richard Diebenkorn, who rejected abstraction in favor of a return to realism, and chose the human form as the best medium for the expression of feelings. The photographic collection includes the works of the region's leading photographers – Watkins, Lange, Weston and Cunningham ● *54*. Further south, Highway 880 passes through the industrial towns of San Leandro, Hayward and Fremont, where you can see the Mission San José de Guadalupe.

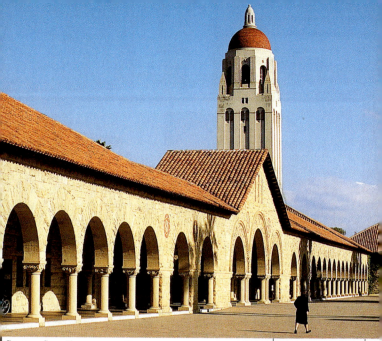

South San Francisco Bay ◆ B A1

San José. The newly acquired wealth of the town's population has favored the patronage enjoyed by such institutions as the Museum of Art, which specializes in contemporary works by local artists, while the Tech Museum of Innovation ▲ *147* explains some of the mysteries of computer technology. Visitors to the Winchester Mystery House will be reminded of the region's dangerous passion for weapons. This amazing house was built by the widow of Oliver Fisher Winchester (1810–80), who was convinced her husband had been carried off by the souls of the men killed by the rifle he invented. She had one room built for each of the supposed 160 souls! Work had to continue at any price, even at the risk of evoking these malevolent spirits, resulting in the many strange structures that gave the house its name. No less strange is the Rosicrucian Museum, with its rather kitsch decor, mainly devoted to Egyptian antiquities. As you head north along Highway 280 toward San Francisco, you pass through towns made famous by the computer technology boom, for example Cupertino, home of Apple Computer, Inc.

Santa Clara. The Santa Clara district is one of the oldest built-up areas in California and its Spanish culture is still very much alive in spite of the success of Silicon Valley ▲ *146*. Thus the remains of the Mission Santa Clara de Asis, built in 1777, largely destroyed and then restored in the 19th century, can still be seen on the campus of Santa Clara University. Various objects and ornaments from the original mission can be seen in the De Saisset Museum.

Palo Alto. This small town positively exudes opulence, with its attractive houses set in gardens planted with trees. At the end of a long avenue stands the campus of Stanford University, a model university and the envy of students throughout the world.

STANFORD UNIVERSITY (Palo Alto) The university is named for Leland Stanford, one of the 'Big Four' ▲ *156*, who founded the university in memory of his son, who died at the age of sixteen. Its huge buildings, which are surrounded by vast lawns and groves of trees, rival those of Berkeley ▲ *143*. The most remarkable is Stanford Memorial Church, a Byzantine-style church built in 1891 and rebuilt after the 1906 earthquake. Its decor includes a huge mosaic by Maurizio Camerino, a reproduction of one of the frescos in the Sistine Chapel. The adjacent cloister (above) has beautiful neo-Romanesque lines. The wealth of the campus is reflected in the collection of paintings and Asian art in the Cantor Arts Center (top left), opened in 1999. It is surrounded by gardens adorned with some of Rodin's most famous sculptures.

145

SGI, in Mountain View, produces 3D special effects for Hollywood on computer.

In 1938, William Hewlett and David Packard founded an electronics company in Palo Alto, and Silicon Valley was soon to change the world. There was an influx of brilliant immigrants from countries worldwide, drawn by the vast numbers of info-tech companies, educated at the universities of Stanford and Berkeley, and attracted by the Californian lifestyle. They innovated like mad, founded start-up companies and made money. The microprocessor was developed by Intel and its offshoot, the microcomputer, by Apple. The Internet took off with Netscape and Sun. According to investor John Doerr, Silicon Valley – the name was coined by a journalist in 1971 – represents 'the greatest legitimate creation of wealth in history'.

THE PARTNERSHIPS OF SILICON VALLEY

The magical partnership between an engineer and businessman of genius is the secret of Silicon Valley's success. In 1938, William Hewlett and David Packard founded a company in the garage of a house in Palo Alto, which can still be seen at 367 Addison Avenue. Over thirty years later, two more 'garage technicians', Steve Jobs and Stephen Wozniak, former hippies and Beatles fans, launched the Apple Macintosh Computer. In 1995, Stanford students Jerry Yang and David Filo created the Internet search engine Yahoo!

PALM, A POCKET COMPUTER

In 1992, Jeff Hawkins had the idea of creating a hand-held computer. He designed and made a wooden model in his garage, carried it in his shirt pocket and asked people's opinion. In 1996, he and Donna Dubinsky launched the Palm Pilot. The Personal Digital Assistant (PDA) overtook the Sony Walkman as the most widely sold new product in history. It is easy to use and replaces diaries and personal organizers.

A café in South Park.

ITINERARY ◆ B A1 FOR COMPUTER BUFFS SAN FRANCISCO: 'MULTIMEDIA GULCH'

A day in the megalopolis that stretches for 50 miles to San José simply has to begin in a café in South Park ◆ E E6, the center of what is known as 'Multimedia Gulch'. With its hundreds of companies (from Macromedia to C/Net and Looksmart to Wired), attracted by the dynamism of San Francisco, the Gulch, to the south of Market Street, is the cultural soup of the Internet.

PALO ALTO: THE HEART OF SILICON VALLEY

Take Highway 280 in a southbound direction and then the Page Mill Road exit and make a left. The road running down through the hills to the bay leads to Stanford Research Park. Created by the University of Stanford in 1951 for Hewlett-Packard, the 690-acre park with its 140 companies and research centers is where Silicon Valley all began. Inventions developed here, in the famous Xerox PARC, include the mouse and the operating system that inspired the Macintosh and Windows systems. The head office of Hewlett-Packard, the world's second largest info-tech company, is at 3000 Hanover Street, on the corner of Page Mill.

SANTA CLARA: INTEL AND SILICON CHIPS

Carry straight on toward Highway 101 South and take the Great America Parkway exit. Make a right onto Mission College Boulevard (in front of Nortel) and Intel is at 2220. As well as tracing the history of the semiconductor giant, the Intel Museum also highlights the technology used in PCs, automobiles and space shuttles. The explanation of how ordinary beach sand is transformed into silicon chips is particularly fascinating.

SAN JOSÉ: CISCO AND THE INTERNET HIGHWAYS

Turn back toward Great America Parkway and make a right. A series of boldly designed buildings, including Verifone and Techmart, run right to the campus of 3Com. Turn back the way you came and make a left onto Tasman Drive, at the Hilton. From 250 Tasman Drive the forty buildings of Cisco Systems run for over half a mile. The company's 35,000 employees construct the infrastructure of the Internet.

DOWNTOWN SAN JOSÉ: THE TECH MUSEUM

Make a right onto North First Street, another 'corridor' of high-tech companies, toward downtown San José. At 201 South Market Street, the primary colors of the Tech Museum of Innovation light up the Center Plaza. With more than 200 interactive exhibitions and its IMAX movie theater, the Tech is a microcosm of Silicon Valley's spirit of innovation.

BACK TO PALO ALTO: THE BREEDING GROUND OF NEW TECHNOLOGY ▲ 145

In the late 1930s, Stanford University became the breeding ground of the 'new economy', in particular of H-P, Yahoo!, Cisco and Sun. Head back to San Francisco on Highway 101 North and take the Ralston Avenue exit toward Belmont. Make a right onto Marine Parkway and a left toward the towers of Oracle, the database software giant. Its founder, Larry Ellison, competes with Bill Gates (Microsoft) for the title of the richest man in America.

DRY CREEK VINEYARDS
(Healdsburg). Very fine, long-lasting Zinfandels top the range from this elegant estate. Old bush-vines hug the red hillsides while white varieties such as Chardonnay, Sauvignon Blanc, and even Chenin Blanc, thrive further down the slopes.

The Gold Rush in 1849 ● *34* reinforced the presence of the mission vineyards, which by then extended into the foothills of the High Sierra: the gold diggers and panners had ferocious thirsts to slake. The gold was eventually exhausted, but the vines stayed, their presence firmly established in newly formed vineyard areas, first Sonoma and then Napa, fueled by demand from nearby towns, not least San Francisco ● *56*. Today, the wineries in the two valleys welcome visitors and offer lots of opportunity to taste. Napa's are glamorous venues where you receive the most attentive hospitality. There's more family-scale charm in Sonoma. Both are worth a visit: Sonoma, 'The Valley of the Moon', is ruggedly beautiful, while Napa is gently rural.

SONOMA VALLEY ◆ **A** B5-B6 ● *56*

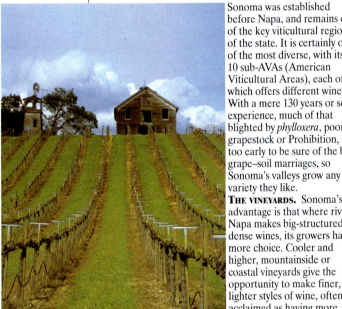

Sonoma was established before Napa, and remains one of the key viticultural regions of the state. It is certainly one of the most diverse, with its 10 sub-AVAs (American Viticultural Areas), each of which offers different wines. With a mere 130 years or so experience, much of that blighted by *phylloxera*, poor grapestock or Prohibition, it's too early to be sure of the best grape–soil marriages, so Sonoma's valleys grow any variety they like.

THE VINEYARDS. Sonoma's advantage is that where rival Napa makes big-structured, dense wines, its growers have more choice. Cooler and higher, mountainside or coastal vineyards give the opportunity to make finer, lighter styles of wine, often acclaimed as having more finesse. The smaller scale of Sonoma wineries often means a hairpin-bend country road to get there, but they are less commercial, and you're more likely to meet the winemaker!

OTHER INTERESTING WINERIES
SIMI WINERY Historically a region-leader winery, with good Chardonnay.
KENWOOD VINEYARDS (Kenwood) Big, bold reds from the Jack London range are especially attractive.
LANDMARK (Kenwood) Look out for the range of fabulous Chardonnays.
GUNDLACH-BUNDSCHU (Vineburg) Watch out for great Merlots, Pinots and Zins.

RODNEY STRONG (Healdsburg). Dramatic octagonal winery built in the 1970s, worth seeing for its striking retrospective pose. Winemaker Rick Sayre produces a full range, but Cabernets and Zinfandels are particularly interesting.
PEDRONCELLI (Geyserville). Historic old redwood winery buildings, worth the visit to step back in time. Zinfandel is the tradition here at this fourth-generation estate, but the aim is for finesse rather than blockbusting monsters.
GEYSER PEAK (Geyserville). Australia has an influence here in approachable, fruit-forward wines. The list runs the gamut from Chardonnay to rich, intense Cabernets, and there's some fine Syrah. Good visitor facilities.
HEALDSBURG. Delightful Sonoma wine town with a charming central square – there are wine stores, restaurants and plenty

to browse around. A good place to lunch before exploring the
RUSSIAN RIVER WINE ROAD, with 75 wineries.
SONOMA. The town still shows the signs of its Spanish
and Mexican heritage. The BEAR FLAG MONUMENT
commemorates the revolt here in 1846. You can also visit
LACHRYMA MONTIS, Vallejo's beautiful house. Nearby, the
SAN FRANCISCO MISSION SOLANO, now well restored, was the
most northerly Mexican outpost in California.

CARNEROS ◆ A B6 ● 56

Carneros, between the two valleys, is also a cool-climate
region and particularly successful with sparkling wines.
THE VINEYARDS. SCHUG. Charming Germanic timber-framed
winery run by Walter Schug, who has turned his back on an
illustrious career making cult Napa wines (Insignia and Eisele

SONOMA
The Spanish and
Mexican influences
on this busy wine
town are still
apparent, and
indicative of less
tranquil times. The
leafy Plaza was, in
1846, the scene of an
uprising against the
Mexican government
in which Colonel
Guadalupe Vallejo
● 25 and his men
were overthrown.
Only a month after
this 'Bear Flag
Revolt', the US

at Joseph Phelps) to get back to his roots and focus on Pinot
Noir. Also fine are Schug's Sauvignon and Bordeaux blends.
DOMAINE CARNEROS. A glamorous outpost of Champagne
Taittinger, receiving visitors for cellar tours and tastings of the
full Champenois range (by log fires in the winter, on an
elegant terrace with vineyard views in the summer). The non-
sparkling Pinot Noir also well worth trying.
JACK LONDON STATE HISTORIC PARK (GLEN ELLEN). Ten
minutes from Sonoma is the densely forested 140-acre ranch
that was the home of Jack London ▲ 144. He lived and wrote
here during the last ten years of his adventurous life, in 'the
most beautiful, primitive land in California'. After his death,
his wife Charmian built THE HOUSE OF HAPPY WALLS which is
now a Jack London museum. A half-mile walk takes you
to the ruins of London's dream home, THE WOLF HOUSE,
which burnt down in 1913 before he ever had the chance
to live there.

declared war on
Mexico and
proceeded to annex
California without
firing a single shot.
Ironically, Colonel
Vallejo had already
suggested an
American takeover,
so the revolution was
almost needless. The
Bear Flag monument
on Sonoma's Plaza
marks the site of the
uprising and it's also
possible to visit
Lachryma Montis,
Vallejo's ornate
home, a short
walk away.

▲ WINE COUNTRY
NAPA VALLEY

NAPA VALLEY, THE QUINTESSENCE OF CALIFORNIAN WINE ✪

When you make a visit to the Napa Valley you will enjoy a combination of many pleasures. The delights of its wines, whether heavy or light, are mingled with the peace of the gently rolling countryside, the architecture, both ancient and contemporary, and the collections of international art. To explore by automobile, it is best to use Highway 29, the main artery of Napa Valley, or follow the 'Silverado Trail', which is quieter and offers more exciting views. You can even go up in a balloon to enjoy a magnificent panorama, or take a trip round the vineyards on the Wine Train, which leaves from McKinstry Street in Napa.

Frog's Leap Winery.

OAKVILLE GRADE. To get from Napa to Sonoma and vice versa you have to cross the Mayacamas Mountains. While on the map this looks like a simple straight road, the Oakville Grade is actually a switch-back adventure through glorious Californian countryside. It offers stunning views and beautifully unspoilt forestland, but there are quicker routes.

NAPA VALLEY ◆ **A** B5-B6 ● *56, 96*

Think Californian wine, think Napa Valley. Napa has come to epitomise Californian wine, despite being one of the last viticultural regions to be established. What really brought it to the forefront was being first out of the blocks after Prohibition. A handful of progressive wineries had kept themselves quietly ticking over during Prohibiion by producing communion wines. These took the lead in reestablishing viticulture, and inspired such enthusiasm that the 1970s and 1980s saw a host of devoted followers. By the end of the 1980s, the original six survivors had increased to 200. Napa's vineyards now stretch in a long, thin arc for 40 miles, and are so densely established that there's little room for further expansion. Newer vineyards are still being planted, up in the less fertile foothills, and many growers say that these higher vineyards are in fact better than the prized valley-floor plots. It's too early to know for sure.

THE VINEYARDS. Cabernet Sauvignon is the grape that gains Napa most fame, and it makes up nearly a third of all plantings, followed by Chardonnay and Merlot. Cabernet is behind many of the valley's small-production, 'cult' wines, and every grower wants to plant it for the high prices its wines fetch. Merlot grows well in Napa, as does Zinfandel, but Chardonnay, Pinot Noir and Sauvignon Blanc, though widely planted, tend to produce less impressive wines from this region.

Hess Collection (Napa). The project of Swiss art collector Donald Hess, it is home to impressive Mount Veeder Cabernet Sauvignon and fine Chardonnay, but is equally distinguished for its spectacular art and museum displays.

Mondavi (Oakville). A distinctive Spanish Mission-style winery well worth a visit. The high quality range of Mondavi varietal wines includes top Cabernet Sauvignon, Pinot Noir and Chardonnay, but also look out for the La Famiglia range of Italian varieties and Opus One, the Bordeaux-style Rothschild joint venture with its own very striking winery. Tours are available.

Frog's Leap (Rutherford). Housed in what used to be a frog-rearing farm, Frog's Leap is now home to very fine Zinfandel and other wines. Its distinctive red barns are worth visiting to take in the unstuffy (and organic) side of Napa winemaking.

Mumm Napa Valley (Rutherford). Take part in a fascinating tour to discover the secret to making sparkling wine in what is ostensibly Cabernet Sauvignon territory.

The grapes are actually collected from cooler areas, but the blend is similar to those used for Champagne, and the end result is great.

St Helena. An interesting old town with plenty of shops to browse around and some good restaurants. The Silverado Museum (1490 Library Lane) charts Robert Louis Stevenson's ● *98* time in the area. He and his new American wife Fanny Osborne stayed in an abandoned miners' bunk house on the mountainside, being too poor to afford anything else. He recorded his impressions of the visit in The Silverado Squatters. Just opposite is the Napa Valley Wine Library.

Calistoga. The town's natural hot springs have given rise not only to mineral water but a collection of spas, where you can indulge in a mud bath (buried up to your neck) and a massage, ideal treatment for aching muscles after touring the wine country. There are plenty of shops and restaurants to explore too.

Sterling. A tour of Sterling includes a cable-car ride which takes you up to the hill-top winery to enjoy views across the valley and a wide range of interesting wines.

Clos Pegase. This is worth visiting not only for its Cabernet and Chardonnay. Clos Pegase is a visitor attraction noted for its modern art displays, sculptures and fine winery (above right). The winery was created by Michael Graves, the winner of an architecture competition, and you either love it or hate it.

Old Faithful Geyser. Just north of Calistoga, Old Faithful faithfully spouts 60 feet of boiling sulphurous water into the air at 40–50 minute intervals. (The 'fainting goats' housed near to the geyser, while impressive, don't necessarily time their antics to that of the eruptions.)

Petrified Forest. A stand of redwoods which were felled and covered by a volcanic eruption were preserved and petrified by the lava. Then, after years of natural erosion, they were exposed. They were discovered in 1870.

OTHER INTERESTING WINERIES
Trefethen (Napa) Fine wines and beautiful gardens to explore.
Chateau Potelle (Rutherford) Hillside winery benefiting from French influence; great wines.
Beringer (St Helena) Stunning historic buildings with tours and free tastings.
Joseph Phelps (St Helena) Beautiful vineyard setting and impeccably-made selection of wines from unusual grapes.
Sutter Home (St Helena) Famed for sweet, white Zin, but the bigger, bolder red version is better.

POSTMODERN CLOS PEGASE
This postmodern ensemble was conceived in 1986 by Michael Graves, the winner of a competition run by the owner and SFMoMA. The pediments and columns refer to Greco-Roman antiquity. Love it or hate it, no one can be indifferent to it.

Point Arena (above);
Mendocino (right).

SOMBER BEAUTY ✪
Driving along Highway 1 between Jenner and the edge of the sequoia forests is a sheer delight. Once beyond the town of Mendocino, most tourists turn back.

Only seasoned travelers know they should continue northward, through a fairytale landscape, between dark forests of giant sequoias and cliffs pounded by the surf.

The clock in Fort Bragg.

The north coast of California is often swathed in fog, especially in summer. Far from concealing its charm, it enhances the mystery and wildness of its cliffs, its reefs pounded by the Pacific surf and its age-old sequoia forests.

BODEGA BAY ◆ A B6. This fishing port at the northern end of Tomales Lagoon has experienced an increase in activity since aficionados of seafood, peace and quiet and sea air began to flock here from San Francisco. The town was made famous by the great movie-maker, Alfred Hitchcock ● 91, who chose it as the setting for sequences from *The Birds*.
Highway 1 continues northward, along the edge of beautiful beaches such as SALMON CREEK, to Jenner.

JENNER ◆ A B6. The town stands on the mouth of Russian River, named for the Russian immigrants who came here to hunt sea otters for their valuable pelts. The navigable river is today used by canoe and kayak enthusiasts.

FORT ROSS ◆ A A5. About 30 miles north of Jenner, Fort Ross is a legacy of the strong Russian presence in the region until the mid 19th century. When they abandoned the fort, built to defend the community against the Mexicans who came from San Francisco Bay, they had virtually exterminated otters on this stretch of coast. It took over 150 years to reestablish the population. All that remains of these hunter-traders are a few traditionally built log *isbahs* and an Orthodox chapel overlooking the ocean.

FORT ROSS TO POINT ARENA ◆ A B5. The coast is dotted with charming little villages, with cafés and imaginative houses whose gardens are filled with Oriental-style sculptures reminiscent of the hippie era. If you want to see this coastline from a high vantage point, make your way to Point Arena and climb to the top of the lighthouse. The road leading to the lighthouse offers some spectacular views as it winds its way across windswept heathland.

MENDOCINO ◆ A A4. Mendocino (above) was founded in the 1850s during the forestry boom. At the time, the industry was run by emigrants from New England, which explains the town's distinctive style, inspired by the East Coast. A century later, when timber supplies ran out and the sawmills closed, Mendocino became a haven for artists. Although they have since been driven out by the rising cost of living, the town manages to survive on its reputation. It has preserved its rows of wooden Western-style houses on Main Street, reminiscent of the works of such artists as Edward Hopper ● *84*. The former red-painted church has been converted into an organic grocery store, proof positive that the hippie culture is still alive in the town, which is also renowned for its chocolate. The promenade along the ocean offers some beautiful views: on one side the rocks constantly pounded by the waves, and on the other the rows of houses dominated by water towers.

FORT BRAGG ◆ A A4. The high price of accommodation in Mendocino often leads visitors to seek refuge in Fort Bragg, about 12 miles to the north. At Caspar, the road runs through the JUGHANDLE STATE RESERVE and its amazing stunted forest, which occupies three terraces leading down to the sea. The trees are 100,000, 200,000 and 300,000 years old respectively. The impoverished soil prevents the trees from growing normally and so they are reduced to the size of bonsais. Fort Bragg, which acquired the nickname 'Fort Drag' when American conscripts leaving for Vietnam were sent here as part of a rigorous training program, is today trying to open up to tourism. It is a strange city, whose old center is located in a quadrilateral bounded by Redwood, Laurel, Main and Franklin Streets, but its antique stores are much less expensive than those in Mendocino. The huge, late-19th-century railroad station is the point of departure for the 'Skunk Line' which runs through the magnificent redwood forests. The town's fishing industry has been replaced by tourism and its former whaling boats have been converted for whale watching.

REDWOOD COUNTRY
About 30 miles north of Fort Bragg, the little town of Leggett ◆ A B4, lies on the edge of redwood country. These giant redwoods, *Sequoia sempervirens*, are over 330 feet tall. Their massive trunks are broad enough for an automobile to pass through a tunnel hollowed out of the base (Chandelier Drive-Thru Park). Another 30 miles further north, the Humboldt Redwoods State Park ◆ A A3 is famous for its Avenue of the Giants, over 30 miles long. The tall trees seem to form the nave of some gigantic cathedral.

The entire region of Humboldt County survives on the memory of a more prosperous era. From the 1850s, its small towns witnessed the over-exploitation of the sequoia forests, as evidenced by the wooden 'palaces' built for the forestry magnates in the late 19th century. Eureka, in particular, is famous for Carson Mansion (1886) ● 66, undoubtedly one of the most ornate houses in California, the pink Queen-Anne mansion opposite, and Carter Mansion (below) a little further on. Although the region's forestry and fishing industries began to decline in the 1930s, new technology and a flourishing tourist industry have boosted the local economy.

As you leave redwood country, you have a choice of two routes north of Leggett ◆ **A** B4. The simplest is to follow the beautiful Highway 101, which winds around hillsides planted with trees and swathed in mist, to the Ferndale junction. The more adventurous takes you along the minor road that runs from Garberville toward the King Range and the village of Shelter Cove – the only point of vehicular access to the ocean. Beyond this, you walk on paths overlooking sheer, somber cliffs that fall steeply to the ocean below. The road follows the 'Lost Coast' as closely as possible and passes through the small towns of Honeydew and then Petrolia on the Mattole River. It is not unusual to come across former hippies, living in the style of the 'good old days' and in accordance with their ecological philosophy. If you double back to Scotia, you will see the bone of contention – an active timber industry which threatens to destroy a fragile ecosystem.

FERNDALE ◆ **A** A2. Like Scotia, Ferndale owes much of its prosperity to the exploitation of the giant redwoods, once used by cabinet-makers throughout the world. Today, Ferndale is a quiet town which is best visited on foot. The GINGERBREAD MANSION (1899) is the best-known of its attractive Victorian houses.

EUREKA ◆ **A** A2. The town grew up around its port – which specialized in timber shipment – built on Humboldt Bay, the only flat part of the coast. Its past has been preserved in the streets of the Old Town, with their cafés, antique and book stores. On F and 9th Streets, the Orthodox Church of St Nicholas is a reminder of the long-standing presence of Russian settlers on this coast. On the island of Samoa, the SAMOA COOKHOUSE, the last surviving cookhouse in the West, displays tools and photographs of the lumbermen who once ate there.

ARCATA ◆ **A** A2. A few miles north of Eureka, the town of Arcata overlooks the broad Humboldt Bay. The town is the home of Humboldt State University, which specializes in biological and agronomic research. Street musicians and travelers hitchhiking along the coast tend to gather beneath the statue of President William MacKinley in the main square, on the corner of H and 9th Streets.

BEYOND ARCATA. Highway 101 runs through a landscape of redwood forests that becomes increasingly spectacular as it nears Klamath. Rangers organize visits to these vast forests, especially the Redwood National and State Parks ▲ 258, south of Klamath. CRESCENT CITY ◆ **A** B1 is really only of any interest in spring when migrating whales can be seen from the shore, although the best vantage point is provided by KLAMATH OVERLOOK.

The Gold Country

▲ Sacramento and the Gold Country

JOHANN A SUTTER
In 1839, the Swiss-born pioneer Johann Sutter (1803–80) was granted land concession of several hundred thousand acres. He named it Nueva Helvetia (New Switzerland) and built Sutter's Fort, which served as a staging post for the first immigrants. He could not have imagined the catastrophe that would befall him one January morning in 1848. The tragedy of the Swiss general, ruined by an event that made California's fortune, was described by the Swiss writer Blaise Cendrars in *L'Or* (Gold).

THE BIG FOUR AND THE RAILROAD ADVENTURE
Collis Huntington, Mark Hopkins, Leland Stanford and Charles Crocker, all from Sacramento, became famous when they financed the construction of the Transcontinental Railroad ● *26.* They stopped at nothing, not even the Rocky Mountains, the misappropriation of funds and the exploitation of Chinese laborers during the laying of the 1765 miles of track. The railroad made a fortune for the Big Four ▲ *122.*

SACRAMENTO ◆ A D6, CAPITAL OF CALIFORNIA

The history of Sacramento is inseparable from that of Johann Sutter, who settled there in 1839. All that remains of his reign as a prosperous landowner is the building known as Sutter's Fort, his main residence. For a long time several towns fought to have the honor of becoming the capital of the new state of California, each claiming economic supremacy during the turbulent period of the Gold Rush. Sacramento was finally chosen in preference to Auburn, Sonora and Nevada City, since it seemed better organized and less dominated by the violent law of the West which held sway in the mining towns.
STATE CAPITOL. Part of the building has been converted into a state history museum. The Capitol is open to the public and a public gallery offers an opportunity to see the Californian Parliament in session.
CROCKER ART MUSEUM. The museum, situated behind the Capitol, on 2nd and O Streets, was named after its generous founder, Judge Edward Bryant Crocker, brother of Charles Crocker, the railroad magnate. He acquired this beautiful building in 1870 to house the rich collection of paintings (especially German Romantics) brought back from a lengthy trip to Europe. The collection was enlarged by commissions placed with such artists as Charles Nahl, to provide heroic illustrations of the greatest hours of the Gold Rush.

> 'In the days of old, in the days of gold, How oftentimes I repine,
> For the days of old when we dug up the gold,
> In the days of '49.'
>
> Old Put's Golden Songster

CALIFORNIA STATE RAILROAD MUSEUM. This vast museum, to the north and only a few minutes' walk from the Crocker Art Museum, houses what all Western fans really ought to go and see: the famous locomotives, complete with 'cow-catcher' grilles, that conquered the West. In summer, some even take to the tracks once again.

OLD SACRAMENTO. The OLD SACRAMENTO HISTORIC DISTRICT, on the banks of the Sacramento River, has been restored to its former glory and given a DISCOVERY MUSEUM. The district's wooden houses, old schoolhouse, stores and saloons are a reminder that this was originally a town of pioneers and gold prospectors. This is also reflected in SUTTER'S FORT STATE HISTORIC BUILDING, on the corner of L and 26th Streets, on the east side of town. The restoration work carried out in recent years has tried to give this beautiful museum complex an air of authenticity, which is highlighted each spring during the Living History festival, when local volunteers dress up and reenact life in the fort in the 1850s. Visitors can see the blacksmith, home distiller and apothecary going about their business in their reconstructed stores. On K Street, Behind Sutter's Fort, is the CALIFORNIA STATE INDIAN MUSEUM, remarkable for its presentation of the state's history from the point of view of its early inhabitants.

THE GOLD COUNTRY ● 34

The small towns of the Gold Country, forgotten for almost 100 years, are being revived by a tourist industry in search of nostalgia. Modern tourists, sitting at the wheel of their air-conditioned 4 x 4 or snuggling under the duvet in a hotel, like to think of the thousands of men who spilled their sweat and blood to tear a few ounces of precious metal from the mountains in the hope of a better life. They came from the East Coast, Europe and China. Many died on the way, burned by the searing desert sun, perishing of exposure in the high Rocky Mountain passes, or victims of snake bite, poison oak or Indian arrows. In 1848, news of the discovery of a gold nugget on the land of a Swiss general named Sutter traveled round the world. In the space of a few years, thousands of men (more than 90 percent of California's immigrants) and a few women and children completely changed the face of what had been a rural landscape. Towns sprang up overnight and sometimes disappeared as quickly, leaving the disjointed wooden ghost towns that are visited so reverently today. Tunnels were dug through mountains, rivers were diverted, forests uprooted and peoples exterminated. All this so that every last ounce of precious metal could be extracted from the deposit known as the Mother Lode. The history of the Gold Rush is also the history of California, and the whole of America, with its moments of glory and heroism, its cruelty and its bloody appetite for conquest, and its obsessive desire always to push back the last frontier, in the largest intermingling of races ever known to humanity.

A MONUMENTAL STATE CAPITOL
The neoclassical building of the State Capitol was designed by the architect Miner Butler. Its 125-foot dome, completed in 1874, was inspired by the dome in Washington. The Californians placed the building under the protection of Minerva, Roman goddess of the professions and the arts, who appears on the bas-relief of the pediment, as well as on the state seal.

THE GOLD COUNTRY ✪
The small towns strung out along Highway 49 are among the prettiest and quietest in the state of California. Most of the gold prospectors have left (though not all!) making way for more peaceful tourists, artists, poets, seniors and travelers. However, the memory of that heroic age is still very much alive, scored out of the mountainsides and reflected in the Western-style streets.

COLOMA, THE SITE OF THE MIRACLE
Little remains of the original sawmill where Sutter's employee, James Marshall, found the famous gold nugget on January 24, 1848. Sutter Mill was painstakingly reconstructed down to the last detail, even the attractively worm-eaten beams, after it was burned to the ground. A nearby gunsmith's, which has changed little over the years, sells old rifles and Indian craft objects made on the spot by charming mixed-race women. Gold washers (below) still go down to the river to sift their claim. The town of Coloma is full of memories of this bygone era, from the miner's cabin to the prison, and the two wooden churches, Methodist (1856) and Catholic (1858).

Highway 49, which winds its way through the Gold Country from north to south, is named after the Gold Rush of 1849 that followed the discovery of gold in the region.
COLOMA ◆ A D6. The first nuggets were discovered by Sutter's employee ● 34 in this modest community on the banks of the American River.
PLACERVILLE ◆ A D6. The town owes its prosperity to the activities associated with the Gold Rush, rather than to the gold itself, and its many industrial buildings evoke this wealthy past. After experiencing a certain decline, Placerville has turned its hand to the second-hand trade.
SUTTER CREEK A D6. Along with its neighbor Jackson, the peaceful town of Sutter Creek is part of Amador County, famous for its rich subsoil. Before his dream of a friendly agricultural society was dashed by the hordes of gold prospectors, Sutter must have seen a resemblance between these undulating landscapes at the foot of high mountains and his native Switzerland. Today it is one of the best-preserved towns in the Gold Country, with its rows of brightly painted Victorian houses.

JACKSON A D6. Jackson (above and opposite) has a number of antique stores, and the fascias of some of its wooden houses, like those in Placerville and Sonora, still bear the insignia of the many guilds of miners, carpenters and metalsmiths who once lived in the region. On a hill overlooking the Western-style main street, the Catholic (St Patrick, 1868) and Methodist (1869) churches face each other, as if to reflect the spirit of religious tolerance that prevailed in these immigrant communities.
MOKELUMNE HILL A D6. You occasionally have to leave Highway 49 to visit some of the delightful hillside villages that lie off the beaten track. One of these is Mokelumne Hill which welcomes visitors in its beautiful LEGER HOTEL. The hotel's French name is a reminder that the region was once the scene of confrontations between miners who had already staked their claims and groups of French miners who wanted to work what was then regarded as the richest gold deposit in California. It was here that Mark Twain wrote

> 'But nature herself [...] seemed to have had an eye to nothing besides mining; and even the natural hillside was all sliding gravel and precarious boulder.'
>
> *From Scotland to Silverado*, Robert Louis Stevenson

The Celebrated Jumping Frog of Calaveras County (1865), the story that brought him overnight fame. It is great fun to take part in the contests, kneeling behind a frog and trying to make it jump as far as possible.

COLUMBIA B C1. A short detour off Highway 49 brings you to the town of Columbia and the Columbia State Historic Park. The park has been reconstructed with great attention to detail, down to the very hay eaten by the horses hitched to the wagons, which are the only form of vehicle allowed on the streets. At its height, Columbia produced around 100 million dollars' worth of gold, enough to build a town solid enough to stand the test of time. It appears they are still finding gold down here, on the banks of the streams and in the foothills.

SONORA B C1. With Highway 49 passing right through the

JACKSON, A TOUCH OF THE OLD WEST
The streets of the Gold Country towns are bordered with traditional Western-style wood or brick houses. Their second-hand stores sell gold nuggets – dating from the 1950s – in the form of juke boxes and 45s.

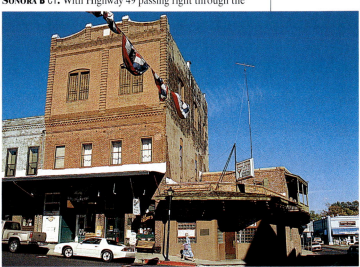

center, this is one of the region's busiest towns. All day long, there is a constant stream of 4 x 4s, old jalopies being driven until they give up the ghost, and trucks transporting timber to sawmills that are slightly more modern than the one owned by Johann Sutter. The historic buildings that have been preserved include the delightful Gothic ST JAMES EPISCOPAL CHURCH (1857) and the prison, which houses TUOLOMNE COUNTY MUSEUM and its collections of Gold Rush photos and memorabilia.

MARIPOSA B C2. South of Sonora, Highway 49 passes through the magnificent gorges of the Merced River en route to Mariposa, gateway to the Yosemite National Park ▲ *254*. The remarkable white-painted wooden courthouse, the embodiment of a law that was not always respected, was built in 1854 and is still in use today. The CALIFORNIA STATE MINING AND MINERAL MUSEUM has a collection of thousands of different types of minerals, and also offers visitors an opportunity to admire some real gold nuggets.

COLUMBIA STATE HISTORIC PARK
The visit, which covers a distance of several miles, is made by stagecoach. The park also has a number of small museums, including the building that houses the *Columbia Gazette* with its rotary presses.

THE EMPIRE MINE OF GRASS VALLEY

Visitors can still see the impressive equipment used in the mine, including the wheel invented by Lester Pelton to drive the engines and activate the water cannons used to bore into the mountainside. The perpetuation of their traditions by miners from Cornwall (England) ensured the cohesion of the group entrusted with a very difficult task. The owner of the mine, William Bourn Jr, had his house, the Empire Cottage, designed and built in 1890 by Willis Polk, architect of a number of houses in San Francisco.

Nevada City.

AUBURN ◆ A D5. This delightful town, which stands on the intersection of Highway 49 and the very busy Interstate 80, is the county town of Placer County and a major market town. A fair held here in September trades American Indian crafts and gold nuggets set as jewelry. The town is dominated by an impressive COURTHOUSE (1894), located near the very attractive ST LUKE'S EPISCOPAL CHURCH (1862). However, visitors tend to head for the old town, founded in 1849, with its painted wood façades and antique and second-hand stores.

GRASS VALLEY ◆ A D5. This is the first major town north of Auburn on Highway 49. Visitors can stay at the HOLBROOKE HOTEL (1851) whose decor has barely changed since Mark Twain used to stay there. The town's main attraction is the vast domain of the Empire Mine State Historic Park, but don't leave without paying your respects to the memory of Lola Montez, the legendary singer and dancer who lived on Mill Street around 1852.

NEVADA CITY ◆ A D5. Nevada City is right next to Grass Valley, but it has preserved its links with the past more jealously and its Western-style saloons are virtually intact. It has also become more middle class as increasing numbers of city dwellers in search of authenticity – or what passes for it – have chosen to live there. You can go bargain hunting in the second-hand book stores or visit the foundry that produced mining tools. In 1947, it was converted into a factory that made the now much sought-after Little Willie fruit presses.

MALAKOFF DIGGINS ◆ A D5. About 12 miles further north on Highway 49, you come to the Tyler-Foote Crossing Road leading to Malakoff Diggins. The landscape looks as if it has suffered a heavy bombardment. For fifteen years, miners' water cannons dug deep into the mountains, washing away millions of tonnes of gravel into the nearby Yuba River. Faced with an ecological disaster, the authorities were forced to ban this type of mining in 1894. In contemplating this landscape, visitors can see the scars left by obsessive greed, a wound that will take thousands of years to heal.

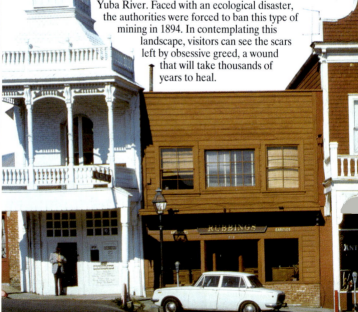

The nearby VILLAGE ANANDA represents a very different California, that of the advocates of non-violent Eastern philosophies ● 47. The school of yoga founded by Paramahansa Yogananda stands in a tree-filled park grazed by deer. Highway 49 follows the course of the Yuba River, which sometimes flows deep in its gorges, as for example near North San Juan where it is crossed by an ancient covered wooden bridge.

DOWNIEVILLE ◆ A D5. Here the white waters of the Yuba are joined by those of the Downie right in the center of this mining town, which is much more authentic than those of the southern Gold Country. In summer gold washers come here to sift for gold on the water's edge. They still find a little bit of gold here, which they sell for about $250 per ounce. However to do this, they have to have bought a claim measuring only a few square feet for $12,000… But here, as in the neighboring town of SIERRA CITY, people are really more concerned with preserving the spirit of an era, in a setting of wooden houses built between 1850 and 1890. As you go deeper into the mountains, toward the magnificent mountain park of PLUMAS EUREKA, tourists become few and far between, probably deterred by the twists and turns of Highway 49.

TRUCKEE ◆ A E5. The main street, which heads toward nearby Nevada, is bordered by the surviving remains of the age of the pioneers: late-19th-century buildings, wooden sidewalks and the hotel where Charlie Chaplin stayed when he was shooting *The Gold Rush* (a mural records the event).

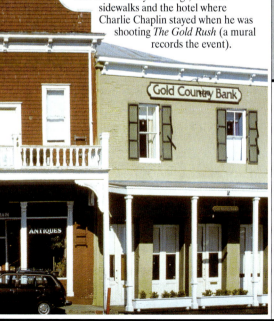

DOWNIEVILLE, A LIVING MUSEM ★
The style of the region reflects a desire for freedom in spite of the cold, which comes early at altitudes of between 3000 and 5000 feet. The men are a cross between bikers and hippies, with their long graying braids, gray beards, ambling bear-like gait, slow deliberate speech and surly friendship, while the women tend to be well-covered. They are loggers, 'grease monkeys', souvenir sellers and even gold diggers, since here in Downieville they are still prospecting for gold! The town is well worth a visit to get some idea of what 'gold fever' was really like, and possibly even negotiate the price of a nugget.

TRAGEDY AT TRUCKEE
Truckee ('excellent') was the nickname given to Chief Winnemuca of the Numa nation by the American explorer and mapmaker John C Frémont (1813–90). However, it is the tragic story of the Donners, a family of white pioneers, that has left its mark on the town. In 1846, suffering from cold and hunger, they were forced to eat their dead companions on the mountain that now bears their name.

Emerald Bay with the El Dorado mountain range in the distance.

En route to Lake Tahoe ◆ A E5-E6, the Interstate 80 passes through a magnificent landscape of mountains planted with fir trees. The waters of the lake are renowned for their purity, coldness and depth, around 1650 feet, which gives them their beautiful blue color.

LAKESIDE CIRCUIT. TAHOE CITY, on the northwest shore, is the lake's busiest town and the closest, in terms of its decor and atmosphere, to those of the Gold Country. Following the shores of the lake is no easy matter. There are many private beaches, and you have to wait until you get to EMERALD BAY, at the southern end of the lake, before you can get down to the shore and enjoy the magnificent views of this vast expanse of water and the solitary Fanette Island. SOUTH LAKE TAHOE, a more affordable town with an abundance of inexpensive motels, is situated just before STATELINE on the Californian border. Across the border, in Nevada, are rows of impressive hotel-casinos whose first floors are filled with slot machines. Nature lovers can leave these depressing places to follow in the footsteps of Mark Twain and explore the magnificent national parks around or overlooking the lake. This is also a popular region for winter sports and the 1960 Winter Olympics were held in SQUAW VALLEY. The surrounding mountains are crossed by marked trails. One route starts in SUGAR PINE POINT STATE PARK, in the north, and crosses into D L BLISS STATE PARK, where you can visit the folly known as EHRMAN MANSION (1903). This landscape provided one of the settings for *The Godfather, Part II*.

EMERALD BAY STATE PARK contains one of the jewels of kitsch architecture built by Californians made rich by the Gold Rush: VIKINGSHOLM, a Viking stronghold built in 1928! The original 'discoverers' of America were indeed Vikings, but they landed on the East Coast. TALLAC HISTORIC SITE, which lies just off Highway 89, near South Lake Tahoe, also has a great many stylish summer residences built by wealthy grandees who wanted to escape the oppressive summer heat of the Central Plain. Those who don't like the idea of long walks or difficult climbs can take the HEAVENLY VALLEY AERIAL TRAMWAY, at the southern end of the lake, which climbs to an altitude of 9850 feet and offers a truly unique viewpoint.

THE JOYS OF GAMBLING ★
Whatever else you do, you should try to cross the border into Nevada and visit the casinos with their foretaste of Las Vegas. In this unique atmosphere, a blend of seriousness and frivolity, faces reflect an infinite range of emotions, from the anxiety of those who have just placed a bet to the joy of the winners and the distress of the losers. If you are reluctant to risk the roulette wheel, can always try your hand at one of the thousands of slot machines, many of which start at 25 cents a game.

San Francisco to
Los Angeles

San Rafael   SAN   Vallejo
             PABLO BAY
      Richmond

San Francisco Oakland

PILLAR   SAN
POINT   FRANCISCO
         BAY   Hayward

Half Moon
    Bay   Fremont

Pescadero   San Jose

PIGEON
POINT

Santa Cruz
Watsonville San Juan
             Bautista

MONTEREY   Salinas
  BAY

3 Monterey

Carmel

Big Sur
BIG SUR
S.P.
JULIA PFEIFFER SP

4   King City
     5843 ft

L. SAN
ANTONIO

LAKE
NACIMIENTO

San Simeon **5**
             Paso Robles
Cambria

Morro Bay
        San Luis
        Obispo
Pismo Beach

Santa Maria

Lompoc

Solvang

1

San Andreas

Stockton   Sonora

DON PEDRO
RES.
Modesto

**Yosemite
National Park** ⊛

Merced   Mariposa   BADGER
                     PASS

                     DEVIL'S
                     POSTPILE N. MON.

                     MAMMOTH
Madera   LAKE

          MILLERTON
          LAKE

Fresno   PINE FLAT
          LAKE

          KINGS
Hanford
        Visalia

        Porterville

ALLENSWORTH
 NATIONAL
  PARK

Wasco

              Bakersfield

Taft

8832 ft

6880 ft

Santa
Barbara **6**

Ojai
Ventura **7**

Thousand
Oaks   San
Oxnard   Fernando

Malibu

Santa Monica

SAN JOAQUIN

SAN JOAQUIN VALLEY

MT HAMILTON
4262 ft

SAN LUIS
RES.

SAN BENITO

COAST

SAN BENITO MT
5240 ft

Coalinga

RANGES

SISQUOC   SAN RAFAEL MTS

L.
CACHUMA

SESPE CR.

SAN MIGUEL I.

SANTA CRUZ I.

SANTA ROSA I.

ANACAPA I.

CHANNEL ISLAND
NATIONAL PARK

SANTA MONICA BAY

Los Angeles ⊛

S I E R R A
N E V A D A

PACIFIC

OCEAN

0   19 miles

For centuries, Central Valley, which stretches from Sacramento to the outskirts of Los Angeles, has produced most of California's agricultural produce.

STOCKTON ◆ B B1. The town's industrial past is still very much in evidence, especially on the wharves of its port. A network of rivers and deep-water canals creates a direct maritime link with San Francisco Bay which lies over 60 miles to the west. Stockton has a reputation for being a tough city and was the subject of John Huston's *Fat City*, a movie about the boxing circuit. The vehicle track known as the 'caterpillar', later used on the first tanks in World War Two, was also invented in the area. Outside downtown Stockton, the HAGGIN MUSEUM houses some beautiful Impressionist works.

MODESTO ◆ B B1. This small, aptly named town has also been in the movies. George Lucas grew up here and chose it as the setting for his *American Graffiti* (1973). You have to go back to the early 20th century to find someone who made a more lasting impression on the town – the billionaire rancher Robert McHenry. His richly furnished Victorian mansion, now the MCHENRY MUSEUM, is open to the public.

MERCED ◆ B C2. The town is worth a visit if only to admire its magnificent COUNTY COURTHOUSE MUSEUM (1875). The surrounding area is also rich in nature reserves, populated by migratory birds and deer, in particular the MERCED WILDLIFE REFUGE.

FRESNO ◆ B C3. At first glance, the principal town of the Central Valley is fairly unprepossessing; you have to stay there for more than a few hours to appreciate its charm. Ignore the pedestrianized FULTON MALL, which is no different from any other shopping mall, and wander beside the station where the former industrial buildings have been colonized by the business sector. It also has the region's best electric train store which sells engines bearing the insignia of local companies. The Art Deco ST JOHN'S CATHEDRAL, with its remarkable stained-glass windows and painted ceiling, attests to Fresno's glorious past. A little further on, on the corner of Tulare and R Streets, is the MEUX HOME MUSEUM. This former mansion, occupied between 1889 and 1970, has remained intact, down to the furniture, soft furnishings and place settings. Seniors dressed in period costume show visitors round the house, where you expect the occupants to appear at any moment. Fresno was also the birthplace of the American-born writer of Armenian descent, William Saroyan, who is remembered in the Armenian church and the exhibitions of the METROPOLITAN MUSEUM. The town pays homage to its large Spanish immigrant community with an ART MUSEUM that exhibits works on the fringe of the more 'official' styles. If you head northward along Van Ness Avenue to Olive Street, you come to the student district of TOWER, with its Mexican and Basque restaurants (owned by the descendants of Pyrenean shepherds) and busy night life. At the end of Olive Street, the trees and shrubs of CHAFFEE ZOOLOGICAL GARDENS offer the inhabitants of Fresno a welcome respite from the oppressive summer heat.

SOUTH OF FRESNO
The vineyards and fruit trees (apples, pears, plums, oranges) of the Central Valley stretch as far as the eye can see. Pick-up trucks carrying Mexican workers run back and forth across the flat landscape. Each town has its own impressive courthouse, a symbol of state authority. Chinese immigration kept pace with the progress of the railroad, as evidenced by the old district of HANFORD ◆ **B** C3 and the Buddhist temple of VISALIA ◆ **B** D3. Further south, Route 43, which runs parallel to Highway 99, runs through the Colonel Allensworth State Historic Park, the haunt of large numbers of migratory birds and birds of prey, where visitors can camp near pioneers' wagons. As you near BAKERSFIELD ◆ **B** D5, the smell of oil pervades a landscape of oil wells and refineries. Some of the best country music is played in the town's bars and nightclubs, and tempers the dullness of this town, whose middle-class residents retreat behind the high walls of their gated communities ● *45*.

A TASTE OF MEXICO IN CENTRAL VALLEY
There is no shortage of missions, *taquerías* – where you can sample the spicy, richly flavored food – and Mexican radio and TV stations. Mexican culture is generally very much in evidence in the Central Valley.

JOHN STEINBECK
John Steinbeck, winner of the Nobel Prize for Literature, was born in the Salinas Valley. After attending Stanford University ▲ *145* he was determined to become a writer. The region is filled with constant reminders of his best-known novel,

The Grapes of Wrath, which describes the harsh existence of agricultural workers from the Midwest ● *39*. Their story was set to music by Woody Guthrie and photographed by Dorothea Lange ● *55*.

The coast stretching from the south of San Francisco to Santa Cruz is punctuated by a series of dunes, sandy cliffs and beautiful beaches, including nudist beaches such as SAN GREGORIO PRIVATE BEACH, about 9 miles south of Half Moon Bay.

HALF MOON BAY ◆ B A1. This charming Victorian resort is named after the crescent-shaped stretch of coast on which it stands. Highway 1 runs past a series of white sandy beaches washed by a fairly cold sea – POMPONIO, PESCADERO, BEAN HOLLOW, AÑO NUEVO – to the cliffs just north of Santa Cruz. Seals and other marine mammals are a common sight, but keep your distance, especially in the mating season when sea elephants weighing several tonnes dispute leadership of the colonies and the right to the females.

SANTA CRUZ ◆ B A2. Since the construction of Highway 17 linking it to the San Jose region, Santa Cruz has become more accessible to people working in the info-tech industries who cannot afford the property prices in San Francisco. Although this has altered the town's liberal and progressive character, it has not destroyed the 'perpetual student' image underscored by the large UCSC campus. In fact, Santa Cruz is the embodiment of the Californian spirit of hedonism and tolerance which tends to be replaced elsewhere by a puritanical productivism. It is well worth stopping to drink in the atmosphere in the town's cafés and music clubs, which remain loyal to the 'folk rock' tradition. Like all university towns, Santa Cruz has a wealth of record and book stores. In a more frivolous vein, the permanent fair on the BOARDWALK has the largest Big Dipper, the Giant Dipper, on the West Coast. The nearby marina evokes the maritime vocation of the original town which has since disappeared. The Mission

EL CAMINO REAL
The 'Royal Way' linked the missions founded
by the Franciscans in the late 18th century ● *32,
62*. It is still marked by the occasional bell.

Santa Cruz (1791), alternately pillaged by pirates and
devastated by earthquakes, was reconstructed on a one-third
scale in 1931. It is decorated with the architectural elements
recovered from the original site, now occupied by the
neo-Gothic HOLY CROSS CHURCH (1889). Don't leave Santa
Cruz without visiting the MYSTERY SPOT, where the laws of
gravity cease to apply and the effect of distorted perspectives
creates an impression of complete disorientation.

SAN JUAN BAUTISTA ◆ B A2. Continue south on Highway 1 to
Watsonville and take the 129 and then the 156 to Hollister.
Movie buffs will recognize the mission bell-tower which
features in Alfred Hitchcock's *Vertigo* ● *91*. The mission was
founded in 1797 and dedicated to St John the Baptist. The
altar was painted by Thomas Doak of Boston, who jumped
ship and became the first American to settle in the region.
The mission complex is impressive, with a convent which once
had the most famous choir on the *El Camino Real*, while its
garden and cemetery are dotted with plain wooden crosses.
A reconstruction of a 19th-century village lies on the far side
of a vast square, while a well-stocked agricultural museum has
exhibits ranging from the most basic tools to tractors and
combine harvesters. Highway 156 passes close to the San
Andreas Fault ● *18*, the cause of the region's disturbing
seismic activity. Hell's Angels fans will recall the motorbike-
gang rampage that took place in the small town of Hollister
and inspired the movie *The Wild One*.

THE SALINAS VALLEY ◆ B A2. As you head south on US-101,
wall paintings illustrate the works of John Steinbeck ● *102*. In
Salinas, the modern building of the NATIONAL STEINBECK
CENTER presents exhibitions, movies and memorabilia
evoking the writer's life and works. The house where he was
born, at 132 Central Road, is now a restaurant.

A GREEN ROUTE
(Highway 84)
At San Gregorio,
between Half Moon
Bay and Santa Cruz,
the 84 takes you to
the village of La
Honda, the base for
Ken Kesey's Merry
Pranksters ▲ *114* in
the mid 1960s.
The landscape is
unchanged, and
footpaths enable
visitors to enjoy its
wild natural beauty.

HIGHWAY 1 ✪
Highway 1,
undoubtedly the most
spectacular highway in
the Californian road
network, is an
American legend. It
follows the extremely
rugged coastline,
twisting and turning
high above the ocean.
To enjoy the scenery
to the full, use the
many stopping places
overlooking the coast
and the ocean.

On the outskirts
of Salinas.

The Grapes of Wrath

MONTEREY CANNING COMPANY

In the early 20th century, Monterey's economic prosperity was based on its canning industry. Millions of sardines caught off the Californian coast were processed in these factories, as well as other fish and marine mammals, including whales. The canners' activity gradually declined as the supply of fish became exhausted in the 1940s. The cannery buildings have remained intact, but the workers, predominantly Sicilian, have long since moved to other regions of California.

CANNERY ROW

'Early morning is a time of magic in Cannery Row. In the grey time after the light has come and before the sun has risen, the Row seems to hang suspended out of time in a silvery light. The street lights go out, and the weeds are a brilliant green. The corrugated iron of the canneries glows with the pearly lucence of platinum or old pewter. No automobiles are running then. The street is silent of progress and business. And the rush and drag of the waves can be heard as they splash in among the piles of the canneries… Cats drip over the fences and slither like syrup over the ground to look for fish-heads.'
Cannery Row, John Steinbeck

The town of MONTEREY ◆ **B** A2 occupies an enviable location at the start of the magnificent section of Highway 1 that runs south along vertiginous cliffs. All traffic heading south along the coastal route has to pass through Monterey, at the risk of yielding to one of its many temptations. The town was founded in 1602 by Sebastián Vizcaíno ▲ 218, the captain of a merchantman exploring this part of the Californian coast on behalf of the king of Spain. It was named Monte Rey after a Mexican viceroy and was one of the oldest settlements in what was to become the United States. Junípero Serra ● 24 completed the Hispanicization of the town in 1770 , a century before California was annexed

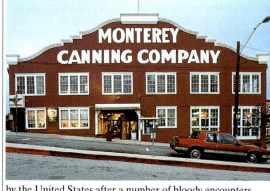

by the United States after a number of bloody encounters with the Mexican garrison. In the late 18th century a major fishing industry developed, whose subsequent industrialization led to the establishment of canneries. This is the famous CANNERY ROW described in the novels of John Steinbeck ▲ 166, the region's famous son. Previously regarded as the principal town of California, Monterey was 'demoted' during the Gold Rush ● 34, when the honor was bestowed on the port of San Francisco ▲ 115.

CANNERY ROW AND FISHERMAN'S WHARF. The former canneries have been converted into workshops of various kinds and only the exteriors, which have been preserved in their original style, have retained a degree of authenticity. Tourists venture onto nearby Fisherman's Wharf in the hope of discovering a good cheap restaurant where they can enjoy clam chowder, seafood platter, grilled sardines or fresh salmon. En route, they will encounter the bust of John Steinbeck erected at the entrance to the wharf.

MONTEREY STATE HISTORIC PARK AND OLD TOWN. This contains many wonderful old buildings which have survived in perfect condition. The best way to visit Monterey State Historic Park and Old Town is on foot, since it is impossible to find parking spaces. The best place to start is the CUSTOMS HOUSE, traditionally believed to be the place where California was first declared a member of the United States. It is the oldest official building in the region and has retained all its original Western charm. About a hundred yards away, the MARITIME MUSEUM traces the history of the fishermen and other seamen who made the fortune of Monterey. Opposite, The PACIFIC HOUSE museum is devoted to the port's sardine fishing and canning industry.

This sign acts as a reminder that from November to March, colonies of monarch butterflies, with their characteristic reddish-brown wings, fly across the highway at Pacific Grove as they migrate to Mexico.

LARKIN HOUSE ● *63*, further south, near the corner of Jefferson and Pacific Street, offers an insight into the relative comfort of the lives of the cannery owners. The house was built in the Mexican style that was fashionable in the 19th century, in beautiful ocher-colored adobe (sun-dried brick). Nearby COLTON HALL, in all its Victorian pomp and glory, is an interesting example of a more classic architectural style. It was here, in 1849, that the Constitution of what would become the State of California was drawn up and signed. A museum commemorates the event.

STEVENSON HOUSE, with its more romantic history, acts as a reminder that Robert Louis Stevenson, the famous author of *Treasure Island*, lived in Monterey c. 1879 and was married here to Fanny Osbourne, the American woman he met in France and followed out to California. His old rooming house at at 530 Houston Street contains a number of souvenirs, especially those he picked up during his travels. Don't leave the district without visiting the ROYAL PRESIDIO CHAPEL, the well-preserved remains of a mission built in 1795.

MONTEREY BAY AQUARIUM. For most visitors, Monterey's main attraction is its magnificent aquarium, a model of its kind. Its many tanks provide an informative visit that appeals to everyone, from the very young to the more seasoned observers of marine flora and fauna. A superb kelp forest (similar to the seaweed washed up on the shore) harbors dozens of different species of fish. Visitors can also see the delightful sea otters living in an imaginative reconstruction of their natural habitat, while respectably sized tunny fish, sharks and barracudas can swim freely in an enormous tank the size of a cavern. Don't miss feeding time, when the tanks' occupants are fed by divers.

GIANT JELLYFISH IN MONTEREY BAY AQUARIUM
These giant jellyfish float so gracefully in the skillfully lit aquariums that it is hard to imagine they are dangerous.

PEACEFUL PACIFIC GROVE (below)
If Monterey seems too touristy, take time out to visit the neighboring town of Pacific Grove. You can enjoy beautiful walks along the waterfront and watch seabirds dip and dive above the breakers.

A DELIGHTFUL MARINE SPECTACLE
The barking of seals and sea lions can be heard a long way off. The sea lions raise their pups at the foot of Cypress Point, proof positive that this is a tranquil spot. Sea otters ▲ *241* are also a common sight, swimming on their backs. In the past, these delightful creatures were killed for their pelts, but the population is now definitely on the increase.

HENRY MILLER AT BIG SUR
Like many other Zen converts, Henry Miller lost and found himself in the landscape of Big Sur. The striking contrast between the violence of the ocean tearing at the coast and the tranquillity of the foliage clinging to the mountainside inspired the author – who returned to the region after his escapades in Paris in the 1920s – to write *Big Sur and the Oranges of Heironymous Bosch* (1957). Today, people come from all over the world to share the experience, and the simple joy of spending a few moments on these cliffs.

17-MILE DRIVE ◆ B A2. Surprising as it may seem to many visitors, you have to pay a toll to drive along the famous '17-Mile Drive'. The road is bordered along much of its length by private residences prohibiting public access to the shore, the whole purpose of the visit. But when you finally catch a glimpse of the Pacific Ocean, it is a sheer delight. The rugged coastline is bordered by cypress trees, including the Lone Cypress that served as a model for Edward Weston ● *55*, the guru of fine art photography. Since then, many amateur photographers have flocked here to take their own shots of this legendary site. The rocks and the few islands scattered along the shore are inhabited by an abundance of noisy marine creatures and seabirds, even pelicans! On the mainland, tame prairie dogs 'pose' for photographers in the hope of being rewarded with scraps of bread and, across the road, small deer graze on the golf course. To the south of 17-Mile Drive, Pebble Beach is the site of one of the world's most famous golf courses. Several times a year, it also hosts prestigious automobile events where enthusiasts can admire rare American pre-war models, as well as Italian and British classics that are auctioned for small fortunes.

CARMEL ◆ B A2. Nearby Carmel has a fashionable bohemian community of artists and actors, and a movie-star mayor in Clint Eastwood. The town makes every effort to preserve its original atmosphere. There are numerous craft stores and galleries, one of which, at the very least, is named after Edward Weston and dedicated to the work of Weston and the other members of the Group *f.64* ● *54*. The 'Friends of Photography' society, founded by Ansel Adams, was originally based in Carmel before being relocated in the San Francisco gallery. The town also attracts many tourists who come to see the delightful Mission Carmel, founded in 1770 by Junípero Serra ● *24,* who is buried here. In striking contrast to the simplicity of the site, his tomb is a small mausoleum, with four life-size monks watching over a recumbent statue of the priest.

BIG SUR ◆ B A2. South of Carmel, Highway 1 passes through a landscape of breathtaking natural beauty: somber cliffs plunging steeply into the sea and mountainsides covered with forests of laurel, eucalyptus and sequoias. Hitchhikers still follow this route, no doubt inspired by the works of Henry Miller and Jack Kerouac, the legendary heroes of a landscape that was much poorer and wilder then than now. Today, much of Big Sur has become the property of wealthy actors and businessmen. Even so,

> '…The blue sea behind the crashing high waves
> is full of huge black rocks rising like old ogresome
> castles dripping wet slime…'

Big Sur, Jack Kerouac

Big Sur has managed to retain its unique atmosphere. Its mystery still envelops the footpaths of the PFEIFFER BIG SUR STATE PARK, where you can walk among the ancient trees, breathe in the scents of the forest and listen to the wind singing in the high branches, mingled with the constant sound of the surf far below. On a bend in Highway 1, a few hundred yards from the hilltop site of NEPENTHE with its complex of cafés, restaurants and stores, the tiny HENRY MILLER LIBRARY nestles in a delightful garden decorated with modern sculptures. It has a collection of first editions of his work, as well as mementos of his life here. It is an ideal place to stop and chat with the warden, who reminisces about the good old days and the long-forgotten libertarian adventures from the 1930s to the 1960s.

MISSION CARMEL ★

If you can visit only one Californian mission, then it has to be Mission Carmel, with its beautiful cloisters surrounding a flower-filled garden. The mission, with its various adjoining rooms, has been more tastefully restored than most, with great respect for its original character.

WELL-BEING AT BIG SUR

The Esalen Institute
● *47* pursues its New Age mission by reconciling mind and body through yoga, massage and baths in hot springs. The prices, which have spiraled since the 1960s, are rather more difficult to reconcile!

Henry Miller at Big Sur, by Henri Cartier-Bresson.

Morro Bay (below). The pool
(top right) and the Casa Grande
(bottom) of Hearst Castle.

WILLIAM RANDOLPH HEARST (1863–1951)

Hearst's larger-than-life personality inspired one of Orson Welles's major works, *Citizen Kane* (1941) ● *90*.
The model was as eccentric as the character created by the great moviemaker.
Hearst, the son of a miner who made his fortune when he discovered rich gold deposits, began his career in 1887 as the proprietor of the *San Francisco Examiner*. He soon found himself running a media empire that was the first of its kind. In 1919, his wealth and thirst for power led him to build a castle intended to impress the booming entertainment industry. His mistress, actress Marion Davies, was 'queen of the castle'.

THE CASA GRANDE OF HEARST CASTLE

The castle was designed by Julia Morgan, the first woman architect to qualify at the École des Beaux-Arts in Paris. Using the most advanced techniques, her team worked closely with Hearst, who wanted to give added luster to his classical pool (top right), theater, reception rooms and 40 guest rooms. At the time, national heritage was still a vague concept, and so the press magnate seems to have had little difficulty in furnishing his castle with architectural elements taken from a Spanish cathedral, a French chateau and an Italian *palazzo*.

SAN SIMEON AND HEARST CASTLE ◆ B B4. As you head south on Highway 1, it is impossible to miss the main attraction of San Simeon. Not only is Hearst Castle signposted well in advance, with the help of numerous publicity hoardings, but it can also be seen from a long way off. Although first impressions conjure up combined memories of the Sleeping Beauty and Louis II of Bavaria, visitors will soon be reminded that they are well and truly in America. Visits are organized with a paramilitary precision that leaves no room for daydreaming: anyone who wanders off from the main group is soon called to order. After visiting this artificial environment,

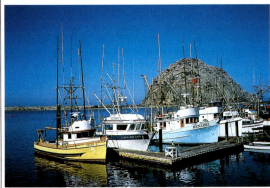

where you are certainly not allowed to linger, a healthy walk along the waterfront comes as a welcome relief. The coast between San Simeon and Morro Bay is punctuated by a series of beautiful beaches where a wide variety of marine creatures (including seals, sea elephants and sea lions) enjoy a siesta in the sun, occasionally interrupted by spectacular confrontations between the males.

CAMBRIA ◆ B B4. About 5 minutes' drive south of Morro Bay, the small town of Cambria seems to have been specially created for the tourist industry. Here you will find attractive antique stores, and art galleries exhibiting variations on the theme of landscapes. The atmosphere is friendly and Californians flock there to find knick-knacks to decorate their suburban villas in Los Angeles.

MORRO BAY ◆ B B4. The beautiful coastal route comes to an end in this little fishing village. Its attractively rounded, volcanic rocks are a favorite haunt for peregrine falcons. This is a good place to stop and sample the seafood in one of the quayside restaurants. You would be well advised to eat here or in Cambria, rather than at San Simeon, which only sells fast food at exorbitant prices. Beyond Morro Bay, Highway 1 continues to San Luis Obispo, where it merges temporarily with US-101.

SAN LUIS OBISPO ◆ B B4. Visitors can stay in the MADONNA INN, owned by the mayor of San Luis Obispo … Mr Madonna. This is undoubtedly one of the most eccentric places on the West Coast (which is saying a lot!) with its completely different and violently colored rooms,

distant echoes of the heroic age of the Hollywood epic. Once a quiet town that you simply passed through, San Luis Obispo is in the process of becoming a fashionable retreat for the stars, along the lines of Santa Barbara ▲ *174*. It also has a dynamic cultural life due to its student population and the attendant cafés, movie theaters, music clubs and book stores. The Mission is surrounded by a pleasant park which is particularly busy at weekends when the Farmers' Market is held on Higuera Street, near the corner of Chorro Street. A few blocks to the east, on the corner of Pacific and Santa Rosa, is the elegant, modern residence built by the architect Frank Lloyd Wright in 1955.

PISMO BEACH ◆ B B5. It is hard to believe that this landscape, so redolent of wealth and the joy of living, witnessed in the 1930s the tragedy of immigrants from Oklahoma and Arkansas driven from their land by dust storms and the greed of the big farming companies ● *39*. Today, the sound of 4 x 4 machines driven by tourists has replaced the noise of the farmers' rickety lorries at the end of the street. Pismo Beach is now a vast playground, where people hurtle down the dunes by every mechanical means imaginable.

BEYOND PISMO BEACH ◆ B B5. At Lompoc, 18 miles south of Santa Maria, visitors can choose between science fiction and ancient history. If you turn west to the aptly named coastal village of SURF, at the end of the 246, you can see the occasional rocket take off from the Vandenberg military base. On the other hand, if you drive a few miles to the east of Lompoc, still on the 246, you will come to LA PURISIMA MISSION STATE HISTORIC PARK. The mission itself appears to have been specially built as decor for a Sergio Leone western. Every effort has been made to recreate, as accurately as possible, the rustic Mexican charm of the original building (1787), destroyed by earthquakes and uprisings.

SOLVANG, THE DANISH EXPERIENCE ◆ B B5 (less than a mile from the US-101, on the 246)
The visitor will appreciate this astonishing reconstruction, which is one of the better ones. Founded by Danish immigrants in 1911, it brings together everything that could possibly remind them of their homeland, from the roughcast half-timbered houses painted in different colors to the working mill, not forgetting the pastry shops and the bars where you can drink beer.

Besides its attractive architectural style, the County Courthouse ● 65 (below) has the advantage of a clock tower tall enough to offer a panoramic view of the town.

SANTA BARBARA, QUEEN OF THE SITCOMS
Sitcom fans worldwide know the name 'Santa Barbara', not because of its mission or its monuments dating from the colonial period, but for the 2000 or so episodes of the popular television series. Some of the scenes were shot on location in the town, but the rest of the series was shot in the Hollywood studios. However, it seems that the region is fast becoming an extension of the prolific movie industry ● 50 ▲ 180. Many stars live here, although they tend to prefer the surrounding area, away from the center and the waterfront, which is also used as a setting for other series. These sitcoms portray a particular view of America: pleasure seeking but also callous and deeply materialistic.

The first thing you notice in Santa Barbara ◆ B C6, renowned for its wealth and the exclusiveness of some of its districts, is the consideration shown toward the marginal sections of society. The lawns which stretch along the waterfront accommodate the sleeping bags of travelers of all ages, beach bums and down-and-outs who have come to end their days under the Californian sun, in a mild climate. The road once traveled by the poets of the Beat Generation is now frequented by movie stars in voluntary exile, within reach by helicopter of the Hollywood studios, and retired politicians such as former US president Ronald Reagan.

STEARNS WHARF. On the promenade along the waterfront you'll meet beautiful young people going surfing, or cleaving the air on roller blades, skateboards or bicycles. At the end of Stearns Wharf, the oldest wooden pier in California (1872), are seafood restaurants and the inevitable ice-cream stalls – the ice-cream is excellent, by the way!

DOWNTOWN SANTA BARBARA. The best way to see Downtown Santa Barbara is on foot, since most of the monuments you are likely to visit lie within a radius of a few hundred feet. Most of the buildings are in the Spanish Colonial style characteristic of the region. If you walk along the main street, STATE STREET, you come to a vast shopping mall in pink adobe, EL PASEO, a classic mall where you can buy everyday items as well as more or less tasteful souvenirs. Two blocks further along, toward the northwest, the MUSEUM OF ART houses collections of Greek and Egyptian antiquities, together with French Impressionists and a few fine American works by artists such as Edward Hopper and John Singer Sargent, donated by wealthy local collectors. On the next block, the ARLINGTON THEATER evokes some of the greatest hours of pre-war California, when projection rooms were 'temples' erected to the cult of legendary movie stars. Next door, on Anapuma Street, the COUNTY COURTHOUSE ● 65 is reputedly one of the most beautiful buildings in Spanish Colonial Revival style, freely inspired by the early missions.

THE PRESIDIO. Turn back toward the waterfront along Santa Barbara Street. The PRESIDIO DE SANTA BARBARA and the surrounding district is the last surviving architectural souvenir of an 18th century that has been reasonably well overlaid, or imitated, elsewhere.

MISSION SANTA BARBARA. About ten minutes' walk to the north stands the magnificent Mission Santa Barbara ● *62*, founded in 1786 and completed in 1820. The 'queen of missions' certainly lives up to its name in terms of its sheer size, architectural balance and the beauty of the surrounding landscape. Before entering the mission, it is worth taking a walk in the huge plaza planted with banks of flowers and bordered by attractive rococo buildings which are a successful pastiche of various Spanish architectural styles. They provided the inspiration for a number of Hollywood mansions. The cemetery adjoining the mission is by far the most moving part of this impressive complex. The Roman-style portico recalls the origins of Saint Barbara, put to death by her pagan father in the first century AD. The church is simply decorated, with baroque-style frescos inspired by traditional motifs of the

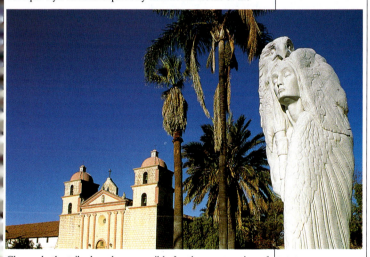

Chumash, the tribe largely responsible for the construction of the mission. It is said that the candles lighting the altar have burned continuously since it was built. Nearby, a small museum describes the life and work of the present-day Franciscan friars, in particular with the American Indian communities of the southwest. In summer, the cool freshness of a shady patio in the center of the cloister provides a welcome respite from the heat.

MUSEUM OF NATURAL HISTORY. Only a short distance from the mission, the museum takes an educational and informative look at the geological formation and evolution of life in this part of California.

BROOKS INSTITUTE OF PHOTOGRAPHY. On the way back down the Alameda, lovers of contemporary art must pay a visit to the Institute of Photography at 1321. Apart from a fine collection of old cameras, there are also exhibitions of the works of some of the most prestigious names in a field that is becoming increasingly highly prized by American collectors.

AMERICAN INDIAN ART: CHUMASH PAINTED CAVE STATE HISTORIC PARK
About 9 miles north of Santa Barbara, these Chumash caves are decorated with well-preserved paintings, thought to be 400 years old. The pictograms have not been deciphered, but are believed to have a religious significance. The Santa Barbara Museum of Natural History also has a collection of items belonging to the Chumash tribe.

Mission Santa Barbara.

THE EDUCATIONAL ROLE OF THE MISSIONS
In the 19th century most missions had an educational as well as a religious role. In the school of the Mission Santa Barbara, the flower of Spanish colonialism was educated by the Franciscan friars.

OLD
COURTHOUSE
MISSION
SAN BUENAVENTURA
HISTORICAL LANDMARK NO. 310 & NO. 847

DRILL PUMPS
These strange drill pumps can be seen throughout the region, relentlessly boring into the earth. Their older counterparts are on display in the Ventura Museum of History and Art. Their slow, balanced rhythm is reminiscent of the movements of wading birds.

VENTURA ◆ B C6. Ventura has all the old-fashioned charm of the coastal towns that have escaped the influence of the large cities. Its main attraction, the MISSION SAN BUENAVENTURA (1782), has been restored to the former glory of its pale yellow roughcast exterior. It has the traditional adjoining museum exhibiting religious objects and clothing, a reminder of the golden age of the missions ● *32*. As in so many other places, a statue of Junípero Serra ● *24* stands in a garden of Mediterranean plants. On the other side of Main Street, an attractive complex of terraced cafés and stores makes a pleasant place to take a break, amidst reminders of a Chinese presence dating from the time of the construction of the railroad. From here, you can walk to the nearby ALBINGER ARCHEOLOGICAL MUSEUM, whose valuable collections trace the life of the American Indians before the arrival of the first Spanish settlers, and the MUSEUM OF HISTORY AND ART, whose exhibits reflect a more contemporary era. From the port of Ventura, a boat takes visitors to the Channel Islands ● *240*, renowned for their abundant wildlife – sea lions, seals, pelicans and whales.

A THEOSOPHICAL ADVENTURE AT OJAI
The town is above all famous for its Krotona Institute of Theosophy. After traveling the world to spread his message of divine wisdom, Jiddu Krishnamurti ● *47* taught in this center from 1969 until his death in 1986. As a strong critic of 'guru mania', he probably had his work cut out trying to enlighten minds after the 1960s. A mile or so from the institute a library perpetuates his memory at 1130 McAndrew Road, a road that leads to the Los Padres National Forest.

OJAI ◆ B C6. About 12 miles north of Ventura, at the intersection of Routes 33 and 150, the little town of Ojai (which the locals pronounce O-eye) seems to have prospered in a time warp. For the last fifty years, it has been a refuge for city dwellers weary of Western materialism. Indian philosophies have gained a number of followers, who have often come from Los Angeles to rebuild their spiritual health ● *46*. The charm of Ojai is immediately apparent, with its tiny ST THOMAS AQUINAS CHURCH and its main street bordered by a magnificent pergola built in 1917 and rebuilt in 1999. There is no shortage of parks and green spaces, and hummingbirds, which feed on the nectar of the magnificent convolvulus flowers, are a common sight. Beyond Ojai lie the green swathes of the LOS PADRES NATIONAL FOREST, one of the few remaining natural areas in a region continually under threat from the sprawling megalopolis of Los Angeles.

The Mission St Thomas (right) is today the Ojai municipal library.

Los Angeles
and Orange County

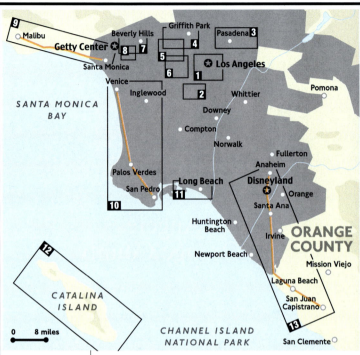

It is hard to believe that when California became a member of the United States of America in 1850 ● *26*, the city of Los Angeles had a population of only 1610. By 1970, the Spanish *pueblo* founded in 1781 had become the second largest city in the United States.

LOS ANGELES: THE EARLY YEARS. In the 19th century, the region's vast cattle ranches ● *33* were transformed into irrigated farms (the French even introduced vines) and Southern California was soon making a major contribution to the American economy by exporting milk and oranges. After 1870, the different languages spoken on the streets of Los Angeles were dominated by English when the completion of the railroad linked the city to the East Coast ● *26* and led to a massive influx of Yankees.

AMENITIES AND INDUSTRY. The city embarked upon a policy of constructing aqueducts, while simultaneously annexing the neighboring territories. Two aqueducts supplied Los Angeles with water from the Sierra Nevada and Colorado. The city's economy was based on property promotion, agriculture, the exploitation of oil, the movie industry ▲ *180* (from the early 20th century) and the aeronautics industry ● *50*.

HOUSES AND FREEWAYS AS FAR AS THE EYE CAN SEE. Unlike the East Coast cities, which had acquired the status of European colonial cities before receiving a major influx of European immigrants, Los Angeles welcomed Americans from the East Coast and the Midwest. These American migrants were seeking a different urban environment, a mild climate and private housing in a natural setting, in accordance with the rural ideals promulgated in the United States during the second half of the 19th century. From the early 20th century,

> 'In Los Angeles, distances are so great that
> anyone on foot is regarded with suspicion.'
>
> Frédéric Dard (*San Antonio*)

therefore, Los Angeles became a city of houses and gardens
with a well-developed public transport system ● *78*. From
1910, the automobile ● *48* began to be widely used by citizens
who saw it as a means of preserving their landscape. In 1939,
Los Angeles acquired a freeway linking it to Pasadena and, in
the late 1950s, a program for the construction of a vast freeway
network received state backing. Today, a car-share (*car-pool*)
system and two subway lines have failed to free up the network
and the population suffers increasingly from smog.

MODERN LOS ANGELES. The city has joined the ranks of the
major American cities (it now rivals New York) and has
expressed this new status by acquiring a 'skyline' of
skyscrapers. Its economic dynamism is based on the service
sector, high-tech industries, defense and the leisure industries
● *50* which are mainly linked to the movie industry.

LOS ANGELES: AN INTERNATIONAL CITY ● *42*. Los Angeles has
always been inhabited by Mexican, Chinese and Japanese
ethnic minorities, who built its infrastructure ● *38*. Following
the Watts riots ● *43*, in 1965, Thomas Bradley became the
city's first black mayor. However, his policies were swept aside
by the South Central riots ● *43*, in 1992, which highlighted
tensions between an established black community and more
recent Spanish and Asian immigrants competing in the job
and housing markets. Today, Los Angeles does not see itself
as a WASP community but as a 'majority-minority city' in
which the ethnic minorities have to form 'rainbow coalitions'
to gain any form of power. However, this cultural coalition is
not reflected in the urban landscape which is characterized by
the juxtaposition of these ethnic communities.

**VENTURING INTO
LOS ANGELES ✪**
Los Angeles, vast,
frightening and
fascinating, is not easy
to understand. You
have to work at it,
since there are
none of the usual
landmarks. Although
it has a downtown in
the sense of a historic,
financial and
administrative heart,
it doesn't really have a
center. The city is a
series of separate
districts reached by
bus or automobile
via the freeways.
These 'villages' are
all very different,
offering a complete
change of atmosphere
within a relatively
short space of time –
from the outmoded
Hollywood to the
elegance of Beverly
Hills, from the
seriousness of
downtown to the
frivolity of Santa
Monica, from the
beach district of
Venice to the
residential Silver
Lake.

The famous
MGM lion.

American cinema originated in New York in 1896, but from 1912 the industry began to look for a region where the weather was good and labor was cheap. The climate and beautiful landscapes around Los Angeles made it the ideal choice. From then on, the tiny village of Hollywood generated thousands of jobs, while the big companies of Warner Bros, Metro-Goldwyn-Mayer, 20th Century Fox and Columbia established their reputations. Not even the advent of television has been able to destroy an industry of which Hollywood remains the international symbol.

SILENT MOVIES

The success of cinema in its early years led producers to make an increasing number of short films which dealt candidly with a wide range of subjects, from romance to social conflict. David W Griffith's *The Birth of a Nation* (1915) marked a major turning point. This long ambitious film dealt with the reconstruction of the South after the Civil War. At about the same time, certain churches managed to persuade the industry to introduce the principle of censorship, to be exercised by the local authorities.

FINANCIAL PARTNERS IN THE MOVIE INDUSTRY

Although Oscars are still awarded on a regular basis, Hollywood has changed greatly since the 1970s. The studio system has disintegrated and been replaced by big financial groups, with Coca-Cola and the Seagram group – which sold out to the French group Vivendi in 2000 – becoming two of the industry's major partners. However, smaller studios such as Disney or Steven Spielberg's Dreamworks have asserted themselves, and actors are now independent and much better paid.

THE HOLLYWOOD MACHINE

With its huge market and a formula for success, Hollywood's organization is extremely fine tuned. In the big studios, work is divided by occupation – the director is not the decision-maker, the scriptwriter doesn't always recognize his/her script and the actors are bound by contracts.

THE GOLDEN AGE

From the late 1920s to the 1960s, Hollywood was in the full glare of censorship and produced conventional, entertaining films with happy endings. The age of the 'talkies' was marked by *The Jazz Singer* (1927) which combined technical innovation and an interesting plot.

The self-censorship imposed by producers led moviemakers to work hard to please the public without shocking them. Some films from this period, defined as 'classics', are among the finest in the history of cinema: *Gone with the Wind* (1939, left), *Casablanca* (1941), *Singin' in the Rain* (1952) and *High Noon* (1952).

THE STAR-SYSTEM

The display of vast amounts of resources exerts an irresistible attraction. The promotion of stars, past and present, has established the worldwide reputation of American actors and actresses. One of the principal outlets for the glitz of the US movie industry is the Academy Awards ceremony, established in 1938.

TODAY, A DIVIDED PUBLIC

Self-censorship was replaced by film categories based on the age of the audience. Today, few films are produced for a universal public (U). Young audiences are treated to a deluge of increasingly sophisticated special effects, from *Star Wars* (1977) to *Independence Day* (1996), while older audiences prefer low-budget films such as *Driving Miss Daisy* (1989) and *Thelma and Louise* (1991). There are obvious exceptions such as *Titanic* (1997, above) and *Gladiator* (2000), which were huge international successes. However, the trend is irreversible, especially with the development of digital television and the Internet.

Los Angeles architecture is a metaphor for the city itself: eclectic, dynamic, helter-skelter, innovative and bewildering. All styles are represented, from simple adobe houses of the Mexican rancho days to the high-tech glass and steel towers of the 21st century. The city's progressive attitude and willingness to experiment, as well as its sunny climate, have acted as a magnet for avant-garde architects for more than a century.

VICTORIAN ● 66:
This style is characterized by heavily detailed façades, fairytale turrets, frilly scrolls, gables and large porches. In LA, a slightly more subdued version survives in several private homes, notably in the 1300 block of CARROLL AVENUE ◆ **G** E4, in Angelino Heights, north of downtown. Faithfully restored, they offer sublime views over the sprawling city.

CRAFTSMAN ● 68:
This style, which evolved from the Arts and Crafts movement, reached its peak in the early decades of the 20th century. Its architects tried to create buildings in harmony with their natural surroundings, partly through the use of organic materials such as wood and rock. Courtyards, balconies and sun porches provided a transition from indoors to outdoors. The brothers Charles and Henry Greene defined the style, notably in their masterpiece the GAMBLE HOUSE (1908) ▲ *191*, at 4 Westmoreland Place in Pasadena ◆ **H** A1. The mansion, formerly the residence of an heir to the Procter & Gamble conglomerate, features exquisite wooden floors, mahogany furniture, period lighting and stained glass.

MODERNIST ● 70:
'Form follows function' is the basic tenet of Modernist architecture. With its origins in 1920s Europe, most notably the Bauhaus school in Germany, Modernism quickly conquered the world, signaling a new age in aesthetics. Its practitioners took a rational, minimalist approach to living spaces through such design elements as flat roofs, angular outlines and glass façades. Concrete and steel were common building materials. In LA, architects extended the style to the outdoors through terraces and courtyards. One of the Modernist pioneers was Frank Lloyd Wright, who came in 1917 to work on HOLLYHOCK HOUSE in Barnsdall Park ◆ **G** D3. Commissioned by oil heiress Aline Barnsdall, it takes its name from her favorite flower which appears as a stylized motif throughout. In 1920 Wright turned over the project to the Austrian Rudolph Schindler, one of his associates. Schindler's PRIVATE HOME (1921–22) ◆ **G** A3 at 835 N Kings Road in Hollywood sports numerous progressive features, including a flat roof, poured concrete flooring and integrated indoor and outdoor areas. Schindler's friend,

associate and fellow Austrian Richard Neutra also lived on Kings Road between 1925 and 1930, before building his own residence ◆ **G** E3 at 2300 E Silver Lake Boulevard in Silver Lake. But Neutra's seminal work was his 1929 experimental LOVELL HOUSE (featured in *LA Confidential*) ◆ **G** D2 at 4616 Dundee Drive overlooking Griffith Park ▲ *192*. Also of note is the so-called NEUTRA COLONY ◆ **G** E3, a group of houses built between 1949 and 1960 near his own home.

CONTEMPORARY ● *74*. FRANK O GEHRY

The best known and most widely respected living American architect is LA-based Frank O Gehry. Born in Toronto, Gehry came to LA at age 17, attended USC ▲ *189* and Harvard and opened his own design firm in 1962. He has received numerous prestigious awards, including the coveted Pritzker Prize in 1989. Many of his ground-breaking creations dot the LA landscape. Gehry's buildings have a sculptural quality and often make use of unconventional materials. For his PRIVATE RESIDENCE ◆ **J** B1 in Santa Monica, the architect turned a two-story clapboard structure into a postmodern deconstructivist vision of corrugated aluminum, particle board, glass and a chain-link fence. Other creations have the look and feel of a collage, such as the structure that houses the West Coast headquarters of the CHIAT/DAY ◆ **J** B3 ● *74* advertising at 340 Main Street in Venice. A giant pair of black binoculars (designed by Claes Oldenburg and Coosje van Bruggen) forms a visual anchor

and is flanked by a white structure resembling an ocean liner and a grove of angular copper-clad columns – an abstract interpretation of a forest. Gehry also drew the plans for the dramatic WALT DISNEY CONCERT HALL ▲ *185*, the future home of the LA Philharmonic, set to open on Grand Avenue downtown in 2003. Its warped and folding façade, which will be covered in brushed stainless steel sheets, has the appearance of a galleon with billowing sails. The theme continues inside, where tiered and sectioned seating completely surrounds the central orchestra platform.

New York-based **RICHARD MEIER** is the other major architect who has put his stamp on the LA landscape, notably with the GETTY CENTER ◆ **F** C2 ▲ *204*. But Meier's signature style of angled and linear buildings bathed in crisp white inside and out is best exemplified by the MUSEUM OF RADIO & TELEVISION ◆ **I** C2 ▲ *202* in Beverly Hills.

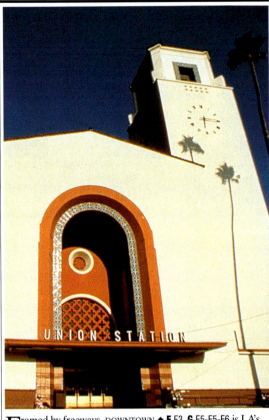

The religious fervour of the hispanic population can be seen in the streets of El Pueblo.

Framed by freeways, DOWNTOWN ◆ **F** E3, **G** E5-F5-E6 is LA's historic and business center. Modern glass-and-steel office high-rises dwarf bustling shopping districts, and ethnic neighborhoods reflect the city's diversity.

CIVIC CENTER. The Civic Center area, bordered by Figueroa Boulevard and San Pedro Street and the Hollywood Freeway and 1st Street, is home to administrative offices, the courts and such cultural institutions as the MUSIC CENTER and the CHILDREN'S MUSEUM. The most prominent building here is the landmark City Hall (1928) at 200 N Spring Street.

EL PUEBLO DE LOS ANGELES. This 44-acre state historic park, on the northeastern edge of downtown, roughly occupies the area where the city was founded in 1781. It preserves some of its oldest buildings and has a central plaza where *fiestas* celebrate LA's Mexican heritage. Nearby, the town's first church, the IGLESIA DE NUESTRA SEÑORA LA REINA DE LOS ANGELES (1818), is still the spiritual center of a large congregation of Spanish-speaking Roman Catholics. Leading away from the plaza, OLVERA STREET is a block-long alleyway lined by restaurants and stores selling Mexican handicrafts and souvenirs. Also here is the AVILA ADOBE (1818), the city's oldest surviving home. Its rooms, furnished to reflect the lifestyle of its original owner, a wealthy rancher and mayor, are open for free self-guided tours. The nearby Victorian SEPULVEDA HOUSE contains the park's visitor center.

UNION STATION. This 1939 structure at 800 N Alameda Street, southeast of the Pueblo, was the last of the grand central stations to be built in the USA. For the exterior, architect Donald B Parkinson drew inspiration from the early Spanish missions ● *64*, reflected in the tiled roofs, stucco walls and bell tower. The interior has Streamline Modern ● *73* touches and features marble floors, arched windows and giant chandeliers.

CHINATOWN. The first Chinese came to Los Angeles in the mid 19th century as railroad workers, servants or farm hands. They first lived in a ghetto on the site of Union Station before being forced to relocate several blocks to the northwest. Today, most of the city's Chinese Americans live in the eastern suburbs of Monterey Park and Alhambra, but New Chinatown remains their cultural center. Its main thoroughfare is NORTH BROADWAY, which erupts in colorful festivities during such major holidays as the Chinese New Year. At its northern end, GIN LING WAY is a small tourist-oriented mall, but authentic restaurants and stores selling exotic spices, herbs, teas, produce and even live chickens can be found throughout the district. Upstairs at 931 Broadway is a small Chinese Buddhist temple.

LITTLE TOKYO. Downtown's Japanese enclave is situated along 1st Street between San Pedro Street, Central Avenue and Alameda Street. Few Angelenos of Japanese descent actually call the area home, but many frequent the stores and restaurants in LITTLE TOKYO PLAZA and JAPANESE VILLAGE PLAZA with its landmark tiled-roof fire tower. The JAPANESE AMERICAN CULTURAL & COMMUNITY CENTER, 244 S San Pedro Street, contains an art gallery and library as well as the JAPAN AMERICA THEATER where kabuki performances and other events are held. Nearby, at 505 E 3rd Street, is the Higashi Honganji Buddhist temple.

JAPANESE AMERICAN NATIONAL MUSEUM (JANM). Located at 369 E 1st Street, this is the country's first museum to document the story of Japanese immigrants. It illustrates more than 100 years of the Japanese American experience, including the painful chapter of the World War Two internment camps ● *29*. The museum is housed in a beautiful building that blends American and Eastern aesthetics and also contains a tranquil garden.

GEFFEN CONTEMPORARY. Just north of the JANM, at 152 N Central Avenue, this exhibition space (named for entertainment mogul and major donor David Geffen) is an adjunct to the Museum of Contemporary Art (MOCA) at California Plaza ▲ *186*. The former warehouse, artfully converted by Frank Gehry ● *74*, originated as a temporary exhibition space during the construction of MOCA and is now used primarily for large-scale installations.

NEW DOWNTOWN LANDMARKS
Scheduled to open in 2003, the Walt Disney Concert Hall ● *75*, on Grand Avenue at 1st Street, will be the new home of the Los Angeles Philharmonic. The building, designed by Frank O Gehry, has a dramatic stainless steel skin and is an architectural representation of the opening of a rose. Nearby, on Temple between Hill Street and Grand Avenue, the new Cathedral of Our Lady of Los Angeles is expected to start welcoming worshipers in 2002. A work of Spanish architect José Rafael Moneo, it will be fronted by a plaza, topped by a large lighted cross and entered through bronze doors designed by LA artist Robert Graham.

The entrance to Chinatown.

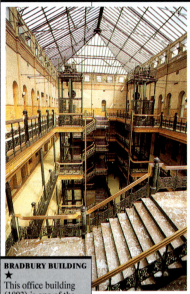

BRADBURY BUILDING
★
This office building (1893) is one of the most beautiful achievements of LA's Victorian architecture. Bradbury had entrusted his concept to a well-known architect's practise, but finally he chose draughtsman, George H Wyman, to see the project through. The restrained façade opens onto an atrium five stories high, bathed in the muted light streaming in through a tented glass roof. Wrought-iron balustrades, red marble floors and open-cage elevators are among the most charming details.

ALSO WORTH SEEING
The WELLS FARGO HISTORY MUSEUM, 333 S Grand Ave, is a paean to the Old West. In Alhambra ◆ **F** F2 the restored 1771 MISSION SAN GABRIEL ARCHANGEL, 428 S Mission Drive, has a museum as well as the original kitchen, cemetery, winery and water cisterns.

PERSHING SQUARE. LA's oldest public park (1866) was named for World War One General John J Pershing. Bordered by Olive, 5th, 6th and Hills Streets, it has received numerous face-lifts and is currently distinguished by walkways, public art and a lavender-colored tower. South of here, along Hill and Olive, is the city's JEWELRY DISTRICT with hundreds of vendors ensconced in such historic structures as the 1920 Pantages Theater on Hill at 7th Street. Stop on the way at the REGAL BILTMORE HOTEL. This palatial Spanish-Italian edifice looms above Pershing Square. The lavish interior evokes the stylish excesses of European palaces, with marble floors, gilded ceilings and works of art. A highlight is the ceiling painting by Giovanni Smeraldi in the Crystal Ballroom.

BROADWAY. In the late 19th century this was downtown's main shopping street, flanked by retail and big department stores. Entertainment in the form of vaudeville and movie theaters also brought in steady swarms of people. Places like the Orpheum, the Los Angeles Theater, the United Artists Theater and the Million Dollar Theater were all built between 1913 and 1931 in a flamboyant medley of styles borrowed from several historical periods, including classical, Gothic and rococo. In the early heyday of film making, they hosted major movie premieres, including Charlie Chaplin's 1931 *City Lights*. The Los Angeles Conservancy offers guided tours of the Broadway Historic Theater District on Saturday mornings. These days, the theaters are flanked by budget retail stores catering primarily to LA's large Latin American population ● *38*. Between 3rd and 4th Streets is the bustling 1917 GRAND CENTRAL MARKET, where artfully arranged fruit and vegetable displays, as well as fish, meat, spice and bakery counters, line the network of aisles. Several eateries offer inexpensive Mexican, Chinese, Salvadoran and other meals.

BRADBURY BUILDING ● *67*, on Broadway at 3rd Street, is the most magnificent of downtown's historic buildings (1893). An unassuming exterior gives way to a five-level atrium with a glass roof. The building has been featured in several movies, mostly memorably *Blade Runner*.

FINANCIAL CENTER. Banks, law firms, insurance companies and corporations of all sorts are installed in the high-rises that have mushroomed along downtown's northwestern edge, primarily in an area called BUNKER HILL. In the late 19th century, this was a residential neighborhood dotted with upscale Victorian mansions, torn down in the 1950s in the name of progress. The recently restored ANGELS FLIGHT FUNICULAR (1901), which connects Hill Street with California Plaza, is the sole reminder from that era. Another approach to the plaza is via the BUNKER HILL STEPS from 5th Street.

MUSEUM OF CONTEMPORARY ART (MOCA). Housed in a red sandstone building by Arata Isozaki, at 250 S Grand Avenue,

Financial district by night.

is this superb collection of art since 1940. The permanent collection includes leading lights of abstract expressionism, pop art, minimalism, post-minimalism and other genres, including Roy Lichtenstein, Mark Rothko, Jackson Pollock and Piet Mondrian. The museum mounts about 20 exhibitions annually, from retrospectives to themed shows and new works in both traditional and new media.

LOS ANGELES CENTRAL LIBRARY ● 72. LA's main repository of some 2.5 million books, photographs, maps and other materials is at 630 W 5th Street, in a 1928 building by Bertram Goodhue. The discovery of King Tutankhamun's tomb that same year inspired the pyramid atop the central tower and other Egyptian motifs. Inside are several murals, including an epic retelling of the history of California in the domed Loderick Cook Rotunda. The MAGUIRE GARDENS on its northern side are full of visual surprises and public art.

GARMENT DISTRICT. This area in southern downtown, roughly bordered by Broadway, Wall and 7th Streets and Pico Boulevard, is the hub of LA's fashion industry. Both original designs and brand-name knock-offs are manufactured here and sold, often at bargain prices, in retail stores, shopping emporia such as the Cooper Building or bazaar-like pedestrian malls such as Santee Alley. On Wall Street, between 7th and 8th, the FLOWER MARKET is a veritable feast for the senses. It's open to noon only.

HISTORIC MOVIE THEATERS IN SOUTH BROADWAY
At 307, the MILLION DOLLAR THEATER (1918), in Spanish baroque style ● 65, was built by theater magnate Sid Grauman.
The LOS ANGELES THEATER at 615 was built in Louis XV style for the world premiere in 1931 of Charlie Chaplin's City Lights
At 842 is the ORPHEUM (1931), in neo-Gothic style, and at 933 is the UNITED ARTISTS THEATER, created by Mary Pickford, Douglas Fairbanks and Charlie Chaplin.

EASTERN COLUMBIA BUILDING
This Art Deco building (left) stands at Broadway between 8th and 9th Streets. With its turquoise tile façade it is particularly eye-catching.

187

CALIFORNIA SCIENCE CENTER

Visitors can test the principles of gravity by taking a bicycle ride through the air, or learn about basic body functions during a multimedia show starring a giant doll named Tess. Exhibits are divided into two themed areas. The WORLD OF LIFE explains how all living organisms, from ants to human beings, engage in the same fundamental processes (eating, reproduction, etc) in order to survive. The CREATIVE WORLD focuses on human innovations in the fields of communications, structures and transportation. The educational emphasis throughout the museum is on 'learning by doing' and many of the exhibits are experiential rather than merely explanatory. An adjacent IMAX THEATER shows mostly nature-themed films on its giant screen, some of them in 3D.

About 3 miles south of downtown, the expansive Exposition Park ◆ **F** D3, **G** D6, has the city's greatest concentration of top-notch museums and sports facilities. An agricultural fairground in an earlier incarnation, it was turned into a park around 1910. One of the most enchanting places is the ROSE GARDEN, which stretches for over 7 acres on its northern flank. This colorful and fragrant sunken garden, with some 15,000 plants, is a popular wedding spot, as it is an ideal backdrop for photography.

NATURAL HISTORY MUSEUM OF LOS ANGELES COUNTY.
A pair of fighting dinosaurs greets visitors as they enter the lobby of this sprawling museum which, since 1913, has chronicled the earth's 4.5 billion-year history and the evolution of its species. Exhibits are drawn from an enormous collection of specimens – said to rival that of the Smithsonian Institution – and displayed in an ornate Spanish Renaissance-style building with marble and stained glass accents. Life and earth sciences, anthropology and history are the overarching thematic divisions. The Dinosaur Hall, with its *Tyrannosaurus rex* skull and full cast skeleton of a *Mamenchisauraus*, is among the biggest crowd pleasers. Other highlights are *megamouth*, the world's rarest shark, and the Gem & Mineral Hall which sparkles with gold, diamonds, emeralds and other precious and semi-precious stones. Another wing sheds light on the customs and living conditions of Native American peoples in the southwest. A prized collection of Navajo baskets and textiles forms one of the centerpieces. Smaller-scale exhibits include the Insect Zoo with dozens of crawling live exhibits, including an ant farm and tarantulas. Finally, there's the Discovery Zone, a play environment for small children.

CALIFORNIA AFRICAN AMERICAN MUSEUM. The main mission of this museum, housed in a handsome space in the park's northeast corner, is to raise awareness of the contributions made to culture, history and society by African Americans. Most exhibits are temporary and many focus on historical figures from fields as diverse as politics, science, art, athletics and music. In addition, samplings from the museum's permanent collection of fine art are on view on a rotating basis, supplemented by a busy year-round schedule of lectures, theater, music and other performances.

CALIFORNIA SCIENCE CENTER. The mysteries of science are unraveled in a playful and entertaining way at this innovative museum. Some of its exhibits are so imaginative, they seem to have sprung direct from the minds of theme park designers.

USC (UNIVERSITY OF SOUTHERN CALIFORNIA). Founded in 1880, USC is the oldest private research university west of the Mississippi. Landmark buildings on its 150-acre campus at 850 W 34th Street, just north of Exposition Park, include the 1930 MUDD HALL, instantly recognizable by its bell tower, inspired by a Tuscan monastery, and the Italian Renaissance-style DOHENY MEMORIAL LIBRARY (1932), home to an important collection of American literature. The FISHER GALLERY in Harris Hall showcases the work of young emerging artists, many from USC's own School of Fine Arts.

USC'S CINEMA-TELEVISION SCHOOL
The prestigious SCHOOL OF CINEMA-TELEVISION, founded in 1929, had DW Griffith and Ernst Lubitsch among its original faculty. Many of its alumni (such as John Wayne, George Lucas and Robert Zemeckis) have had illustrious careers in Hollywood. Other famous ex-students include astronaut Neil Armstrong and architect Frank Gehry ● *74* ▲ *183*. USC has about 28,000 students, half of them in undergraduate programs. Many of its sixteen graduate schools are top ranked, including those in law, business and public administration.

LOS ANGELES MEMORIAL COLISEUM
This grand arena, at the heart of Exposition Park, is one of the nation's most famous sports facilities. Dating back to 1923, it has witnessed such historic moments as the first ever Super Bowl in 1967 (and another in 1973) and is the only stadium to have hosted two Olympic Games (1932 and 1984). It suffered significant damage during the 1994 Northridge earthquake, but has since been restored and refitted. It is also the home base of the football team of the University of Southern California.

One of the entrances to the Memorial Coliseum.

Pasadena City Hall (below).
The Long Leg by Edward Hopper (below right) in the Huntington Art Collection.

PASADENA, ROSE PARADE & ROSE BOWL
A tradition since 1890, the flower-festooned floats of Pasadena's Tournament of Roses Parade are beamed into the world's living rooms every New Year's Day. Since 1902, an American football classic has followed the parade. And since 1922, the game has been played at the historic Rose Bowl Stadium, 1001 Rose Bowl Drive. Designed by Myron Hunt, it has room for 100,000 spectators.

CALIFORNIA INSTITUTE OF TECHNOLOGY (CALTECH) ◆ **H** B2
Founded in 1891, Caltech has become one of the world's foremost scientific research universities. No fewer than twenty-seven of its faculty and alumni have won the Nobel Prize. Caltech is best known for its achievements in seismology; earthquakes around the world are recorded and measured here. It also manages the JET PROPULSION LAB (JPL), the main center for robotic exploration of the solar system.

Pasadena ◆ **F** E2-E3, about 10 miles northeast of downtown LA, is a classy haven of art, culture, architecture and science. In the late 19th century it became a fashionable winter resort for rich but sun-starved visitors from the Midwest and the East Coast. Their lavish mansions still dot the city's tree-lined streets. Civic pride has always loomed large here, expressed as much in the glistening dome of the 1927 CITY HALL as in the more recent metamorphosis of OLD PASADENA into one of Los Angeles' premier arteries of shopping, dining and entertainment.

HUNTINGTON LIBRARY, ART COLLECTIONS AND BOTANICAL GARDENS ◆ **H** C3. Set in genteel San Marino, this spectacular compound started life in 1908 as the private estate of railroad tycoon Henry Huntington. Today it is a stunning repository of his personal collection of British and American art, books and objects, surrounded by 150 acres of gardens that are a year-round delight.

THE LIBRARY. This is primarily a research library filled with some 5 million volumes, but fortunately some major highlights are on public display. They include early editions of Shakespeare plays, Geoffrey Chaucer's Ellesmere manuscript of *The Canterbury Tales* (1410) and a Bible printed by Johannes Gutenberg in 1455.

ART COLLECTIONS. The refined ambience of the original Huntington residence forms the ideal backdrop for the collection of British and French art from the 18th and 19th centuries, including Gainsborough's famous *Blue Boy* (1770) and works by Constable, Reynolds and Turner. In another building, the Virginia Steele Scott Gallery of American Art displays paintings from the Colonial period to the 1930s Depression. Another permanent exhibit showcases the work of Charles and Henry Greene, architects of the Arts & Crafts Gamble House ▲ *182*.

BOTANICAL GARDENS. Henry Huntington himself began landscaping the magnificent gardens that now encompass more than 15,000 plant species. The rose, Japanese and desert

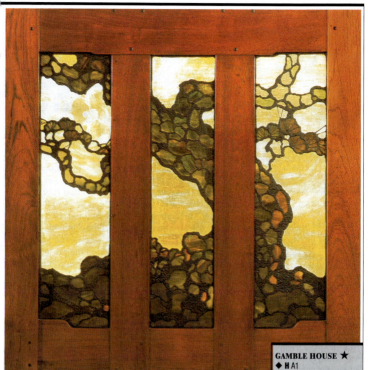

gardens are the biggest draws among the dozen themed gardens which are accented by benches, bridges and ponds.
PACIFIC ASIA MUSEUM ◆ H B2. Located at 46 N Los Robles Avenue, the building that houses this eclectic collection of Asian art and artifacts from five millennia was originally the home and gallery of Grace Nicholson, one of the city's first dealers in art from the Far East. Resembling a Chinese imperial palace, it is filled with symbolic architectural elements and has a tranquil courtyard garden with a pond, statues and rocks. The permanent collection includes Buddhist sculptures, jade carvings, ceramics, textiles and paintings reflecting the traditions and history of India, Tibet, China and Japan.
NORTON SIMON MUSEUM ◆ H A2. This world-class private collection, at 411 W Colorado Boulevard, represents a roll-call of some of the world's finest artists. At its core are six centuries of European painting and sculpture, with an emphasis on Old Masters, including Raphael, El Greco, Rubens, Rembrandt and Tiepolo. A survey of French Impressionists is another highlight, with Degas, Monet, Manet and Renoir among the leading lights represented. Other galleries house South Asian sculpture from India, Thailand, Nepal and Cambodia. Museum founder Norton Simon (1907–93), the head of a business empire, began amassing his prized collection in the 1950s, and in the 1970s he donated it to the Pasadena Art Institute. A major remodel under the auspices of architect Frank Gehry now allows natural light to bring out the mastery in the art works.

GAMBLE HOUSE ★ ◆ H A1
The Arts and Crafts masterpiece of the Greene brothers, the Gamble House (1908) ● 68 ▲ 182 seems to be a celebration of nature. This is partly because wood is a primary element here. But it is also because the architecture, inspired by Japan and Switzerland, creates a flow with its terraces between interior and exterior, adapting to the way of life and climate of southern California. You can make a tour of the house even outside the strict opening hours (Thu.–Sun., 12–3pm). The garden with its Japanese theme is an invitation to serenity, while the ingenious lighting inside the house allows you to see the refined Arts and Crafts decor with its stained glass and furniture.

▲ LOS ANGELES GRIFFITH PARK

A poster in the Autry Museum of Western Heritage.

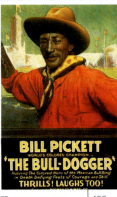

HOLLYWOOD SIGN ◆ G C1

They are the world's most famous nine letters, standing 50 feet high on Mount Lee, a hillside on the western edge of Griffith Park. The original sign, erected in 1923 by *Los Angeles Times* publisher Harry Chandler, spelled 'Hollywoodland' and was merely an advertising gimmick to sell real estate. But it soon became synonymous with the entertainment industry and a symbol of hope, glamour and success. Some of the best views are from the northern end of Beachwood Drive and from the Griffith Park Observatory, but alas, the hiking trail affording close-ups is now closed.

Griffith Park ◆ **F** D2 is the country's largest city park with 4044 acres of rugged hills and canyons cloaked in chaparral ● *20*. It was donated to the city in 1896 by mining millionaire Colonel Griffith Jenkins Griffith who envisioned 'a place of recreation and rest for the masses'. He got his wish: today, more than 10 million people annually use the park as their local playground. It is crisscrossed by scenic drives, 53 miles of hiking trails, 43 miles of bridle paths and dotted with museums, golf courses and picnic areas.

LOS ANGELES ZOO ◆ G D1. When the LA Zoo opened in 1966, it was the city's third animal park. The first, named Selig Zoo, delighted visitors as early as 1885, while the second, Griffith Park Zoo, became a refuge for retired circus animals in 1912. Today's LA Zoo, at 5333 Zoo Drive, is home to 1200 animals representing 400 species. The Chimpanzees of the Mahale Mountains (in Tanzania) is among the newest exhibits and part of a planned Great Ape Forest. Another highlight is the Ahmanson Koala House which simulates dawn and dusk when these animals are most active. The zoo is also involved in the preservation of endangered species, including the California condor.

AUTRY MUSEUM OF WESTERN HERITAGE ◆ G D1. The American West is the focus of this history museum at 4700 Western Heritage Way. Its main donor, Gene Autry (1907–98), was a legendary actor and singer known as the 'Singing Cowboy'. A huge bronze statue of him on horseback greets visitors in the museum courtyard. Inside, seven permanent galleries look at such subjects as the western migration of the 19th-century pioneers; the deadly conflict between the native Indians and the new settlers; and the ethnic, religious and social diversity of the new residents.

GRIFFITH OBSERVATORY & PLANETARIUM ◆ G C2. Clinging to the southern slope of Mount Hollywood, this 1935 Art Deco landmark at 2800 East Observatory Road offers one of the best views of the 'city of stars'. But even more spectacularly, it also looks up at the real stars, as well as planets and moons. The gleaming white complex is topped by a trio of copper cupolas; two contain telescopes, while the central one holds the planetarium theater. The Hall of Science on the ground floor is a free astronomy museum sporting a 1934 ceiling mural by Hugo Ballin which traces the history of science.

GRIFFITH OBSERVATORY

Film buffs will recognize the Griffith Observatory from many movies, including Arnold Schwarzenegger's *The Terminator* and the classic *Rebel Without a Cause,* starring James Dean. A memorial bust of the latter star stands on the western edge of the lawn.

SILVER LAKE & LOS FELIZ SOUTH OF GRIFFITH PARK These two neighborhoods have evolved into LA's epicenters of bohemian chic over the last decade. In Los Feliz, the action centers on Vermont Avenue where vintage clothing stores rub shoulders with coffee houses, retro bars, independent bookstores and eccentric gift boutiques. Silver Lake has a similarly eclectic assortment of one-of-a-kind establishments, especially along Sunset Boulevard. It is also noteworthy for its abundance of Modernist architecture ● *70* ▲ *182.*

FOREST LAWN MEMORIAL PARK ◆ G B1-C1. The final resting place of Lucile Ball, Buster Keaton, Sammy Davis Jr, Clark Gable and other celebrities, this sprawling 1917 cemetery in the park's northwestern corner features rolling lawns and immaculate landscaping. Monumental sculptures with patriotic themes stand alongside extravagant tombs and copies of famous works of art. There is also a Great Mausoleum where many movie stars are buried. Its founder, Hubert L Eaton, revolutionized the funeral business, a subject wonderfully satirized by Evelyn Waugh's 1948 novel *The Loved One.*

TRAVEL TOWN MUSEUM ◆ G C1. The Golden Age of the railroad comes alive at this outdoor museum at 5200 W Zoo Drive on the park's northern edge. Children and those young at heart can fancy themselves railroad engineers as they clamber over some of the vintage rolling stock on view here. Fourteen steam locomotives – the oldest from 1864, the 'newest' from 1925 – form part of the collection, along with trolleys, passenger and freight cars. On the first Sunday of the month, volunteers offer rides aboard an old caboose, while guided tours of some of the rarer cars run on the third Sunday.

▲ MOVIE AND TELEVISION STUDIOS

During the Golden Age of Hollywood (mid 1920s to early 1950s), seven major studios dominated the industry: the so-called *Big Five* (MGM, RKO, Paramount, 20th Century Fox, Warner Bros) and the 'Little Two' (Columbia and Universal). Except for RKO, all continue to exist in spite of mergers and takeovers. Many studios run tours that offer a partial look behind the scenes. The tours usually include peeks at such departments as wardrobe, make-up, props and set construction and, sometimes, visits to outdoor lots and sound stages. Several studios also offer free tickets to live tapings, available through Audiences Unlimited (tel. 818 753 3470, www.tvtickets.com).

WALT DISNEY STUDIOS ◆ G B1

1937 was a turning point for Walt Disney when *Snow White and the Seven Dwarfs*, the first full-length animated film, was a box office hit. With the money Disney built an animation studio in Burbank which became the dream factory of such classics as *101 Dalmatians* and *Jungle Book*. An addition to the original building pays homage to the *Seven Dwarfs*, with giant versions integrated into the façade as roof supports.

NBC TELEVISION STUDIOS ◆ G B1

The LA branch of this huge TV network, at 3000 West Alameda Avenue in Burbank, is where the *Tonight Show with Jay Leno* is recorded most weekdays at 5pm. NBC is the only major TV network that offers tours of its facilities. These are a 70-minute no-nonsense look at the inner workings of a television studio, including a visit of the *Tonight Show* set. Entrance is free

UNIVERSAL STUDIOS ◆ G A1

Universal is the world's largest film and television studio. In its amusement park visitors can relive scenes from such famous films as *Back to the Future* and *Jurassic Park* during high-tech adventure rides and live action shows. Universal was founded by German immigrant Carl Laemmle in 1909 and moved to its present location in 1915. Today, the studio where productions are filmed is off-limits to the public.

Metro Goldwyn Mayer

WARNER BROS STUDIOS ◆ G B1

Founded in 1918, the studio revolutionized the industry with the world's first 'talkie': *The Jazz Singer* (1927). In 1929 the studio moved from Sunset Boulevard to Burbank where its star actors included Humphrey Bogart, Errol Flynn and Bette Davis. Unforgettable hits include *Casablanca* and *Rebel without a Cause* and the more recent neo-noir *LA Confidential*.

PARAMOUNT STUDIOS ◆ G C3-C4

This is the oldest Hollywood movie studio, and the only one still located in Hollywood proper, at 5555 Melrose Avenue. Paramount looks back on a most illustrious history. Founded in 1914, its successes range from *Son of the Sheik* with Rudolph Valentino to Hitchcock's *Psycho,* and *Forrest Gump.* Its ornate wrought-iron gate was made famous in *Sunset Boulevard* with Gloria Swanson.

SONY PICTURES ◆ F C3

This fortress-like domain at Culver City is the kingdom of Columbia/TriStar Pictures (today owned by Sony). From 1924 to 1986 it housed the studios of MGM. With actors such as Gene Kelly, Greta Garbo and Katharine Hepburn, MGM could boast in their famous slogan, 'Only the sky has more stars than us'. *The Wizard of Oz* is one of their best-known and most enduring successes.

195

**HOLLYWOOD
BOULEVARD** ✪
Hollywood Boulevard
should not be missed,
for its star-studded
pavements, Mann's
Chinese Theater
(above) with its
emotive hand- and
footprints, and the
exotic Egyptian
Theater, and above all
because it is the
legendary center of
the Hollywood myth.
Weary tourists can
stop for refreshment
at the equally
legendary Musso
Frank's Grill at 6667,
patronized in the past
by Mary Pickford,
Douglas Fairbanks
Snr, Raymond
Chandler ● *105*,
Nathanael West
● *104* and Dashiell
Hammett, and today
by Bruce Willis.

Dream factory, Tinseltown,
home of the stars – no other
Los Angeles neighborhood
captures the imagination as much
as Hollywood ◆ **F** D2, **G** B3-C3 ▲ *180*.
Created in the late 19th century by
Methodist migrants from Kansas,
the area established itself as the
center of early film making in the
1920s. Some 40 years later,
following the exodus of most of the
big studios and stars, it plunged into
a serious economic slump. Vigorous
revitalization efforts over the last
decade, especially along Hollywood
Boulevard, have returned at least
some pockets of bygone glory.
HOLLYWOOD BOULEVARD. Allowed
to go from glamorous to seedy,
one of LA's most famous streets is
once again poised to kindle
excitement among visitors.
Developers and city boosters
hope that the cornerstone of
the district's rebirth will be the
new entertainment complex –
named HOLLYWOOD & HIGHLAND
for its location – that opened in
2001. Its centerpiece is a dramatic
plaza with a view of the Hollywood
Sign ▲ *192* flanked by shops, restaurants, a small TV studio
and a hotel. Also here is the state-of-the-art Premiere
Theater, which will bring the Academy Awards ceremony
back to Hollywood.
HOLLYWOOD WALK OF FAME. Thanks to businessman Harry
Sugarman, sections of Hollywood are, quite literally, paved in
stars. Since 1960, the names of about 2500 celebrities from
film, TV, radio or theater have been engraved in bronze and
embedded in the sidewalks of Hollywood Boulevard and
Vine Street. Newcomers are added monthly.
HOLLYWOOD ENTERTAINMENT MUSEUM. Props, movie star
memorabilia, make-up and costumes are among the items
offering a glimpse of the glamor and history of movie making
at this small museum. Ensconced in the basement
of the Galaxy Mall at 7021 Hollywood Boulevard, it also
contains an excellent scale model of Hollywood in the 1940s,
a multimedia presentation and interactive learning stations.
The highlight, though, is a guided 'studio tour' which includes
visits to the original sets of the USS *Enterprise's* command
bridge from *Star Trek* and the bar from the classic sitcom
series *Cheers*.
MANN'S CHINESE THEATER ● *73*. The world's most famous
movie theater, at 6925 Hollywood Boulevard, opened in
1927 as a fantastical pagoda-style structure festooned with
exotic decoration inside and out. In the 1940s it hosted the
Academy Awards, and gala movie premieres still take place
here regularly. The concrete slabs in its famous FORECOURT
are imprinted with the hand- and footprints of many
legendary stars (left). Douglas Fairbanks and Mary Pickford,

The pneumatic Angelyne, purely an invention of the Hollywood publicity machine, appears on all the billboards simply for the sake of being famous.

HOLLYWOOD STUDIO MUSEUM ◆ G B3
In 1913, Cecil B DeMille rented a horse barn to shoot his first feature film *The Squaw Man*. Thus was born the first film studio in Hollywood. Now a museum devoted to the pioneer days of the film industry, the barn stands at 2100 N Highland Ave.

ALSO WORTH A LOOK
RIPLEY'S BELIEVE IT OR NOT ▲ *127*, the HOLLYWOOD WAX MUSEUM and the GUINNESS BOOK OF RECORDS are a trio of tourist attractions just east of Hollywood and Highland Boulevards.
The HOLLYWOOD ROOSEVELT HOTEL, built in 1927, hosted the first Academy Awards ceremony two years later. Allowed to decay after the 1950s, it once again welcomes guests to its sunken Spanish Colonial lobby decorated with a painted ceiling and Moorish arches. The ghost of Montgomery Clift supposedly haunts room 928.

the original theater owners along with Sid Grauman, started the tradition back in the 1920s.

EL CAPITAN THEATER. Built in 1926, this has had a complete overhaul. From the lavish entrance and box office area to the glittering silver curtain in the auditorium and the state-of-the-art sound system, this place turns movie going into a celebration. Many Disney premieres take place here, sometimes preceded by a live stage show.

EGYPTIAN THEATER. The 1922 EGYPTIAN THEATER, at 6712, was the first built in Hollywood, its theme inspired by that year's discovery of King Tutankhamun's tomb. Following a faithful restoration, it reopened in 1998, complete with sphinx's heads, hieroglyphics and stately columns. It is now home to the American Cinemateque, a nonprofit film organization.

CELEBRITY LINGERIE HALL OF FAME. What would Hollywood be without a little naughtiness? This eccentric collection of celebrity undergarments is tucked away in the back of Frederick's of Hollywood, the original branch of the famous lingerie emporium. Madonna's conical bra, Robert Redford's boxer shorts, and panties from Zsa Zsa Gabor and the entire cast of *Beverly Hills 90210* are among the items on display. Definitely not your grandma's underwear!

CAPITOL RECORDS TOWER. A Hollywood landmark since 1954, this circular structure at 1750 N Vine Street was Los Angeles' first air-conditioned office building. Many people feel that it resembles a stack of vinyl records topped by a needle, but its architect Welton Becket insisted that this was merely coincidental.

DON'T MISS ON SUNSET STRIP...
At 8358 the ARGYLE HOTEL in Art Deco style; at 8440, the MONDRIAN HOTEL, inspired by the painter's work; and at the corner of Marmont Lane, the sumptuous CHÂTEAU MARMONT, a copy of one of the châteaux of the Loire and a favorite of Greta Garbo.

SUNSET STRIP ◆ G A3. The Sunset Strip, which generally refers to Sunset Boulevard between Crescent Heights and Doheny Drive, is LA's epicenter of cool, with the densest concentration of trendy night clubs, boutiques, bars, comedy clubs and hotels. Historic places like The Whisky à Gogo, where the Doors began their career, are here along with new arrivals like the House of Blues. The chic restaurants along Sunset Plaza, in the 8600 block, are great for watching the steady stream of humanity passing beneath giant billboards, often touting upcoming movie releases, that are a trademark of the Strip.

FARMERS' MARKET ◆ G A4. LA's most famous farmers' market has been at the corner of Fairfax Avenue and 3rd Street since 1934. These days, some 160 vendors hawk a wide range of wares, including produce, souvenirs, jewelry and curios.

Some have been here for generations, but Magee's House of Nuts is the only remaining original merchant. Popular eateries include KoKoMo and the Gumbo Pot. In the late 1930s, what is believed to be the world's first self-service gas station, called GAS-A-TERIA, opened next to the market. The landmark clock tower was added in 1941.

CBS TELEVISION CITY ◆ G A4. Some of the network's favorite soap operas and game shows are taped in the mammoth building with the familiar logo at 7800 Beverly Boulevard. Tickets to shows with a live audience are free. The 1952 structure sits on the site of the Gilmore Stadium, built in 1934 for midget car races and later the home of the Bulldogs, LA's first professional football team.

MELROSE AVENUE ◆ G A4-B4. There are few places in LA where walking is as much fun as along this wacky haven of hip, especially between Highland and Fairfax Avenues. Stores with fronts emblematic of the city's creative spirit sell everything, from the bizarre to the exquisite, the banal to the eccentric. People-watching is a great sport here, as trend-conscious locals mingle with international visitors. The scene is liveliest on weekends.

HOLLYWOOD FOREVER MEMORIAL PARK ◆ G C3. It's fitting that LA's most star-studded cemetery lies just north of Paramount, the only remaining big movie studio in Hollywood ▲ 195. A mecca for mourners since 1899, this beautifully landscaped burial ground of the rich and famous features ornate headstones, statues and monuments. Rudolph Valentino and Douglas Fairbanks are the biggest names in the Cathedral Mausoleum, while Tyrone Power, Jayne Mansfield and John Houston are among those buried near a picturesque lake. Free maps are available.

Melrose Avenue.

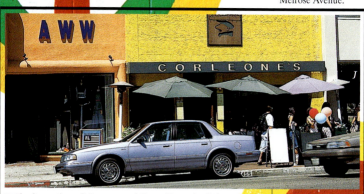

The invention of the automobile ● *48* sparked the decentralization of Los Angeles and the emergence of shopping districts away from the downtown area. Conceived in the 1920s by developer AW Ross, the Miracle Mile ◆ **F** D3, along Wilshire Boulevard between La Brea and Fairfax Avenues, was the first such suburban haven of commerce ● *76*. These days, several cultural institutions have replaced most of the shops, hence the nickname 'Museum Row'.

GEORGE C PAGE MUSEUM AT LA BREA TAR PITS ◆ **G** B4. The La Brea Tar Pits are among the world's richest fossil sites. Thousands of now extinct animals, including mammoths, saber-toothed cats and wolves, became trapped in the tar during the last Ice Age between 40,000 and 10,000 years ago. Excavation on the land, which was then part of an oil field owned by G Allan Hancock, began in 1875 and continues to this day. More than one million bones representing 231 species have been unearthed so far, including the skeleton of a Chumash Indian woman. The most impressive are on display at the GEORGE C PAGE MUSEUM located at 5801 Wilshire Boulevard, right next to the tar pits.

CRAFT AND FOLK ART MUSEUM (CAFAM) ◆ **G** B4. For centuries, people from diverse cultures have found ways to express their identity and traditions through hand-made art and objects. Since 1976, CAFAM has hosted a multitude of exhibits showcasing such work created by both local and international artisans. The museum also presents workshops, lectures and conferences and organizes the biannual International Festival of Masks.

PETERSEN AUTOMOTIVE MUSEUM ★ This museum (below), at 6060 Wilshire Boulevard, is a hymn to the automobile and how it defined the culture of Southern California ● *48*. On the first story visitors take a trip along memory lane with a faux LA street set in the first half of the 20th century. Major inventions, such as gas stations, drive-in restaurants, giant billboards and mini-malls, are recreated as charming dioramas and replicas. Hot rods, race cars, classic cars, vintage vehicles and those used in movies and owned by celebrities take center stage in the upper galleries. On the third story, children can learn about basic scientific principles at the interactive May Family Discovery Center.

▲ LACMA (Los Angeles County Museum of Art)

As the population of Los Angeles expanded westward shortly before and after World War Two, the Los Angeles County Museum of Art – LACMA – was carved from the existing Museum of History, Science and Art at Exposition Park, and opened in 1965 at its current location between Hollywood and Beverly Hills on Wilshire Boulevard. LACMA occupies six buildings, in a park-like setting, that were designed by such architects as Hardy Holzman Pfeiffer, Bruce Goff and Bart Prince. The museum's collection of 110,000 works from around the world span the history of art from ancient times to the present and is the largest 'encyclopedic' visual arts museum west of Chicago. LACMA also offers an ever-changing selection of exhibitions of the world's leading artists, tours, lectures, music and films, and a gallery designed specifically for children.

A UNIVERSAL COLLECTION

Among the museum's many departments, special mention must be made of the prints and drawings collection, which has more than 30,000 pieces spanning 500 years. The photography collection includes the work of Alfred Stieglitz, Edward Weston and Ansel Adams ● *54*. A leading collection of decorative arts, costumes and textiles round out the rich visual experience for more than one million visitors each year.

AMERICAIN ART

LACMA's significant collection of American art covers the period from the start of the 18th to the end of the 20th centuries. Of particular note are works by John Singleton Copley (1738–1815), John Singer Sargent (1856–1925), Mary Cassat (1844–1926), Henri Ossawa Tanner (1859–1937) and George Bellows (1882–1924). *The Cotton Pickers* (above), by Winslow Homer (1836–1910), no doubt draws upon a European tradition. The painter renders his unmistakable American subject with the same respect and sympathy the French artists had for their nation's peasants. The highly saturated hues of *An American Oriental* (left) became the hallmark of paintings by Guy Pène du Bois (1884–1958), a critic as well as a painter, who focused his entire painting career on contemporary city life.

EUROPEAN PAINTING AND SCULPTURE

This department's works date from the 17th to the early 20th centuries. Among its many masterpieces are those from the Middle Ages, the Renaissance (Titian, Veronese), 17th-century Flanders and Holland (Rembrandt) and 17th-, 18th- and 19th-century France (Le Nain, Delacroix, Corot), as well as those of impressionists (Degas, Monet – *Water Lilies*, below) and postimpressionists (Cézanne, Gauguin).

MODERN AND CONTEMPORARY ART

This part of the museum, certainly the most important, features 20th-century works from around the world. The modern art collection includes galleries devoted to Russian avant-garde, Parisian Fauvism, New York Expressionism and Mexican Modernism. Among its treasures is *Flower Day* (1925, left), by Diego Rivera (1886–1957), who became fascinated with the Native American and mestizo way of life. The contemporary art collection, while increasingly global, maintains a special commitment to established and emergent Californian painters, such as David Hockney ● 85 and Edward Ruscha. Its holdings of the last thirty years are often displayed thematically or conceptually rather than classified into schools and national styles.

EASTERN ART

The museum also has particularly strong collections of Islamic, South and Southeast Asian and Far Eastern art, including the largest and highest quality Korean art outside of Korea. The Japanese collection is dramatically displayed in the architecturally unique Japanese Pavilion (designed by Bruce Goff), a blend of traditional Japanese design and modern technology. *Crowned Buddha* (left), a 18th-century Burmese sculpture.

DECORATIVE ARTS

This collection, who's works range from the medieval period to the present day, include silver and metalwork, ceramics and furniture. It is divided into European, American and modern and contemporary sections. The electric lamp (1910, above) by the Charles P Limbert Company owes its hipped roof and architectonic base to Prairie school designs, while the meandering vine on the shade is inspired by Japanese arts.

Rodeo Drive (the most expensive street in the world), Santa Monica and Wilshire Boulevard, delimit the Golden Triangle of Beverly Hills, where they sell haute couture and rivers of diamonds.

CELEBRITY MANSIONS
Beverly Hills has been studded with the palatial homes of the stars ever since Douglas Fairbanks and Mary Pickford built their Pickfair Estate in 1919. Here's a small sampling of the mansions on view: Hugh Hefner's Playboy Mansion is at 10236 Charing Cross Road, while the producer Aaron

Synonymous with wealth, fame and a lavish lifestyle, Beverly Hills ◆ **F** C2-C3 works hard to live up to the clichés it has engendered. Opulent mansions with immaculate gardens line its tree-shaded avenues. Chic, trendy restaurants teem with perfectly coiffed and bejeweled patrons. Most clients are decked out in the latest haute couture creations, acquired in the international designer emporia of RODEO DRIVE and its side streets. Even the public buildings, modest and functional in most cities, here cling to architectural flights of fancy. The 1932 City Hall, for instance, part of the CIVIC CENTER ◆ **I** C2 on the corner of Santa Monica Boulevard and Crescent Drive, is a sumptuous Spanish baroque edifice topped by a gilded cupola.

Spelling's compound is at 594 S Mapleton Drive. Jayne Mansfield's former home stands at 10100 Sunset Boulevard, a large pink confection last owned by the singer Engelbert Humperdinck. The best way to visit the area is undoubtedly to join a guided tour. As you might imagine, there are no names on the gates to help identify these well-guarded homes of the famous.

ALSO WORTH SEEING
At 507 Rodeo Drive, the O'NEIL HOUSE (1989) is built in generous curves after the style of Gaudí.

MUSEUM OF TELEVISION & RADIO ◆ **I** C2. Much more an interactive archive than a traditional museum, this Richard Meier-designed facility pays homage to the two media that revolutionized communication in the early 20th century. Visitors can completely personalize their experience by choosing screenings of popular programs in the auditorium or listening to preprogrammed radio broadcasts. The heart of the museum is the Stanley Hubbard Library, where more than 100,000 historic radio and TV broadcasts are available for viewing at private consoles.
FAMOUS HOTELS. When visiting celebrities, dignitaries and royalty visit Beverly Hills, there are two hotels where many choose to stay. Those in love with the limelight pick the BEVERLY HILLS HOTEL ◆ **I** B1, 9641 Sunset Boulevard, nicknamed the 'Pink Palace'. A major celebrity playground since 1912, it has hosted a galaxy of stars, from Douglas Fairbanks to Katherine Hepburn, Liz Taylor to Paul McCartney. Movie deals and romantic affairs are often conducted poolside or in its famous Polo Lounge restaurant. Those wanting to get away from the attention prefer the secluded HOTEL BEL-AIR ◆ **I** A1 at 701 Stone Canyon Road. The 1922 mission-style mansion is surrounded by 11 acres of lovely gardens with winding streams and splashing waterfalls. It's a romantic retreat with a fairy-tale setting.

VIRGINIA ROBINSON GARDENS ◆ I B1. This oasis of palms, azaleas, camellias and other exotic plants at 1008 Elden Way is one of Beverly Hills' best-kept secrets. The lush gardens, connected by brick walkways and punctuated by Spanish-style fountains, surround one of the city's oldest estates. Originally owned by the Robinson family of department store fame (now Robinsons-May), the 1911 Beaux Arts mansion and grounds opened to the public in 1982.

GREYSTONE PARK & MANSION ◆ I C1. Driving through the wrought-iron gates onto the Greystone estate at 905 Loma Vista Drive is like entering a different world. Given to his son by local oil baron Edward L Doheny, the now empty 55-room Tudor-style mansion (1928) sits almost forlornly on its hillside perch. The building itself is off-limits to the public but is a

popular location for weddings and movie shoots (scenes from *The Bodyguard* and *Indecent Proposal*, among many others, were filmed here). The rambling gardens, with their secluded courtyards, open lawns and fountains, offer the occasional dramatic glimpse over the cityscape below.

MUSEUM OF TOLERANCE ◆ I C3. An adjunct of the LA branch of the Simon Wiesenthal Center, this multi-media museum has a two-fold mission: to teach visitors about the horrors of the Holocaust and to make them confront their own prejudices. The tour covers such topics as the civil rights struggle in the US, current hate group activity and the horrors of the Nazi concentration camps.

THE MUSEUM OF JURASSIC TECHNOLOGY (MJT) ◆ F C3. Natural history museum or elaborate joke? The MJT, at 9341 Venice Boulevard in Culver City, south of Beverly Hills, takes visitors on a bizarre journey where the borders between reality, imagination and perception become mesmerizingly intertwined. Displays range from the obscure to the unusual to the absurd: while one examines the qualities of the stink ant of the Cameroons, another explores the relationship between an opera singer and a neurophysiology professor that resulted in breakthroughs in memory research. Truly impressive are the micro-sculptures inserted into the eye of a needle. This place must be seen to be believed.

MUSEUM OF TOLERANCE
Displays include a bunk bed from Majdanek concentration camp and letters by Anne Frank. The Hall of Testimony plays videos of camp survivors recalling their experiences. To learn more you can visit the multi-media learning center (below).

CENTURY CITY ◆ I B3
This is an urban island, built in the 1960s on the backlot of 20th Century Fox Studios. The Century City Shopping Center, on Santa Monica Blvd, is one of the most chic places in LA. At 2020 Avenue of the Stars, the ABC Entertainment Center houses the famous Shubert Theater, one of the leading live theaters in LA. It is also the location of Harry's Bar & American Grill, a replica of the one in Florence. As for the Century Plaza hotel opposite, it tends to be used by heads of state who are passing through.

The collections of the billionaire J Paul Getty were for a long time housed in his 'Roman' villa in Malibu. In 1989, the Getty Trust, which inherited his fortune in 1976, decided to build a complex which incorporated a museum and various research institutes (including research into the conservation of works of art) and which would also make art more accessible to the general public. The project was a huge success. Since 1997, the Getty Center, designed by the architect Richard Meier, has echoed the rounded contours of the Santa Monica Mountains – a masterpiece of contemporary architecture.

J PAUL GETTY (1892–1976)
At the age of 23, J Paul Getty inherited the fortune of his oil-magnate father. He used it to build up a major collection of paintings, French furniture and antiques.

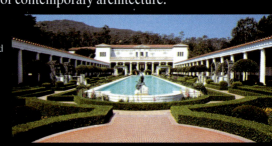

A SPECTACULAR PIECE OF ARCHITECTURE ✪
The Getty Center attracts visitors for the setting as much as for its collections. Everything conspires to make it a haven of light: the five, modestly sized wings that open onto the interior courtyard, the pink and beige stone, the metal panels and the use of mirrors. The crowning glory of this masterpiece of contemporary architecture is the fact that it blends perfectly with the site in the Santa Monica Mountains, offering a spectacular view of Los Angeles, the San Gabriel Mountains and the Pacific Ocean. Visitors can appreciate the dazzling beauty of the site and its surroundings as they take a break in the cafeteria. NB: if you go by car, remember to reserve a parking space in advance: tel: 310 440 7300.

Irises (left)
by Van Gogh (1889).

THE GETTY VILLA IN MALIBU

From 1954, J Paul Getty housed his collections in his Malibu ranch. However, the ranch proved too small and he decided to build a museum based on the layout of a Roman villa. The Getty Villa, a faithful reconstruction of the Villa of the Papyri in Herculaneum, buried during the eruption of Mount Vesuvius in AD 79, was completed in 1974, two years before Getty's death. It has recently been refurbished, and when it reopens will house Greco-Roman antiquities as well as a research center.

THE COLLECTIONS

Two of the collections from the Getty Villa are today housed in the Getty Center: French decorative *objets d'art* and European paintings. The museum also houses medieval miniatures, manuscripts, drawings and photographs. Its most famous works include Andrea Mantegna's *The Adoration of the Magi*, Van Gogh's *Irises* and the collection of 17th- and 18th-century French furniture. Interesting temporary exhibitions are also held there.

THE GARDENS

The gardens, inspired by traditional Californian gardens and the gardens of ancient Greece and Rome, were as carefully designed as the buildings. The extremely detailed arrangement of plants and minerals is designed to maximize the interplay of light and color. Visitors are drawn irresistibly to the Central Garden, a masterpiece by Robert Irwin, described as 'a sculpture in the form of a garden'.

THE ARCHITECT

Richard Meier, who was greatly inspired by the early works of Le Corbusier, expresses himself via the architecture as much as the design. Both reflect the same requirement for purity, the same preoccupation with the contrast between form and color, and the same awareness of balanced proportions.

Westwood village was a popular pedestrian-oriented shopping district until gang-related shootings in the 1980s plunged it into near-oblivion. Recent revitalization efforts have begun to whittle away at the negative image, emphasizing its beautiful streets of Spanish Colonial architecture ● *64*. Westwood is home to numerous movie theaters, including the historic FOX VILLAGE THEATER (1931) and the BRUIN THEATER (1937), which frequently host star-studded movie premieres. Evenings and weekends are the best times to explore the village.

SKIRBALL CULTURAL CENTER ◆ F B2

This museum and educational facility at 2701 N Sepulveda Boulevard is dedicated to chronicling and explaining Jewish history, from ancient times to Jewish America. It is housed in a dramatic steel, slate, stone and concrete structure designed by Moshe Safdie. The museum contains photographs, archeological artifacts, ceremonial objects, sound recordings, paintings and sculptures. Perhaps the most important document in the collection is the original 1935 Nuremberg Laws, signed by Hitler, that deprived Jews and other non-Aryans of their citizenship and civil rights in Nazi Germany. There are also hands-on exhibits for children, an art gallery and frequent lectures.

This westside community, anchored by the University of California, Los Angeles (UCLA), was developed in the 1920s by the Janss Investment Corporation. Its commercial heart is WESTWOOD VILLAGE ◆ F C2, I A2, just south of campus, a favorite with the students.

UCLA ◆ I A2. The largest of the nine-campus University of California system, UCLA is one of the top learning and research institutions in the country. Founded as a teachers' college in 1882, it moved to Westwood in 1929 and now enrolls 36,500 undergraduate and graduate students in more than 100 academic programs.

ROYCE QUADRANGLE. This rectangular plaza is framed by the four original campus structures, including two major landmarks built in Italian Renaissance style: Royce Hall, modeled after a cathedral in Milan, which houses an auditorium; and Powell Library, distinguished by an octagonal tower inspired by a church in Bologna.

FOWLER MUSEUM OF CULTURAL HISTORY. West of Royce Hall, this museum offers an insight into the customs, arts, religious beliefs and lifestyles of non-western cultures. Changing exhibitions present the museum's rich collection in a kaleidoscope of contexts and themes, ranging from the role of music in the life of African peoples, to folk art made from recycled materials. On permanent view is European and American silver from the collection of the Fowler family, the museum's major donor.

FRANKLIN D MURPHY SCULPTURE GARDEN. Northeast of Royce Quad, this five-acre outdoor gallery gives a comprehensive overview of 19th- and 20th-century American

Westwood Village by night.

and European sculpture. More than 70 pieces by such notable artists as Alexander Calder, Jacques Lipschitz, Gerhard Marcks, Henri Matisse, Joan Miró, Auguste Rodin, Francisco Zuñiga and David Smith dot a grassy area shaded by mature trees.

MILDRED E MATHIAS BOTANICAL GARDEN. Tucked away in the southeast corner of campus (entrance on Tiverton Avenue), this seven-acre garden teems with native and exotic plants and flowers. Paths invite quiet strolls and there are benches for relaxing and reading. Koi fish tumble lazily in a pond fed by a little stream. The newest addition to the 70-year-old garden is a public outdoor classroom, affectionately nicknamed 'The Nest'.

UCLA HAMMER MUSEUM. An imposing black and white marble edifice at the corner of Wilshire and Westwood Boulevards, this museum has emerged as an important venue for showcasing cutting-edge art by contemporary artists, many of them from California. Other exhibits are drawn from the permanent collection, most of which was donated by museum founder Armand Hammer (1898–1990). The oil magnate's main interest was in Impressionist and Post-Impressionist European art, including masterpieces by Claude Monet, Mary Cassatt, John Singer Sargent and Van Gogh. Hammer also amassed an impressive number of lithographs, paintings and sculptures by French satirist Honoré Daumier and his contemporaries. Integrated within the museum is the Grunwald Center for the Graphic Arts, comprised of 35,000 prints, drawings and photos by such prominent artists as Albrecht Dürer, Paul Cézanne and Carlos Almaraz.

GETTING LOST IN LOS ANGELES

Los Angeles will divert you, literally as well as metaphorically! But don't be discouraged by the numerous twists and turns on the autoroutes, and the streets that can be more than 30 miles long. Whether you are visiting Westwood Village or Hollywood Boulevard, getting lost is part of the journey, and enables you to make all sorts of unexpected discoveries, such as a charming residential quarter, or an oil field in the heart of town! And don't forget that even the Angelinos sometimes get lost.

UNIVERSITY OF THE STARS

UCLA is the *alma mater* of numerous celebrities, including James Dean, Jim Morrison, Tim Robbins, Heather Locklear, Rob Reiner, Lloyd Bridges and former long-time LA mayor, Tom Bradley ▲ *179*.

WESTWOOD MEMORIAL PARK

Some of Hollywood's brightest stars are buried in this small, secluded cemetery at 1218 Glendon Avenue. Oddly, many of them died either young, or tragically: Marilyn Monroe died in 1962 at age 36; Natalie Wood drowned in 1981 at age 43; Roy Orbison died suddenly in 1988 at age 52; Frank Zappa died of cancer in 1993 at age 53; and Dominique Dunne, who appeared in *Poltergeist*, was strangled in 1982 by her boyfriend at age 23.

PEACE, LUXURY AND PLEASURE AT MALIBU
The idea of the beach as a resort originated back in the 1920s when oil heiress May Rindge, who owned all of Malibu, was forced to sell off some of her land in order to support her lavish lifestyle. Clara Bow and Gloria Swanson were among the first to buy property here. Home

to such A-List stars as Barbra Streisand, Tom Hanks and Mel Gibson, they still prize the privacy of this illustrious enclave, which is off-limits to the public. It is, however, legal to walk along the beach, but only below the high-tide mark.

ALSO TO SEE AT MALIBU
The Getty Villa ▲ *204* is being renovated and will soon reopen.

One of the strange things about Los Angeles is that as you travel through the 'towns' which line the coast for 50 miles, seeing only the sea and the beaches, you tend to forget that you are at the heart of a giant megalopolis.

MALIBU ◆ F A3. Malibu follows the coastline for 27 miles all the way to the Ventura County line. The views of the ocean and ribbon of sandy beach are priceless, but the villas along here are not, which is why many of them are in the hands of well-to-do industry insiders. In fact, the MALIBU COLONY is among the most exclusive residential areas in LA.

SANTA MONICA ◆ F B3-C3. The most popular of the area's coastal towns, Santa Monica has grown from a laid-back beach community into a sparkling seaside resort in less than a decade. Luxury hotels now overlook the Pacific, gourmet restaurants have mushroomed, and pedestrianized THIRD STREET PROMENADE ◆ **J** A2 draws the crowds with its smart boutiques, movie theaters and free street entertainment.

Cliff-top PALISADES PARK has a view of the ocean. Its avenue lined with palms is popular with joggers, strollers and t'ai chi practitioners.

SANTA MONICA PIER ◆ J A2. The lighted neon arch at the entrance of this historic pier has greeted visitors for more than fifty years and has been featured in countless movies and TV programs. Right beneath the carousel, at beach level, is the UCLA OCEAN DISCOVERY CENTER, intended to familiarize children with the eco-scape of the Santa Monica Bay. Jellyfish and sharks are among the denizens of the aquariums, while touch tanks provide the opportunity for close encounters with such exotic ocean creatures as sea cucumbers and starfish.

MAIN STREET ◆ J A2. Along with Third Street Promenade and Montana Avenue, Main Street, flanked by boutiques and galleries, is a major Santa Monica shopping destination. The classic Victorian home at 2612 contains the CALIFORNIA HERITAGE MUSEUM with early 20th-century period rooms and changing exhibits with historical themes. The dramatic EDGEMAR COMPLEX at 2415 was designed as a mall by Frank Gehry ● *74*.

MUSEUM OF FLYING ◆ J C2. Within Santa Monica Airport, this three-story museum occupies the grounds of the historic Douglas Aircraft Corporation, which built planes for military and civilian use between 1920 and 1967. A self-guided tour explores the origins of flight and pays homage to pioneers and heroes of the skies before bringing visitors face to wing with some historic flying machines. Among the highlights are several rare World War Two fighter planes, such as a Messerschmitt

BF 109, one of the most lethal aircraft in the history of aerial warfare, and the Hawker Hurricane, which did serious damage to German aircraft during the Battle of Britain.

BERGAMOT STATION ARTS CENTER ♦ **J** B1. For an immersion in LA's art scene, there's no more convenient place than this complex at 2525 Michigan Avenue where nearly three dozen galleries cluster. Bergamot Station was originally a stop on the Red Line trolley which ran from downtown LA to Santa Monica between 1875 and 1953. It went through incarnations as an ice-making plant and a water heater factory before being abandoned and finally resurrected in 1994. Galleries, most of them well respected in the art world, present the full spectrum of media and artists, from traditional to avant-garde. Also part of the center, which has preserved its industrial look, is the SANTA MONICA MUSEUM OF ART **J** B1. This avant-garde exhibit space presents group and solo shows of emerging and established artists working primarily in new and experimental media, many of them from Southern California. Museum curators also run a lively community program, including the popular Friday evening salons of discussions, performance art and film presentations.

WALKING IN LOS ANGELES ✪
At first sight Third Street Promenade, in Santa Monica (above), Westwood Village ▲ *206* or City Walk at Universal Studios ▲ *194* have nothing extraordinary about them. And yet these are some of the favorite meeting places of Angelinos, who enjoy strolling around. Because the automobile is king in this city, streets where people are free to walk have the charm of the unusual.

SANTA MONICA PIER
Visitors and locals alike flock to the pier to stroll the wooden planks, enjoy the sunset, listen to street musicians, or patronize the bars and restaurants. First built in 1909 as a fishing pier, it was expanded into an amusement park in 1916. The most charming reminder of that era is a classic CAROUSEL with colorfully painted horses. The park was revamped as PACIFIC PARK in the 1990s and a roller coaster, ferris wheel and other rides once again attract thrill seekers.

The most muscular men and women in LA show off at Muscle Beach, an open air weightlifting club, especially popular on Sundays.

VENICE BOARDWALK
◆ J B3
The funky VENICE BOARDWALK offers front row seats to a unique street spectacle: bikini-clad inline skaters, chainsaw-juggling street performers, buffed and oiled musclemen (and women), fortunetellers and henna artists, all against the backdrop of the bright blue bay. Fitness enthusiasts can rent skates, bicycles or surfboards to blend into the quintessential Southern California beach scene ▲ 225.

VENICE'S SUCCESSFUL STUDIOS
The brand-new Manhattan Beach Studios, at 1600 Rosecrans Avenue, which began operation in 1998, is the first film studio to open in Los Angeles in some 60 years. The brainchild of Roy Disney, Walt Disney's nephew, the studio's sound stages are used to produce such hit TV series as *Ally McBeal* and *The Practice*.

THE BIRTH OF SURFING IN SOUTHERN CALIFORNIA
Surfers gather near Manhattan Beach Pier and at Redondo Beach, which was the birthplace of surfing in Southern California. George Freeth, the man who pioneered the sport in 1907, is honored with a memorial statue on the Old Historic Pier. He was brought over from Hawaii by Henry Huntington to launch the art.

VENICE ◆ F C3 ▲ *183.* Just south of Santa Monica, Venice enjoys a reputation as LA's bohemian playground, peopled by a motley mix of balding hippies, New Age gurus, artists and students. In such a free-wheeling climate, public art has thrived and numerous large-scale MURALS now grace Venice's façades: Rip Cronk's *Venice Reconstituted*, just off the boardwalk, is world famous. Also of note is the eccentric sculpture *Ballerina Clown* by Jonathan Borowsky at the corner of Main Street and Rose Avenue.

MARINA DEL REY ◆ F C4. Yachts, cruisers, speed and pleasure boats bob lazily in what is the country's largest small-craft marina with space for 6000 vessels. The boats are surrounded by monolithic apartment buildings and hotels whose design reflects the no-nonsense aesthetics of the 1960s. BURTON CHACE PARK is popular with picnickers and outdoor recreationists, while Cape Cod-style FISHERMAN'S VILLAGE has a few tourist restaurants and bars.

SOUTH BAY ◆ F C5. Manhattan Beach, Hermosa Beach and Redondo Beach collectively make up the communities of the South Bay. Of the three, Manhattan is the most affluent enclave, Hermosa has lively student vibes and Redondo a more down-to-earth ambience. Attractions here are recreational rather than cultural.

Beach volleyball is big, as are swimming, inline skating and surfing. Some of the best surfers gather near the Manhattan Beach Pier.

RANCHO PALOS VERDES ◆ F C6. This highland area, jutting dramatically into the Pacific Ocean, is an exclusive enclave of Mediterranean-style homes, quiet streets and horse trails, sandy coves and majestic cliffs. Besides spectacular coastal views, it offers surprise encounters with its resident peacocks, first introduced in the 1920s. The peninsula's POINT VICENTE INTERPRETIVE CENTER, 31501 Palos Verdes Drive West, is a prime spot for watching the migration of the Pacific gray whale, which travels from Alaska to Baja California and back between December and April. Adjacent to the 1926 Point Vicente Lighthouse, the center has an exhibit about local history and the coastal terrain.

SAN PEDRO ◆ F D6. In many ways San Pedro, which clings to the southern portion of the Palos Verdes Peninsula, is the exact opposite of its swanky neighbor. Gritty, working-class and inhabited by a rainbow of races, it is a colorful community with a down-to-earth spirit and some pretty stellar sights. Among them is the CABRILLO MARINE AQUARIUM in a Frank Gehry-designed building at 3720 Stephen M White Drive. It has taught visitors about the underwater creatures of Southern California for nearly sixty years. There are around forty aquariums divided into three main habitats: rocky shores, beaches and mudflats, and the open ocean. A 1941 car ferry terminal at 6th Street now functions as the home of the LOS ANGELES MARITIME MUSEUM, with more than 700 ship models, including an 18-foot one of the *Titanic*. Historical exhibits cover such varied subjects as early navigation by Native Americans, the whaling industry and tall ships.

VENICE'S EXOTIC CANALS ◆ J B3
Venice's other distinctive feature is its network of six idyllic CANALS, the brainchild of developer Abbot Kinney. In 1904, inspired by the Italian city, Kinney set out to create a superior, elegant theme park, called Venice of America, complete with canals, gondoliers and high-brow entertainment. But the public wanted more down-to-earth amusements and so Kinney obliged by giving them a roller coaster, indoor salt water swimming pool, camel rides and other diversions.
All these popular entertainments have now disappeared, but the VENICE CANAL WALKWAY enables visitors to meander through what's left of Kinney's original vision.

WAYFARER'S CHAPEL, RANCHO PALOS VERDES
A few miles south, at 5755 Palos Verdes Drive South, the 1951 WAYFARER'S CHAPEL is the most famous creation of Lloyd Wright (son of Frank). Made entirely from glass, redwood and stone, this almost ethereal meditation chapel is a memorial to the 18th-century Swedish religious reformer Emanuel Swedenborg. Thanks to its location, with splendid views over the Pacific, it is also a popular wedding spot. Jayne Mansfield and Mickey Hargitay were married here in 1958.

THE *QUEEN MARY*
Like the *Titanic*, the *Queen Mary* was an elegant city afloat, a stately vessel that allowed its many illustrious passengers (including such notables as Winston Churchill and Greta Garbo) to cross the Atlantic in style and comfort. Self-guided tours start with a video, then take in the engine room, various staterooms and dining rooms as well as the wheel room and the officers' sleeping quarters. The most spectacular sections, such as the first-class swimming pool and the grand Art Deco dining hall, can be seen only on a guided tour. Throughout the ship, exhibits and photographs further bring to life this bygone era of ocean travel.

T he southernmost community of LA County, Long Beach ◆ **F** E6 is the fifth largest city in California and home to the nation's busiest commercial port. It offers several attractions, including a newly revamped waterfront and a popular eating and entertainment mile along downtown's Pine Avenue.

LONG BEACH AQUARIUM OF THE PACIFIC ◆ K A2. This innovative complex reveals the beauty and mystery of the underwater world of the Pacific. The figures are staggering: 17 major habitats plus 30 smaller exhibits; 12,000 ocean creatures representing 500 species; tanks that range in size from 5000 to 350,000 gallons. But of course numbers say nothing about the visual surprises that await visitors. The journey of discovery kicks off dramatically in the GREAT HALL OF THE PACIFIC, where a full-scale model of a blue whale dangles from the ceiling and a three-story tank holds 400 predatory fish, including sharks and giant spiny sea stars. The stars of the section devoted to SOUTHERN & BAJA CALIFORNIA are the denizens of the fast-growing kelp forests ▲ *234* – endangered sea turtles, jellyfish, sea lions and seals. Next are the frigid waters of the NORTHERN PACIFIC, where typical residents include giant octopuses, sea otters and Japanese spider crabs. The most dramatic galleries are those of the TROPICAL PACIFIC, which recreate the lagoons and reefs of the Palau archipelago in the South Seas. The highlight is the tropical reef tank, home to more than 1000 creatures.

THE *QUEEN MARY* ◆ K A3. Launched in 1936, 25 years after the *Titanic's* disastrous maiden voyage, it was even larger and more luxurious. More than 1000 feet long, it catered for 1957 passengers and crossed the Atlantic 1001 times before being retired in 1967. Moored since then in Long Beach, the *Queen Mary* has been converted into a hotel.

NAPLES ◆ K C2
Around the same time that Abbot Kinney dreamed up his Venice of America ▲ *211*, Arthur Parsons dredged marshland in Alamitos Bay, in southern Long Beach, and built three islands linked by a network of canals. A private company offers gondola rides through this superior neighborhood.

LONG BEACH MUSEUM OF ART ◆ K B2. This small but choice collection sits adjacent to its original quarters, a 1912 Arts and Crafts house ● *68*, on a cliff at 2300 E Ocean Boulevard. The changing exhibits are drawn from the permanent collection, whose strong points are American decorative arts, early-20th-century European art, California Modernism and contemporary art (especially videos). In summer, the museum runs a popular concert series.

Served by ferry from Long Beach and San Pedro ▲ *211*, Catalina Island ◆ **C** A5 is a popular weekend getaway offering fresh air, clean water and a relaxed Mediterranean ambience. Catalina, which lies about 20 miles off the coast, is one of the rare, easily accessible islands in the Channel Islands chain, whose isolation has favored the development of unique plants and animals, now protected in a National Park.

AVALON. The main 'town' is tiny Avalon, about one mile square, where nearly all the hotels, restaurants, bars and outfitters are located. William Wrigley Jr, the chewing gum magnate from Chicago, bought the island in 1919 and hosted lavish parties for his Hollywood friends in the stylish circular Casino. Still a major landmark today, it contains a small historical museum and an Art Deco movie theater and ballroom. The ballroom, which is still used, had its heyday in the 1940s when the jazzband music played there was broadcast on the radio. The murals, which were painted by John G Beckman, notably in the movie theater, depict the underwater world of the region (including mermaids!) and the history of Southern California.

WRIGLEY BOTANICAL GARDEN. About 2 miles inland from Avalon is a beautiful botanical garden which contains plants unique to the island. Here too stands the rather bombastic Wrigley memorial, erected to the former owner of the island.

MAGIC KINGDOM ✪
It's easy to spend several days at Disneyland, especially in summer when long lines make it impossible to see everything in one day. Savvy visitors arrive early in the morning and head to the most popular attractions first. Lines are also shorter during lunchtime.

THE NEWEST DISNEY 'LAND'
Just south of the original Disneyland is the brand-new DISNEY'S CALIFORNIA ADVENTURES park whose seven themed areas celebrate the state's heritage and landmarks (separate admission). In between the two is DOWNTOWN DISNEY, a walking mall and fun zone lined by restaurants, stores, dance clubs and movie theaters (free).

Beautiful coastline, family-oriented amusement parks and large shopping malls are among the attractions that bring about 40 million visitors to Orange County each year. The county has 2.7 million inhabitants and is a mosaic of 34 independent cities, including Anaheim, home to Disneyland and the center of the tourist industry.

DISNEYLAND ◆ **C** B4. Opened in 1955, Disneyland, 1313 Harbor Boulevard, is the original of the giant theme parks and a product of the vision of animation pioneer Walt Disney ▲ *194*. Over the years, the attractions, which are updated periodically to reflect recent additions to the Disney stable, have become increasingly high-tech and special effects-oriented. Each year, millions of people stream through the gate and onto Main Street USA, an idealized version of an early-20th-century American high street. Employees disguised as Mickey Mouse, Roger Rabbit or other Disney characters often greet visitors as they stock up on souvenirs and candy before venturing into the park's several themed 'lands'. The undisputed highlight here is the thrilling Indiana Jones Adventure, a virtual breakneck journey to the mythical Temple of the Forbidden Eye aboard four-wheel-drive vehicles.
TOMORROWLAND features Space

Mountain, a hair-raising roller coaster ride through complete darkness, and Star Tours, a wild and wacky high-tech space adventure. New Orleans Square houses the Haunted Mansion, with an imaginative labyrinth as enchanting as it is creepy, as well as Pirates of the Caribbean, a gentle cruise through underground caves where hilariously drunken buccaneers celebrate, having buried their booty. The park's other sections are especially suited for younger children. FRONTIERLAND takes visitors back to the early days of America, complete with Tom Sawyer Island and a sternwheeler named for Mark Twain. The Big Thunder Mountain Railroad is a roller coaster most people will be able to stomach. At MICKEY'S TOONTOWN little ones can visit the homes of their favorite Disney cartoon characters and take a CarToonSpin with Roger Rabbit. Finally, there's FANTASYLAND, complete with the Sleeping Beauty's Castle.

KNOTTS BERRY FARM ◆ C B4. Older than Disneyland by more than two decades, Knotts was built around an Old West theme but there's nothing 'old' about the thrill rides and roller coasters dotting the 150-acre park at Buena Park. Some are clearly not suited for the faint-hearted: Supreme Scream plunges passengers down thirty stories in three seconds, while Boomerang sends them through six loops in less than a minute. Others are tamer if not without surprises, such as Big Foot Rapids, a drenching white water ride. Small children will delight in meeting Charlie Brown and other Peanuts characters at the charming Camp Snoopy. The park's original theme comes alive at Ghost Town, erected with buildings from actual historic mining towns from the West. Live shows, shops and restaurants round out the experience.

SANTA ANA ◆ C B4. The BOWERS MUSEUM OF CULTURAL ART seeks to explain the cultural complexity of African, Asian, Native American, Precolumbian and Oceanic peoples through their arts. The nearby Kidseum offers hands-on exhibits and experiences for children.

CRYSTAL CATHEDRAL ◆ C B4
(13280 Chapman Ave) This stunning house of worship, designed by American Philip Johnson, is a symphony in steel and glass and home to the congregation of televangelist Robert Schuller. Johnson chose a four-pointed star as the basis of the cathedral design, then filled out its towering façades with more than 10,000 panes of glass. It holds almost 3000 people.

Laguna Beach.

LAGUNA BEACH ART FESTIVALS

Laguna's artistic heritage is kept alive today by numerous galleries as well as several popular summer festivals. The most unusual and surprising festival is the Pageant of the Masters. Famous paintings are recreated on a large scale by locals, accurately dressed in period costumes and make-up. The actors then take up the exact position of the figures depicted in the painting and remain motionless to create the illusion of a tableau in two dimensions. The Festival of the Arts and the Sawdust Festival are both exhibitions that run parallel to the pageant, with the former focusing on fine arts and the latter on crafts. Laguna Beach is also famous for its theater, the Laguna Playhouse.

LAGUNA BEACH ◆ C B5. The prettiest of the Orange County coastal towns, Laguna Beach wouldn't look out of place if it was magically lifted off the map and transported to the French Riviera. Red-tiled villas cling to hillsides lush with vegetation that, in places, cascades all the way down to the edge of the Pacific. Cliffs and coves are connected by a band of white sand, and a relaxed ambience reigns throughout. Laguna Beach looks back on a long tradition as an artists' colony. Norman St Claire was among the first painters to be inspired by the village and its scenery in 1903. His presence drew other painters who liked to work in the open air, thus following the influence of Claude Monet and fellow French Impressionists. The Laguna Beach Art Association, founded in 1918 by Edgar Payne, grew out of this collection of artists and is the origin of the LAGUNA ART MUSEUM. This museum, situated on the beach at 307 Cliff Drive, has accumulated an impressive collection of American art – with an emphasis on works by Californians – from the late 19th century to the present. Curators mount several exhibits annually, representing both traditional art and such cutting-edge media as computer and performance art.

MISSION SAN JUAN CAPISTRANO ◆ C B5. Often called the 'Jewel of the California Missions', this beautiful complex at 31882 Camino Capistrano in the town of San Juan Capistrano, was the seventh in the chain of missions created by Franciscans in the 18th century. Padre Junípero Serra ● *24* himself officiated over its founding on November 1, 1776, and it grew into one of the largest and most important of the missions. The restored chapel named in Serra's honor contains a Spanish baroque altarpiece, smothered in gold leaf. A museum, book store and gift shop are also on the grounds. The museum contains religious objects, tools and vestments belonging to the first colonists. The town of San Juan Capistrano itself is famous for the swallows which return here each year in mid March to nest after wintering in South America. Their arrival is celebrated by popular festivals and parades.

San Diego

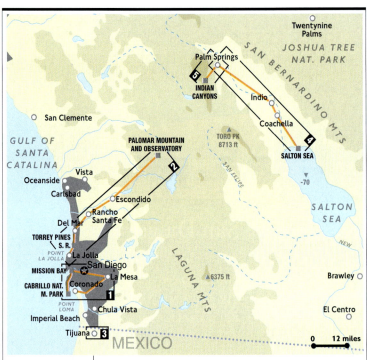

Just as today, San Diego's earliest inhabitants were drawn to the region some 20,000 years ago by its mild climate and fertile soil. The earliest culture, known as the San Dieguito Paleo-Indian, lived around 7500 BC along the coast and river valleys. The mountains and deserts formed a natural barrier from other tribes, and they lived peacefully, existing mainly on fruits and vegetables, acorns, small game and shellfish.

THE FIRST EUROPEANS. In September 1542, explorer Juan Rodríguez Cabrillo ▲ 224 landed at Point Loma and claimed the land for Spain. But Spain was busy establishing a trade route to the Philippines, and so the area was forgotten. In 1602, Don Sebastian Vizcaíno came in search of a safe harbor for Spanish galleons and named it for San Diego de Alcalá de Henares, a 15th-century saint.

THE MISSION PERIOD. In 1697, to exert control over its territory, Spain allowed the Jesuits to build 21 missions ● 32 from San José del Cabo to within 120 miles of San Diego. However, fear of the Jesuits' growing influence in Europe and strong Russian interest in the region led Spain to expel the priests in 1767 and establish new Franciscan missions every 30 miles along the coast. One of the first expeditions included Junípero Serra ● 24, a Franciscan friar who founded the first mission in Alta California on Presidio Hill on July 16, 1769, the date associated with the founding of San Diego. The missions helped Spain to extend its control over California, converted thousands of Indians to Christianity, introduced Spanish colonial architecture and helped to create the first highway, the Royal Road or *El Camino Real*. The Spanish also introduced European diseases that eventually wiped out 50 percent of the native Indian population.

THE RANCHOS. When Mexico began its battle for independence, payments to the San Diego military post dried up. Their reaction was to seek compensation in land grants from Spain. Some 33 land grants totaling about 950 square miles were made between 1822 and 1846. These grants (mostly of mission lands) were developed into sprawling cattle ranches that produced great wealth for a small elite. The bulk of San Diego's population of 800 remained in the *pueblo* of the Old Town beneath the Presidio.

SAN DIEGO, PART OF THE UNITED STATES. In 1850, California became the 31st state. San Diego grew slowly until the arrival of Alonzo Erastus Horton, a San Francisco businessman. Horton purchased 960 acres of waterfront property in 1867 for 33 cents an acre, and began development of New Town, the present downtown San Diego. The arrival of the railroad in the mid-1880s brought further growth to San Diego and the region. By the early 1900s, the city had became a major port for the US Navy and one of the main centers of aircraft manufacture, powerful industries that helped boost the city's economy throughout the 20th century.

OLD TOWN ◆ **P** B3

Situated beneath the mission and Presidio established by the Spanish in 1769, Old Town thrived until the 1870s when the city center was moved to its present location.

OLD TOWN STATE HISTORIC PARK. Some 20 historic adobe buildings, mostly from the mid-1800s, house museums, shops, galleries and restaurants, forming a square around the lovely Old Town plaza with its towering eucalyptus trees.

BAZAAR DEL MUNDO. Once the home of Pío Pico, California's last Mexican governor, Bazaar del Mundo with its tropical plants, strolling musicians, exotic drinks and the *tortilla* lady (making fresh tortillas on a hot stone) is what many San Diegans associate with Old Town today.

PRESIDIO PARK. In 1929, philanthropist George W Marston donated the majestic Presidio Park to the city. The park, situated on an emerald-green hill, offers dramatic views of San Diego, the Pacific and the mountains. The massive JUNIPERO SERRA MUSEUM, designed by William Templeton Johnston in 1928, occupies the site of the original fort and mission built by the Spanish in 1769. The museum's exhibits, artifacts and art, including Father Serra's vestments and records, trace San Diego's history prior to 1850.

SAN DIEGO AND ITS SURROUNDINGS ✪
San Diego and its surrounding region is an absolute must, with its endless beaches swept by the mighty Pacific and the rollers which delight the surfers, the Spanish-influenced architecture, new and old, and of course the nearby desert. This town, the second biggest in California, also has an intensely active cultural life. Tijuana ▲ *227* is close by, and offers the opportunity to cross the border into Mexico and sample its attractions.

MISSION SAN DIEGO DE ALCALÁ ● *62*
◆ **P** C2
The first Franciscan mission in California ● *24* was founded by Father Serra in 1769 on Presidio Hill. In 1774 the mission was moved to Valle del Rio San Diego where land was more fertile, and there were more potential converts. But the Kumeyaay Indians resisted, and in 1775 the mission was burned and nearly destroyed. It was rebuilt in 1781 and has since undergone several restoration projects. It remains an active parish church today.

219

**SAN DIEGO
BY NIGHT ★**
You must drive
through San Diego
at night because it is
then that downtown
seems to look its best.
The skyscrapers
are all lit up,
especially the neon
lights at the top of the
towers of Emerald
Plaza, while the
tramway snakes
across town in a
surrealist fashion.
The Coronado Bay
Bridge, outlined
in the sky by subtle
lighting, leads
straight to the hotel
of the same name.
Here in this Victorian
palace, you can
enjoy a drink and
reflect on the
great epoch when
Marilyn Monroe,
Tony Curtis and
Jack Lemmon
performed there
in the classic film
Some Like It Hot
● *90.*

DOWNTOWN, THE BUSY CITY

HORTON PLAZA SHOPPING CENTER ◆ Q B2. Horton Plaza, a
small square in center of downtown San Diego, was laid out in
1870 by San Diego developer Alonzo E Horton ▲ *219* to
provide a pleasant view for guests at his luxurious Horton
House Hotel. In 1985, the Plaza was transformed into a
bustling, multi-level shopping center with over 140 shops,
restaurants, boutiques and bistros.
US GRANT HOTEL ◆ Q B2. The Horton House Hotel was
razed in 1905 by Ulysses S Grant Jr, son of the 17th President
of the United States, to make way for a massive Italian-
Renaissance hotel in marble, steel and cement dedicated to
the late president. Although there have been many changes
over the years (the swimming pool is gone, the number of
rooms reduced to 280), the historic hotel with its crystal
chandeliers retains an elegant, genteel atmosphere.
GASLAMP QUARTER ◆ Q C2. Just to the southeast of Horton
Plaza lies the historic Gaslamp Quarter, a lively district of
over 100 restaurants, nightclubs and coffee shops. The
quarter was established as San Diego's business center in
1867, but by the end of the century it had become a seedy red-
light district known as the 'Stingaree' (where one could be
stung just as badly as by the local sting rays). A massive
facelift in the mid-1970s halted further neglect and
deterioration, restoring many of the buildings to their turn-of-
the-century glory. Today, this charming quarter, with its gas

The three hexagonal
towers of Emerald
Plaza, crowned at
night by their
sparkling neon rings.

street lamps, draws tourists and locals alike to enjoy the blend
of fine food, fun and culture.
EMERALD PLAZA. Brilliant emerald neon rings crown the
three hexagonal towers of Emerald Plaza, one of the most
distinctive skyscrapers in downtown San Diego. Designed by
C Kim in 1990, the hotel's lobby includes a dramatic 100-foot-
high atrium and a chandelier of green glass panels.
MUSEUM OF CONTEMPORARY ART. This is the permanent
second home of the Museum of Contemporary Art in La Jolla
▲ *225*. Permanent and traveling exhibits of modern painting,
sculpture and design are displayed among four small galleries
on two levels of this all-glass building in America Plaza.

SANTA FE RAILWAY DEPOT ◆ Q A2. The Santa Fe Railway Depot, designed by San Francisco architects Blakewell and Brown, was completed in 1914 just in time for the opening of the 1915–16 ▲ 222 Panama–California International Exposition. The largest railway station building in the US used by a single company, it was also the first successful adaptation of Spanish Mission Colonial Revival ● 64 style in a modern building. Borrowing design elements from California missions, Latin American churches and Roman basilicas, its most notable feature is its blue, yellow and white Hispano-Moorish tiled dome. The depot is the terminus of the nation's second-busiest Amtrak railway corridor, the Coaster commuter trains, and the San Diego Trolley light rail system.

EMBARCADERO ◆ Q A3-B3. In 1911, the tidelands along San Diego's bayfront were filled in for industrial use and a commercial pier was constructed at the foot of Broadway. It was not until the mid 1980s that the city redeveloped the Embarcadero and Harbor Drive into the present cultural and recreational waterfront. San Diego's MARITIME MUSEUM, at the northern end of the Embarcadero, is housed in the Berkeley, an 1898 ferryboat that connected Oakland with San Francisco for almost half a century. The *Berkeley's* decks include numerous models and exhibits of maritime history, a research library, an active ship model shop and a bookstore. The museum also includes the *Medea*, a steam-powered luxury yacht built in Scotland in 1904, and the *Star of India*, the oldest square-rigged sailing ship in the world. Built in 1863, the Star of India made 21 circumnavigations of the globe and is still fully operational.

SEAPORT VILLAGE ◆ Q A3-B3. Quaint Seaport Village lies in a landscaped harborside park where Kettner Boulevard meets West Harbor Drive. Three themed plazas representing harbor villages of a century ago include gift and clothing stores, restaurants and several specialty food and coffee shops. Seaport Village is also home to a late 19th century carousel built by Charles Looff

CORONADO ◆ P B4

Originally known as Peninsula of San Diego, separating San Diego Bay from the Pacific Ocean, the 'enchanted isle' of Coronado was purchased for $110,000 in 1885 by a syndicate headed by railroad promoter Elisha Babcock. A team of architects was hired to build the sprawling Hotel del Coronado, a $1 million, 399-room luxury resort that opened in 1888. The historic 'Del' as it is affectionately known, remains the island's centerpiece and continues to draw visitors to its gracious Victorian atmosphere. Today, Coronado is accessible via the San Diego–Coronado Bay Bridge, a two-mile long span built in 1969, with 30 concrete towers shaped like mission arches. Orange Avenue, the charming main street of Coronado, is known for its restaurants, galleries, bookstores and theater.

VILLA MONTEZUMA, A VICTORIAN PAINTED LADY ◆ P C3
Perched high above San Diego on Golden Hill, the ornate Villa Montezuma, built in Queen Anne style in 1887, is the unique artistic creation of Jesse Shepard, a British spiritualist, musician and author. It is a superb example of Victorian architecture, with its onion dome, stained-glass windows, and redwood shingles, and was carefully restored after years of neglect and fire damage in the mid-1980s. Today Shepard's 'Palace for the Arts' is a monument to the exotic and romantic styles of the late 19th century, and is open as a museum.

'THE DEL' ● 67
The luxurious Victorian hotel, opened in 1888, was one of the first hotels in California to have electricity. Thomas Edison himself was in charge of the installation. It was here too that the future King Edward VIII first met Wallis Simpson in 1920.

SAN DIEGO
BALBOA PARK

The California Building
(below).

In 1868, the Board of Trustees of the city of San Diego set aside some 1400 acres for the city park. The barren mesas and canyons above the city were transformed by horticulturist Kate Sessions. She began in 1892, operating a private nursery in exchange for planting 100 trees a year in the park and donating another 300 to plant throughout the city. Two international expositions held in the park in 1915 and 1935 helped to put the city on the map and created the concentration of architecturally significant buildings and museums that draws millions of visitors to San Diego today.
THE SAN DIEGO ZOO ◆ R A1-B1. Concerned about the fate of about 50 animals in cages left over from the Panama-California Exposition of 1915–16, Dr Harry Wegeforth and two fellow doctors created the San Diego Zoological Society. Today, it is the largest zoo in North America, some 4239 specimens representing 816 species and subspecies, including many endangered animals, live among 100 acres of tropical and subtropical vegetation. The animals are displayed in open-air enclosures similar to their natural habitat, ranging from Tiger River, Hippo Beach and Sun Bear Forest to the African Rock Kopje, Rain Forest Aviary and Gorilla Tropics.
REUBEN H FLEET SPACE THEATER AND SCIENCE CENTER ◆ R B2. The world's first tilted dome theater and planetarium is just across the Plaza de Balboa from the San Diego Natural History Museum. Planetarium shows and sensational films made in the Omnimax large format are presented daily,

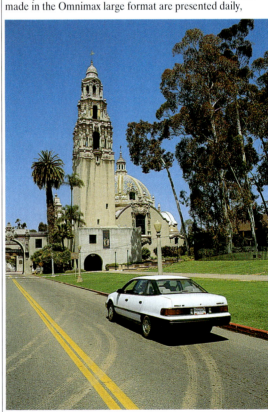

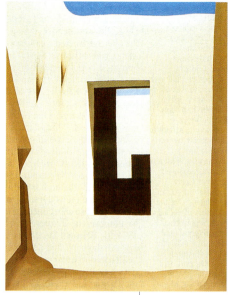

In the Patio I (1946) by Georgia O'Keeffe
(San Diego Museum of Art).

though the film themes, like many of the exhibits in the adjacent Science Center, are not always strictly scientific .

CASA DE BALBOA ◆ R B2. The Casa de Balboa was designed in Spanish Renaissance-style for the 1915–16 Panama-California Exposition. Today, this ornate building houses four museums, dedicated to history, sports, model railroading and photographic arts.

TIMKEN MUSEUM OF ART ◆ R B2. One of the more recent buildings in Balboa Park, the Timken Museum of Art was opened in 1965 to house a small collection of Spanish and Italian masters. The collection now includes works by other European masters, such as Rubens, Corot, Frans Hals and Fragonard. There is also a small but superb collection of Russian icons.

SAN DIEGO MUSEUM OF ART ◆ R B2. Inspired by works of art in the Exposition of 1915–16, San Diego decided to build its own museum of art. In 1924, architect William Templeton Johnson was given carte blanche to create a museum. The ornate Spanish Colonial building on the Plaza de Panama was completed two years later, and today holds a large collection of American, European, Asian and modern art.

SAN DIEGO MUSEUM OF MAN ◆ R A2. This museum is housed in the 1915 California Building ● *65* with its tiled dome and 100-bell carillon tower. The original emphasis on the story of man through the ages has been narrowed to concentrate on the peoples of the Western Hemisphere.

SPRECKELS ORGAN PAVILION ◆ R B2. Donated by Adolph Spreckles ▲ *131*, the sugar magnate, in 1915, the Pavilion boasts one of the largest outdoor organs in the world. The organ, which contains 4400 pipes ranging in size from 4 centimeters to 10 meters, is perched on a raised stage and is protected from the elements by a massive metal curtain. Recitals are held every Sunday afternoon, rain or shine, and on Monday evenings in the summer. The pillared walkways, designed by Harrison Albright, form Corinthian colonnades in a semicircle around seating for 2400.

SAN DIEGO AEROSPACE MUSEUM AND HALL OF FAME ◆ R A3. Designed in 1934 by Walter Teague, the circular Ford building was more Modernist in spirit that any other exhibition space in Balboa Park. The building that once housed the Ford Motor Company's automobile assembly line today is home to the Aerospace Museum and International Aerospace Hall of Fame. Exhibits trace the history of flight to early space travel and include a replica of Charles Lindbergh's *Spirit of St Louis* (the original was built in San Diego). Biographies and photographs of famous aviators are also displayed in the Hall of Fame.

ALSO WORTH SEEING

SAN DIEGO NATURAL HISTORY MUSEUM ◆ R B2 Traveling exhibitions on reptiles, wild cats, dinosaurs and bears occupy the ground floor. Permanent exhibits include a walk-through mine tunnel, a hall of desert ecology and an insect zoo.

SAN DIEGO AUTOMOTIVE MUSEUM ◆ R A3 On display are historic, collectible, and unusual automobiles and motorcycles, mostly from private collections.

MARSTON HOUSE ◆ R A3 Built by George W Marston, founder of Presidio Park ▲ *219* and Anza Borrego State Park ▲ *246*. The elegant house was designed by Irving J Gill ● *70* and William Hebbard in 1905 and today is a showplace for the decorative furnishings and art of the American Arts and Crafts movement ● *68*.

JUAN RODRÍGUEZ CABRILLO
Spanish explorer Juan Rodriguez Cabrillo landed on what is now Point Loma in September 1542 and claimed the area for the King of Spain. Cabrillo had been sent by Viceroy Antonio de Mendoza in Mexico City to explore the Californian coast and find the supposed Strait of Anián between the Atlantic and Pacific Oceans. A summary of his log from September 23 tells of 'good land with great valleys' and 'a very good enclosed port' to which he gave the name of San Miguel, the name of one of his ships. After a stop of about 10 days, Cabrillo continued exploring the Californian coast, but never returned. He died in January 1543 of wounds received in a skirmish with Indians on one of the Channel Islands ▲ *240* off Santa Barbara.

SHELTER ISLAND ◆ P A3. Shelter Island, in the lee of Point Loma, was created when dredged silt and mud from San Diego Bay was deposited on a submerged shoal. Ever since the city constructed a causeway to Point Loma in 1950, the island, which forms a shelter for thousands of small boats, has become a popular spot for restaurants, hotels and marinas, as well as the home of the San Diego Yacht Club.

POINT LOMA ◆ P A4. This narrow peninsula of land some 500 feet high juts out into San Diego Bay and protects the harbor from winter storms. One of the city's most beautiful neighborhoods, Point Loma is also home to Fort Rosecrans National Cemetery and several military installations.

CABRILLO NATIONAL MONUMENT PARK. The park, which is named for Juan Rodríguez Cabrillo, the Spanish explorer who first set foot on the coast in 1542, offers a dramatic panorama of San Diego, the harbor and the mountains of Mexico. A small museum tells the story of Cabrillo's voyage, and his statue stands a short distance from the Old Point Loma Lighthouse, the southernmost beacon on the Pacific Coast 1854–91. Between December and March, enormous Pacific gray whales can often be viewed from Whale Overlook as they head south to calve in the warm lagoons of Baja California. A nature trail around the point leads to a series of pools along the Pacific side where marine life can be seen, especially during the very low tides of December.

MISSION BAY ◆ P A2-B2. This tidal marshland was originally named 'False Bay' by a party of Spanish sailors who thought their ship had sailed without them. As they began walking toward La Paz, 800 miles to the south, they found the ship still at anchor in San Diego Bay. Today, channels guide the San Diego River to the Pacific, marshlands are dredged to form coves, islands and sandy beaches and Mission Bay is an aquatic recreational center. Some 90 acres of public parkland and 27 miles of shoreline surround this water park where families come to ride bicycles, picnic, fly kites, sail, swim and water ski. The nearby communities of Mission Beach and

Ocean Beach cater to a colorful mix of students and surfers, and offer a variety of lively eating establishments.

SEA WORLD. The key attraction of Mission Bay is Sea World, a 150-acre marine-life theme park on the southern shore. A cross between entertainment and education, Sea World offers a variety of attractions such as its Shamu killer whale, penguin and shark encounters, a white-water thrill ride, and bottle-nosed dolphins.

FROM LA JOLLA TO PALOMAR MOUNTAIN

From Coronado's Silver Strand to Trestles, the famous San Onofre surfing break on Orange County border, the rugged coastline alternates between charming seaside towns and sandstone bluffs overlooking wide, sandy beaches, clear aquamarine water and the never-ending waves of the Pacific.

LA JOLLA ◆ P A1. Contemporary guides describe it as 'the Jewel of the Sea,' mistakenly deriving 'Jolla' from the early Spanish word *joya* (meaning 'jewel') when in fact it comes from the word *hoya* (meaning 'hollow'). To many, this gem of a village set above dramatic cliffs and sea caves, represents both. Originally created as a summer colony in the late 19th century, La Jolla owes much of its charm to Ellen Browning Scripps who began buying land in 1896. Heiress of a newspaper business, Scripps hired San Diego architect Irving Gill ● 70 to design the elegant buildings that are her legacy to the town.

MARINE GROTTOS. Around a promontory at the extreme north of the town are seven grottos accessible from the sea. You can hire kayaks at nearby La Jolla Shores in order to explore, but SUNNY JIM'S CAVE can be reached from the Cave Store, by a staircase of 144 steps built in 1902.

THE ART OF BEACH LIFE ● *45, 47* Immortalized in the 1960s by the ballads of the Beach Boys ● *52*, typical beach scenes range from the oiled bodies and volleyball heaven of Mission Beach to secret surfer spots accessible only by way of steep, twisting tracks. The beach is a sacred place that highlights the difference between the East and West coasts. Every weekend people come here to see and be seen, and to practice their favourite sport, be it surfing, jogging, cycling …

SAN DIEGO MUSEUM OF CONTEMPORARY ART, LA JOLLA Once the oceanfront home of Ellen Browning Scripps, the 1916 building designed by Irving Gill ● *70* is now the cultural centerpiece of La Jolla. Like its downtown branch ▲ *220*, the MCA offers exhibitions of post-1950s art and hosts concerts by the La Jolla Chamber Orchestra and an annual Animation Film Festival. Tucked behind the museum, within a stone's throw of the sea, is Pacific Union, an unusual miniature park designed by George Trakas in 1989.

ALSO WORTH SEEING
STEPHEN BIRCH
AQUARIUM MUSEUM
◆ **P** A1 Perched high
above La Jolla
Shores, the Aquarium
offers educational
exhibits, an outdoor
tidepool and more
than 30 tanks
containing marine
creatures from the
whole Pacific coast.
Le SAN DIEGO WILD
ANIMAL PARK in the
San Pasqual Valley,
near Escondido
◆ **C** C5 was established
in 1972 as a breeding
sanctuary for
endangered species.
It is home to over
3000 creatures on
some 1800 acres.
Asian and African
animals roam freely
through areas similar
to their native
habitats.

**MISSION SAN LUIS
REY DE FRANCIA**
(on the north coast
of Del Mar ◆ **C** B5)
Founded in 1789,
San Luis Rey was the
18th Californian
mission and the last
to be established by
Fermín Francisco de
Lasuén, the
Franciscan friar who
succeeded Junípero
Serra ● *24*. Named
for the 13th-century
King Louis IX of
France (St Louis), the
mission was one of
the largest and most
important of the
Californian mission
chain. It flourished
for many years, aided
by some 3000 Native
American Indians
who lived and worked
there, raising
livestock and growing
small crops. Age and
neglect took its toll in
the mid 19th century,
but today San Luis
Rey has been
restored, and many of
its religious artifacts
are on display in a
small museum.

SALK INSTITUTE FOR BIOLOGICAL STUDIES ◆ C B6. Across
from the University of California, San Diego campus on
North Torrey Pines Road is the biological research institute
founded by Jonas Salk in 1960. Renowned architect Louis
Kahn designed the stark, reinforced concrete buildings
around a smooth marble plaza, broken only by a thin sluice of
water flowing toward the Pacific. A controversial addition by
Anshen + Allen was completed in 1995.

TORREY PINES STATE RESERVE ◆ C B6. First discovered by
European mariners in the 16th century, the Punto de los
Arboles was the only pine-covered bluff for miles along the
coastline and was used as a navigational aid. Charles Parry, an
American doctor and botanist for the US–Mexico Boundary
Survey, discovered the unknown species and named it *Pinus
torreyana* after John Torrey, an eminent botanist. Established
as a reserve in 1922, the park's spectacular trails traverse
canyons and sandstone cliffs studded with the peculiar, long-
needled pine. Wooden platforms along the trails offer
spectacular views of the ocean.

DEL MAR ◆ C C6. A quaint seaside resort and chic residential
community, Del Mar is a favorite coastal destination. The
Del Mar Plaza, a Mediterranean-inspired piazza with endless
views, boutiques, gourmet restaurants and a marvelous
bookstore café, has become the stylish center of the town.
Del Mar is often overwhelmed in the summer months because
of its famed thoroughbred race track, the annual Del Mar
Fair and its bathing and surfing beach.

RANCHO SANTA FE ◆ C C5. Rancho San Dieguito was
purchased by the Santa Fe Railroad in the early 20th century
to grow millions of eucalyptus trees for railroad ties. When
the wood was discovered to be unsuitable, the land was sold
to shareholders. Now this elegant enclave of large homes and
horse farms has been ranked as one of the most desirable
places to live in the United States. Architect Lillian Rice
designed the historic Inn at Rancho Santa Fe in 1923 as well
as most of the whitewashed adobe buildings that line the main
street. Rancho Santa Fe boasts one of the finest restaurants in

California (Mille Fleurs) as well as one of the country's foremost specialty produce farms, the Chino family's vegetable shop.

PALOMAR MOUNTAIN AND OBSERVATORY ◆ C C5. Since 1948, Mount Palomar, with its prominent white dome high in the Cleveland National Forest, has been best known for the Hale Telescope. Astronomical exhibits and a photo gallery at the facility explain how the giant telescope (one of the largest in the world) operates, and how it captures views of the universe over one billion light years away. Below in the village of Palomar Mountain lies the entrance to the PALOMAR MOUNTAIN STATE PARK. The park offers trout fishing and marvelous hiking trails that wind through coniferous forest and flowering trees, offering spectacular views toward the coast on clear days. Rains on the valley floor often result in extreme weather shifts on the mountain (10,000 feet above sea level), ranging from hoar frosts to driving blizzards.

THE MEXICAN FRONTIER

TIJUANA ◆ C C6. Fifteen minutes south of downtown San Diego, the freeway becomes Mexico's Highway 1, sweeping drivers into another world. Tijuana, Mexico's second-largest city (above), is a bustling metropolis of stark contrasts, from crowded shopping arcades, sophisticated restaurants and colorful markets, to cardboard shantytowns and other signs of poverty. Its economy is based on tourist dollars seeking out bargains, drinks and nightlife, and the multinational manufacturing industries that operate along the border.
AVENIDA REVOLUCIÓN. Along the traditional tourist shopping street, Avenida Revolución, and among its many arcades, visitors can purchase (and haggle for) items such as perfume, arts and crafts and silver and leather goods.
CENTRO CULTURAL TIJUANA. Designed by Pedro Ramírez Vasquez and Manuel Rosen Morrison, this modern, sand-colored building has been the cultural center of the city since 1982, offering everything from art exhibits, classical music, modern dance and experimental theater, to seminars, outdoor concerts and giant-screen movies.

CROSSING THE BORDER ✪
The border crossing is one of the busiest in the world. Crossing the border by car requires inexpensive Mexican automobile insurance, which can be purchased before the border. Although most vehicles are waved through without formality, travelers returning to the USA will need proof of US citizenship or a passport. Most non-American citizens require passports but no visas to enter Mexico, but it is advisable to check with the Mexican consulate in your home country before departure. Once inside Mexico, directions for drivers can become confusing. For those who prefer to cross by foot, there are many parking lots on the US side of the border where visitors may leave their vehicles, cross the pedestrian bridge, and take a taxi into downtown Tijuana. The San Diego Trolley also runs directly from downtown San Diego to the border.

COUNTLESS DATES
In 1912, date palms from Algeria were introduced into the Coachella Valley, and today they produce about 17,500 tonnes of dates a year. The National Date Festival, held at Indio every February since the end of the 1940s, celebrates the end of the harvest for ten days.

Palm Springs, with palm trees stretching off into the distance.

From Salton Sea to Palm Springs

Twenty-five miles east of San Diego, the landscape changes dramatically. Green valleys and boulder-strewn hillsides change to pine- and oak-forested mountains that plunge down some 7000 feet to the gullies and badlands of the Anza Borego desert. Named for Spanish explorer Juan Bautista de Anza and the Spanish *borrego*, or bighorn sheep, this state park is the largest in the nation. Once home to the San Dieguito and Cahuilla tribes of Native Americans, the desert later became little more than an inhospitable stretch of the all-season Sonora Road (renamed the Southern Emigrant Trail) that brought settlers to California during the 1849 gold rush. Today, the Anza Borego Desert State Park ◆ C D6 ▲ *246* offers winter and spring visitors a window onto an intriguing geologic past and thriving desert ecosystem.

SALTON SEA ◆ C D5. The Salton Sea lies at the northeastern corner of the Anza Borego Desert State Park, some 228 feet below sea level. This inland sea was created in 1905 when a Colorado River dike broke during construction of the All-American Canal. Despite concerns at the water's extreme salinity, the Salton Sea today is a popular site for boaters, water-skiers, anglers and birdwatchers.

COACHELLA VALLEY ◆ C D5. From the Salton Sea, Highway 86 runs north through the Coachella Valley to Indio and Palm Springs. This rich agricultural valley produces grapefruit, watermelon and other produce, especially dates.

PALM DESERT LIVING WILDLIFE RESERVE AND BOTANICAL PARK ◆ C D5. Established in 1970, the wilderness hiking trails (or guided tram) offer views of some 400 desert animals representing over 150 species, including coyotes, bighorn sheep, oryx, golden eagles, mountain lions and wolves. The park's lush botanical gardens represent ten different North American desert ecosystems.

PALMS TO PINES HIGHWAY ◆ C C5-D5. From the cacti, sage and creosote bush of the low desert to the 5000 feet Santa Rosa Summit, this spectacular scenic driving tour passes

through several ecosystems ● *20* and offers dramatic views along the way. From Mountain Center, Highway 234 continues on to the quaint alpine village of Idyllwild, a popular vacation spot with lodges, restaurants, shops, campgrounds and Idyllwild Arts Academy, the renowned college and summer arts academy.

PALM SPRINGS AND ITS SURROUNDINGS ◆ **C** C4-C5

For thousands of years, Native American Indians lived beside the natural hot springs and crystal clear waters of the Coachella Valley's palm canyons. Diseases brought by Spanish and, later, American settlers, all but wiped out the original inhabitants of what had become known as Agua Caliente. The heated mineral waters bubbling out of the ground did not go unnoticed by settlers heading to the gold fields of California. The site was a popular stage-coach stop, and by the late 19th century, hotels and homes had been built, and Palm Springs had become a fashionable health spa.

DESERT FASHION PLAZA. The chic life style of Palm Springs is evident in its many specialty shops, trendy restaurants and art galleries. The boutiques in the new Desert Fashion Plaza, a pedestrian mall in the city center, rival those on Rodeo Drive ▲ *202* in Beverly Hills. Although private clubs and bougainvillea-draped walls screen much of the city's glamour from visitors, the rich and famous are often spotted along the palm-lined downtown shopping streets, Indian Canyon and Palm Canyon.

VILLAGE GREEN HERITAGE CENTER. Four historic buildings in a quiet downtown oasis offer views of Palm Springs' frontier past. The oldest building, the McCallum Adobe, was built in 1884 by Judge John Guthrie McCallum, founder of the Palm Valley Colony. His house, moved brick-by-brick from its original site in 1952, is now home to the PALM SPRINGS HISTORICAL SOCIETY. The MISS CORNELIA WHITE HOUSE, built in 1893 of railroad ties, displays early-20th-century antique furnishings. RUDDY'S GENERAL STORE MUSEUM features some 6000 unused dry goods on shelves exactly as they would have been in the 1930s. The AGUA CALIENTE CULTURAL MUSEUM features artifacts, jewelry, music and photographs of the indigenous Cahuilla Indians.

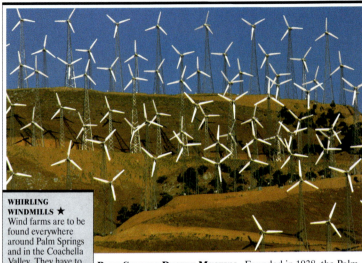

WHIRLING WINDMILLS ★
Wind farms are to be found everywhere around Palm Springs and in the Coachella Valley. They have to be seen, as they look like elegant figures marching across the hills in rhythm. With the desert as a backdrop, these giant figures with their pure lines make a beautiful and unforgettable sight.

WINDMILLS TOUR
The Wintec Wind Farm, about 15 minutes west of Palm Springs near Interstate Highway 10, is one of the area's most unique environmental and educational attractions. A forest of giant turbines, positioned to catch the winds rushing through the San Gorgonio Pass, produces pollution-free electricity. Electric buses (powered by windmills) take visitors on a tour of this fascinating 21st-century energy source, one of only six such massive wind farms in the world.

PALM SPRINGS DESERT MUSEUM. Founded in 1938, the Palm Springs Desert Museum offers collections, exhibitions and programs dealing with natural science, art and the performing arts. The museum's permanent collection features 19th- and 20th-century works focusing on contemporary Californian, western American, Native American and Precolumbian art. The McCallum Natural Science Wing features a diorama of the Coachella Valley and exhibits of desert life. Ballet, modern dance, classical music and drama performances are held in the impressive state-of-the-art ANNENBERG THEATER. Two marvelous nature trails leading from the museum into the Mount San Jacinto State Park, as well as the museum's sculpture gardens, fountains, café and store, make for a fascinating cultural experience.

PALM SPRINGS AERIAL TRAMWAY. One of Southern California's most popular attractions, the Palm Springs Aerial Tramway, opened in 1963, has just undergone a $7 million renovation. The 2½-mile trip to the top is the largest vertical cable rise in the United States and the second largest in the world. Two new Swiss gondolas (with rotating floors) take 80 passengers to the top of Mount San Jacinto (8500 feet) in less than 15 minutes, offering 360° views of five different ecosystems ranging from Sonoran Desert to Alaskan alpine wilderness. Hiking, cross-country skiing (in winter), camping and picnicking are available at the top, as well as superb views on a clear day.

INDIAN CANYONS. Long before the arrival of Europeans, the abundant water and plant life in the Palm, Murray, Andreas, Tahquitz and Chino Canyons (5 miles south of Palm Springs) supported several communities of Agua Caliente Cahuilla Indians. Today, visitors hiking through these spectacular oases of desert fan palms (Palm and Andreas Canyons contain the most wild palm trees in the world) can see traces of the Cahuilla people in rock art, mortars and metates used for preparing food. Bighorn sheep, wild ponies and other animals can be viewed on the rocky slopes above the canyons. A trading post near the entrance to the 15-mile Palm Canyon offers hiking maps, refreshments and Indian arts and crafts.

National Parks of California

▲ NATIONAL PARKS OF CALIFORNIA
INTRODUCTION

In 1890, the first three American national parks were created, all in California. These included Yosemite ▲ 254, Sequoia and Grants Grove National Parks, later regrouped in the Sequoia and Kings Canyon National Parks ▲ 250, in large part due to the inspirational writings of John Muir. These parks were conceived to preserve both nature and natural resources, such as watersheds, whose value went beyond the purely aesthetic. However, the National Park Service was not established until 1916, with the mandate to preserve the country's most spectacular natural areas in perpetuity.

HISTORY OF LOGGING IN CALIFORNIA AND CREATION OF PARKS. The state of California has long been exploited for its vast and valuable natural resources. The first European settlers recognized the prairies, oak and other woodlands and grasslands as potential grazing sites and soon were raising large herds of cattle and sheep throughout the state. The Gold Rush of 1849 ● 34 brought thousands of new settlers who sought quick wealth in the 'Mother Lode'. Those who were unsuccessful in the pursuit of gold found other ways to prosper from the natural environment. The vast wetlands of the Central Valley ● 21 were diked and drained for conversion to rich and fertile agricultural fields. The vast mountain forests were logged for their timber. The giant sequoia and redwood groves were considered by the early loggers to be an unending supply of fine lumber for construction and carpentry ▲ 154. The harvesting swept through northern California and the Sierras, only slowing down in the latter part of the 20th century due to diminishing resources, and public pressure to preserve the meager remnants of the old forests still standing. The work of John Muir and other early visionaries led to the concept of setting aside large tracts of natural areas to be preserved for future generations to enjoy. The national and state park systems resulted, and have successfully maintained, studied and restored remarkable natural areas that can be enjoyed today.

DAMS AND WATER DIVERSION IN CALIFORNIA. Water is a valuable commodity in this highly populated and drought-ridden state. California is a web of waterways, with many streams and rivers flowing down from the Sierra Nevada and Cascade Range to the Central Valley. These once wild rivers are

> 'Climb the mountains and get their good tidings.
> Nature's peace will flow into you as sunshine flows into trees.'
>
> John Muir

now tapped extensively for agriculture and city water supplies. Dams have been built in the Sierra to provide water supplies for the major cities. Streambeds have been diverted to direct water to irrigation canals. The vast wetlands of the Central Valley have been drained and converted to farmland. Today, government agencies work to preserve the scant remaining natural river habitats and wetlands, and to restore waterways and their native fish populations.

Types of protected areas. Within the state of California are a variety of natural protected areas, all with a well-defined status. The eight National Parks have the greatest level of protection. The federal government also manages a national seashore, five marine sanctuaries, five national monuments of historical or geological importance, thirty wildlife refuges, one national reserve, twenty-two national forests with fifty-five wilderness areas and three recreation areas, two of these in Los Angeles and San Francisco. In addition, there are two hundred state parks and beaches. The national forests and sanctuaries are managed for wise use and conservation (including recreation and education) as well as resource utilization (such as fishing, grazing and timber harvesting).

The multiplicity of nature. The National Parks are part of the Californian myth, because they remind people of the epoch when the West was virgin territory, still to be tamed and conquered. Today, these parks still arouse awe because their very huge and amazing diversity evoke strong feelings: in one and the same state you can experience the intense heat of the desert, the deep shadow and majesty of the sequoia forests, the strange beauty of lava flows or geysers and the vertiginous thrill of the mountain peaks.

John Muir's Legacy
John Muir, the pioneering conservationist and naturalist, visited Yosemite for the first time in 1868 and remained for the rest of his days, exploring the vast wilderness of the Sierra Nevada. He observed and described nature in keen detail. He wrote of its wonders, moving the political powers of the day to preserve the most spectacular parts of these mountains as national parks for perpetuity. His early ecological vision inspired the concept of a national park system in America and saw beyond the mere preservation of scenic wonders to the protection of entire ecosystems.

John Muir (below, right) with the naturalist John Burroughs.

The 1100-mile-long
coastline and offshore waters of
California display a great diversity of
marine life and terrain. Biological productivity is
high here, in large part due to the cold California Current
mixing with deeper, nutrient-rich water along the central coast,
where the narrow continental shelf is dissected by deep
submarine canyons reaching toward the shore. More types
of life occur in the Southern California Bight, where the
cold northern waters meet the subtropical current from the
south. Thus in California's offshore waters can be found
typically northern temperate species as well as subtropical
marine species.

KELP FORESTS

The underwater habitat is the realm of the largest, fastest growing marine algae, the giant kelp. This algae can grow up to a foot a day, reaching 100 feet in length, with graceful fronds reaching toward the surface, swaying with the current. It grows on rocky bottoms close to shore, which provide a solid anchor. Invertebrates use the kelp for shelter and as a food source. Rockfish raise their young in the protection of the fronds.

BLUE WHALE

HUMPBACKED WHALE

GRAY WHALE

DOLPHIN

KILLER WHALE

MARINE MAMMALS

Six species of seals and sea lions and over 27 species of dolphins and whales occur in Californian waters. From the shore, the visitor can view gray whales migrating, catch glimpses of dolphins surfacing, spot sea otters feeding, and observe seals and sea lions resting on the rocks. A boat trip provides even more opportunities for seeing whales, dolphins and porpoises, as well as sea birds and perhaps sharks and sea turtles.

There are five national marine sanctuaries along the Californian coast. These contain unique biological and geological resources and habitats, which are protected and managed by the federal government. Public education programs strive to interpret these areas for visitors who want to learn more about such marine environments.

A herd of tule elk lives on the northern point of the peninsula.

PENINSULA RESULTING FROM SAN ANDREAS FAULT ● 18
The San Andreas Fault runs along the eastern border of the park, forming the long, narrow Tomales Bay and Olema Valley. The 100-square-mile Point Reyes Peninsula is on the west side and has a different geology and vegetation from the east side of the park, a result of the slow northwestward movement of the Pacific Plate (a total of 280 miles in the past 30 million years). Point Reyes juts out ten miles into the Pacific Ocean, making it a natural stopping-off point for migrating birds and an excellent whale-watching area. Recreational pursuits include hiking, biking, kayaking, horseback riding and backpacking. The climate is amazingly constant all year round, with only a ten degree temperature variation between the foggy, windy summers and the moderately stormy winters.

Point Reyes National Seashore ◆ **A** B6 is much more than a seashore: it is a nature lover's paradise. Trails crisscross the 71,000 acre park, and habitats include marshy wetlands, rolling grassy hillsides, oak woodlands and forested coastal slopes, together with long sandy beaches, rocky cliffs and tide pools. The land was designated as a national seashore to protect the rural nature of the landscape, including the late-19th-century dairy farms, and to prevent future loss of natural areas.

BEAR VALLEY VISITORS CENTER. Realistic natural history displays explore the many habitats and species. The EARTHQUAKE TRAIL demonstrates the geological forces that shaped the region. It leads the walker round a dramatic circuit with rifts in the ground and a barn knocked off its foundations, striking evidence of the moment during the 1906 San Francisco earthquake ● *28* when the land moved 20 feet north.

MULE DEER
Russet in summer and brown in winter, the color of its coat varies with the seasons. The male develops its antlers in the summer.

Cultural history is explored through exhibits at the KULE LOKLO MIWOK VILLAGE, a restored Native American coastal settlement. One of the most popular hiking trails, the Bear Valley Trail, begins at the center. It is an easy eight-mile circular trail through wooded hillsides to the beach.

SIR FRANCIS DRAKE BOULEVARD. The main scenic road runs for 20 miles north-south through the park, passing through rolling pasturelands with historic dairy farms. It passes the Great Beach, one of the longest beaches in the state. Its wind-swept dunes, rough waves and treacherous surf make for dramatic beach walks, but swimming is dangerous. The road leads to the POINT REYES LIGHTHOUSE (right). To reach the lighthouse, you must park and hike up the road to the tiny visitors center, and then down a hefty set of stairs out onto a rugged point. DRAKES BEACH, another long, sandy beach, was named for Sir Francis Drake, who landed here in 1579. It has an informative visitor center.

NORTH OF POINT REYES. In the northern section of the park, take PIERCE POINT ROAD towards TOMALES POINT to observe elk, watch for whales, visit tide pools, or hike the easy-to-moderate TOMALES POINT SHORELINE TRAIL for rugged shoreline vistas and elk-sighting. A herd of over 400 reintroduced tule elk roam the meadows in this region. The trail to ABBOTS LAGOON is an easy three-mile round trip that leads through a marshy area with excellent birdwatching.

SOUTH OF THE PARK. Drive to the southern end of the park by taking Highway 1 from Olema to Bolinas Lagoon. At low tide, you can explore the tide pools at DUXBURY POINT. Serious birdwatchers can visit the POINT REYES BIRD OBSERVATORY at the end of the road. The park is known to be home for over 350 species of birds, including migratory birds, seabirds, shorebirds and birds of prey. Here also is the trail head for the COAST TRAIL which offers striking views, cliffs, small lakes, meadows and a waterfall cascading down a 40-foot bluff onto the beach. The hike is an easy to moderate seven-mile round trip.

POINT REYES LIGHTHOUSE
The historic lighthouse, whose lens was imported from France, was built in 1870. It is more often foggy and windy here than sunny. The rare clear days are a delight for photography and wildlife viewing. Migrating gray whales, sea lions resting on the rocks and a variety of seabirds can be spotted from this vantage point.

Marbled godwit

Black turnstone

Great egret

Sandpiper

American black oystercatcher

Willet

Big Sur
(below and right).

The rare Monterey cypress can be seen at Point Lobos (below), along the 17-Mile Drive ▲ 170.

The Monterey Bay National Marine Sanctuary is over 300 miles long and 50 miles wide. It connects with the Gulf of the Farallones National Marine Sanctuary on its north edge. Highway 1 ▲ 167 hugs most of the scenic shoreline stretching south from San Francisco to San Simeon. The first section, known as DEVIL'S SLIDE, is precipitous, with steep cliffs plummeting down to wave-swept rocky shores. The coastline has everything: spectacular scenery and an abundance of marine life, including sea lions, seals, sea otters, whales, birds and fish. Offshore, its waters conceal the massive Monterey Submarine Canyon with its deep-water habitats. The lush kelp forests provide shelter for the southern sea otter. Recreational opportunities along the coast include tide pool exploration, surfing, kayaking, birdwatching, hiking and scuba diving.

HALF MOON BAY ▲ *166* ◆ **B** A1. The south shore of this bay is where 'Mavericks', the largest surf roller on the west coast breaks on

ALSO WORTH A VISIT
Boat trips to the FARALLON ISLANDS and whale-watching trips offer close-up views of whales and sea birds. Stop at PESCADERO MARSH for excellent birdwatching, or to walk the long sandy beach. The PIGEON POINT LIGHTHOUSE offers tours at weekends and inexpensive accommodation at the youth hostel. AÑO NUEVO STATE RESERVE has an elephant seal rookery, which should not be missed.

BROWN PELICAN
Rather clumsy on the ground, the pelican is an elegant glider, its long neck seeming to disappear.

BIG SUR ✪
There is nothing but inlets, cliffs plunging down to the sea, crashing waves and fog concealing the green landscape. Stop at the café in Nepenthe for a drink – you will still be able to admire the view.

a reef one-mile offshore when the swell is high. Surfers from all over the world seek out this famous 30-foot wave. Whale-watching trips depart from the harbor during the early spring to observe the gray whale migration. Watch for gray whale spouts on the horizon from November through May ▲ *235*.

SANTA CRUZ ▲ *166* ◆ **B** A2. Marine life viewing opportunities abound in the Santa Cruz area at the top of Monterey Bay. Stop at the LONG MARINE LAB DISCOVERY Center to view marine aquaria and tour the marine mammal research facility. Next door is NATURAL BRIDGES STATE PARK, a beach with good tide pools and a eucalyptus grove aflutter with monarch butterflies each winter ▲ *169*. WEST CLIFF DRIVE has an excellent path to walk, skate or bicycle along the ocean. Keep watch for sea otters, sea lions, harbor seals, whales and dolphins.

POINT LOBOS STATE RESERVE ◆ **B** A2. Here you will discover perhaps the most striking and beautiful natural area along the whole coast of California. Take the CYPRESS GROVE and NORTH SHORE TRAILS to view the magnificent granite outcrops, twisted cypress trees and dramatic wave-swept coves. Serious scuba divers can dive (by reservation) into the glorious underwater kelp forest reserve with its colorful rocky pinnacles at the mouth of WHALER'S COVE. ▲ *234*.

BIG SUR ▲ *170* ◆ **B** A3. A scenic wonderland. Stops should include the numerous scenic viewpoints along the highway: PFEIFFER BIG SUR STATE PARK for hiking, PFEIFFER BEACH just to the south, and the JULIA BURNS PFEIFFER STATE PARK, where a short trail leads to a picturesque waterfall plunging onto the beach below. The marine sanctuary ends at San Simeon, home to Hearst Castle ▲ *172* and the historic lighthouse. A northern elephant seal breeding beach was recently established here, providing a dramatic finish to the scenic journey along the central Californian coastline.

CALIFORNIA SEA LION
These animals often rest packed together on land, or float together on the ocean as 'rafts'.

NORTHERN ELEPHANT SEAL
Thousands of these immense seals gather in colonies during the winter.

▲ CHANNEL ISLANDS NATIONAL PARK AND MARINE SANCTUARY

Horned puffin

Tufted puffin

Double-crested cormorant

Brandt's cormorant

Pelagic cormorant

Puffins nest in the cliffs, while cormorants prefer steep slopes. Brandt's cormorant is the most common.

Colonies of elephant seals and sea lions.

The Channel Islands ◆ C form a chain of eight islands off southern California's coast. They are accessible only by boat or small plane and have limited camping facilities. The climate can be harsh, with high winds, fog and rough seas, but the wildlife is outstanding. The Channel Islands National Park encompasses five of the islands and extends one nautical mile offshore of each one, while the National Marine Sanctuary extends the protection to six miles around each island. The islands have been separated from the mainland – and each other – since sea levels rose at the end of the last Ice Age. This isolation has resulted in the evolution of new species and the exaggeration of size and coloration in certain species compared to their mainland counterparts. Recent activities, such as livestock grazing and introduced species, are now threatening much of the native flora and fauna. The islands are tucked into a pocket off the coast of southern California known as the Southern California Bight. Here, warm and cold water masses meet to form a biological transition zone with a great diversity of marine species. The California Current ▲ 234 brings cold water south from Alaska, influencing the northwestern islands, while warm water currents from Baja California influence the more southerly islands. The islands are a valuable breeding ground for five different species of seals and sea lions and also birds, including the brown pelican. There are six species of pinnipeds and twenty-seven species of cetaceans (whales and dolphins). The waters surrounding the islands support lush kelp forests with their corresponding communities of fish and invertebrates.

ACCESS
Apply to the National Park Visitors Center at Ventura (Channel Islands National Park), and to the Sea Center at Santa Barbara (Marine Sanctuary). Although it doesn't belong to the park or the reserve, the island of Catalina ▲ 213 is the most accessible of all, being only two hours by boat from LA.

SANTA ROSA. Santa Rosa Island, the second largest of the islands, is known for its windswept sandy beaches, rocky terraces and grassy hillsides, which cover over 85 percent of the island. It has two groves of Torrey Pines, Chumash middens and fossil beds where the pygmy mammoth was discovered. Day hiking and overnight camping trips can be arranged. Diving features include rocky pinnacles and thick kelp forests with abundant fish and invertebrate life representative of colder northern waters.
SAN MIGUEL. San Miguel Island is known for the bizarre Caliche forest. Plan a half day visit to see this forest where ancient tree trunks have been preserved in sand casts, as the wind-blown sand hardened around them as calcium carbonate. This is the best island to view pinniped rookeries.

SEA OTTER
This captivating mammal breaks open shellfish on its stomach, with the aid of pebbles. It is a rare example of a mammal using tools.

Coreopsis in flower on Anacapa.

DIVING IN THE CHANNEL ISLANDS
Diving in the Channel Islands is highly recommended as the visibility is generally better than the mainland coastal waters. Colorful fish, lobster, rocky ledges and reefs, kelp forests, rocky pinnacles, sea caves, sea lions, rockfish and colorful invertebrates are just a few reasons to make the plunge.

Take a ranger-led 15-mile hike to Point Bennett and allow a full day to view the northern elephant seals ▲ *239*, California sea lions, harbor seals and northern fur seals.

SANTA CRUZ. Santa Cruz Island is the largest island of the chain, 24 miles long. The diverse habitats can be explored on Nature Conservancy day trips, which must be arranged in advance. The island is home to the endangered island gray fox and large sea bird rookeries. Diving offers scenic sea caves and reefs with generally favorable conditions.

SANTA BARBARA. Santa Barbara Island is the southernmost and smallest of the islands, only one square mile. This island has the best birdwatching, with brown pelican, Xantu guillemot and colonies of Western gulls. California sea lions and northern elephant seals also breed on its beaches. Diving offers a chance to swim with wild and sometimes playful California sea lions ▲ *239*, as well as extensive kelp forests, underwater archways, caves, pinnacles and rocky reefs.

ANACAPA. Anacapa Island is only 14 miles from the mainland off Ventura. The island is quite small and partially closed to the public, but it offers excellent diving with an ecological reserve, large shellfish and colorful fish, sea caves and arches. A major brown pelican rookery is located on the island.

TURKEY VULTURE
Widely distributed, these vultures fly over open spaces looking for refuse and dead animals, which they live on.

The deserts which cover 25 percent of California are all in the south and east of the state. The two major southern deserts include the Mojave and the Colorado. Here the temperatures soar, and the precipitation is extremely low, with some regions receiving only one inch of rain in dry years. Much of these deserts consists of hard, flat terrain with the occasional shrubs and cactus, although there are some sand dune areas. The Joshua tree (below), ocotillo and cholla cactus predominate as vegetation. The ephemeral spring wildflower bloom can be spectacular in good years.

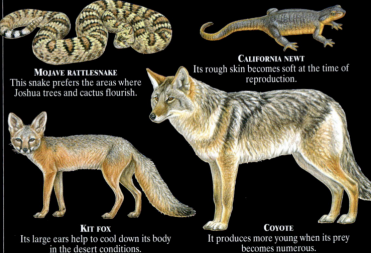

MOJAVE RATTLESNAKE
This snake prefers the areas where Joshua trees and cactus flourish.

CALIFORNIA NEWT
Its rough skin becomes soft at the time of reproduction.

KIT FOX
Its large ears help to cool down its body in the desert conditions.

COYOTE
It produces more young when its prey becomes numerous.

TARANTULA
Its powerful fangs inject venom
that is painful but not fatal.

ANIMAL ADAPTATIONS
Most desert animals have adopted a nocturnal lifestyle. Many burrow underground or seek cover under rocks and shrubs during the day. They have adapted efficient kidneys in order to conserve what little water they obtain from seeds and berries. Some may become dormant during the hot summer months. Most are light colored to avoid absorbing the sun's rays and some have large ears to help radiate away body heat.

JOSHUA TREE
This striking plant grows in extensive stands in the Mojave Desert. It grows to 30 feet tall and sports a broad crown with long, dagger-like spine-tipped leaves. It blooms in early spring, with clusters of yellowish flowers. The Joshua tree is not actually a tree, but a large yucca. It belongs to the agave family, which is related to the lilies.

DESERT TORTOISE
It takes 15 to 20 years for this species
to reach maturity.

KANGAROO RAT
It is active at night in the sand
dunes, except at full moon.

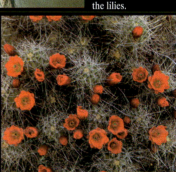

PLANT ADAPTATIONS
Plants living in the desert must have the ability to conserve and retain moisture. Their adaptations include deep roots, tough, waxy skin and leaves, and water storage in their stems. Many shed their leaves in summer to avoid losing moisture.

Badwater (below) and the characteristic
dunes of Death Valley.

DEATH VALLEY, A DELIGHTUL HELL ✪

Deep canyons, seas of sand, gaping craters, enormous dunes: everything here is amazing, disconcerting stupifying… People go in the spring for the amazing bloom of flowers. In winter, temperatures are bearable, but there are crowds. In summer you can only go in an air-conditioned vehicle. To cope with the heat it is advisable to wear long sleeved shirts and trousers, thick-soled shoes and a hat. Get yourself a parasol, or even an umbrella, and take plenty to drink with you.

Death Valley ◆ **C** holds a peculiar fascination. Its history reminds us of the ordeals of the Wild West, especially the Gold Rush pioneers who died trying to find a southern route to California avoiding the Sierras. At 1,200,000 acres it is the largest National Park. It has the driest and hottest climate in North America. Temperatures average 115°F in the shade in summer, with a record maximum of 134°F. Rainfall is less than two inches annually. Amazingly, there is great species diversity in this harsh environment, with 900 plants, 350 birds, 51 mammals and 36 reptiles. The variety of habitats include barren saltpans, desert scrub, ponds and springs, rock canyons and even coniferous forests at the higher elevations. The ephemeral spring wildflower blooms can be spectacular.

FURNACE CREEK ◆0 B2. The Visitor Center here is the first stop for visitors. Park staff provide information on trails, programs and even daily wildflower blooms. The small BORAX MUSEUM explains the mining history of the valley.

NORTH OF FURNACE CREEK. SCOTTY'S CASTLE ◆0 B1. This was the desert oasis retreat of millionaire Albert Johnson and his friend Walter Scott, a local prospector and cowboy. Here, rangers in 1930s garb lead visitors through the Mediterranean

CHUCKWALLA
This lizard puffs itself up to avoid being dislodged from its rocky hiding place.

hacienda with its decorated tiles and crafted furniture.

UBEHEBE CRATER ◆0 A1. From the castle it is a short drive to the moonscape-like Ubehebe Crater, half a mile wide, the result of a volcanic eruption 1000 years ago. Take a moderate hike through a field of smaller craters and volcanic gray badlands for even more dramatic views.

TITUS CANYON NARROWS ◆0 B1. Heading back towards Furnace Creek, visit Titus Canyon Narrows. An easy three-mile hike and a four-wheel drive road take you through a narrow rock-walled canyon with oasis springs scattered along the ravine. The rock walls are ablaze with orange and black volcanic sediment streaked with threads of gleaming white calcite.

SOUTH OF FURNACE CREEK. HARMONY BORAX WORKS **◆0** B2. Two miles south of Furnace Creek is the 1880s refinery where over 20 million pounds of the 'white gold' were refined and transported via twenty mule teams during this profitable era in Death Valley's history.

DEVIL'S GOLF COURSE ◆ 0 C2
This dried-up lake bed has salt creations of spikes, pits, craters and jagged ridges. Walk away from the parking areas to see the natural salty white surfaces.

ALSO VISIT
The SAND DUNES are a great place for photographers. MOSAIC CANYON features a short hike through a marble canyon with white, gray and black mosaic. SALT CREEK NATURE TRAIL is an easy hike on a boardwalk through salt marshes.

ZABRISKIE POINT ◆0 B2. Plan your drive to Zabriskie Point at dawn or sunset for the best photographs of the colorful badlands and a good view of the pale mudstone hills of Golden Canyon.

ARTIST'S DRIVE ◆0 B2. This is an eight-mile circular drive with views of hills with brilliant swaths of color from volcanic mineral deposits. At ARTIST'S PALETTE you can scramble through pink, blue, red, orange and green patches from the parking lot after the scenic view.

DANTES VIEW ◆0 B2. A classic Death Valley view of the lowest and highest points in the park. It is over 5000 feet above the salt flats of BADWATER, itself below sea level, and directly across from TELESCOPE PEAK, the highest peak in the park at 11, 049 feet. Arrive here at sunrise for spectacular lighting effects.

BADWATER ◆0 C2. This is the lowest spot in the Western Hemisphere, at 282 feet below sea level. Here the land subsided due to the seismic action of a subsiding fault between the Panamint Mountains to the west and the Black Mountains to the east. A short hike leads to spring-fed pools with extremely salty water.

RAVEN
This large member of the crow family can adapt to many different environments. It is omniverous, and so can find its food from many different sources. It makes its nest in the cavity of a rock face.

Woodpecker.

ANZA BORREGO STATE PARK ◆ C D6 ▲ 228
Lying to the west of the Colorado Desert, this is the largest state park, with over half a million acres. Visit the fan palm groves, especially on the Canyon Trail. Look for bighorn sheep in the summer near the canyon floor. See also the wild flowers in March and the butterflies in the fall after the rains.

Gambel's quail and the cactus wren.

ALSO VISIT
Take the Pinto Basin Road which bisects the park from top to bottom, beginning at the higher Mojave Desert and ending in the hotter Colorado Desert.

Joshua Tree National Park ◆C D4-E4 is a park with deserts at both ends. The northwest end is part of the Mojave Desert, and is renowned for its Joshua Tree Forest. The Colorado Desert at the southeast end is hotter, drier and lower in elevation with creosote bush, stands of ocotillo and teddy bear chollas. There are five California fan palm oases and intriguing geological oddities, including large boulder gardens. The fabulous ephemeral spring wildflower bloom lasts for several weeks. Desert wildlife includes bighorn sheep, the desert tortoise, roadrunners, cougars and coyote.
TWENTY NINE PALMS. Start your visit with a stop at the Oasis Visitor Center in Twenty Nine Palms. The easy half-mile OASIS OF MARA NATURE TRAIL leads through palm trees, small ponds and abundant wildlife. Close by, the 29 PALMS OASIS HIKE is a strenuous three-mile-long trail leading to a rock canyon with a spectacular oasis of fan palms, cottonwood trees and clear green pools.
PARK BOULEVARD. Park Boulevard begins at the northwest edge of the park and crosses boulder-strewn terrain and stands of Joshua trees. The HIDDEN VALLEY NATURE TRAIL is great for photographers, and for kids who enjoy scrambling over rocks. Follow the road to BARKER DAM to view American Indian petroglyphs. WONDERLAND OF ROCKS is twelve square miles of massive jumbled granite. Groves of Joshua trees and small pools are hidden in the maze of rocks. KEY VIEW POINT offers sweeping panoramic vistas from a mile-high vantage point. The three-mile, three-hour hike to RYAN MOUNTAIN has some of the best scenery in the park. Finally, Park Boulevard leads through the wonderfully scenic JUMBO ROCKS area, with its vast array of rock formations and Joshua tree forest.

This reserve ◆**C** E3 boasts the world's largest Joshua tree forest, spectacular canyons, limestone caverns, volcanic formations, tabletop mesas, a dozen mountain ranges and abundant wildlife. In ancient times, water carved out canyons, minerals were deposited on drying lake beds and ancient oceans deposited colorful mineral layers now visible in the mountains. After the last Ice Age the area turned to desert. The flora is predominately creosote bush, several species of cacti, including the cholla, and several species of yucca, including the Joshua tree.

KELBAKER ROAD. This road provides the best scenic route through the reserve. The road passes through lava beds and cinder cones, the KELSO DEPOT (a Spanish-Revival-style train station) and the KELSO DUNES. A three-mile hike leads to the 45 square miles of golden towering mounds, some up to 700 feet high. These dunes are known for their 'singing sands', which emit a low rumble as blowing sands pass over the underlying layer. Near the south end of the route is a fine view of the jagged Granite Mountains with their rosy-colored boulders.

KELSO–CIMA ROAD. Another scenic drive is along the Kelso–Cima Road, which takes you to Cima Dome, an almost perfectly rounded batholith (large volcanic rock) rising 1500 feet above the desert floor. It is blanketed by the largest Joshua tree forest in the world. A four-mile circular hike to TEUTONIA PEAK gives a view of Cima Dome and hillsides of Joshua tree woodland, mojave yucca and cholla cactus.

MITCHELL CAVERN. Situated at the southern region of the reserve, this is a limestone cave with fantastic stalactite and stalagmite formations. Rangers offer daily tours during the summer.

CHOLLA CACTUS
This cactus may look soft and fluffy from a distance, but its fine, sharp needles stick so well (and painfully) to skin and clothes that it is known as the 'jumping cactus'.

Roadrunner.

Six major mountain ranges in California support almost all of its forests, which cover 35 percent of the entire state. The two main mountain ranges are the Coast Range and the Sierra Nevada Range. The Coast Range runs 600 miles along the western edge of the state and averages peaks of 2000 to 4000 foot elevations. It includes Redwood National Park. The Sierra Nevada runs north–south along the eastern side of the state for 400 miles and is the most prominent topographic feature in California, with six peaks over 14,000 feet high. It includes Yosemite, Kings Canyon and Sequoia National Parks. Additional extensive forests are found in the Klamath and Cascade ranges to the north and the Peninsular and Transverse ranges in Southern California.

BRISTLECONE PINES
These pines with their spiny cones and contorted shapes can live as long as 4700 years. They are found on the slopes of the White Mountains ▲ 263 , in dry, rocky regions. There, the environment and harsh climate have encouraged the growth of these conifers which can withstand a limestone soil.

DESCRIPTION OF FORESTS
Most of the trees found in California are evergreen and many are conifers. Evergreens can conserve moisture during the long, dry summers with their needles and scale-like leaves, and can also tolerate the winter cold and snow. There are fifty-six species of conifers in the state, including the largest (giant sequoia ▲ 250), tallest (coast redwood ▲ 258) and oldest (bristlecone pine) trees in the world.

SIERRA NEVADA

Traveling up the slope of the Sierra Nevada is similar to traveling north towards the Arctic tundra. The vegetation changes at each 1000 feet correspond climatically to a move north of 300 miles. The oak woodland gives way to mixed conifer forest from 3500 to 6000 feet, consisting mainly of ponderosa pine, Jeffrey pine, incense cedar and Douglas fir. In the upper montane zone from 6000 to 8500 feet, lodgepole pine, red fir, whitebark pine and western juniper predominate. The sub-alpine zone is above 8500 feet, with low-growing, twisted trees. Rainfall and snowfall is mainly on the western slope, due to the rain shadow effect. Here the giant sequoia grows along with vast stands of yellow pine and fir. The east slope is much starker, due to the drier conditions. The sub-alpine zones of both slopes have twisted, contorted pines and junipers, adapted to survive in this harsh environment.

▲ SEQUOIA AND KINGS CANYON NATIONAL PARKS

GIANT SEQUOIA
The giant sequoia, *Sequoiadendron giganteum*, grows only on the western slope of the Sierra Nevada, mostly between 5000 and 7000 feet in elevation. The immense, column-like trunk grows to over 30 feet in diameter. The huge, stout branches themselves are larger than most trees. The distinctive cinnamon-colored bark is fire-resistant and up to 18 inches thick. Sequoias reproduce from seeds, which require bare mineral soil with the duff cleared away by wildfires in order to germinate and sprout.

PIKA
The pika harvests, dries and stores hay during the short summer growing season. During the long winter it lives under the snow-pack inside a rock pile, eating this dried hay.

The trunk of a giant sequoia can reach a diameter of 30 feet.

Sequoia and Kings Canyon National Parks S◆ B E3, known for their high peaks, steep canyons, powerful rivers and giant sequoia groves, are located in the southern Sierra, bounded on the east by the Sierra Nevada crest. The parks contain twelve peaks over 14,000 feet. Within the park you can walk around the base of the largest tree in the world and climb Mount Whitney, the tallest mountain in the US (14,494 feet). Recreational pursuits include sightseeing, hiking, cross-country skiing, mountain climbing, camping, backpacking, fishing, caving and photography. Sequoia National Park was created in 1890, the same year as Yosemite, as a result of the devoted efforts of conservationists such as John Muir ▲ *233*. Within these two parks are found 67 of the 75 remaining giant sequoia groves, along a 60-mile stretch of the western Sierra slope. A day's visit is the minimum, and should include the drive through Kings Canyon from the Giant Forest to Grants Grove. Driving the Kings Canyon Highway is an awesome experience. It is the deepest canyon in the US, with steep mountains plunging to the raging Kings River below. The purplish-gray granite walls rise from 2500 feet to nearly a mile above the valley floor.

SEQUOIA NATIONAL PARK ◆ N A3-B3-C3

LODGEPOLE, GIANT FOREST AND GENERAL SHERMAN TREE.
The Visitor Center at Lodgepole includes new exhibits on the giant sequoia, park history, geology, wildlife and the southern

Sierra environment. Visit CONGRESS GROVE for a magnificent two-mile hike through one of the most impressive giant sequoia groves in the park. The GENERAL SHERMAN TREE, 275 feet high and 36 feet wide, is the largest living thing on the planet, named after one of the generals in the American Civil War. Though not the tallest nor the widest, its total mass of 1400 tonnes is greater than any other tree. It is around 2000 years old and still growing. Giant Forest, named by John Muir, is a second spectacular grove in the park.

CRYSTAL CAVE. A visit to Crystal Cave will take half a day, and you must reserve in advance through the visitor center, but it is well worth the effort. This exquisite cavern is a wonderland of crystalline limestone formations and magical underground pools. The hike down the wooded canyon crosses a lovely cascading stream and leads to an awesome cavern entrance with a spider web iron gate gaping from the rocky hillside. Cave guides lead tours along a path through the various lighted chambers. There are over one hundred caves in the two parks, a terrain riddled with limestone caverns, but only two, Crystal Cave and Boyden Cave, are open for public tours.

CRESCENT MEADOW AND LOG MEADOW. These are lovely, unspoiled meadows filled with wildflowers and surrounded by giant sequoias and fir trees. The CRESCENT LOG MEADOW LOOP TRAIL leads around the meadows to THARP'S LOG, an historic cabin built into a fallen sequoia hollowed out by fire that was home to the first white settler in the area, Hale Tharp, a cattle grazer. Fallen sequoias provide natural boardwalks to venture out into Log Meadow without trampling flowers or sinking into the bog-like terrain. The road to Crescent Meadow actually passes through a tunnel carved out of a fallen sequoia log.

HUCKLEBERRY TRAIL. The Huckleberry Trail is an attractive, moderate four-mile circular hike through beautiful forest and meadow, passing an old cabin and an old American Indian village ▲ 253.

MORO ROCK. This is a large granite dome with a spectacular view of the Sierra that can be reached via a steep half-hour hike up hundreds of stairs. The view during a fall full moon is magical as moonlight reflects off the mountain peaks.

SIERRA HIGH COUNTRY
For adventurous hikers, a trek up to the alpine areas of the High Sierra – at an altitude of more than 9000 feet – is like visiting the Arctic. The life here is adapted to severe winds, cold and lack of moisture. The zone just below the tree-line, at 11,000 feet, supports only twisted, contorted trees of a few species, such as the western juniper and whitebark pine. Above the tree-line, only low-growing dwarf shrubs and seasonal herbaceous plants grow on the thin, rocky soil. Here, animals such as the marmot and pika must be able to endure long periods of winter snow cover and no plant growth. Prairie falcons and other raptors are often spotted hunting small mammals in this open terrain.

◢ SEQUOIA AND KINGS CANYON NATIONAL PARKS

GOLDEN EAGLE
It makes its enormous nest either in a large tree, or on the slope of a cliff.

FOOTHILLS. The visitor center focuses on the oak woodland habitats and local Native Americans. Visit Hospital Rock to view ancient pictographs painted by the Monache American Indians and nearby grinding rocks where acorns were smashed into flour. Take the short trail down to the KAWEAH RIVER to view rapids and deep, clear pools with a fine swimming hole.

KINGS CANYON NATIONAL PARK ◆ N A1-B1

GRANT GROVE. A grove of majestic giant sequoias, this is the most popular tourist site in the park, in part due to its proximity to the park entrance and the excellent visitor facilities available. Visitors can park right by Grant Grove and take a short circular hike to view the most impressive trees. The Grant Grove Visitor Center includes exhibits on giant sequoias and the effects of logging and wildfire on the groves. For a sobering view of the destruction that logging reaped on the area in the 19th century, take the Big Stump Trail with its century-old leftover piles of sawdust and giant stumps.

KINGS CANYON HIGHWAY. The Kings Canyon Highway is a spectacular ride. It twists and winds down a steep canyon with massive granite slopes arising from the turbulent Kings River below. Gouged out by glaciers, the canyon, which is nearly a mile high, is ten miles long and half a mile wide. John Muir labeled it a 'rival to Yosemite Valley'. Stop along the way to visit BOYDEN CAVE, an impressive limestone cavern that is open to the public and right above the road. A rather steep walk up the hillside takes you to the cave entrance where a tour guide leads the group through a series of lighted chambers with striking limestone formations.

GENERAL GRANT TREE
This tree measures 267 feet tall and 107 feet in diameter, and is approximately 2000 years old. It is the 'Nation's Christmas Tree' and is the centerpiece of a magical Christmas celebration in the snow-covered grove.

CEDAR GROVE. This is the base for exploring the vast wilderness of the Kings River Canyon. This portion of the park has been protected from tourist development to avoid the problems of overcrowding that have plagued Yosemite, so there are only modest amenities available, which include a simple lodge and campgrounds. Here, in this remote pocket of the Sierra, nature lovers can find plenty of solitude and communion with nature amidst gorgeous scenery, including tumbling waterfalls, lush forests and abundant wildlife. Visit CANYON VIEW, one mile east of the Cedar Grove Village, for a good view of the glacially carved U-shape of Kings Canyon. Take the ZUMWALT MEADOW NATURE TRAIL, a scenic one-mile easy loop around a meadow bordered with ponderosa pine and incense cedar. Keep your eyes open for black bear, which frequent this lush meadow ▲ 257. The path to ROARING RIVER FALLS is a 5-minute easy walk, though it may be quite wet from the spray where a short but powerful waterfall crashes through a narrow granite chute into a deep green pool below. Cedar Grove is also the point of departure for more demanding hikes which enable you to explore the regions around JENNIE

MARMOT
It builds up reserves of fat before hibernating for the winter.

LAKE and MONARCH WILDERNESS. You must first get an excursion permit from the Grant Grove Visitors Centre. Here are sub-alpine meadows dotted with juniper trees, their trunks knotted and twisted, river torrents full of trout and impressive granite outcrops.

ROADS END. Roads End has various trails which lead down to the Kings River where kids can clamber up huge granite boulders. When the river level is at its lowest in late summer, they can also find shallow areas to swim in the cold, clear water. Climb up onto historic MUIR ROCK, an enormous flat granite boulder from which the conservationist and explorer John Muir ▲ *233* expounded on the wonders of his beloved Sierra Nevada to rapt audiences.

BIGHORN SHEEP
In winter they divide into small groups of the same sex, three to five in each male group and five to fifteen in the female ones. In the summer, the two sexes join up again in large herds. The males then take part in ritual combat with each other, clashing their horns. These displays can last up to 20 hours, the noise echoing for miles.

THE MONACHE
Originally from around Mono Lake, the Monache resided in these mountains until the 1870s, living by hunting, fishing and gathering berries. Their permanent encampment was near the Kaweah River, in the foothills. But in the summer they climbed up to Crescent Meadow, where they could enjoy the cooler environment of the sequoia forests.

Kings Canyon National Park at sunset.

YOSEMITE NATIONAL PARK

The impressive monolith El Capitan (below).
Winter fog in Yosemite (right).

YOSEMITE ✪
Staggeringly beautiful, Yosemite is one of those well-known sites whose very name conjures up dreamlike images. How many places in the world can boast, all in a totally natural, wild setting, one of the largest monoliths in the world, the largest trees on the planet and a unique collection of waterfalls, some more than 2000 feet high?
The best way to explore Yosemite is on foot or by mountain bike, especially during the summer months when it is crowded and traffic movement is restricted.

Yosemite is a park of superlatives. The grandeur and scale of Yosemite's peaks, valleys and waterfalls is awe-inspiring. Here you can find spectacular valleys carved by glaciers, granite monoliths and domes, leaping waterfalls, alpine meadows, lakes, forests (including giant sequoia groves) and abundant wildlife. The first humans to revere and settle in this valley were Native Americans of the Miwok tribe. These hunter-gatherers lived in the valley during the summer, subsisting on the wealth of seeds, acorns, bulbs, deer and trout, and migrated down to the Sierra foothills for the harsh winters. The valley was first viewed by white soldiers in 1851 who described it in terms of awe. As early as 1859, daguerreotype photographers ● *54* documented the splendor of Yosemite for the rest of the world to marvel at. These images helped convince President Abraham Lincoln to place the valley and the Mariposa Grove of giant sequoia in public trust for protection even as the Civil War was raging. John Muir ▲ *233*, who first came to Yosemite in 1868, became entranced with the valley and the majestic mountains

> 'It is by far the grandest of all the special temples of
> Nature I was ever permitted to enter.'

John Muir

AHWAHNEE HOTEL
An elegant historic inn designed by the renowned architect Julia Morgan ▲ *172*. It has a majestic stone façade and wooden beams, and a rustic yet elegant interior with each window framing an exquisite view.

surrounding it, and spent the rest of his life here. He devoted himself to exploring the wilderness, and to studying, describing and saving Yosemite for prosperity. Muir's passion for preserving not only Yosemite Valley but the surrounding mountains as well, resulted in the creation of Yosemite National Park ◆ **B** D1 in 1890.

YOSEMITE VALLEY ◆ M B3.

Allow at least one day for a visit. The best approach is along Highway 140. You wind along the Merced River Canyon, which narrows as you approach the park entrance. Upon entering the valley itself, the view is breathtaking, with granite cliffs towering above the lushly forested valley floor.

BRIDAL VEIL FALL. The first stop is the misty Bridal Veil Fall, which flows from a hanging valley 620 feet high above the valley floor.

EL CAPITAN. This is a massive granite monolith, carved out by glaciers, rising 3604 feet straight up from the valley floor. Look carefully for the ant-like climbers high up on the sheer rock face. The climb may take several days, with climbers slinging hammocks from the cliffs to spend the night suspended precariously.

YOSEMITE FALLS. These are the highest falls in the United States. The upper one is 1430 feet tall and the lower one 320 feet. A hike to the lower fall is easy, but plan on getting wet from the spray at the base. The upper fall is a strenuous 7-mile round-trip hike that climbs 2700 feet and offers excellent views.

YOSEMITE VILLAGE. The Valley Visitor Center provides fine displays, maps and ranger programs. The Miwok Indian Village is a recreation of an 1870s village and includes a ceremonial roundhouse. Visit the Happy Isles Nature Center for engaging, child-friendly exhibits and to admire the Merced River as it tumbles over rounded boulders and around rocky islets.

This view of Yosemite Valley taken from Half Dome lets you imagine the vertiginous sensations of the climbers.

CHIPMUNK
It lives in the pine forests and hibernates from October to May.

SKIING AT YOSEMITE
The ski resort of Badger Pass is located along this road and offers fine downhill and cross country skiing during the winter.

VERNAL/NEVADA FALLS MIST TRAIL. This is an exceptional hike up to a pair of staircase falls where the Merced River plunges into Yosemite Valley. The trail follows the river to a bridge with a lovely view of the Vernal Fall, 80 feet wide, and continues, shrouded in mist, up slippery granite steps to the top of the fall. For a longer hike, continue along the Merced River to the top of beautiful Nevada Fall. Back down on the valley floor, take the mile-long hike to Mirror Lake.

SOUTH YOSEMITE VALLEY ◆ M B3. Take the Wawona Road south and stop at Tunnel View overlook for a wonderful vista of Yosemite Valley stretching out below with Bridal Veil Fall ▲ 255 in the foreground. Turn north on Glacier Point Road to reach the most spectacular vantage point in the park. Glacier Point is 3200 feet above the valley floor and offers a fine view of Yosemite Falls, the valley below and Half Dome. A trail leads from here to the top of Half Dome and other overlooks. The best times to visit are at sunset and on nights with a full moon.

MARIPOSA GROVE. This is the largest giant sequoia grove in Yosemite, located in Wawona. The road has been closed to traffic to protect the grove, so you must walk the 2½ mile trail or take the tram tour to view the grove of 500 trees which

COUGAR
You can spot its presence by claw marks on the trees and the round paw prints with four pads. This solitary hunter lives on deer, rabbit and rodents.

MIRROR LAKE
The lake no longer acts as a mirror for Half Dome, as it is filling in with marsh vegetation, in a process of natural succession. Half Dome is the classic Yosemite formation, a massive granite dome rising 4748 feet above the valley floor, its 2000 foot cliff face carved flat by glaciers. Sunset on Half Dome, with its sheer granite face lit in a golden glow, is an unforgettable experience.

The lake at the foot of Sentinel Rock (right) is turning into a marsh, in the same process that is affecting Mirror Lake.

includes one over 300 feet tall with a 50-foot circumference. The historic Wawona Lodge situated in a picturesque meadow offers fine accommodation.

NORTH YOSEMITE VALLEY ◆ M A2-B2-C2. To experience the High Sierra, head up the Tioga Road. From there, paths lead to smaller groves of giant sequoia, the Merced and the Tuolumne groves. Crane Flat is one of the best places to view the magnificent great gray owl at night. Continue driving up through stands of stately red firs at heights of 7–8000 feet. Stop at Olmsted Point for a wonderful view of the valley, including Half Dome and Cloud's Rest. Granite rock faces rise straight up from the road, speckled with junipers and green mats of low-growing manzanita. The rocks are streaked with vertical strips of gray, black and tan due to erosion, which causes the granite to peel off in shell-like layers. Tenaya Lake, one of the largest in the park, is surrounded by glacier-polished granite and moraine. It is named after Chief Tenaya, a Yosemite American Indian. TUOLUMNE MEADOWS. The magnificent high meadows (8600 feet) are strewn with wildflowers and surrounded by granite domes and formations. The Soda Springs trail leads to a natural mineral spring with effervescent water. TIOGA PASS. At 9943 feet, this is the highest point you can drive to in the state. At Tioga Lake you notice the thin, cold air and low-growing vegetation. This is the only spot where the road climbs high enough to reach the alpine zone above the tree-line. Here, snow remains on the peaks all year round. Mount Dana rises to 13,053 feet, just south of the pass, the second highest peak in the park. A steep and strenuous hike up Mount Dana rises 3000 feet in a mere three miles and offers stupendous views from the top.

CLARK'S NUTCRACKER
It lives in the sub-alpine mountains (left) in southern California.
On the ground, it walks rather than jumps, like the crow family to which it belongs. It is often seen in parking places, where it comes to pick up the crumbs from picnickers.

TO EXPLORE THE HIGH SIERRAS
The best way to explore the alpine regions is to take the relatively short and easy paths to May Lake, Dog Lake and Glen Aulin.

BLACK BEARS OF YOSEMITE
The black bear is alive and well in the national and state parks of California. In fact, it is considered a menace, due to its attraction to campers' food stashes. Black bears are remarkably good at breaking into cars, trailers, tents and ice chests if they detect food. Visitors should heed the warnings of park rangers and never leave any food items in their car while visiting the park. Black bears do not usually pose a threat to humans, but you should never approach one, as their behavior can be unpredictable, especially if they have have cubs. Consider yourself lucky if you chance to see one, but keep your distance!

257

▲ REDWOOD NATIONAL AND STATE PARKS

REDWOOD. It produces tiny cones less than one inch long.

STELLER'S JAY
Its raucous cry is typical of the sequoia forests. It lives on acorns, insects, eggs and baby birds.

BANANA SLUG
Its horrible taste protects it from predators.

PACIFIC RHODODENDRON
This semi-evergreen shrub has large, attractive flowers and

The northern coast of California is green, lush, moist, misty and primeval. This region is known as temperate rainforest. These coastal mountains, most famous for their old redwood groves, host a variety of northern coniferous trees, which reach their southern limits here. Although many parks along the extensive coast range contain redwood groves as far south as the Big Sur, this northern region contains the largest and wildest expanses of old redwoods in the state. It is here, in the 50-mile stretch of coastline running south from the Oregon border, that four contiguous parks were joined to create the Redwood National and State Parks ◆ **A** B1 in 1994. These 40,000 acres hold almost half of the remaining old redwood groves. The creation of the national park was spurred in the late 1960s, when conservationists became concerned about the rapid destruction of the old redwood forests. The beautiful and durable wood has long been prized for construction. The original 200 million acres of coast redwoods in California had been depleted to a mere 300,000 by 1965 due to intensive logging, so Redwood National Park was created in 1968 to protect some of what remained. Along this route there are many opportunities for scenic drives and hikes, the most popular and spectacular of which are listed in this itinerary. The coast redwood thrives on plenty of moisture and cool temperatures, so expect mostly fog and rain in the realm of the redwoods.

REDWOOD NATIONAL PARK ◆ L B3. The original park is the southernmost portion of the park and includes the world's tallest trees. Stop at the Interpretive Center just west of Orick for maps and information. The LADY BIRD JOHNSON GROVE LOOP is an easy self-guided circular trail through an exceptional stand of lush old redwoods. The tallest tree in the world is located in this section of the park. To view the 368-foot tree, a special permit must be obtained from the ranger station. It takes four hours to drive out along a remote road to the steep TALL TREES TRAIL which leads along REDWOOD CREEK to the tree.

PRAIRIE CREEK REDWOODS STATE PARK ◆ L B3. Imagine a camping ground where you wake up with huge Roosevelt elk grazing a few yards from your tent. This is Prairie Creek, a combination of open coastal prairie, lush, temperate rain

is characteristic of these damp pine forests. It flowers profusely between May and June.

forest and long, expansive wild beaches. After visiting the elk meadow and ranger headquarters by the campground, backtrack a few miles south on Highway 101 and take a drive out to GOLD BLUFFS BEACH on the coast. Here elk may be seen grazing next to the beach. Take the short easy trail along

GIANT PACIFIC SALAMANDER
It is active at night and after rain.

a creek to FERN CANYON, where steep 50-foot-high rock walls are covered with six different species of dense green ferns. Giant horsetails and moss cover the forest floor. Back out on Highway 101, the NEWTON B DRURY SCENIC PARKWAY takes you through an eight-mile bypass of scenic redwood forest and elk meadows. Along the way, take the CAL BARREL ROAD spur, a three-mile circular gravel road through another spectacular grove. Look for trails to two famous redwoods: BIG TREE and CORKSCREW TREE.

DEL NORTE COAST REDWOODS STATE PARK ◆ L B1.
To view an incredibly rugged rocky coastline, drive and hike this section. DAMNATION CREEK TRAIL leads through dense forest to a rocky beach with impressive offshore sea stacks and a small natural arch. Tide pools can be explored during low tides. Stop at the northern park headquarters in CRESCENT CITY ▲ *154* for maps and information.

SPOTTED OWL

JEDEDIAH SMITH STATE PARK ◆ L B1. The northernmost of the parks and mostly old redwood forest. Walk the half-mile long SIMPSON REED DISCOVERY TRAIL or drive HOWLAND HILL ROAD which follows the last major free-flowing river in California, the SMITH RIVER, and has some of the best old redwood stands. Look for the STOUT GROVE TRAILHEAD, which leads to a stand of ancient redwoods almost 2000 years old.

ROOSEVELT ELK

▲ VOLCANIC LANDSCAPES

The Pacific Ocean is bordered by the great Ring of Fire. Volcanic activity along this portion of the Pacific Rim has created a dramatic terrain in northeastern California. This is a zone of volcanos and earthquakes resulting from the collision of tectonic plates. As the heavier oceanic plate is pushed under the continental plate into the Earth's mantle, the water and carbon dioxide in the ocean sediments seep up through the pressurized rock above and cause it to melt, forming hot gas-charged magma. Periodically, this magma bursts through the surface in huge eruptions of volcanic ash, sometimes followed by thick flows of lava. Here in Cascade Range, huge eruptions have occurred twice in the 20th century.

MONO BASIN ▲ 262
The Mono Basin lies east of the central Sierras and on the west of the Great Basin. It is noted for the enormous saline Mono Lake. This region has the youngest chain of lava domes and craters in the US, with potential for future volcanic activity. Twenty volcanic eruptions have occurred here in the last 2000 years, the most recent in the late 1800s. Mammoth Mountain is a dormant volcano, with steam occasionally rising from the summit.

MODOC PLATEAU AND THE CASCADES

The Modoc Plateau is located at the southeast edge of the Cascade Range and on the west edge of the Great Basin. The Modoc Plateau sits on volcanic terrain formed as lava oozed out of long cracks in the Earth's surface, known as fault flows.

It includes Lassen Volcanic National Park ▲ 264, Lava Beds National Monument ▲ 266 with many lava tube caves to explore, and Klamath Basin ▲ 266 with its vast wetlands offering exceptional wildlife viewing opportunities.

Mount Shasta.

FLORA AND FAUNA

These volcanic regions, although appearing hostile and barren, support a rich flora, as the mineral-laden volcanic rocks and ash break down to form fertile soils. The dominant vegetation on the dry, flat plateaus is sagebrush prairie, with western juniper and single leaf pinyon pine on the lower slopes. Here in the high desert-like plateaus you can spot remnants of pronghorn herds, sage grouse making mating displays, and prairie falcons nesting in rocky cliffs and hunting in open areas.

Bumpass Hell Trail ▲ 265 in Lassen Volcanic National Park. The smoke, gas and pools of bubbling mud are due to the upsurge of boiling water from underground pockets of magma.

MONO LAKE
Mono Lake is
ancient – over
700,000 years old –
and has no outlet.
Over the centuries,
salts and minerals
have been washed
into the lake from
streams and have
concentrated as the
water evaporates.
The lake is now two
and a half times
more salty and
eight times more
alkaline than
seawater. The
resulting brine has
provided a unique
habitat for a short
but productive food
chain. Bacteria feed
algae, which feed
huge populations of
brine shrimp and
brine flies. Large
flocks of migrating
and nesting water
birds depend on the
brine shrimp and
flies for food,
making the lake an
exceptional
birdwatching spot.
The color of
Mono Lake
changes with the
season. During
winter and spring it
is green with algae
and in summer and
fall it turns blue as
the brine shrimp
and flies consume
the algae.

W hen you cross the crest of the Sierra at Tioga Pass
▲ 257 and begin descending the eastern slope, you have
entered a different world, reminiscent of a lunar landscape.
Forested canyons open onto a high, arid basin riddled with
cinder cones, craters, ancient lava flows and hot springs.
MONO LAKE ◆ **B** D1-E1. In 1941, a huge aqueduct was
constructed to transport Mono Basin water to southern
California, followed by a second in 1970, and in the ensuing
years the lake level dropped dramatically. The colony of
nesting California gulls was threatened when the waters
dropped and a land bridge was exposed for predators to cross.
Efforts by environmentalists have turned the tide on water
diversion and currently the lake is protected.
MONO BASIN AREA VISITORS CENTER. This is off Highway 395,
just north of Lee Vining, and provides an informative
introduction to the area and a good view of the lake. Just north
of the center is COUNTY PARK, where a boardwalk provides
access across marshlands to the lakeshore for excellent
birdwatching and there are fine examples of tufa formations.
SOUTH TUFA AREA. On the south shore is the greatest density
of the fantastic tufa formations unique to this lake. Tufa forms
underwater when calcium-bearing freshwater wells up

Views of Mono Lake (below and left).

through the alkaline lake water and limestone precipitates in formations. The lowering of the water level only exposed these eerie formations in the late 1900s. Swimming in the lake is a unique experience, as the high alkaline content increases your buoyancy. Kayak tours take visitors out to the islands for a close look at birds and rock formations.

BODIE STATE HISTORIC PARK ◆ B D1-E1. Bodie is an authentic mining town, preserved just as it was abandoned in the 1930s. Here the visitor can stroll through the largest unrestored ghost town of the American West, with buildings including a variety of shops, saloons, churches, hotels, a school and many old homes, a cemetery, and old tools and equipment scattered about. A peek through the windows reveals the furnishings and possessions that were left behind as the town died following the exhaustion of the mineral resources.

JUNE LAKE ◆ B D1 **AND MAMMOTH LAKES ◆ B** D2. The area southwest of Mono Lake is reminiscent of the heights of nearby Yosemite. Here, striking granite formations and Jeffrey pine forests border brilliant blue lakes. JUNE LAKE is a quaint scenic village, which provides a comfortable overnight base for exploring the area. Hiking and fishing opportunities abound. MAMMOTH LAKES offers more tourist amenities and a large ski resort for winter recreation. MAMMOTH MOUNTAIN is a dormant volcano, with hot springs and steam vents. DEVIL'S POSTPILE NATIONAL MONUMENT is a fine example of columnar-jointed basalt. This is an ancient lava flow which cracked in long post-like columns as it was cooling and later was quarried away on one side by a glacier, exposing a sheer wall of three heptagonal columns 60 feet high.

WHITE MOUNTAINS ◆ B E2 The real destination for those seeking botanical wonders is the ANCIENT BRISTLECONE PINE FOREST ▲ *248* in the White Mountains. The dramatic 6000 foot ascent takes 25 miles along the winding road east of Big Pine. You go through shadscale scrub, then pinyon pine and juniper woodland. Finally, near the tree-line at 9500 to 12,000 feet, you reach the bristlecone forest. SCHULMAN GROVE at 10,000 feet has a mile-long discovery trail and an interpretive center. PATRIARCH GROVE at 11,000 feet has some of the most picturesque trees, among them the Patriarch, the largest known bristlecone pine.

Devastated Area
and Bumpass Hell Trail
(below right).

ERUPTION HISTORY

Mount Lassen is the only volcano in California that has erupted in recent history. The 20th-century volcanic activity began in 1914, when a 1000-foot-wide crater was excavated over the course of a year as the volcano spewed out. In May 1915, thick black glassy lava emerged in a dome, followed by an explosion two days later that spewed out hot lava. The resulting avalanche created a devastating mudflow. Two days later an explosive eruption of ash and pumice sent a cloud 25,000 feet up into the sky and created a huge ash flow, avalanche and mudflow wreaking even more devastation. Smaller steam explosions occurred into 1917.

Lassen Peak (right).

PRONGHORN

This incredible animal is capable of running for 15 miles at 30 mph. It keeps its mouth open when running to take in more oxygen.

At Lassen Volcanic National Park you can experience the earth's forces in a tangible way. The earth steams and bubbles, sulfur fumes fill the air and barren slopes remind you of past violent eruptions. The main road ◆ **A** D3 takes you past sweeping volcanic vistas, slopes devastated by eruptions, dense coniferous forests, flower-filled meadows, subalpine lakes, volcanic domes, cinder cones and steaming, bubbling hydrothermal vents. To appreciate the natural wonders, you should walk the trails. The park roads are closed from the first snows in November to late spring.

FROM THE SOUTHWEST ENTRANCE. Most visitors begin their tour of the park from the southwest entrance. Pick up a map and Road Guide from the entrance gate. A small café and store just past the entrance are the only amenities on this side of the park. The observation deck provides a good view of the SULPHUR CREEK VALLEY and surrounding peaks, some of which are the remains of a massive ancient volcano. As you drive up the road, you climb from 6700 feet to 8512 feet. The sub-alpine terrain and flora are strikingly beautiful. Stop at the SULFUR WORKS and wander up the short boardwalk trail through the steaming, bubbling terrain. Here below the earth's surface, a magma intrusion, or pocket of molten rock

SAGE GROUSE
In autumn and winter sage leaves are their chief source of food. In spring, the males display in groups.

Female

Male

with entrapped volcanic gases, heats the ground water to almost 200°F. The fumaroles (vent holes) and hot springs emit sulfur and carbon dioxide gases, causing the wet clay to bubble. Next stop at the beautiful EMERALD LAKE, which fills a rock basin carved out by glaciers. The emerald color is due to algae growing on the shallow sunlit lake bottom.

BUMPASS HELL TRAIL. For three miles you see nothing but springs and pools of bubbling sulphurous mud, swathed in clouds of vapor.

BUMPASS HELL TRAIL
View boiling pools and bubbling mud pots, with rising mists of steam. Kendall Bumpass, the man who discovered this site, had the misfortune to fall through the crust of a boiling mud pot and lose his leg. So keep to the trail! The next stop for hikers is the trail to Lassen Peak (10,457 feet). It is also a good stop for a snowball fight, even in late summer. Annual snowfall can

KINGS CREEK FALLS TRAIL. A recommended hike is the Kings Creek Falls Trail, which leads through dense forests and exquisite mountain meadows with mid- to late-summer wildflower blooms.

DEVASTATED AREA. Following the road around the mountain, you reach the area which was completely barren following the 1915 eruption. It has taken nearly a century for the forest to regenerate. The story of the eruption is told along the Devastation Trail and through historic photographs at the LOOMIS MUSEUM a few miles up the road. The road continues past the CHAOS CRAGS, jagged peaks where lava domes were pushed up through the earth's surface 1000 years ago. The pink volcanic rubble seen along the road was brought down by a huge avalanche 300 years ago.

exceed 40 feet here, with snow pack reaching 20 feet.

ALSO WORTH A VISIT
Hikers should visit the eastern side of the park. Recommended hikes include: Cinder Cone, Juniper Lake, Warner Valley, Mill Creek Falls Trail and Drakesbad (Boiling Springs Lake Trail and the Devil's Kitchen Trail).

▲ KLAMATH NATIONAL WILDLIFE REFUGES LAVA BEDS NATIONAL MONUMENT

In winter, Tule Lake and Lower Klamath Lake (below) shelter the most important concentrations of water birds in the region.

KLAMATH NATIONAL WILDLIFE REFUGES ◆ A D1

The high Klamath Basin on the Oregon border supports a patchwork of marshes, lakes and ponds, meadows, grasslands, farms, sagebrush prairies and coniferous forests which are home to an abundance of wildlife. The freshwater marshes swarm with insect life, which provides food for the numerous amphibians, fish and birds. Sadly, 75 percent of the original wetlands were converted to agriculture, and so the Klamath Basin National Wildlife Refuges were created to protect and maintain this remaining wetland area, including TULE LAKE, LOWER KLAMATH and CLEAR LAKE. The first two refuges have auto-tour routes, a visitor center, observation points and a photoblind. CLEAR LAKE also has a white pelican breeding colony. The grasslands support a sage grouse breeding ground where a lucky visitor may observe their elaborate courtship display ▲ 265. Look for pronghorn, mule deer and black-tailed jackrabbits.

BALD EAGLE
Klamath Refuges have the largest population of these birds of prey in the US, especially in January and February.

LAVA BEDS NATIONAL MONUMENT ◆ A D1

Lava Beds National Monument contains 430 lava tube caves, the highest concentration in North America. It sits on the north face of Medicine Lake Volcano, which has erupted periodically over the last half million years. The lava spread over a wide area, building a gently sloped mountain. As hot lava continued to pour through cracks in the slope, hundreds of long lava flows formed. As the molten lava cooled and hardened on the

Canada goose

BATTLE SITES
Near the Lava Beds National Monument, Captain Jack's Stronghold is a lava tube cave. This is where the last free Modocs held out over the winter of 1872–3, in their last stand against the white military advances.

OTHER PLACES TO VISIT AT THE LAVA BEDS NATIONAL MONUMENT
On the road to Mammoth Crater see HEPPE ICE CAVE, which has a pond and ice on the cave floor. FLEENER CHIMNEYS is a 50-foot splatter cone with unusual colors and textures. The easy hike to BIG PAINTED CAVE and SYMBOL BRIDGE TRAIL winds past interesting lava tube collapses. There are Modoc pictographs at the bridge and cave. SCHONCHIN BUTTE trail offers late spring and summer wildflowers and panoramic views. THOMAS WRIGHT BATTLEFIELD TRAIL offers interesting geology, wildflowers and history. Visit PETROGLYPH POINT for petroglyphs and nesting raptors.

outside, the inner core of hot lava continued to flow after the eruption ended until the tube hollowed out, leaving tunnel-like caves. The lava tube caves here range in size from a few hundred feet to a mile long. Some of the caves have been developed for visitors with paths, ladders and steps, while others are open for wild exploration. A few provide valuable roosting areas for bats, including the threatened Townsend's big-eared bat.

THE CAVES. Stop at the Visitor Center for information on visiting the caves. To explore a safe, easy cave on your own, try the lighted Mushpot Cave next to the visitor center, or take one of the ranger-led tours. The more adventuresome can explore the mile-long CATACOMBS, which involves some crawling.

MAMMOTH CRATER. Three miles from the Visitor Center is the trail up to the rim of Mammoth Crater, the enormous crater from which most of the lava originated.

At Klamath National Wildlife Refuges the population of migrating birds is at its height in March and November, when there are sometimes more than a million birds there.

Sandhill crane

Snow goose

Whistling swan

Great blue heron

Ross goose

Adult

Young

▲ MOUNT SHASTA

M ount Shasta is the most striking volcano in California, rising up above the surrounding mountains of the Cascade Range at 14,162 feet. It is an almost perfectly cone-shaped volcano, with five glaciers, old lava flows, and thermal sulfur springs. The snow-capped summit can be seen from hundreds of miles away on a clear day.

SHASTA NATIONAL FOREST ◆ A C2. Mount Shastina is the 12,330-foot subpeak cinder cone on the west slope. The mountain is on national forest lands and offers excellent hiking, climbing and camping, as well as downhill and cross-country skiing. Take the road up the west side of the mountain from the small town of Mount Shasta through majestic stands of white and red fir to reach the Forest Service trailheads and the winter sledding slope. In July and August trails are open for hikes to upper montane meadows and sub-alpine forests of

ALSO VISIT
North of Mount Shasta, in the small town of Yreka, an old steam train ride takes visitors across the spacious open northern plateau stretching out from the base of Mount Shasta.

MCARTHUR BURNEY FALLS STATE PARK
Burney Falls (129 feet) is one of the most beautiful falls in the state, surrounded by maples, dogwood, alders and Douglas firs. It flows consistently all year round as it is spring-fed. Black swifts nest under the falls. Bald eagles and ospreys can be seen at Lake Britton.

whitebark pine and mountain hemlock. Southeast of Mount Shasta is the historic logging town of McCloud, which has several good hotels and is the route to the Shasta Ski Resort.

SOUTH OF MOUNT SHASTA. CASTLE CRAGS STATE PARK has towering crags and spires of granite. Further south is SHASTA LAKE, a man-made lake which is popular for boating, fishing and camping. A spectacular limestone cave, SHASTA CAVERNS, is located above the lake. Tours are offered from the lakeshore via a boat and bus ride to the cave entrance high up on a steep slope above the lake. Bald eagles ▲ 266, ospreys and falcons may be spotted along the way.

◆ GETTING THERE

ANZA BORREGO STATE PARK

AIR TRAVEL FROM ABROAD
There are regular flights from London and most other major cities direct to San Francisco and LA. Duration: 10–12 hours.

→ **UK NUMBERS**
■ **British Airways**
Tel. 0845 222 111
www.britishairways.com
■ **American Airlines**
Tel. 020 8572 55 55
www.aa.com
■ **Also**
www.cheapflights.com

CLIMATE
California has a pleasant climate all year round. The average temperature in Los Angeles is around 70°F, although daily highs can reach well over 90°F in summer, while winter temperatures can fall as low as 50°F. Rainfall is heaviest between October and April. The San Francisco region has a micro-climate characterized by fog and cool temperatures, even in summer.

COST OF LIVING
The cost of living is high, especially in the large towns and cities.

→ **ACCOMMODATION CHARGES**
■ **Budget prices**
Accommodation: $50–100
Lunch: $10–15
Dinner: $15–25
■ **Average prices**
Accommodation: $100–200
Lunch: $20–30
Dinner: $45
■ **Above-average prices**
Accommodation: $200+
Lunch: $60
Dinner: $100
■ **Some prices**
1 cup of coffee: $1.50
1 breakfast: $3–10
1 soda: $1–1.50
1 postcard: $1–1.50
1 pack of cigarettes: $4.50
Standard car rental: $35–45 per day.

CUSTOMS
Plants and perishable goods are subject to rigorous controls by the *Food and Drug Administration*. Adults over the age of 21 can import 2 pints (1 liter) of alcohol, 200 cigarettes or 50 cigars (except Cuban). If you are carrying more than

$10,000, you must declare it at US customs.

DISCOUNTS
■ **Student Card**
Reductions on public transport and free admission to certain tourist sites and museums are available on presentation of an international student identity card.
■ **Youth Hostel Card**
Entitles the holder to reductions in youth hostels.
American Youth Hostels
733 15th Street, NW
Suite 840
Washington DC 20005
Tel: 202 783 6161
www.hostelweb.com

FORMALITIES
→ **PASSPORT**
Overseas visitors must have a valid passport and a return ticket (except for those travelers entering the country overland), as well as proof of sufficient resources to cover your stay in the country.

→ **VISA**
A visa is not necessary for British tourists or business travelers wishing to stay in the US for less than 90 days.

→ **VACCINATIONS**
No compulsory inoculations.

→ **ANIMALS**
Dogs must have an anti-rabies inoculation more than one month and less than one year before traveling.

HEALTH
→ **MEDICATION**
Standard medication is available from supermarket drugstores. Visitors with special requirements will need to obtain a prescription.

INSURANCE
→ **HEALTH INSURANCE**
Take out comprehensive health insurance cover as medical costs are high in the United States.

→ **BY CREDIT CARD**
Visa and MasterCard offer health insurance schemes, including repatriation under certain circumstances.

MONEY
→ **CURRENCY**
US dollar ($).
Rates of exchange are published in the national press.
US$1 = £0.65 and €1.14

BAY BRIDGE, SAN FRANCISCO

→ CASH
There is no need to take large amounts of cash – automatic teller machines are widely available. However, a credit card is indispensable.

→ CREDIT CARDS
MasterCard and Visa are accepted everywhere; American Express and Diners Club are widely accepted.

→ TRAVELER'S CHECKS
Traveler's checks can be obtained from most banks. Don't forget to make a note of the numbers – they can be replaced if they are lost or stolen.

TIME DIFFERENCE
California is 8 hours behind Greenwich Mean Time and 3 hours behind Eastern Standard Time. If it's noon in California, it's 8pm in London and 3pm in New York.

WHAT TO TAKE
■ **Clothing**
Pack a pullover and windcheater whatever the season – it can turn chilly and wet at any time of year, especially in northern California. For the desert, take long sleeves and light pants. In summer, take sunglasses, hat, bathing suit and sun block.
■ **Binoculars**
A must if you're visiting the national parks.
■ **Footwear**
Comfortable walking shoes or boots for the parks – with thick soles for the desert, in summer.
■ **Electricity**
Flat-pin plugs. Voltage: 110 V, 60 MHz. Adapters may be necessary for foreign appliances.

WHEN TO GO
The best time to go depends on the region you are visiting. It's best to visit the north between May and October to avoid the cold winters. The south Is less popular with tourists and therefore pleasanter in winter, autumn or spring.

→ AUTUMN
One of the best times to go. The weather is fine but not too hot and the light is beautiful. The parks are quieter and you can see blue whales migrating southward along the coast. But be warned, winter comes suddenly in the north.

→ WINTER
The best season for winter sports and seeing marine mammals – gray whales along the coast November–May and elephant seals January–March. However some sites in the Great Basin are closed and mountain parks are often inaccessible due to snow.

→ SPRING
An ideal time to admire waterfalls as the snow melts, and to see the desert in flower.

→ SUMMER
In spite of the unbearable desert heat, high temperatures on the coast and further inland, and dense fog, you will still enjoy your visit.

USEFUL ADDRESSES
→ AMERICAN EMBASSY IN THE UK
24 Grosvenor Square
London
W1A 1AE
Tel: 020 7499 9000
www.usembassy.org.uk
■ **Visa Information Line**
Tel. 09068 200 290 24-hour. 60p per min; only available in the UK.

→ AMERICAN CONSULATES IN THE UK
3 Regent Terrace
Edinburgh
EH7 5BW
Tel. 0131 556 8315
Queen's House
14 Queen Street
Northern Ireland
BT1 6EQ
Tel. 028 9032 8239

WEBSITES
www.go calif.gov
Official California Government Tourist Office website. A great place to start planning your trip. You can download scenic driving tours, make hotel reservations and check out the calendar of seasonal events. This site also offers links to other useful sites, such as bed and breakfast tours and restaurant listings.
www.winezone.com
For lodgings, maps and information about the Napa Valley and Sonoma County wine country.
www.citysearch.com
For hotels, restaurants and events in the major cities. The site has listings for the Bay Area, Los Angeles, Sacremento, San Diego, San Francisco and San Jose.

ARRIVAL

Tourist information offices (*Travelers Aids*) are located in each airport.

→ LOS ANGELES

■ **LAX Shuttles**
Free shuttles – white with green and blue stripes – providing a 24-hour link with bus stops and car rental agencies.

■ **Cabs**
Allow $28 to Downtown, $32 to Hollywood.

■ **Shuttle service**
These minibuses are less expensive than cabs and drop passengers at the door.

■ **Buses**
The LAX shuttle (C) runs to the LAX Transit Center, where you can take a bus. Downtown: n° 439. West Hollywood and Beverly Hills: n° 220.

■ **Subway**
The LAX shuttle (G) drops passengers at the Aviation subway station, on the Green Line, situated on Vicksburg Avenue and 96th Street.

→ SAN FRANCISCO OAKLAND

■ **Cabs**
Allow $35 to the city center from San Francisco International Airport (SFO) and $55 from Oakland Airport (OA). Journey time: approx. 30 mins.

■ **Shuttle service**
There are several private shuttle companies. Shuttles leave every 20 mins. Price: $15

■ **Buses**
The KX ($3; 30 mins) and 292 lines operate between SFO and Transbay Terminal (1st Street/ Mission Street).

■ **Car rental**
The main car rental agencies have desks in the arrival halls.

ACCOMMODATION

High season: May–September. Breakfast often not included. Some hotels are non-smoking; some don't accept children or animals. Phone if you are going to arrive after 6pm or you may find that the hotel has canceled your reservation.

■ **Inns**
Country inns and B&Bs with character along the coast and in the towns of the Gold Country. Prices vary.

■ **Youth Hostels**
Shared rooms and bathrooms, refectory and laundromat. Sheets may not be provided, so bring a sleeping bag. There is no age limit. $9–26 per person. Reductions with an international youth-hostel card.

For information and reservations contact:
Hostelling International America Youth Hostels
Tel. (202) 783 6161
www.hiayh.org

■ **Camping**
In the national parks, State parks, national forests and on private camp sites. $7–30 per space. It is advisable to book in advance. Lists of camp sites available from Tourist Offices. Wild camping is prohibited.

■ **Bed & Breakfast**
More expensive than motels ($60–190) and not always as comfortable, but they certainly have more charm. Prices depend on the number of people, not the number of rooms. It is advisable to book in advance. B&B International Tel. 800 872 4500 or 408 867 9662
www.bbintl.com

■ **Hotels**
Very expensive: at least $150 per night.

■ **Motels ▲ 296**
Good value for money. Guaranteed clean and comfortable (TV and bathroom). Many don't have a restaurant or serve breakfast. Several categories: $50–190.

BRITISH CONSULATES

→ LOS ANGELES
11766 Wilshire Blvd
Suite 400
Los Angeles
CA 90025
Tel: (310) 477 3322
Fax: (310) 575 1450

→ SAN FRANCISCO
1 Sansome Street
Suite 850
San Francisco
CA 94104
Tel: (415) 617 1300
Fax: (415) 434 2018

EMERGENCIES

■ **Emergency numbers (Police, Fire, Ambulance)**
911 (toll free)

■ **Emergency services**
Very expensive. For non-emergency treatment, use the urgent care clinics located in the hospitals.

LOCAL TIMES

Californians tend to get up and go to bed early. Many people are at work by 8am. People in the film industry, in particular, often have early call hours.

■ **Mealtimes**
Lunch: 11.30am–2pm
Dinner: 6.30pm–8pm
Most restaurants serve until 10pm or 11pm.

■ **Office hours**
Open Mon.–Fri. 9am–5pm.

■ **Rush hours**
7–10am; 3–5pm.

■ **Stores**
Open 10am–6pm.
Malls sometimes
stay open later.

MAIL
■ **Stamps**
On sale in post
offices. Also
available (but
they cost more)
from airports,
supermarkets and
newsdealers.
For Europe: first
class (80 cents)
takes a minimum
of 5 to 10 days.
Post stamped mail
in the blue mail
boxes.
■ **General
delivery**
You can have mail
sent to the main
post office in major
towns and cities.
Letters must be
addressed c/o
General Delivery,
include the zip
code of the post
office, and bear the
name of the
recipient and the
address of the
sender.

MONEY
→ **CURRENCY**
$1 = 100 cents (¢).
Currency is
available in notes
(bills) – $1, 5, 10,
20, 50 and 100 –
and coins –
1 (penny), 5 (nickel),
10 (dime), 25
(quarter) cents.
Avoid $50 bills as
they are not
accepted by some
stores. Make sure
you have a good
supply of quarters
for parking meters
and public
transport.

→ **CREDIT CARDS**
Accepted almost
everywhere, even
for modest
amounts. They
are indispensable
for phone
reservations
and car rental.
When paying by
credit card, you can
ask for the amount

to be rounded up
and receive the
difference in cash
(this is known as
cashback).

→ **CASH DISPENSERS**
Banks and ATMs
(Automatic Teller
Machines) are
widespread, and
may even be sited
in small stores (such
as drugstores,
souvenir stores,
gas stations, etc.).
There is a charge
of between $2
and $3 for each
withdrawal.

NEWSPAPER DISPENSERS

→ **FOREIGN CURRENCY
EXCHANGE**
Banks are open
Mon.–Fri. 9am–4pm.
They are sometimes
until open 5pm and
on Saturdays.
Foreign exchange
offices are open
9am–5pm or 6pm.

PLACES TO SEE
Tourist sites and
cultural events are
listed in the free
weeklies available
from Visitors
Centers and other
places in main
towns and cities.
LA Weekly
www.laweekly.com

San Francisco Bay
Guardian
www.sfbg.com
San Francisco
Weekly
www.sfweekly.com
San Diego Reader
www.sdreader.com

PRESS
The *Los Angeles
Times* and *San
Francisco Chronicle*
are the most widely
read of the
Californian dailies.
They include Sunday
supplements
for the arts and
entertainment.

SPECIAL NEEDS
Public buildings
have wheelchair
access. Free parking
and admission to
national parks.
At theme and
amusement parks,
wheelchair patrons
can often go to
the head of the
lines.

TAX
Tax is not included
in prices shown in
stores or, as a
general rule, hotels
and restaurants.
You should allow
for 8.25% of the
total. Tax is included

in the price of
transport, cabs, gas
and telephone.
For accommodation,
an additional
tourist tax (14%) is
added to the
standard 8.25%.

TELEPHONE
Phone booths
take coins or
cards. Use a
phone card in
hotels, where
calls can cost up
to 70% more.
■ **Phone cards**
Phone cards
can be used for
public or private
phones. They are
generally good
value for money
depending on
the company.
Cards are on
sale at airports,
newspaper kiosks,
drugstores, gas
stations and
Visitors Centers.
■ **Calling the UK
from the US**
Dial 011 44 +
the number you
require (omitting
the initial 0)
■ **Toll-Free
Numbers**
800 numbers
are free within
the United States
only.

TIPPING
Compulsory but
not included in
the bill (*tab*).
Bars and restaurants:
add 15 20%.
Taxis: add 10–15%.
When paying by
credit card, you
can add the
amount of the
tip to the total
before signing.

TOURIST OFFICES
**California Division
of Tourism**
801 K Street
Sacramento
CA 95814
Tel. 916 322 2881
Visitors Centers
and Conventions
Bureaux in towns
and cities and main
tourist sites.

BY AIR

→ AIRPORTS
■ **International Airports**
Los Angeles (LAX)
Tel. (310) 646 5252
San Francisco (SFO)
Tel. (415) 761 0800
Oakland (OAK)
Tel. (510) 577 4000
San Diego (SAN)
Tel. (619) 213 7361
■ **Regional Airports**
San Jose (SJC)
Tel. (408) 277 4759
Sacramento (SMF)
Tel. (916) 929 5411
Orange County
Tel. (949) 252 5000
Palm Springs
Tel. (619) 323 8163

→ INTERNAL FLIGHTS
In view of the distances between cities, internal flights are a practical way to travel.
■ **American Airlines**
Tel. 800 433 7300
■ **America West Airlines**
Tel. 800 235 9292
■ **Continental Airlines**
Tel. 800 525 0280
■ **Delta Airlines**
Tel. 800 221 1212

→ PACKAGE DEALS
Special *passes* can be obtained for a 'package' of internal flights. See your local travel agents for details. Itineraries can be booked in advance but dates can remain flexible.

BY BUS

■ **Greyhound Bus Lines**
Greyhound buses operate throughout the United States. Special 7-, 15- or 30-day passes offer an unlimited number of journeys.
Tel. (213) 629 8401
■ **Green Tortoise**
Tourist coach tours from San Francisco to the northeastern United States, Central America and Alaska.
Tel. (415) 956 7500

BY CAB

Relatively inexpensive per mile, but the total cost of each journey is high due to the distances involved. Use only within cities.
■ **Los Angeles**
Yellow Cab
Tel. (800) 200 1085
■ **San Francisco**
Yellow Cab Bay Area
Tel. (650) 361 1234

BY CAR

→ CAR RENTAL
■ **Conditions**
Drivers must be over 25 (sometimes 21 if you pay a supplement) and must have held a driving license for over 1 year.
An international driving license is required only for visits lasting more than three months.
■ **Insurance**
Be warned! Insurance is not always included in the rental price. Two options: CDW (Collision Damage Waiver) and LDW (Loss Damage Waiver), comprehensive insurance.
■ **Type of vehicle**
All cars are automatic.

→ DRIVING IN CALIFORNIA
■ **Safety belts**
Compulsory in both front and back seats.
■ **Speed limit**
25 mph in urban areas, 55–70 mph on freeways and Interstates, 35–55 mph on other roads. NB: you can get a ticket for driving too slowly.
■ **Priority**
There is no priority to the right. At an intersection, the first car there has right of way. Give way to pedestrians.

■ **Traffic lights**
They are sometimes positioned on the far side of the intersection. In towns, unless otherwise indicated, you can turn right at a red light – but give way to oncoming traffic.
■ **Road signs**
They are often (especially in Los Angeles) positioned above the roads they are indicating, which can cause confusion.
■ **Road markings**
Xing
Xing – an abbreviation for crossing – means you are approaching an intersection and must slow down.
A double yellow line
Can be crossed to turn left.
Two double yellow lines
Cannot be crossed.
Central lane bounded on either side by a single and a broken line
Reserved for vehicles turning left.
Diamond line
An outside lane on freeways, reserved for the car pool, i.e. car-sharing by two or more people.
Right lane exit
(*freeways and Interstates*)
The right-hand lane is a slip road. To remain on the freeway, stay in the center lanes. If there is a 'thru traffic merge left' sign, keep to the left.

→ PARKING
Don't ignore parking signs. In this domain, the police are impressively efficient.
■ **Coloured sidewalks**
Red
No parking or stopping.
Yellow
Deliveries only.

Blue
Reserved for special needs.
White
Stopping allowed to drop or pick up passengers.
Green
Maximum stopping time 20 mins.
■ **Parking signs**
Parking
Each street has signs indicating authorized times and duration of parking. If you ignore them you can expect a fine.
No Parking, No Standing or No Stopping
This means you can't park or stop.
Tow-away
You run the risk of having you car impounded.

→ DRUNK DRIVING
Limit: blood-alcohol concentration of 0.08%. It is an offense to carry alcohol inside the car – keep it in the boot (trunk).

→ GAS
Gas is cheap in the US, making driving an inexpensive way to travel.

FINDING YOUR WAY ON FREEWAYS AND INTERSTATES
→ PREPARE YOUR ROUTE
Place names are not always well-marked. Before setting out, it is therefore important to find the name or number of the freeway you want, the direction you will be taking (North, South, East, West) and the name or number of the exit.

■ **In urban areas**
Even numbers run east–west, odd numbers run north–south.

→ ROAD MAPS
Available from gas stations, book stores and supermarkets. For Los Angeles, *The Thomas Guide*, the most comprehensive road atlas, is highly recommended.

→ THE ROAD NETWORK
The road network consists of national roads (US Roads), state roads (SR), county roads (CR), national Interstates (I), freeways and highways.
Only Tollways and some bridges (such as the Golden Gate Bridge) charge a toll.

■ Freeways and Highways
Identified by their green and white signs. These freeways can be quite challenging to drive on, with numerous lanes.

■ Interstate Freeways
Identified by their blue, white and red signs.

■ US Federal Highways
Identified by their black and white sign in the form of a shield. They are as fast as the Interstates, with the exception of Highway 1 (the Pacific Coast Highway) a picturesque highway that winds its way along the coast.

RAIL TRAVEL
The Amtrak network is not widely used by the Americans. A few lines are well worth the detour.
Coast Starlight
Runs along the coast between Seattle and San Diego.

California Zephyr
Runs through the Sierra Nevada and along Lake Tahoe.
Tel. (800) 872 7245
www.amtrak.com

URBAN TRANSPORT
→ LOS ANGELES
■ Subway
Three lines open 5am–11pm. Trains run every 15 mins. Tickets cost $1.35.
Blue Line
Downtown–Long Beach.
Red Line
Downtown–Universal City.
Green Line
Redondo Beach–Norwalk.

■ Buses
208 routes run by several companies. General map available from the Los Angeles Convention and Visitors Bureaus. Individual route maps available from information kiosks and main tourist sites.

→ SAN FRANCISCO
Two public transport networks.
■ MUNI (San Francisco Municipal Railway)
Tel. (415) 673 6864
Services all districts with its bus, subways, trams and cable cars.
Tickets (each): $1 (buses and trams), $2 (cable cars).
Travel cards (passes): 1-day ($6), 3-day ($10), 7-day ($15).

■ BART (Bay Area Rapid Transit)
Tel. (650) 992 2278
Rail network linking San Francisco to the East Bay (Oakland, Berkeley, etc.). Tickets available from automatic ticket machines in stations.

◆ FESTIVALS AND EVENTS

FESTIVALS AND EVENTS

JAN. 1	PASADENA	Tournament of Roses
JAN.	SAN JOSE	Vietnamese New Year
MID JAN.	PALM SPRINGS	Palm Springs International Film Festival
END JAN.	COLOMA	Gold Discovery Day
JAN.–MAY	SAN FRANCISCO	Symphony Orchestra Season
FEB. 13.	MAJOR CITIES	Chinese New Year
	LOS ANGELES	Golden Dragon Parade
FEB 20–27	SAN FRANCISCO	Chinese New Year Celebration
FEB	INDIO	Napa Valley International Mustard Festival National Date Festival
	RIVERSIDE	Dickens Festival
MARCH	EUREKA	Redwood Coast Dixieland Jazz Festival
	MENDOCINO	Whale Watch Festival
	SAN FRANCISCO	Saint Patrick Day's Parade
	SAN JUAN CAPISTRANO	Return of the Swallows
	SANTA BARBARA	International Film Festival
	TAHOE CITY	Snowfest
APRIL	JAPANTOWN	Cherry Blossom Festival
	LOS ANGELES	Academy Awards Ceremony
	PALM SPRINGS	Agua Cahuilla Indian Heritage Festival
	LOS ANGELES	Broadway Fiesta
	SAN FRANCISCO	Commemoration of the 1906 Earthquake International Film Festival
MAY	ANGELS CAMP	Calaveras County Fair (rodeo) Jumping Frog Jubilee
	HEALDSBURG	Wine Festival
	LA, SAN FRANCISCO	Cinco de Mayo (Mexican festival)
	OXNARD	California Strawberry Festival
	SANTA ROSA	Rose Parade
	SELMA	Raisin Festival
3RD W/E MAY	SACRAMENTO	Jazz Jubilee
END MAY	SAN FRANCISCO	Carnaval
MAY–JUNE	SAN DIEGO	Mainly Mozart Festival
JUNE	OJAI	Music Festival
	HOLLYWOOD	Playboy Jazz Festival
	SAINT HELENA	Napa Valley Wine Auction
	THOUSAND OAKS	International Pow Wow
	TUOLUMNE	Lumber Jubilee
	SAN FRANCISCO	Gay Pride
END JUNE	MONTEREY	Blues Festival
	OAKLAND	Juneteenth (Jazz and Gospel Festival)
JUNE–SEP.	SAN DIEGO	Shakespeare Festival
JUNE–AUG.	SAN FRANCISCO	Music Festival
JULY	GILROY	Gilroy Garlic Festival
	MAMMOTH LAKE	Jazz Festival
	SALINAS	California Rodeo
	SAN JOSE	Olbon Festival (Japanese-American Festival)
	LAGUNA BEACH	Festival of the Arts (Festival of the Arts and *Tableaux Vivants*) Pageant of Masters (*Tableaux Vivants* of Old Masters) Sadwust Festival (Festival of Creative Crafts)
AUGUST	CARMEL	Bach Festival
	COSTA MESA	Native American Pow Wow (Indian festival)
	SANTA BARBARA	Old Spanish Days Fiesta
	LONG BEACH	International Sea Festival
	LA (LITTLE TOKYO)	Nisei Week (Japanese festival)
	SALINAS	Steinbeck Festival
AUG.–SEP.	SACRAMENTO	Country State Fair
SEP.	POMONA	Los Angeles County Fair
SEP. 10	NAPA	Napa Valley Music & Wine Festival
MID-SEP.	LOS ANGELES	Mexican Independence Day
	GUERNEVILLE	Jazz Festival
	MONTEREY	Jazz Festival
	SAN FRANCISCO	Blues Festival

END SEP.	SAN DIEGO	Cabrillo Festival
	SAN FRANCISCO	Art Festival
SEP.–OCT.	TORRANCE	Oktoberfest (Beer Festival)
SEP.–NOV.	SAN FRANCISCO	Opera season
OCT.	CARMEL	Tor House Poetry Festival
	OAKLAND	Black Cowboy Heritage Festival
	SANTA ROSA	Sonoma County Harvest Fair
OCT. 1	SAN FRANCISCO (FISHERMAN'S WHARF)	Blessing of the Fishing Fleet
	BRIDGEPORT	Mountain Man Rendez-vous (Open-air barbecue)
1ST SUN. OCT.	SAN FRANCISCO	Gay Pride Festival
MID OCT.	NEWPORT BEACH	Motor Show (classic car event)
	HALF MOON BAY	Pumpkin Festival
END OCT.	LOS ANGELES	International Festivals of Masks
31 OCT.	NATIONAL EVENT	Halloween
END OCT.– BEG. NOV.	SAN FRANCISCO	Jazz Festival
	DALY CITY	Grand National Rodeo
NOV. 2	NATIONAL EVENT	Dia de los Muertos (Day of the Dead)
NOV. 6	NAPA VALLEY	Wine Festival
MID NOV.	PASADENA	Doo Dha Parade (parody of the Rose Parade)
END NOV.–DEC.	MAJOR CITIES	Christmas Parades
DEC.	SAN JUAN BAUTISTA	Nativity Play
	GUERNEVILLE	Russian Heritage Christmas Celebration
	INDIO	International Tamale Festival (Mexican festival)

SPORTING EVENTS

MARCH	LOS ANGELES	Marathon
APRIL	LONG BEACH	Toyota Grand Prix
MAY	SAN FRANCISCO	Bay to Breakers (marathon)
APR.–SEP.	MAJOR CITIES	Major League Baseball (start of the baseball season)
	SAN FRANCISCO	Marathon
END JULY	LOS ANGELES	International Surf Festival

PUBLIC HOLIDAYS

JAN. 1		New Years Day
3RD. MON. JAN.		Martin Luther King Day
3RD. MON. FEB.		Presidents' Day
APRIL		Easter Sunday
APRIL 15		Memorial Day (firework display)
JULY 4		Independence Day (firework display)
1ST. MON. SEP.		Labor Day
2ND. MON. OCT.		Colombus Day
NOV. 11		Veterans' Day
4TH THU. NOV.		Thanksgiving
DEC. 25.		Christmas Day

◆ PLACES TO VISIT

PLACES TO VISIT (IN ALPHABETICAL ORDER) EXCLUDING PARKS

ANAHEIM ◆ C B4

| DISNEYLAND
1313 Harbor Blvd
Tel. (714) 781 4565 | Open daily
Information: www.disney.go.com
and www.disneyland.com | ▲ 214 |

BERKELEY ◆ A B6

BERKELEY ART MUSEUM 2626 Bancroft Way Tel. (510) 642 0808	Open Wed., Fri.–Sun. 11am–5pm, Thu. 11am–9pm. Closed Mon.–Tue. Information: www.bampfa.berkeley.edu	▲ 143
PHOEBE HEARST MUSEUM OF ANTHROPOLOGY 103 Kroeber Hall Bancroft Way Tel. (510) 643 7648	Open Wed.–Sun. 10am–4.30pm (Thu. 9pm). Closed during university vacations. Information: www.qal.berkeley.edu/~hearst	▲ 143
UNIVERSITY OF CALIFORNIA VISITORS CENTER 101 University Hall 2200 University Ave Tel. (510) 642 5215	Information: www.berkeley.edu	▲ 143

BIG SUR ◆ B A3

| PFEIFFER BIG SUR STATE PARK
47225 Hwy 1
Tel. (831) 667 3100 | Open daily 10.30am–10.30pm. | ▲ 170,
239 |
| HENRY MILLER LIBRARY
Hwy 1
Tel. (831) 667 2574 | Open Tue.–Wed. 2–6pm, Thu.–Sun. 11am–6pm.
Information: www. henrymiller.org | ▲ 170 |

BORREGO SPRINGS ◆ C D6

| ANZA BORREGO DESERT STATE PARK
200 Palm Canyon Drive
Tel. (760) 767 5311 | Visitors Center open Oct.–May daily 9am–5pm;
June–Sept. Sat.–Sun. and public holidays.
Information: www.anzaborrego.statepark.org | ▲ 246 |

BUENA PARK ◆ C B4

| KNOTT'S BERRY FARM
8039 Beach Blvd
Tel. (714) 220 5200 | Open daily except Dec. 25.
Phone for opening hours
or visit the website: www.knotts.com | ▲ 215 |

CALISTOGA ◆ A B5

CLOS PEGASE 1060 Dunaweal Lane Tel. (707) 942 4981	Open daily 10.30am–5pm. Guided tours daily 11am, 2pm. Information: www.clospegase.com	▲ 151
OLD FAITHFUL GEYSER 1299 Tubbs Lane Tel. (707) 942 6463	Open daily 9am–5pm in summer; 9am–6pm in winter. Information: www.oldfaithfulgeyser.com	▲ 151
STERLING VINEYARDS 1111 Dunaweal Lane Tel. (707) 942 3344	Open daily 10.30am–4.30pm. Book in advance for guided tours, lunches and dinners. Information: www.sterlingvyds.com	▲ 151

CARMEL ◆ B A2

| MISSION CARMEL
3080 Rio Road and Lasuen Drive
Tel. (831) 624 3600 | Guided tours Mon.–Sat. 9.30am–4.15pm,
Sun. 10.15am–4.15pm and June 1–Aug. 31 daily
9.30am–7.15pm. | ▲ 171 |

CASPAR ◆ A A4

| JUGHANDLE STATE RESERVE
Caspar Tel. (707) 937 5804 | Visitors Center open Mon.–Fri. 8am–4.30pm. | ▲ 153 |

CATALINA ISLAND ◆ C A5

| CATALINA ISLAND VISITORS BUREAU
General Information
Tel. (310) 510 1520 | Information: www.visitcatalina.org | ▲ 213 |
| CATALINA EXPRESS
Tel. (800) 481 3470 | Departure from San Pedro, Long Beach and Dana
Point. Information: www.catalinaexpress.com | |

ESCONDIDO ◆ C C5

| SAN DIEGO WILD ANIMAL PARK
15500 San Pasqual Valley Road
Tel. (760) 747 8702 | Open daily 9am–4pm.
Information: www.sandiegozoo.org | ▲ 226 |

EUREKA		◆ A A2
SAMOA COOKHOUSE 1 Cookhouse Road Tel. (707) 442 1659	*Open daily except Dec. 25. Breakfast: 7am–11am. Lunch: 11am–13.30pm. Dinner: 5–9pm. Information: www.humboldtdining.com/cookhouse*	▲ 154
FRESNO		◆ B C3
ALLENSWORTH STATE HISTORIC PARK Hwy 99 Tel. (661) 849 3433	*Visitors Center open daily 10am–4pm.*	▲ 165
ART MUSEUM 2233 N 1st Street Tel. (559) 441 4221	*Open Tue.–Fri. 10am–5pm, Sat.–Sun. noon–5pm. Closed Mon., Thanksgiving, Dec. 25, Jan. 1. Information: www.fresnoartmuseum.com*	▲ 165
CHAFFEE ZOOLOGICAL GARDENS 894 West Beelmont Ave Tel. (559) 498 2671	*Open daily (except safari days) Mar.–Oct. 9am–5pm; Nov.–Dec. 10am–4pm. Information: www.chaffeezoo.org*	▲ 165
MEUX HOME MUSEUM 107 R Street Tel. (209) 233 8007	*Open Fri.–Sun. noon–3.30pm. Closed January. Information: www.meux.mus.ca.us*	▲ 165
METROPOLITAN MUSEUM 155 Van Ness Ave Tel. (559) 441 1444	*Open Tue.–Wed., Fri.–Sun. 11am–5pm, Thu. 11am– 8pm. Closed Mon., Thanksgiving, Dec. 25, Jan. 1, Labor Day, Easter. Information: www.frestnomet.org*	▲ 165
ST JOHN'S CATHEDRAL 2814 Mariposa Street Tel. (559) 485 6210		▲ 165
GARDEN GROVE		◆ C B4
CRYSTAL CATHEDRAL 13280 Chapman Ave Tel. (714) 971 4000	*Guided tours Mon.–Sat. 9am–3.30pm. Sunday service 9.30–11am. Information: www.crystalcathedral.org*	▲ 211
GEYSERVILLE		◆ A B5
GEYSER PEAK WINERY 22281 Chianti Road Tel. (800) 255 9463	*Open daily 10am–5pm. Information: www.geyserpeakwinery.com*	▲ 148
PEDRONCELLI WINERY 1220 Canyon Road Tel. (707) 857 3531	*Open daily 10am–4.30pm except public holidays. Information: www.pedroncelli.com*	▲ 148
GLEN ELLEN		◆ A B6
JACK LONDON STATE HISTORIC PARK 2400 London Ranch Road Tel. (707) 938 5276	*Open daily 10am–5pm (7pm in summer). Guided tours 11.30am–3.30pm. Closed Thanksgiving, Dec. 25, Jan. 1.*	▲ 149
GRASS VALLEY		◆ A D5
EMPIRE MINE STATE HISTORIC PARK 10791 E Empire Street Tel. (530) 273 8522	*Disabled access, cycle tracks.*	▲ 160
HOLBROOKE HOTEL 212 W Main Street Tel. (530) 273 1353	*Bar, hotel, restaurant. Information: www.holbrook.com*	▲ 160
HEALDSBURG		◆ A B5
DRY CREEK VINEYARDS 3770 Lambert Bridge Road Tel. (800) 864 9463	*Open Mon.–Fri. 10.30am–4.30pm except public holidays. Information: www.drycreekvineyard.com*	▲ 148
RODNEY STRONG VINEYARDS 11455 Old Redwood Hwy Tel. (707) 431 1533	*Guided tours and wine tastings daily 10am–5pm. Information: www.rodneystong.com*	▲ 148
SIMI WINERY 16275 Healdsburg Ave Tel. (800) 746 4880	*Open daily 10am–5pm. Guided tours daily 11am, 1pm, 3pm. Information: www.simiwinery.com*	▲ 148
KENWOOD		◆ A B5
KENWOOD VINEYARDS 9592 Sonoma Hwy Tel. (707) 833 5891	*Wine-tasting daily 10am–4.30pm except vacations. Picnic area. Information: www.kenwoodvineyards.com*	▲ 148
LANDMARK VINEYARDS 101 Adobe Canyon Road Tel. (707) 833 0053	*Open daily 10am–4.30pm. Wine tasting and picnic area. Information: www.landmarkwine.com*	▲ 148

◆ PLACES TO VISIT

LAGUNA BEACH		U C C5
LAGUNA ARTS MUSEUM 307 Cliff Drive Tel. (949) 494 8971	*Open daily 11am–5pm except Wed. Guided tours 2pm. Artwalk open 6–9pm 1st Thu. of the month. Free admission Tue.* *Information: www.lagunaartmuseum.org*	▲ 216

LA JOLLA		U C B6
CAVE STORE 1325 Coast Blvd Tel. (858) 459 0746		▲ 225
SAN DIEGO MUSEUM **OF CONTEMPORARY ART** 700 Prospect Street Tel. (858) 454 3541	*Open Mon.–Tue., Fri. 11am–5pm (8pm in summer); Thu. 11am–6pm; Sat.–Sun. 11am–5pm. Closed Wed.* *Information: www.mcasandiego.org*	▲ 225
STEPHEN BIRCH AQUARIUM MUSEUM 2300 Expedition Way Tel. (828) 534 3474	*Open daily 9am–5pm.* *Closed Thanksgiving, Dec. 25, Jan. 1* *Information: www.aquarium.ucsd.edu*	
TORREY PINES STATE RESERVE 12600 N Torrey Pines Road Tel. (858) 755 2063	*Open daily 8am–dusk.* *Visitors Center open 9am.* *Information: www.torreypine.org*	▲ 226

LOMPOC		◆ B B5
PURISIMA MISSION STATE HISTORIC PARK 2295 Purisima Road Tel. (805) 733 3713	*Guided tours daily 10am and 11am.* *Information: www.lompoc-ca.com*	▲ 173

LOS ANGELES		◆ C A4-B4
CONVENTION AND VISITORS BUREAU **DOWNTOWN** 685 S Figueroa Street Tel. (213) 689 8822	*Information: www.lacvb.com* *Open Mon.–Fri. 8am–5pm, Sat. 8.30am–5pm.*	
HOLLYWOOD Janes House 6541 Hollywood Blvd Tel. (213) 689 8822	*Open Mon.–Sat. 9am–5pm.*	
BEVERLY HILLS 239 S Beverly Drive Tel. (310) 271 8174	*Open Mon.–Fri. 8.30am–5pm.*	
LONG BEACH AREA I World Trade Center, Suite 300 Tel. (562) 436 3645	*Open Mon.–Fri. 8am–5pm.*	
PASADENA 171 S Los Robles Ave Tel. (626) 795 9311	*Open Mon.–Fri. 8am–5pm, Sat. 10am–4pm.* *Information: www.pasadenacal.com*	
SANTA MONICA 520 Broadway, Suite 250 Tel. (310) 319 6263	*Open Mon.–Fri. 9am–5pm.*	
1400 Ocean Blvd Tel. (310) 393 7593	*Open daily 9am–6pm.*	
ABC ENTERTAINMENT CENTER 2020–2040 Avenue of the Stars Century City Tel. (310) 556 3096	*Information: www.centuryplazatowers.com*	▲ 203 ◆ I B3
ANGELS FLIGHT FUNICULAR 351 S Hill Street Tel. (213) 626 1901	*Open daily 6.30–10pm except 1st and 3rd Tue. of the month 6.30am–8pm.*	▲ 186 ◆ G E5
AUTRY MUSEUM OF WESTERN HERITAGE 4700 Western Heritage Way Griffith Park Tel. (323) 667 2000	*Open Tue.–Sun.10am–5pm (8pm Thurs).* *Admission free 2nd Thu. of the month.* *Information: www.autry-museum.org*	▲ 192 ◆ G D2
AVILA ADOBE HOUSE El Pueblo de Los Angeles 10 Olvera Street Tel. (213) 628 1274	*Open Mon.–Sat. 9am–5pm.* *Admission free.*	▲ 184 ◆ G F5
BERGAMOT STATION ARTS CENTER 2525 Michighan Ave Santa Monica Tel. (310) 586 6488	*Hours vary for each gallery.* *Most are open Tue.–Sat. 10am–6pm.* *Information: www.bergamotstation.com*	▲ 209 ◆ J B1
BRADBURY BUILDING 304 S Broadway Tel. (213) 626 1863	*Open Mon.–Sat. 9am–5pm.*	● 67 ▲ 186 ◆ G E5

BRUIN THEATER UCLA UCLA Ticket Office Alumni Center Tel. (213) 825 2101	*Open daily 10am–5pm.* *Admission free. Car-parking charges.* *Imax: hours vary.*	▲ 206 ◆ I A2
CABRILLO MARINE AQUARIUM 3720 Stephen White Drive San Pedro Tel. (310) 548 7562	*Open Tue.–Fri. noon–5pm, Sat.–Sun. 10am–5pm.* *Information: www.cabrilloaq.org*	▲ 211 ◆ F D6
CALIFORNIA AFRICAN AMERICAN MUSEUM 600 State Drive, Exposition Park Tel. (213) 744 7432	*Open Tue.–Sun. 10am–5pm.* *Admission free.* *Information: www.caam.ca.gov*	▲ 188 ◆ G D6
CALIFORNIA HERITAGE MUSEUM 2162 Main St, Santa Monica Tel. (310) 392 8537	*Open Wed.–Sun. 11am–4pm.*	▲ 208 ◆ J B2
CALIFORNIA INSTITUTE OF TECHNOLOGY 1200 E California Blvd Pasadena Tel. (626) 395 6811	*Visit the website for a program of cultural events:* *www.caltech.edu*	▲ 190 ◆ H B2
CALIFORNIA SCIENCE CENTER Exposition Park, 700 State Dr Tel. (323) 724 3623	*Open daily 10am–5pm. Closed Thanksgiving,* *Dec. 25, Jan. 1* *Information: www.casciencectr.org*	▲ 188, 189 ◆ G D6
CAPITOL RECORDS TOWER 1750 Vine Street Tel. (323) 462 6252		▲ 197 ◆ G C3
CBS TELEVISION CITY 7800 Beverly Blvd Tel. (323) 575 2448	*Information: www.cbs.com*	▲ 198 ◆ B4
CELEBRITY LINGERIE HALL OF FAME FREDERIK'S OF HOLLYWOOD 6608 Hollywood Blvd Tel. (323) 466 8506	*Open Mon.–Thu. 10am–9pm, Fri. 10am–6pm,* *Sat.–Sun. noon–5pm.* *Admission free.*	▲ 197 ◆ G B3
CHILDREN'S MUSEUM 310 N Main Street Tel. (213) 687 880	*Open daily in summer; Sat.–Sun. in winter.* *www.childrensmuseumla.org*	▲ 184 ◆ G E5
CRAFT AND FOLK ART MUSEUM 5800 Wilshire Blvd Tel. (323) 937 4230	*Open Wed., Fri.–Sun. 11am–5pm, Thu. 11am–9pm.*	▲ 199 ◆ G B4
DOHENY MEMORIAL LIBRARY University of South California 3550 Trousdale Parkway Tel. (213) 740 6050	*Opening hours vary.* *Visit the website: www.usc.edu/isd/doheny*	▲ 189 ◆ G D6
EGYPTIAN THEATER 6712 Hollywood Blvd Tel. (323) 467 0163	*Open Tue.–Sun. 1–4pm and 30 min after the start of* *the last show. Guided tours in summer.* *Information: www.americancinematheque.com*	▲ 197 ◆ G B3
EL CAPITAN THEATER 6838 Hollywood Blvd Tel. (323) 467 7674	*Phone for program details.* *Wheelchair access.*	▲ 197 ◆ G B3
FARMERS MARKET 6333 W Third Street Tel. (323) 933 9211	*Open Mon.–Sat. 9am–7pm, Sun. 10am–6pm in* *summer; Mon.–Sat. 9am–6.30pm, Sun. 10am–5pm* *in winter. Information: www.farmersmarketla.com*	▲ 198 ◆ G B4
FISHER GALLERY University of South California 823 Exposition Blvd Tel. (213) 740 4561	*Open Tue.–Sat. noon–5pm during exhibitions.* *Closed during university vacations.* *Information: www.esc.edu/org/fishergallery*	▲ 189 ◆ G D6
FOREST LAWN MEMORIAL PARK 1712 S Glendale Ave Tel. (800) 204 3131	*Museum open daily 10am–5pm. Admission free.* *Information: wwwforestlawn.com*	▲ 193 ◆ G C1
FOWLER MUSEUM OF CULTURAL HISTORY University of California 10899 Wilshire Blvd Tel. (310) 825 4361	*Open Wed.–Sun. noon–5pm (8pm Thu.).* *Closed Mon.–Tue.* *Information: www.fmch.ucla.edu*	▲ 206 ◆ I A2
FRANKLIN D MURPHY SCULPTURE GARDEN University of California 10899 Wilshire Blvd Tel. (310) 443 7000	*Open daily.* *Admission free.*	▲ 206 ◆ I A2
GAMBLE HOUSE 4 Westmoreland Pl, Pasadena Tel. (626) 793 3334	*Guided tours Tue.–Sun. noon–3pm.* *Allow time to buy tickets.* *Information: www.gamblehouse.org*	● 68 ▲ 191 ◆ H A1

◆ PLACES TO VISIT

GEORGE C PAGE MUSEUM **OF LA BREA DISCOVERIES** 5801 Wilshire Blvd Tel. (323) 936 2230	*Open Mon.–Fri. 9.30am–5pm, Sat.–Sun. 10am–5pm.* *Opening hours subject to alteration during* *vacations.* *Information: www.tarpits.org*	▲ 199 ◆ G A4
GEFFEN CONTEMPORARY AT MOCA 152 N Central Ave Tel. (213) 626 6222	*Open Tue.–Sun. 11am–5pm (8pm Thu.).* *Information: www.moca-la.org*	▲ 185 ◆ G F5
GETTY CENTER 1200 Getty Center Drive Tel. (310) 440 7300	*Open Tue.–Wed. 10am–7pm, Thu.–Fri. 10am–9pm,* *Sat.–Sun. 10am–6pm. Closed Mon. and public* *holidays. Parking must be booked in advance.* *Information: www.getty.org*	▲ 204, 205 ◆ F C2
GRAND CENTRAL MARKET 317 S Broadway Tel. (213) 624 2378	*Open daily 9am–6pm.* *Information: www.grandcentralsquare.com*	▲ 186 ◆ G E5
GREYSTONE PARK AND MANSION 905 Loma Vista Drive Tel. (310) 550 4796	*Open daily Oct.–Mar. 10am–5pm; Apr.–Sep.* *10am–6pm.*	▲ 203 ◆ I C1
GRIFFITH OBSERVATORY 2800 E Observatory Road Griffith Park Tel. (323) 664 1191	*Open Tue.–Fri. 2–10pm, Sat.–Sun. and public hols* *12.30–10pm in winter; 12.30–10pm in summer* *(July–Aug.). Closed Colombus Day, Thanksgiving,* *Dec. 25. Information: www.griffithobs.org*	▲ 192 ◆ G C2
GUINNESS BOOK OF RECORDS 6764 Hollywood Blvd Tel. (323) 463 6433	*Open daily 10am–noon.*	▲ 197 ◆ G B3
HOLLYWOOD ENTERTAINMENT MUSEUM 7021 Hollywood Blvd Tel. (323) 465 7900	*Open Thu.–Tue. 11am–6pm in winter;* *Mon.–Sat.10am–6pm, Sun. 11am–6pm in summer.* *Closed Wed., Thanksgiving, Dec. 25, Jan. 1.*	▲ 196 ◆ G B3
HOLLYWOOD FOREVER MEMORIAL PARK 6000 Santa Monica Blvd Tel. (323) 469 1181	*Open Tue.–Fri. 8am–5pm and Sat.–Sun. 9am–4pm.* *Free parking.*	▲ 198 ◆ G C3
HOLLYWOOD & HIGHLAND 6834 Hollywood Blvd, Suite 600 Tel. (323) 460 2626	*Information: www.hollywoodandhighland.com*	▲ 196 ◆ G B3
HOLLYWOOD STUDIO MUSEUM 2100 N Highland Ave Tel. (323) 874 2276	*Open Sat.–Sun. 11am–3.30pm. Admission free.* *Opening hours subject to alteration. Phone for* *details.*	▲ 197 ◆ G B3
HOLLYWOOD WAX MUSEUM 6767 Hollywood Blvd Tel. (323) 462 5991	*Open Sun.–Thu. 10am–midnight,* *Fri.–Sat. 10am–2am.*	▲ 197 ◆ G B3
HOUSE OF BLUES 8430 Sunset Blvd Tel. (323) 848 5100	*Open daily 8pm–1.30 am.* *Information: www.hob.com*	▲ 198
HUNTINGTON LIBRARY, **ART COLLECTIONS** **AND BOTANICAL GARDENS** 1151 Oxford Road, San Marino Tel. (626) 405 2100	*Open Sept.–May Tue.–Fri. noon–4.30pm,* *Sat.–Sun. 10.30am–4.30pm; June–Aug. Tue.–Sun.* *10.30am–4.30pm. Closed Mon., Thanksgiving, Dec.* *24–25, Jan. 1, Apr. 15, July 4, Labor Day.* *Information: www.huntington.org*	▲ 190 ◆ H C3
JAPANESE AMERICAN CULTURAL **& COMMUNITY CENTER** 244 S San Pedro Street Tel. (213) 628 2725	*Information: www.jaccc.org*	▲ 185 ◆ G F5
JAPANESE AMERICAN **NATIONAL MUSEUM** 369 E 1st Street Tel. (213) 625 0414	*Open Tue.–Sun. 10am–5pm (8pm Thu.).* *Closed Mon., Thanksgiving, Dec. 25, Jan. 1.* *Admission free Thu. 5–8pm and 3rd Thu. of the* *month. Information: www.janm.org*	▲ 185 ◆ G F5
LOS ANGELES CENTRAL LIBRARY 630 W 5th Street Tel. (213) 228 7069	*Open Mon.–Thu. 10am–6pm, Fri.–Sat. 10am–8pm,* *Sun. 1–5pm.* *Information: www.lapl.org*	▲ 187 ◆ G E5
LACMA 5905 Wilshire Blvd Tel. (323) 857 6000	*Open Mon.–Tue., Thu. noon–8pm, Fri. noon–9pm,* *Sat.–Sun. 11am–8pm. Closed Wed., Thanksgiving,* *Dec. 25. Information: www.lacma.org*	▲ 200, 201 ◆ G A4
LOS ANGELES MARITIME MUSEUM 84 Berth, Foot of 6th Street San Pedro Tel. (310) 548 7618	*Guided tours in English and Spanish by prior* *arrangement. Wheelchair access.* *Information: www.lamaritimemuseum.org*	▲ 211 ◆ F D6
LOS ANGELES MEMORIAL COLISEUM 3939 S Figueroa Street Tel. (213) 748 6136	*Information: www.stadianet.com/lacliseum*	▲ 189 ◆ G D6
LOS ANGELES ZOO Griffith Park, 5333 Zoo Drive Tel. (323) 644 6400	*Open daily (except Dec. 25) 10am–5pm (6pm* *July–Aug.). Animals cannot be seen 1 hour before* *closing. Information: www.lazoo.org*	▲ 192 ◆ G D1

Place	Details	Ref
LONG BEACH AQUARIUM OF THE PACIFIC 100 Aquarium Way, Long Beach Tel. (562) 590 3100	*Open daily 9am–6pm except Dec. 25 and the weekend of the Long Beach Toyota Grand Prix (April).* *Information: www.aquariumofpacific.org*	▲ 212 ◆ K A2
LONG BEACH MUSEUM OF ART 2300 E Ocean Blvd, Long Beach Tel. (562) 439 2119	*Open Tue.–Sun. 11am–7pm.* *Information: www.lbma.org*	▲ 212 ◆ K B2
MAGEE'S HOUSE OF NUTS 6333 W Third Street Tel. (323) 938 4147	*Open Mon.–Tue., Thu. noon–8pm; Fri. noon–9pm; Sat.–Sun. 11am–8pm.*	▲ 198
MANN'S CHINESE THEATER 6925 Hollywood Blvd Tel. (323) 464 6266	*Program details: www.manntheatres.com*	● 73 ▲ 196 ◆ G B3
MILDRED E MATHIAS BOTANICAL GARDEN University of California 10899 Wilshire Blvd Tel. (310) 285 1260	*Open Mon.–Fri. 8am–5pm (4pm in winter), Sat.–Sun. 8am–4pm. Closed during university vacations.* *Information: www.botgard.ucla.edu*	▲ 207 ◆ I A2
MISSION SAN GABRIEL ARCHANGEL 428 S Mission Drive Tel. (626) 457 3035	*Open daily 9am–4.30pm.* *Closed Thanksgiving, Dec. 25, Easter.* *Information: www.sangabrielmission.org*	▲ 186 ◆ F F2
MOCA 250 S Grand Ave Tel. (213) 626 6222	*Open Tue.–Sun. 11am–5pm.* *Free late-night opening Thu. 8pm.* *Information: www.moca-la.org*	▲ 186 ◆ G E5
MUSEUM OF FLYING 2772 Donald Douglas Loop N Santa Monica Tel. (310) 392 8822	*Open Wed.–Sun. 10am–5pm. Closed Mon.–Tue.* *Information: www.museumofflying.com*	▲ 208 ◆ J C2
MUSEUM OF JURASSIC TECHNOLOGY 9341 Venice Blvd, Culver City Tel. (310) 836 6131	*Open Fri.–Sun. 2–6pm (8pm Tue.). Closed Thanksgiving, Dec. 24–25, Easter, 1st Thu. in May.* *Information: www.mjt.org*	▲ 203 ◆ F C3
MUSEUM OF TELEVISION & RADIO 465 N Beverly Drive Tel. (310) 786 1025	*Open Wed.–Sun. noon–5pm (9pm Thu.). Closed Mon.–Tue., July 4, Thanksgiving, Dec. 25, Jan. 1.* *Information: www.mtr.org*	▲ 203 ◆ I C2
MUSEUM OF TOLERANCE Simon Wiesenthal Plaza 9786 W Pico Blvd Tel. (310) 553 8403	*Open Mon.–Thu. 11.30 am–6.30pm; Fri. Nov.–Mar. 11.30am–3pm, Apr.–Oct. 11.30am–5pm; Sun. 11am–7.30pm. Last admission 2 hours before closing. Closed Sat. and Jewish festivals.* *Information: www.wiesenthal.com*	▲ 203 ◆ I C3
MUSIC CENTER 135 N Grand Ave Tel. (213) 972 7200	*Visit the website for program details: www.musiccenter.org*	▲ 184 ◆ G E5
NATURAL HISTORY MUSEUM OF LOS ANGELES COUNTY 900 Exposition Blvd Tel. (213) 763 3466	*Open Mon.–Fri. 9.30am–5pm, Sat.–Sun. 10am–5pm. Closed Sat., May 12, July 4, Thanksgiving, Dec. 25, Jan. 1.* *Information: www.nhm.org*	▲ 188 ◆ C D6
NBC STUDIO TOUR 3000 W Alameda Ave, Burbank Tel. (818) 840 3537	*Tour lasts 70 mins.*	▲ 194 ◆ G B1
NORTON SIMON MUSEUM OF ART 411 W Colorado Bvld, Pasadena Tel. (626) 449 6840	*Open Tue.–Sun. noon–6pm (9pm Fri.).* *Information: www.nortonsimon.org*	▲ 191 ◆ H A2
PACIFIC ASIA MUSEUM 46 N Los Robles Ave Pasadena Tel. (626) 449 2742	*Open Wed.–Sun. 10am–5pm (8pm Thu.).* *Free parking.* *Information: www.pacasiamuseum.org*	▲ 191 ◆ H B2
PARAMOUNT STUDIOS 5555 Melrose Ave Tel. (323) 956 5000	*Guided tours Mon.–Fri. 9am–2pm.*	▲ 195 ◆ G C3
PETERSEN AUTOMOTIVE MUSEUM 6060 Wilshire Blvd Tel. (323) 930 2277	*Open Tue.–Sun. 10am–6pm.* *Closed Mon., Thanksgiving, Jan. 1, Dec. 25.* *Information: www.petersen.org*	▲ 199 ◆ G A4
POINT VICENTE INTERPRETATIVE CENTER 35501 Palos Verdes Drive West Rancho Palos Verdes Tel. (310) 377 5370	*Open daily 10am–5pm (7pm in summer).* *Closed Thanksgiving, Dec. 24-25, Jan. 1.* *Information: www.palosverdes.com*	▲ 211 ◆ F C6
QUEEN MARY SEAPORT 1126 Queen's Hwy, Long Beach Tel. (562) 435 3511	*Open daily 10am–6pm.* *Information: www.queenmary.com*	▲ 212 ◆ F E6
RIPLEY'S BELIEVE IT OR NOT 6780 Hollywood Blvd Tel. (323) 466 6335	*Open daily 10am–10pm.*	▲ 197 ◆ G B3

PACIFIC PARK Santa Monica Pier Tel. (310) 260 8744	*Hours vary according to exhibitions.* *Visit the website: www.pacpark.com*	▲ 209 ◆ J A2
SANTA MONICA MUSEUM OF ART Bergamot Station 2525 Michighan Ave Building G1, Santa Monica Tel. (310) 586 6488	*Open Tue.–Sat. 11am–6pm, Sun. noon–5pm.* *Information: www.smmoa.org*	▲ 209 ◆ J B1
SEPULVEDA HOUSE 622 Main Street Tel. (213) 628 1274	*Open Mon.–Sat. 10am–3pm; Aug. daily 10am–7pm.* *Closed public holidays.*	▲ 184 ◆ G F4
SHUBERT THEATRE ABC Entertainment Center 2040 Avenue of the Stars Century City Tel. (310) 210 1500	*Reservations: www.telecharge.com*	▲ 203 ◆ I B3
SKIRBALL CULTURAL CENTER 2701 N Sepulveda Blvd Tel. (310) 440 4500	*Open Mon.–Fri. 8am–5pm.*	▲ 206 ◆ F B2
SONY PICTURES 10202 W Washington Blvd Culver City Tel. (323) 520 8687	*Open Mon.–Fri. 9am–5pm.*	▲ 195 ◆ F C3
TRAVEL TOWN MUSEUM 5200 W Zoo Drive Tel. (323) 662 5874	*Open Mon.–Fri. 10am–4pm, Sat.–Sun. 10am–5pm.* *Closed Dec. 25. Admission free.* *Information: www.scsra.org/ttown*	▲ 193 ◆ J C1
UCLA HAMMER MUSEUM 10899 Wilshire Blvd Tel. (310) 443 7000	*Open Tue.–Sat. 11am–7pm (9pm Thu. free), Sun.* *11am–5pm. Closed Mon., July 4, Thanksgiving, Dec.* *25, Jan. 1. Information: www.hamWed.ucla.edu*	▲ 207 ◆ I A2
UCLA OCEAN DISCOVERY CENTER 1600 Ocean Front Walk Santa Monica Tel. (310) 393 6149	*Open Tue.–Fri. 3–5pm, Sat. 11am– 6pm,* *Sun. 11am–5pm in summer; Sat.–Sun. 11am–5pm in* *winter.* *Information: www.odc.ulca.edu*	▲ 208 ◆ J A2
UNIVERSAL STUDIOS TOUR 100 Universal City Plaza Universal City Tel. (818) 508 9600	*Open daily 10am–10pm in summer; 10am–7pm in* *winter.* *Closed Thanksgiving, Dec. 25.*	▲ 194 ◆ G A1
UNIVERSITY OF CALIFORNIA Los Angeles (UCLA) 405 Hilgard Ave Tel. (310) 825 4321	*Visit the website for details of cultural events:* *www.ucla.edu*	▲ 206 ◆ I A2
UNIVERSITY OF SOUTHERN CALIFORNIA University Park Tel. (213) 740 6005	*Guided tours Mon.–Fri. 10am–3pm.* *Every hour, on the hour.* *Information: www.usc.edu*	▲ 189 ◆ G D6
VIRGINIA ROBINSON GARDENS 1008 Eden Way Tel. (310) 276 5367	*Open Tue.–Wed., Fri.–Sun. 11am–5pm, Thu.* *11am–8pm. Closed Thanksgiving, Dec. 25, Jan. 1.*	▲ 203 ◆ I B1
WALT DISNEY STUDIOS 505 S Buena Vista St, Burbank Tel. (818) 560 1000	*Open Mon.–Fri. 8am–6pm.*	▲ 194 ◆ G C1
WARNER BROS VIP TOUR 4000 Warner Blvd, Burbank Tel. (818) 954 1744	*Open Mon.–Fri. 9am–3pm in winter; 9am–2pm in* *summer.*	▲ 195 ◆ G B1
WAYFARER'S CHAPEL 5755 Palos Verdes Drive S Rancho Palos Verdes Tel. (310) 377 7919	*Open daily 7am–5pm.* *Information: www.wayfarerschapel.org*	▲ 211 ◆ F C6
WELLS FARGO HISTORY MUSEUM 333 S Grand Ave Tel. (213) 253 7166	*Open Mon.–Fri. 9am–5pm.* *Information: www.wellsfargohistory.com*	▲ 186 ◆ G E5
WESTWOOD MEMORIAL PARK 1218 Glendon Ave Tel. (310) 474 1579	*Open daily 8am–5pm.*	▲ 207 ◆ I A3
WHISKY À GOGO 8901 W Sunset Blvd Tel. (310) 652 4205	*Open daily 8pm–1am.* *Information: www.whiskyagogo.com*	▲ 198
MARIPOSA		◆ B C2
CALIFORNIA STATE MINING AND MINERAL MUSEUM Tel. (209) 742 7625	*Open daily except Tue. May 1–Sep. 30, 10am–6pm;* *Oct. 1–Apr. 30, 10am–4pm.*	▲ 159

MODESTO ◆ B B1

MCHENRY MUSEUM
1402 I Street
Tel. (209) 577 5366

Open Tue.–Sun. noon–4pm.
Information: www.mchenrymuseum.org

▲ 165

MONTEREY ◆ B A2

VISITORS AND CONVENTION BUREAU
380 Alvaro Street
Tel. (831) 649 1770

Open Mon.–Fri. 9.30am–5pm.
Information: www.monterey.com

COLTON HALL
Madison and Pacific Streets
Tel. (831) 646 5640

Open 10am–5pm.
Information: www.monterey.org/museum

▲ 169

MARITIME MUSEUM
5 Custom House Plaza
Tel. (831) 372 2608

Open Tue.–Sun. 11am–5pm.

▲ 168

MONTEREY BAY AQUARIUM
886 Cannery Row
Tel. (831) 648 4888

Open daily 10am–6pm (9.30am–6pm
Apr. 15–Labor Day and public holidays).
Information: www.mbayaq.org

▲ 169

MONTEREY STATE HISTORIC PARK
20 Custom House Plaza
Tel. (831) 649 7118

Gardens open daily 10am–4pm.
Guided tours 10am, 11am, 2pm.
Closed Thanksgiving, Dec. 25, Jan. 1.

▲ 168

STEVENSON HOUSE
530 Houston House
Tel. (831) 649 7118

Open daily 10am–noon and 1–4pm.
Guided tours by prior arrangement.

▲ 169

MUIR BEACH ◆ A E1-F1

MUIR WOODS NATIONAL MONUMENT
Mill Valley
Tel. (415) 388 7059

Open daily 8am–dusk.
No bicycles, animals, picnics or camping.
Information: www.visitmuirwoods.org

▲ 141

NAPA ◆ A B6

CONVENTION AND VISITORS BUREAU
1310 Napa Town Center
Tel. (707) 226 7459

Open Mon.–Fri. 9.30am–5pm.
Information: www.napavalley.com

CHATEAU POTELLE
3875 Mt Veeder Road
Tel. (707) 255 9440

Sales and wine tastings Thu.–Mon. 11am–5pm.
Information: www.chateaupotelle.com

▲ 151

DOMAINE CARNEROS
1240 Duhig Road
Tel. (707) 257 0101

Open daily 10am–6pm. Guided tours daily
Apr.–Oct. 11am, 4pm; Nov.–March Mon.–Tue.
11am, 1pm, 3pm, Sat.–Sun. 11am, 4pm.
Information: www.doMayne carneros.com

▲ 151

HESS COLLECTION WINERY
4411 Redwood Road
Tel. (707) 255 1144

Open daily 10am–4pm except public holidays.
Information: www.hesscollection.com

▲ 151

TREFETHEN VINEYARDS AND WINERY
1160 Oak Knoll Ave
Tel. (707) 255 7700

Open daily 10am–4.30pm.
Guided tours by prior arrangement.
Information: www.threfethen.com

▲ 151

NEVADA CITY ◆ A D5

ANANDA VILLAGE
14618 Tyler Foote Road
Tel. (530) 478 7560

Information: www.crystalclarity.com

▲ 161

MINERS FOUNDRY CULTURAL CENTER
325 Spring Street
Tel. (530) 265 5040

Open Mon.–Fri. 9am–5pm.

NOVATO ◆ A F1

MARIN MUSEUM
OF THE AMERICAN INDIAN
2200 Novato Blvd
Tel. (415) 897 4064

Closed Mon.
Information: www.marinindian.com

▲ 142

OAKLAND ◆ B E4

OAKLAND MUSEUM OF CALIFORNIA
1000 Oak Street
Tel. (510) 238 2200

Open Wed.–Sat. 10am–5pm, Sun. noon–5pm
(from 9am 1st Fri. of the month). Closed Mon.–Tue.
Admission free 2nd Sun. of the month.
Information: www.museumca.org

▲ 144

PARAMOUNT THEATRE
2025 Broadway
Tel. (510) 465 6400

For times of performances, phone or visit the
website: www.paramounttheatre.com

● 73
▲ 144

◆ PLACES TO VISIT

OAKVILLE		◆ A B6
MONDAVI 781 Saint Helena Hwy Tel. (888) 766 6328	Information: www.robertmondavi.com	▲ 151

OCEANSIDE		◆ C B5
MISSION SAN LUIS REY DE FRANCIA 4050 Mission Ave Tel. (750) 757 3651	Open daily 10am–4.30pm. Information: www.sanluisrey.org	▲ 226

PALM DESERT		◆ C D5
PALM DESERT LIVING WILDLIFE RESERVE AND BOTANICAL PARK 47900 Portola Ave Tel. (760) 346 5694	Open daily 9am–5pm in winter (last admission 4pm); 8am–1.30pm in summer (last admission 1pm). Information: www.livingdesert.org	▲ 228

PALM SPRINGS		◆ C D4
VISITORS CENTER 295 N Sunrise Way Tel. (760) 778 8418	Open daily 9am–5pm. Information: www.palmsprings.com and www.palm-springs.org	
AGUA CALIENTE CULTURAL MUSEUM 245 S Palm Canyon Drive Tel. (760) 323 0151	Open Mon.–Sat.10am–4pm, Sun. noon–3pm. Admission free.	▲ 229
ANNENBERG THEATER 101 Museum Drive Tel. (760) 325 0189	Open Tue.–Sat. 10am–4pm, Sun. noon–4pm and performance days: 10am–start of performance. Information: www.psmuseum.org/performances	▲ 230
MISS CORNELIA WHITE HOUSE 221 S Palm Canyon Drive Tel. 760-323 8297	Open mid Oct.–June Wed.–Sun. noon–3pm, Thu.–Sat. 10am–4pm.	▲ 229
PALM SPRINGS AERIAL TRAMWAY Valley station 1 Tramway Road Tel. (760) 325 1449	Departures every ½ hour Mon.–Fri. 10am–8pm, Sat.–Sun. and public holidays 8am–8pm. Last return trip 9.45pm. Information: www.pstramway.com hour	▲ 230
PALM SPRINGS DESERT MUSEUM 101 Museum Drive Tel. (760) 325 7186	Open Tue.–Sat.10am–5pm, Sun. noon–5pm. Closed Mon. and public holidays. Information: www.psmuseum.org	▲ 230
PALM SPRINGS HISTORICAL SOCIETY 221 S Palm Canyon Drive Tel. (760) 323 8297	Open Oct.–June Wed.–Sun. noon–3pm, Thu.–Sat. 10am–4pm.	▲ 229
RUDDY'S GENERAL STORE 221 S Palm Canyon Drive Tel. (760) 327 2156	Open mid Oct.–June Thu.–Sat. 10am–4pm; July–Sep. Sat.–Sun. 10am–4pm.	▲ 229
VILLAGE GREEN HERITAGE CENTER 219–223 S Palm Canyon Drive Tel. (760) 323 8297	Open mid-Oct.–June Wed.–Sun. noon–3pm, Thu.–Sat. 10am–4pm. Information: www.palmsprings.com/history	▲ 229
WINDMILL TOURS 62–950 20th Ave Tel. (760) 251 1997	Tours daily 9am, 11am, 1pm, 3pm. Information: www.windmilltours.com	▲ 230
WINTEC WIND FARM 25 E Tahquitz Canyon, Suite 201 Tel. (760) 323 9490	See Windmill Tours (above) or visit the website: www.windmilltours.com	▲ 230

PALO ALTO		◆ B A1
STANFORD UNIVERSITY VISITORS INFORMATION CENTER Tel. (650) 723 2560	Open Mon.–Tue. 8am–5pm, Sat.–Sun. 9am–5pm. Guided tours daily 11am, 3.15pm. Closed end Dec. Information: www.stanford.edu	▲ 145

PALOMAR MOUNTAIN		◆ C C5
PALOMAR MOUNTAIN STATE PARK 19952 State Park Road Tel. (760) 742 3462 Observatory: (619) 742 2119	Open daily 8am–dusk. Visitors Bureau open daily from 9am.	▲ 227

RANCHO SANTA FE		◆ C C5
VEGETABLE SHOP 6123 Calcazada del Bosque	Open Tue.–Sat. 9.30am–3.30pm, Sun. 10am–1pm. Closed Mon. and public holidays.	▲ 227

RUTHERFORD		◆ A B6
FROG'S LEAP 8815 Conn Creek Road Tel. (707) 963 4704	Open Mon.–Sat. 10am–4pm. Information: www.frogsleap.com	▲ 151

MUMM NAPA VALLEY 8445 Silverado Trail Tel. (707) 942 3434	*Open daily Nov 1–Apr. 1 10am–5pm, in summer* *10.30am–6pm. Guided tours 10am–3pm.* *Information: mummcuveenapa.com*	▲ 151

SACRAMENTO   ◆ A C6-B6

CALIFORNIA STATE INDIAN MUSEUM 2618 K Street Tel. (916) 324 0971	*Open daily 10am–5pm.* *Closed Thanksgiving, Dec. 25, Jan. 1.*	▲ 157
CALIFORNIA STATE RAILROAD MUSEUM 2nd and I Streets Tel. (916) 445 6645	*Open daily 10am–5pm.*	▲ 157
CROCKER ART MUSEUM 216 O Street Tel. (916) 264 5423	*Open Tue.–Sun. 10am–5pm (8pm Thu.).*	▲ 156
DISCOVERY MUSEUM HISTORY CENTER 101 I Street Tel. (916) 264 7057	*Open Wed.–Sun. and bank holidays 10am–5pm in* *winter; daily 10am–5pm in summer.* *Closed Thanksgiving, Dec. 25, Jan. 1.*	▲ 157
DISCOVERY MUSEUM SCIENCE CENTER 3615 Auburn Blvd Tel. (916) 575 3941	*Same times as for the History Center (above).*	▲ 157
STATE CAPITOL 10th and L Street Tel. (916) 324 0333	*Open daily 9am–5pm. Closed Thanksgiving, Dec.* *25, Jan. 1. Guided tours every hour 9am–4pm.* *Admission free.*	▲ 156, 157
SUTTER'S FORT STATE HISTORIC **BUILDING** 2701 L Street Tel. (916) 445 4422	*Open daily 10am–5pm.*	▲ 157

SALINAS   ◆ B A2

NATIONAL STEINBECK CENTER 1 Main Street Tel. (831) 796 3833	*Open daily 10am–5pm. Closed Thanksgiving, Dec.* *25, Jan. 1, Easter.*	▲ 167

SAN DIEGO   ◆ C C6

CONVENTION AND VISITORS BUREAU 401 B Street, Suite 1400 Tel. (619) 232 3101	*Open Mon.–Sat. 8.30am–5pm.* *Closed public holidays.* *Information: www.sandiego.org*	
INTERNATIONAL VISITORS **INFORMATION CENTER** 11 Horton Plaza Tel. (619) 236 1212	*Open Mon.–Sat. 8.30am–5pm, Sun. 11am–5pm.*	
BAZAAR DEL MUNDO 2754 Calhoun Street Tel. (619) 296 3161	*Open daily 10am–9pm.* *Information: www.bazaardelmundo.com*	▲ 219 ◆ P B3
CABRILLO NATIONAL MONUMENT PARK 1800 Cabrillo Memorial Drive Point Loma Tel. (619) 557 5450	*Visitors Center open daily 9am–5.15pm.* *Museums open daily 9am–5pm.* *Information: www.nps.gov/cabr*	▲ 224 ◆ P A4
CASA DE BALBOA See Museum of Photographic Arts San Diego Hall of Champions San Diego Model Railroad Museum		▲ 223 ◆ R B2
JUNÍPERO SERRA MUSEUM Presidio Park, Old Town 2727 Presidio Drive Tel. (619) 297 3258	*Open Tue.–Sat. 10am–4.30pm, Sun. noon–4.30pm.*	▲ 219 ◆ P B3
MARITIME MUSEUM 1492 N Harbor Drive Tel. (619) 234 9153	*Open daily 9am–9pm (8pm in winter).* *Information: www.sdmaritime.com*	▲ 221 ◆ Q A1
MARSTON HOUSE 3525 7th Ave, N Balboa Park Tel. (619) 298 3142	*Open Fri.–Sun. 10am–4.30pm.*	▲ 223
MISSION SAN DIEGO DE ALCALÁ 10818 San Diego Mission Road Tel. (619) 281 8449	*Museum and gardens opens daily 9am–5pm.*	▲ 221 ◆ P C2
MUSEUM OF CONTEMPORARY ART 1001 Kettner Blvd Downtown Tel. (619) 234 1001	*Open daily 11am–5pm except Wed.* *Guided tours Sat.–Sun. 2pm, 3pm.* *Wheelchair access.* *Information: www.mcasandiego.org*	▲ 220 ◆ Q B2

◆ PLACES TO VISIT

MUSEUM OF PHOTOGRAPHIC ARTS Casa de Balboa 1649 El Prado, Balboa Park Tel. (619) 238 7559	*Open daily 10am–5pm except public holidays.*	▲ 223 ◆ R B2
OLD TOWN STATE HISTORIC PARK San Diego Ave Tel. (619) 220 5422	*Open daily 6am–10pm.*	▲ 219 ◆ P B3
REUBEN H FLEET SCIENCE CENTER 1875 El Prado, Balboa Park Tel. (619) 238 1233	*Open Mon.–Thu. 9.30am–5pm, Fri.–Sat. 9.30am–9pm, Sun. 9.30am–7pm. Information: www.rhfleet.org*	▲ 222 ◆ R B2
SAN DIEGO AEROSPACE MUSEUM AND HALL OF FAME 2001 Pan American Plaza Tel. (619) 234 8291	*Open daily 10am–4.30pm (5.30pm in summer). Closed Thanksgiving, Dec. 25, Jan. 1. Information: www.aerospacemuseum.org*	▲ 223 ◆ R A3
SAN DIEGO AUTOMOTIVE MUSEUM 2080 Pan American Plaza Tel. (619) 231 2886	*Open daily 10am–5pm (6pm in summer). Closed Thanksgiving, Dec. 25, Jan. 1. Information: www.sdautomuseum.org*	▲ 223 ◆ R A3
SAN DIEGO HALL OF CHAMPIONS Casa de Balboa 2131 Pan America Plaza Tel. (619) 234 2544	*Open daily 10am–4.30pm. Information: www.sandiegosports.org*	▲ 223 ◆ R A3
SAN DIEGO MODEL RAILROAD MUSEUM Casa de Balboa, 1649 El Prado Tel. (619) 696 0199	*Open Tue.–Fri. 11am–4pm, Sat.–Sun. 11am–5pm. Information: www.sdmodelrailroadm.com*	▲ 223 ◆ R B2
SAN DIEGO MUSEUM OF ART 1450 El Prado, Balboa Park Tel. (619) 232 7931	*Open Tue.–Sun. 10am–6pm (9pm Thu.). Information: www.sdmart.com*	▲ 223 ◆ R B2
SAN DIEGO MUSEUM OF MAN 1350 El Prado, Balboa Park Tel. (619) 239 2001	*Open daily 10am–4.30pm. Information: www.museumofman.org*	▲ 223 ◆ R A1
SAN DIEGO NATURAL HISTORY MUSEUM 1788 El Prado, Balboa Park Tel. (619) 232 3821	*Open daily 9.30am–4.30pm (5.30pm in summer). Closed Thanksgiving, Dec. 25, Jan. 1. Information: www.sdnhm.org*	▲ 223 ◆ R B2
SAN DIEGO ZOO Balboa Park, 2920 Zoo Drive Tel. (619) 234 3153	*Open daily 9am–4pm. Information: www.sandiegozoo.org*	▲ 222 ◆ R A1
SEA WORLD 500 Sea World Drive Tel. (619) 226 3901	*Opening hours vary, visit the website: www.4adventure.com*	▲ 225 ◆ P A2
TIMKEN MUSEUM OF ART 1500 El Prado, Balboa Park Tel. (619) 239 5548	*Open Tue.–Sat. 10am–4.30pm, Sun. 1.30–4.30pm. Closed Sept.*	▲ 223 ◆ R B2
VILLA MONTEZUMA 1925 K Street Tel. (619) 239 2211	*Admission free. Open Fri.–Sun. 10am–4.30pm.*	▲ 221 ◆ P C3

SAN FRANCISCO ◆ A B6

SAN FRANCISCO CONVENTION AND VISITORS BUREAU 201 3rd Street, Suite 900 Tel. (415) 974 6900	*Information: www.sfvisitor.org*	
AFRICAN AMERICAN HISTORICAL AND CULTURAL SOCIETY Fort Mason Center, Bldg C Tel. (415) 441 0640	*Open Wed.–Sun. noon–5pm. Closed Mon.–Tue.*	▲ 128 ◆ Q Q2
ALCATRAZ ISLAND Pier 41 Tel. (415) 705 5555	*Ferry departures Mon.–Fri. 9.30am–2.45pm, Sat.–Sun. and public holidays 9.30am–2.15pm.*	▲ 126 ◆ D D1
ANSEL ADAMS CENTER 655 Mission Street Tel. (415) 495 7000	*Open daily 11am–5pm (8pm on 1st Thu. of month).*	▲ 117 ◆ E D5
ART INSTITUTE 800 Chestnut Street Tel. (415) 771 2020	*Open daily 9am–5pm. Closed public holidays.*	▲ 122 ◆ E B2
BEACH CHALET VISITORS CENTER Golden Gate Park 1000 Great Hwy Tel. (415) 751 2766	*Open daily 9am–6pm.*	▲ 133
BOOKSMITH 1644 Haight Street Tel. (415) 863 8688	*Open Mon.–Sat. 10am–9pm (6pm Sun.).*	▲ 134

CABLE CAR BARN MUSEUM Powell Station 1201 Mason Street Tel. (415) 474 1887	*Open daily Apr.–Sep. 10am–6pm; Oct.–Mar.* *10am–5pm. Admission free.*	▲ *123* ◆ E C3
CAFE FLORE 2298 Market Street Tel. (415) 621 8579	*Open Mon.–Thu., Sun. 7am–11.30pm,* *Fri.–Sat. 7.30am–midnight.*	▲ *135*
CALIFORNIA ACADEMY OF SCIENCES Golden Gate Park 55 Concourse Drive Tel. (415) 750 7145	*Open daily 10am–5pm in winter;* *9am–6pm in summer (Apr. 15–Labor Day).* *Admission free 1st Wed. of the month.* *Information: www.calacademy.org*	▲ *132* ◆ D B4
CALIFORNIA PALACE OF THE LEGION OF HONOR Lincoln Park 34th Ave and Clement Street Tel. (415) 869 3330	*Open Tue.–Sun. 9.30am–5pm.* *Information: www. thinker.org*	▲ *131* ◆ D A3
CAMERA OBSCURA 1096 Point Lobos Ave Tel. (415) 750 0415	*Phone for details of opening hours.*	▲ *131*
CASTRO THEATER 429 Castro Street Tel. (415) 621 6120	*Phone for program details.*	▲ *135* ◆ D D5
CHINESE CULTURAL CENTER 750 Kearny Street Tel. (415) 986 1822	*Open Tue.–Sun. 10am–4pm. Admission free.*	▲ *119* ◆ E D3
CHINESE HISTORICAL SOCIETY OF AMERICA 965 Clay Street Tel. (415) 391 1188	*Open Mon.–Fri. 10.30am–4pm.* *Information: www.chsa.org*	▲ *119* ◆ E D3
CITY HALL 20 Polk Street Tel. (415) 554 4000	*Open Mon.–Fri. 8am–8pm.* *Admission free.*	▲ *125* ◆ E B6
CITY LIGHTS BOOK STORE 261 Columbus Ave Tel. (415) 362 8193	*Open daily 10am–midnight.*	▲ *120* ◆ E D3
COIT TOWER Telegraph Hill Blvd Tel. (415) 362 0808	*Open daily May–Sep. 10am–7.30pm;* *Oct.–April 10am–6pm.*	▲ *121* ◆ E D2
CONSERVATORY OF FLOWERS Golden Gate Park Tel. (415) 750 5105	*Open Mon.–Fri. 9am–5pm except public holidays.*	▲ *132* ◆ D B4
CRAFT AND FOLK ART MUSEUM Fort Mason Center, Bldg A Laguna Street and Marina Blvd Tel. (415) 775 0991	*Open Tue.–Fri., Sun. 11am–5pm, Sat. 11am–5pm.* *Information: www.mocfa.org*	▲ *128* ◆ D D2
DIFFERENT LIGHT (A) 498 Castro Street Tel. (415) 431 0891	*Open daily 10am–midnight.*	▲ *135* ◆ D D5
EXPLORATORIUM Palace of Fine Arts 3601 Lyon Street Tel. (415) 561 0360	*Open daily 9am–6pm.* *Late-night opening Wed. 9pm.* *Information: www.exploratorium.edu*	▲ *129* ◆ D C2
FILLMORE AUDITORIUM 1805 Geary Blvd at Fillmore St Tel. (415) 346 6000	*Visit the website for program details:* *www.thefillmore.com*	▲ *124* ◆ E A5
FLOOD MANSION 2222 Broadway Tel. (415) 563 2900	*Guided tours by prior arrangement. Phone or visit* *the website: www.floodmansion.org*	▲ *123* ◆ D C2
FORT POINT Marine Drive Tel. (415) 556 1693	*Open Wed.–Sun. 10am–5pm.* *Closed public holidays.*	▲ *128* ◆ D D2
GALERIA DE LA RAZA 2857 24th Street Tel. (415) 826 8009	*Open Wed.–Sun. noon–6pm.*	▲ *139* ◆ D D5
GOLDEN GATE PARK VISITORS CENTER Stanyan St and J F Kennedy Dr Tel. (415) 750 5105	*Open Mon.–Fri. 9am–5pm except public holidays.*	▲ *132*
GRACE CATHEDRAL 1100 California Street Tel. (415) 749 6300	*Open daily 7.30am–6pm. Guided tours Mon.–Fri.* *1–3pm, Sat. 1.30–3.30pm, Sun. 12.30–2pm.* *Phone for details of concert programs.*	▲ *123* ◆ E C4

◆ PLACES TO VISIT

GUINNESS MUSEUM 235 Jefferson Street Tel. (415) 771 9890	*Open Sun.–Thu. 11am–10pm, Fri.–Sat.* *10am–midnight.*	▲ 127 ◆ E B1
HAAS LILENTHAL HOUSE 2007 Franklin Street Tel. (415) 441 3004	*Open Wed. noon–3pm, Sun. 11am–4pm.* *Closed public holidays.*	▲ 123 ◆ E A4
HOLY TRINITY ORTHODOX CATHEDRAL 1520 Green Street Tel. (415) 673 8565		▲ 122 ◆ E A3
JAPANESE TEA GARDEN Golden Gate Park Music Concourse Tel. (415) 668 0909	*Tearoom open daily 8am–6.30pm.*	▲ 133 ◆ D B4
LOIUSE M DAVIS SYMPHONY HALL 201 Van Ness Ave Tel. (415) 864 6000	*Phone for program details.*	▲ 125 ◆ E B6
MARK HOPKINS TOP OF THE MARK 1 Nob Hill Street Tel. (415) 392 3434	*Bar open Mon.–Sat. 3pm–12.30 am,* *Sun. 4.30pm–12.30 am.*	▲ 122 ◆ E C4
MASONIC AUDITORIUM 1111 California Street Tel. (415) 776 4917	*Museum open Mon.–Fri. 10am–3pm.* *Admission free.*	▲ 123 ◆ E C4
MECHANICAL MUSEUM 1090 Point Lobos Ave Tel. (415) 386 1170	*Open Mon.–Tue. 11am–7pm, Sat.–Sun. 10am–8pm.*	▲ 131
METREON 4th and Mission Street Tel. (415) 369 6000	*Open daily 10am–10pm.* *Information: www.metreon.com*	▲ 116 ◆ E D5
MEXICAN MUSEUM Fort Mason Center, Bldg D Tel. (415) 202 9700	*Open Wed.–Fri. noon–5pm, Sat.–Sun. 11am–5pm.* *Closed Mon.–Tue.* *Information: www.mexicanmuseum.org*	▲ 128 ◆ D D5
MISSION DOLORES 320 Dolores Street Tel. (415) 621 8203	*Open daily Nov.–April 9am–4pm; May–Oct.* *9am–4.30pm.*	▲ 138 ◆ D D5
MUSEO ITALO-AMERICANO Fort Mason Center, Bldg C Laguna St and Marina Blvd Tel. (415) 673 2200	*Open Wed.–Sun. noon–5pm. Closed Mon.–Tue.* *Information: www.museoitaloamericano.org*	▲ 128 ◆ D D2
MUSEUM OF THE CITY **OF SAN FRANCISCO** 945 Taraval Street Tel. (415) 928 0289	*Information about the exhibitions:* *www.sfmuseum.org*	▲ 127 ◆ E B1
NAMES PROJECT VISITORS CENTER 284 Sanchez Street Tel. (415) 863 1966	*Information: www.aidsquilt.org*	▲ 135, 136 ◆ D D5
NATIONAL MARITIME MUSEUM Beach Street Fisherman's Wharf Tel. (415) 556 3002	*Open daily 10am–5pm.* *Closed public holidays. Admission free.*	▲ 126 ◆ E A1
OLD ST MARY'S CHURCH 660 California St at Grant Ave Tel. (415) 288 3800	*Open daily 7.30am–5.30pm.* *Admission free.*	▲ 118 ◆ E D4
PACIFIC HERITAGE MUSEUM 608 Commercial Street Tel. (415) 362 4100	*Open Tue.–Sat. 10am–4pm.* *Information: www.pacificheritage.citysearch.com*	▲ 119
PRESIDIO NATIONAL PARK Visitors Center Tel. (415) 561 4323	*Open daily 9am–3pm.*	▲ 129 ◆ D D2
PUBLIC LIBRARY 100 Larkin Street Tel. (415) 557 4400	*Open Mon. 10am–6pm, Tue.–Thu. 9am–8pm,* *Fri. 11am–5pm, Sat. 9am–5pm, Sun. noon–5pm.* *Closed public holidays.*	▲ 125 ◆ E B6
QUEER CULTURAL CENTER 584 Castro Street Tel. (415) 552 7709	*For program of events:* *www.queerculturalcenter.org*	▲ 135 ◆ E B5
RIPLEY'S BELIEVE IT OR NOT MUSEUM 175 Jefferson Street Fisherman's Wharf Tel. (415) 771 6188	*Open daily Sun.–Thu. 10am–10pm,* *Fri.–Sat. 10am–midnight.* *Information: www.ripleysf.com*	▲ 127 ◆ E B1
ROXIE (THE) 3117 16th Street Tel. (415) 863 1087	*Phone for times of performances.*	▲ 139 ◆ D D5

SFMOMA
151 Third Street
Tel. (415) 357 4000

Open daily (except Wed.) 10am–4pm in winter; 11am–4pm in summer (Apr. 15–Labor Day). Late-night Thu. 9pm. Closed Wed., July 4, Thanksgiving, Dec. 25, Jan. 1. Information: www.sfmoma.org

▲ 116
◆ E D5

STRYBING ARBORETUM
Golden Gate Park
9th Ave and Lincoln Way
Tel. (415) 661 1316

Open Mon.–Fri. 8am–4.30pm, Sat.–Sun. and public holidays 10am–5pm. Admission free.

▲ 133
◆ D A4

TRANSAMERICA PYRAMID
600 Montgomery at Colombus
Tel. (415) 983 4100

Panoramic view. Visit the 27th floor during office hours (8.30am–4.30pm).

▲ 117
◆ E D3

UNIVERSITY OF CALIFORNIA
100 Medical Center Way
Tel. (415) 476 4394

Open Mon.–Fri. 9am–5pm. Closed public holidays. Admission free.

WELLS FARGO HISTORY MUSEUM
420 Montgomery Street
Tel. (415) 396 2619

Open Mon.–Fri. 9am–5pm. Information: www.wellsfargohistory.com

▲ 117
◆ E D4

WAR MEMORIAL OPERA HOUSE
301 Van Ness Ave
Tel. (415) 864 3330

Open Mon.–Sat. 10am–6pm. Wheelchair access. Information: www.sfopera.com

▲ 125
◆ E B6

WAX MUSEUM
145 Jefferson Street
Fisherman's Wharf
Tel. (415) 202 04000

Open daily. Opening times subject to alteration. Information: www.waxmuseum.com

▲ 127
◆ E B1

YERBA BUENA CENTER
701 Mission Street
Tel. (415) 978 2787

Open Tue.–Sun. 11am–6pm (Thu.–Fri. 9pm). Admission free 1st Thu. of the month.

▲ 116
◆ E D5

SAN JOSE ◆ B A1

MUSEUM OF ART
110 S Market Street
Tel. (408) 294 2787

Open Tue.–Sun. 10am–5pm (8pm Thu.). Guided tours 12.30pm, 2.30pm (6.30pm Thu.). Closed Mon., Dec. 25, Thanksgiving, Jan. 1. Information: sjmusart.org

▲ 145

TECH MUSEUM OF INNOVATION
201 S Market Street
Tel. (408) 294 8324

Open daily 10am–5pm. Information: www.thetech.org

▲ 145, 147

WINCHESTER MYSTERY HOUSE
525 S Winchester Blvd
Tel. (408) 247 2000

Open daily 9am–5pm (7pm Sat.–Sun. Apr. 27–Oct. 19). Information: www.whinchestermysteryhouse.com

▲ 145

SAN JUAN BAUTISTA ◆ B A2

OLD MISSION
2nd and Mariposa Streets
Tel. (831) 623 4528

Souvenir store open daily 9.30am–4.45pm except public holidays. Information: www.sanjuanbautista.com

STATE HISTORIC PARK
19 Franklin Street
Tel. (831) 623 4526

Visit the website for a program of exhibitions and events: www.sanjuanbautista.com

SAN JUAN CAPISTRANO ◆ C B5

MISSION SAN JUAN CAPISTRANO
31882 Camino Capistrano
Tel. (949) 234 1300

Guided tours by prior arrangement. Phone or visit the website: www.sanjuancapistrano.net

▲ 216

SAN LUIS OBISPO ◆ B B4

MISSION SAN LUIS OBISPO
728 Monterey Street
Tel. (805) 781 8220

Phone for opening hours.

▲ 173

SAN RAPHAEL ◆ A B6

MISSION SAN RAPHAEL
1104 5th Ave
Tel. (415) 454 8141

Mission open daily 9am–5pm. Museum open daily 11am–4pm. Information: saint-raphaels.com

▲ 142

SAN SIMEON ◆ B B4

HEARST CASTLE
750 Hearst Castle Road
Tel. (800) 444 4445

Guided tours daily 8.20am–3.20pm except Thanksgiving, Dec. 25, Jan. 1. Disabled tours by prior arrangement. Information: www.hearstcastle.org

▲ 172

SANTA ANA ◆ C B4

BOWERS MUSEUM OF CULTURAL ART
2002 N Main Street
Tel. (714) 567 3600

Open Tue.–Sun. 10am–4pm. Closed Mon., July 4, Thanksgiving, Dec. 25, Jan. 1. Information: www.bowers.org

▲ 215

◆ PLACES TO VISIT

SANTA BARBARA		◆ B C6
SANTA BARBARA CONVENTION AND VISITORS BUREAU 1601 Anacapa Street Tel. (805) 966 9222	*Information: www.santabarbara.com*	
ARLINGTON THEATER 1317 State Street Tel. (805) 963 4408		▲ 174
BROOKS INSTITUTE OF PHOTOGRAPHY 801 Alston Road Tel. (888) 304 3456	*Guided tours Fri. 11am, noon.* *Information: www.brooks.edu*	▲ 175
CHUMASH PAINTED CAVE STATE HISTORIC PARK Hwy 154 on Painted Cave Road Tel. (805) 686 0855	*Open daily noon–2am.* *Information: www.cal-parks.ca.gov/south/channel*	▲ 175
COUNTY COURTHOUSE 1100 Anacapa Street Tel. (805) 962 6464	*Panoramic view.* *Open Mon.–Fri. 8am–4.45pm, Sat.–Sun.* *and school vacations 10am–4.45pm.*	● 65 ▲ 174
MISSION SANTA BARBARA 2201 Laguna Street Tel. (805) 682 4713	*Open daily 9am–5pm.* *Closed Dec. 25, Thanksgiving, Easter, Jan. 1.* *Information: www.sbmission.org*	● 64 ▲ 175
MUSEUM OF ART 1130 State Street Tel. (805) 963 4364	*Open Tue.–Thu., Sat. 11am–5pm, Fri. 11am–9pm, Sun. noon-5pm. Closed Mon.* *Information: www.sbmuseart.org*	▲ 174
MUSEUM OF NATURAL HISTORY 2559 Puerta del Sol Road Tel. (805) 682 4711	*Open Mon.–Fri. 9am–5pm, Sun. and vacations 10am–5pm. Closed Dec. 25, Jan. 1, Thanksgiving.* *Information: www.sbnature.org*	▲ 175
SANTA CLARA		◆ B A1
DE SAISSET MUSEUM University of Santa Clara 500 El Camino Real Tel. (408) 554 4528	*Open Tue.–Sun. 11am–4pm. Closed Mon.* *Admission free.* *Information: www.scu.edu/deSaisset*	▲ 145
INTEL MUSEUM 2200 Mision College Blvd Tel. (408) 765 0503	*Open Mon.–Fri. 9am–6pm, Sat. 10am–5pm.* *Admission free.* *Information: www.intel.com/intel/intelis/museum*	▲ 146
MISSION SANTA CLARA DE ASIS University of Santa Clara 500 El Camino Real Tel. (408) 554 4023	*Phone for opening times.*	▲ 145
SANTA CRUZ		◆ B A2
MISSION Mission Plaza, High Street Tel. (831) 426 5686	*Open Tue.–Sat. 10am–4pm, Sun. 10am–2pm.* *Closed Mon.*	▲ 166
MYSTERY SPOT 465 Mystery Spot Street Tel. (831) 423 8897	*Open daily 9am–7pm in summer (Apr. 15–Labor Day); 9am–4.30pm in winter.* *Information: www.mystery-spot.com*	▲ 167
SAINT HELENA		◆ A B6
BERINGER VINEYARDS 2000 Main Street Tel. (707) 963 7115	*Open daily 9.30am–5pm (5.30pm in summer).* *Guided tours daily 10am, 4.30pm (5pm in summer).* *Information: www.beringer.com*	▲ 151
JOSEPH PHELPS VINEYARDS 200 Taplin Road Tel. (707) 963 2745	*Open Mon.–Sat. 9am–4pm, Sun. 10am–4pm.* *Information: www.jpvwines.com*	▲ 151
NAPA VALLEY WINE LIBRARY 1492 Library Lane Tel. (707) 963 5244	*Seminars throughout the year. Phone for details.* *Information: www.napawinelibrary.com*	▲ 151
SILVERADO MUSEUM 1490 Library Street Tel. (707) 963 3757	*Open Tue.–Sun. noon–4pm. Closed Mon.*	▲ 151
SUTTER HOME VINEYARDS 277 Street Helena Hwy Tel. (707) 963 3104	*Open daily 10am–5pm.* *Information: www.sutterhome.com*	▲ 151
SAUSALITO		◆ A F1
BAY MODEL VISITORS CENTER 2100 Bridgeway Tel. (415) 332 3870	*Open June–Sep. Tue.–Fri. 9am–4pm, Sat.–Sun. 10am–5pm; Oct.–Mar. Tue.–Sat. 9am–4pm.* *Admission free.*	▲ 140

GREEN GULCH FARM AND ZEN CENTER 1601 Shoreline Hwy Tel. (415) 383 3134	*Phone for details of activities and programs.*	▲ 141
SONOMA		◆ A B6
HISTORIC VISITORS CENTER 1800 Old Winery Route Tel. (707) 938 1266	*Open Mon.–Fri. 8.30am–4.30pm.*	
LACHRYMA MONTIS North Spain Street Tel. (707) 538 8068	*Open daily 10am–5pm.*	▲ 149
MISSION SOLANO Spain Street Tel. (707) 938 9560	*Open daily 10am–5pm except Dec. 25 and Jan. 1.*	▲ 149
GUNDLACH-BUNDSCHU 2000 Denmark Street Tel. (707) 938 9640	*Wine tasting and guided tours daily 11am–4.30pm. Closed Thanksgiving, Easter, Jan. 1, Dec. 24–25. Information: www.gundbun.com*	▲ 148
SCHUG 602 Bonneau Road Tel. (800) 966 9365	*Open 10am–5pm. Information: www.schugwinery.com*	▲ 149
SONORA		◆ B C1
TUOLUMNE COUNTY MUSEUM 158 W Bradford Ave Tel. (209) 532 1317	*Open daily 10am–4pm. Information: tchistory.org*	▲ 159
SOUTH LAKE TAHOE		◆ A E6
VISITORS CENTER 2550 Tahoe Blvd Tel. (530) 542 4200	*Open 8am–6pm.*	▲ 162
TALLAC HISTORIC SITE Visitors Center Tel. (916) 573 2674 Museum Tel. (916) 541 5227	*Open daily 8am–5.30pm (7pm Fri.).* *Open daily 11am–3.30pm except Tue.*	▲ 162
STOCKTON		◆ B B1
HAGGIN MUSEUM 1201 North Pershing Ave Tel. (209) 940 6300	*Open Tue.–Sun. 1.30–5pm. Closed Mon. and public holidays. Information: www.hagginmuseum.org*	▲ 165
TAHOMA		◆ A E6
SIERRA DISTRICT VISITORS CENTER 7360 W Lake Blvd Tel. (530) 525 7232	*Open Mon.–Fri. 8am–4.30pm.*	
D L BLISS STATE PARK Hwy 89 Tel. (530) 525 7277	*Open June–Sep.*	▲ 162
EMERALD BAY STATE PARK Vikingsholm Tel. (530) 541 3030	*Open mid June–mid Sep. 10am–4pm. Guided tours every ½ hour. No camping or animals.*	▲ 162
ERHMAN MANSION Voir Sugar Pine Point State Park		▲ 162
SUGAR PINE POINT STATE PARK Tel. (530) 525 7982	*Open July–Sep. 25. Guided tours daily 11am–4pm.*	▲ 162
TIJUANA (MEXICO)		◆ C C6
CENTRO CULTURAL Paseo de los Héroes and Mina Tel. (66) 87 96 00	*Open daily 10am–7pm. Information: www.cecut.org.mx*	▲ 227
VENTURA		◆ B C6
ALBINGER ARCHEOLOGICAL MUSEUM US Naval Base, Port Huenne Tel. (805) 982 5165	*Open Mon.–Sat. 9am–4pm, Sun. 12.30–4.30pm.*	▲ 176
CHANNEL ISLANDS NATIONAL PARK 1901 Spinnaker Drive Tel. (805) 658 5730	*Park open 8am–dusk. Visitors Center open daily 8.30am–5.30pm except Dec. 25 and Thanksgiving.*	▲ 176
MISSION SAN BUENAVENTURA 211 East Main Street Tel. (805) 643 4318	*Open daily dawn–dusk. Gift store open Mon.–Sat. 9am–5pm, Sun. 10am–4.30pm.*	▲ 176

◆ PLACES TO VISIT

MUSEUM OF HISTORY AND ART 100 East Main Street Tel. (805) 653 0323	*Open Tue.–Sun. 10am–5pm.* *Closed Mon., Thanksgiving, Dec. 25, Jan. 1.* *Information: www.vcmha.org*	▲ 176

WEOTT ◆ A A3

HUMBOLDT REDWOODS STATE PARK Tel. (707) 946 2409	*Open 8am–1am. Park Visitors Center open* *9am–5pm in summer; 10am–4pm in winter.* *Information: www.humboldtredwoods.org*	▲ 153

LIST OF NATIONAL PARKS (IN ALPHABETICAL ORDER)

ANCIENT BRISTLECONE PINE FOREST SCHULMAN GROVE VISITORS CENTER Tel. (760) 873 2500	*Open mid May–Nov. 1*	▲ 263 ◆ B E3
AÑO NUEVO STATE RESERVE New Years Creek Road Pescadero Tel. (800) 444 445	*Park open 8am–dusk.* *Visitors Center open 8.30am–3.30pm.* *Information: www.anonuevo.org*	▲ 238 ◆ B A2
ANZA BORREGO DESERT STATE PARK 200 Palm Canyon Drive Borrego Springs Tel. (760) 767 5311	*Visitors Center open Oct.–May daily 9am–5pm;* *June–Sep. Sat.–Sun. and public holidays only.* *Information: www.anzaborrego.statepark.org*	▲ 246 ◆ C D6
BODIE STATE HISTORIC PARK Bridgeport Tel. (760) 647 6465	*Open 8am–4pm (7pm in summer).* *Museum open in summer Sat.–Sun. 10am–5pm.* *Information: www.desertusa.com/bodie/bodie.html*	▲ 263 ◆ B D1- E1
CASTLE CRAGS STATE PARK Tel. (530) 235 2684	*Open daily*	▲ 268 ◆ A C2
CHANNEL ISLANDS NATIONAL PARK 1901 Spinnaker Drive, Ventura Tel. (805) 658 5730	*Park open 8am–dusk. Visitors Center open daily* *8.30am–5.30pm except Dec. 25 and Thanksgiving.*	▲ 240 ◆ C A5
CHANNEL ISLANDS MARINE SANCTUARY 113 Harbor Way, Santa Barbara Tel. (805) 966 7105	*Information: www.cinms.nos.noaa.gov*	▲ 240 ◆ C A5
DEATH VALLEY NATIONAL PARK Furnace Creek Visitors Center Tel. (760) 786 2331	*Park open daily 24 hours. Visitors Center open daily* *8am–6pm (7pm in summer). Borax Museum open* *8.30am–4pm. Tours of Scotty Castle 9am–5pm.* *Information: www.death.valley.national-park.com*	▲ 244 ◆ C D2, 0
DEVIL'S POSTILE NATIONAL MONUMENT Mammoth Lakes Tel. (760) 872 4881 (winter) Tel. (760) 934 2289 (summer)	*Open 7am–6pm in summer. Closed in winter.* *Information: www.nps.gov/depo*	▲ 263
ELKHORN SLOUGH NATIONAL ESTUARINE RESERVE 1700 Elkhorn Road, Watsonville Tel. (408) 728 2822	*Open Wed.–Sun. 9am–5pm.* *Information: inlet.geol.sc.edu/ELK/home.html*	◆ B A2
GULF FARALLONES NATIONAL MARINE SANCTUARY Fort Manson, Building 201 San Francisco Tel. (415) 561 6622	*Open all year. Camping by prior arrangement.* *Open Sat.–Sun. 8am–5pm in summer; Mon.–Fri.* *8am–5pm, Sat.–Sun. 8am–5.30pm in winter.* *Closed Dec. 25, Thanksgiving.* *Visitors Center open Mon.–Fri. 8.30am–4.30pm.*	▲ 238 ◆ B D2
JOSHUA TREE NATIONAL PARK 74485 National Park Drive Twentynine Palms Tel. (760) 367 5500	*Park open daily.* *Visitors Centers open daily 9am–5pm.* *Information: www.joshua.tree.national-park.com*	▲ 246 ◆ C D4- E4
JULIA PFEIFFER BURNS STATE PARK Tel. (831) 667 2200	*Visitors Center open daily8.30am–5pm.*	▲ 239 ◆ B A3
KLAMATH NATIONAL WILDLIFE REFUGES 4009 Hill Road, Tulelake Tel. (530) 667 2231	*Open Mon.–Fri. 8am–4.30pm, Sat.–Sun. 10am–4pm.* *Information: www.klamathnwr.org*	▲ 266 ◆ A D1
LASSEN VOLCANIC NATIONAL PARK Visitor Information Tel. (530) 595 4444 Southwest Visitors Center Tel. (530) 595 3308	*Visitors Center open Mon.–Fri. 8am–4.30pm except* *public hols. Loomis Museum 8am–5pm summer; May* *25–June 11 and Sep. Sat.–Sun. 8am–5pm. Closed* *winter. Southwest Visitors Center open 9am–4pm in* *summer. www.lassen.volcanic.national-park.com*	▲ 264 ◆ A D3
LAVA BEDS NATIONAL MONUMENT Visitors Center, Tulelake Tel. (530) 667 2282	*Visitors Center open daily 8am–5pm (6pm in* *summer). Closed Thanksgiving, Dec. 25.* *Information: www.nps.gov/labe*	▲ 266 ◆ A D1
MOJAVE NATIONAL MONUMENT 222 E Main Street, Barstow Baker Visitors Center 72157 Baker Blvd Tel. (760) 733 4040	*Open daily 24 hours.* *Baker Visitors Center open daily.* *Information: www.nps.gov/moja*	▲ 247 ◆ C E3

Needles Visitors Center 707 W Bradway, Needles Tel. (460) 326 6322	*Needles Visitors Center open Tue.–Sun.*	
MONO LAKE TUFA STATE RESERVE Visitors Center Lee Vining, Hwy 395 Tel. (760) 647 6331	*Visitors Center open daily in summer.* *Opening days vary in winter.* *Phone for opening times.* *Information: www.monolake.org*	▲ 262 ◆ B D1– E1
MONTEREY BAY NATIONAL **MARITIME SANCTUARY** 299 Foam Street Tel. (831) 647 4201	*Open all year.* *Information: www.mbnms.nos.noaa.gov*	▲ 238, 239 ◆ B A2
MONTEREY BAY AQUARIUM 886 Cannery Row Tel. (831) 648 4800	*Open daily 10am–6pm except Apr. 15–Labor Day* *and public holidays 9.30am–6pm.* *Information: www.mbayaq.org*	▲ 169 ◆ B A2
NATURAL BRIDGES STATE PARK West Cilff Drive, Santa Cruz Tel. (831) 423 4609	*Guided tours Oct.–Feb. daily 10am–3pm.*	▲ 239 ◆ B A2
PFEIFFER BIG SUR STATE PARK Hwy 1 Tel. (831) 667 2315	*Open all year.*	▲ 171, 239 ◆ B A3
PIGEON POINT LIGHTHOUSE **STATE HISTORIC PARK** 210 Pigeon Point Road Hwy 1, Pescadero Tel. (650) 879 2120	*Open daily 8am–dusk.* *Guided tours every hour 10am–3pm in winter* *(Oct.–Mar.);* *every 45 mins. 11am–4pm in summer (Apr.–Sep.)* *Information: www.parks.ca.gov*	▲ 238 ◆ B A1
POINT LOBOS STATE RESERVE Route 1, Carmel Information Station: Sea Lion Point Parking Tel. (831) 624 1909	*Reserve open daily 9am–5pm (7pm in summer).* *Museum open daily 11am–3pm.* *Information Station open daily 9am–4pm.* *Information: pt-lobos.parks.state.ca.us*	▲ 239 ◆ B A2
POINT REYES NATIONAL SEASHORE Bear Valley Visitors Center Tel. (415) 464 5100 Lighthouse Visitors Center Tel. (415) 669 1534	*Open Mon.–Fri. 9am–5pm, Sat.–Sun.* *and public holidays 8am–5pm. Closed Dec. 25.* *Open Thu.–Mon. 10am–4.30pm.* *Closed Tue.–Wed., Dec. 25.* *Information: www.prbo.org*	▲ 236, 237 ◆ A A6
REDWOOD NATIONAL AND STATE PARKS Crescent City Visitors Center 111 2nd Street, Crescent City Hiouchi Information Center US Hwy 199, Hiouchi Jedediah Smith Visitors Center US Hwy 101, Hiouchi Prairie Creek Visitors Center US Hwy 101, along Newton B. Drury Scenic Parkway Redwood Information Center US Hwy 101, Orick Tel. (707) 464 6101	*Park open daily* *Crescent City and Redwood Visitors Centers open* *daily 9am–5pm except Thanksgiving, Dec. 25 and* *Jan. 1.* *Hiouchi and Jedemiah Smith Visitors Centers open* *in summer 9am–5pm. Closed in winter.* *Prairie Creek Visitors Center open Jan.–Feb.* *10am–4pm; March-Oct. 9am–5pm. Closed* *Thanksgiving,* *Dec. 24–25, Jan. 1, Easter.* *Information: www.redwood.national-park.com* *and www.nps.gov/redw*	▲ 258, 259 ◆ A A1– B1, L
SEA CENTER 211 Steams Wharf Santa Barbara Tel. (805) 963 1067	*Open daily in winter noon-5pm; 10am–5pm in* *summer (Apr. 15–Labor Day).* *Information: www.sbnature.org*	▲ 240 ◆ C A5
SEQUOIA AND KINGS CANYON **NATIONAL PARKS** 47050 Generals Hwy Foothills Visitors Center Tel. (559) 565 3135 Grant Grove Visitors Center Tel. (559) 565 4307 Lodgepole Visitors Center Tel. (559) 565 3782	*Mineral King Area (Sequoia Park) and Cedar Grove* *Area (Kings Canyon) open in summer only.* *Crystal Cave closed in winter.* *Foothills Visitors Center open daily 8am–4.30pm.* *Grant Grove Visitors Center open daily* *9am–4.30pm. Lodgepole Visitors Center closed* *Tue.–Thu. in winter.* *Information: www.nps.gov/seki* *and www.sequoia.national-park.com*	▲ 250- 253 ◆ B E3, N
SEYMOUR DISCOVERY CENTER **AT LONG MARINE LAB** Institute of Marine Sciences Univ. of California, Santa Cruz Tel. (831) 459 3800	*Open Tue.–Sat. 10am–5pm, Sun. noon-5pm.* *Closed Mon., July 4.* *Information: www2.ucsc.edu/seymourcenter*	▲ 239 ◆ B A2
YOSEMITE NATIONAL PARK Visitors Center Tel. (209) 372 0200	*Park open 24 hours. Tioga, Glacier Point and* *Mariposa Grove Roads closed mid Oct.–mid May,* *due to bad weather conditions. Visitors Center* *open daily.* *Information: www.yosemitepark.com*	▲ 254- 257 ◆ B D1, M

◆ HOTELS AND RESTAURANTS

The order of major towns, cities and regions is the same as for the Itineraries section of the guide. Towns and districts listed under the main heading are in alphabetical order. An alphabetical list of all locations is given in the Index of Towns, Cities and Parks, below.

MOTEL CHAINS
Motels offer a standard level of comfort: parking, TV, bathroom, telephone and (usually) a pool. They have the advantage of being located on the main highways and of being the most inexpensive form of accommodation. Their main disadvantage is that they are sometimes lacking in character.
Best Western
Tel. 800 780 7234
bestwestern.com
Comfort Inn
Tel. 800 228 5150
comfortinn.com
Days Inn
Tel. 800 544 8313
www.daysinn.com
Econlodge
Tel. 800 553 2666
hotelchoice.com
Motel 6
Tel. 800 466 8356
motel6.com
Travelodge
Tel. 800 578 7878
travelodge.com

SAN FRANCISCO

→**SHOPPING**
Metreon
150 4th Street
With its panoramic movie theater, interactive games area, restaurants and fashion boutiques, the Metreon is part-mall, part-amusement arcade – a temple of electronic leisure.
Union Square
The commercial heart of San Francisco. A wide choice of fashion stores, from international clothing chains to luxury boutiques.

→**NIGHTLIFE**
Bars, nightclubs, theaters and concert halls to suit every taste.
Castro
The gay district has a dynamic night life.
North Beach
Renowned for its restaurants and cafés.
Mission District
The Latin quarter with its *taquerías* and inexpensive restaurants.
Pier 39
A tourist pier with restaurants, stores and street performers.

CHINATOWN
◆ **E** E3-D4
→**RESTAURANT**
House of Nanking
919 Kearny Street
Tel. 415 421 1429
Open daily, lunch and evenings.
This restaurant on the edge of Chinatown is very popular with the Chinese community. It is small and crowded, with a slightly faded decor and a friendly atmosphere. Delicious vegetable, meat and tofu dishes at unbeatable prices.
◻

CIVIC CENTER
◆ **E** B6
→**HOTEL-RESTAURANT**
Renoir Hotel
45 McAllister Street
Tel. 415 626 5200
renoirhotel.com
An unpretentious hotel in a beautiful brick building (1909), well located between the Civic Center and Union Square. Standard comfort.
◻◻◻◻◻◻◻◻

→**RESTAURANT**
Jardiniere
300 Grove Street
Tel. 415 861 5555
Open evenings only.
Even without the jazz concerts, you could be in the heart of New Orleans. The name of the restaurant pays tribute to the chef, Traci Des Jardins, while its walls are decorated with huge cooking utensils. On the menu: potted rabbit, duck sausage with baby turnips, ginger and fruit compote. Choose a mezzanine table for a better view of the comings and goings of the waiters and a very stylish clientele.
◻◻◻◻◻◻◻

EMBARCADERO
◆ **E** E3
→**RESTAURANTS**
Globe
290 Pacific Avenue
Tel. 415 391 4132
Open Mon–Fri. lunch, daily evenings. Closed Memorial Day weekend.
Chefs and waiters from other restaurants meet after hours in this converted house, where they sip its famous Manhattan cocktails and sample dishes from the regularly renewed menu until 1am. Fish and seafood, meat and pizzas.
◻◻◻◻◻

Harbor Village
4 Embarcadero Center
Tel. 415 781 8833
Open daily, lunch and evenings.
This Chinese restaurant is popular with aficionados of the excellent dim sum (steamed appetizers) served from trolleys at lunch. Very affordable.
◻◻◻

Kokkari Estiatorio
200 Jackson Street
Tel. 415 981 0983
Open Mon.–Fri. lunch and evenings, Sat. evening.

HOTELS
- ⬚ < $100
- ⬚ $100–200
- ⬚ > $200

RESTAURANTS
- ⬛ < $15
- ⬛ $15–30
- ⬛ > $30

The symbol ◆ followed by letters and numbers refers to the map section. Other symbols are explained on page 269.

Modern Greek-Californian cuisine. The most popular dishes include pikilia (a plate of Greek appetizers), leg of lamb with ouzo, ice cream with honey, and Greek coffee (prepared like Turkish coffee). Patinated wood decor with sophisticated soft furnishings.
⬛🔳⬛⬛⬛

FINANCIAL DISTRICT
◆ E D4
→ **HOTEL-RESTAURANTS**
Mandarin Oriental Hotel
222 Sansome Street
Tel. 415 276 9888
Fax 415 433 0289
mandarinoriental.com
Magnificent view from each of its 158 rooms. Fitness center with massage. The Silks restaurant serves quality Californian cuisine.
⬛⬛⬛⬛⬛⬛⬛⬛⬛⬛

Park Hyatt
333 Battery Street
Tel. 415 392 1234
Fax 415 421 2433
hyatt.com
Even if you're not staying here, it's worth a visit to see the magnificent atrium and elegant elevators in the form of Japanese lanterns. The rooms are of the usual Hyatt standard, with a bouquet of flowers into the bargain. Guests can also take advantage of the hotel's free chauffeur service to visit Downtown San Francisco in a Mercedes. The Park Grill is a favorite rendezvous for the financial and computer sets.
⬛⬛⬛⬛⬛⬛⬛⬛⬛
⬛⬛⬛

→ **RESTAURANTS**
Aqua
252 California Street
Tel. 415 956 9662

nextcentury
restaurants.com
Open Mon.–Fri. lunch and evenings, Sat. evening.
Chef Michael Mina creates innovative seafood dishes. His specialties include crab cake with crystallized cherry tomatoes, Chilean bass in a miso glaze, warm chocolate tart with cocoa syrup and papaya coulis. There is also a separate cheese menu. An elegant decor of large mirrors and clean lines is set off by sophisticated floral motifs.
⬛🔳⬛⬛⬛

Carnelian Room
555 California Street
52nd floor
Tel. 415 433 7500
carnelianroom.com
Open evenings only.
This restaurant, at the top of a Downtown office tower with a view of the city, is a favorite establishment rendezvous (suits and ties only). The chef has updated such classics as leg of lamb and duck with orange sauce. NB: at lunch time, this is a private business club.
⬛⬛⬛⬛⬛

JACKSON SQUARE
◆ E D3
→ **RESTAURANT**
MC2
470 Pacific Avenue
Tel. 415 956 0666
Open Mon.–Fri. lunch and evenings, Sat. evening. Closed public holidays.
Yoshi Kojima creates an innovative, minimalist cuisine in keeping with the brick and solid-wood decor: fennel salad with tomatoes, salmon in Pinot Noir sauce. Excellent desserts. Lively but rather

noisy atmosphere, popular with the pub set.
⬛⬛⬛⬛⬛

JAPANTOWN
◆ E A5
→ **RESTAURANT**
Iroha
1728 Buchanan St
Tel. 415 922 0321
Open daily, lunch and evenings.
Closed Thanksgiving and Christmas.
Specialty is ramen, a noodle, meat and vegetable soup from China that has become one of the classics of Japanese cuisine.
⬛⬛⬛⬛

MISSION
◆ D D5
→ **RESTAURANTS**
The Slanted Door
584 Valencia Street
Tel. 415 861 8032
Open Mon.–Sun. lunch and evenings.
Brightly colored plates relieve a rather sober decor. Original Vietnamese cuisine. Try the delicious chocolate cake. Well-stocked wine list.
⬛⬛⬛

NORTH BEACH
◆ E C2-C3
→ **HOTEL**
San Remo Hotel
2237 Mason Street
Tel. 415 776 8688
Fax 415 776 2811
sanremohotel.com
No pool or restaurant. Rooms small but clean and tidy, some with bathrooms at the end of the corridor. You can spend a whole week in this charming Victorian hotel for the cost of one night in some of the city hotels. Ideally situated off the beaten tourist track.
⬛⬛⬛⬛⬛⬛

→ **RESTAURANT**
Caffe Malvina
1600 Stockton Street
Tel. 415 391 1290

Open daily, mornings and lunch. One of the best genuine Italian cafés in North Beach. Here, they roast the coffee beans (and also sell them by the pound) and serve very good pizzas, pasta, salads and sandwiches. All-day breakfast.
⬛⬛⬛

OCEAN BEACH
◆ D A4 off the map
→ **RESTAURANT**
Beach Chalet ▲ 129
1000 Great Highway
Tel. 415 386 8439
Open daily, mornings, lunch and evenings.
Situated just above Golden Gate Park Visitors Center. American cuisine (grills, pasta, sandwiches), home-brewed beers and wines bottled by the restaurant. Simple but tasteful decor and a magnificent view of the Pacific.
⬛⬛⬛⬛⬛⬛⬛⬛⬛

RICHMOND
◆ D A3
→ **RESTAURANTS**
Brother's
4128 Geary Blvd
Tel. 415 387 7991
Open daily, lunch and evenings.
The most sought-after Korean restaurant in San Francisco. An unpretentious cuisine: barbecued rib of beef, grilled fish, noodles and soups, sashimi and beef tempura. Lively atmosphere.
⬛⬛⬛⬛

Tommy's Mexican Restaurant
5929 Geary Blvd
Tel. 415 387 4747
tommystequila.com
Open daily, lunch and evenings.
Good Mexican home cooking. The proprietor prides himself on offering the widest selection

◆ HOTELS AND RESTAURANTS

HOTELS
- ▫ < $100
- ▪ $100–200
- ▣ > $200

of 100% agave tequilas outside Mexico. Customers can obtain a tequila drinker's certificate and attend seminars on the history of tequila and the correct way to drink it.
🔲🅿️📶📺♿

RUSSIAN HILL
◆ E B2

→RESTAURANT

Luna Rossa
1556 Hyde Street
Tel. 415 409 3000
Fax 415 929 7014
Open Wed.–Mon. evenings.
A real taste of Italy on the plates and in the restaurant's friendly atmosphere. Traditional Italian dishes with a modern touch – ravioli filled with bass, arugola and ricotta, grilled filet mignon with black truffle sauce – and some very good wines.
🔲♿

SOMA
◆ E D5

→HOTEL

W Hotel
181 Third Street
Tel. 415 777 5300
Fax 415 817 7823
whotels.com
One of the trendy, luxury hotels in the W chain. The rooms have comfortable beds and high-powered Internet access. The staff, dressed in black, are attentive to your every need. Designer decor in the XYZ restaurant and the bar. One of the most high-profile hotels in town.
🔲🅿️📶🗄️📺♿🍴➡️🛗
📶♣️🛗

→RESTAURANT

Azie
826 Folsom Street
Tel. 415 538 0918
Open daily, evenings only.

restaurantazie.com
From the nine appetizers ('nine bites') served on tiny colored glass plates to the lobster roasted in a shallot and ginger sauce, this Asian-French bistro never ceases to impress. The split level dining room is superbly decorated in shades of orange enhanced by the generous use of silk hangings and warm wood paneling. Comfortable tables and stylish service.
🔲🅿️📶📺📶🛗♣️🎵

UNION SQUARE
◆ E C4-C5-D4

→HOTEL-RESTAURANTS

Hotel Diva
440 Geary Street
Tel. 415 885 0200
Fax 415 346 6613
personalityhotels.com
This hotel is extremely popular with the music, pub and fashion sets. As its name suggests, it pays tribute to divas of every kind. Rooms are decorated in Eames style with brushed metal, stone floors in the bathrooms and thick, soft bed linen. Several points for Internet access. Baskets of fruit on the continental breakfast buffet served on each floor.
🔲🅿️📶♿➡️🛗

Hotel Metropolis
25 Mason Street
Tel. 415 775 4600
Fax 415 775 4606
hotelmetropolis.com
The hotel (1910) is based on the theme of water, air, earth and fire. The minibars contain only organic products, while the alarm clocks are programmed to tune into recordings of the sound of the ocean. The holistic meditation room is a piece of pure

California. Don't miss the manager's sherry parties. It is also worth knowing that the hotel helps the district's poor through charitable works.
🔲♿📺🛗📶

Hotel Monaco
501 Geary Street
Tel. 415 292 0100
Fax 415 292 0111
kimptongroup.com
A magnificent Fine-Arts building (1910) whose interior is decorated with floral motifs. Spacious European-style rooms with minibars and, in some cases, a Jacuzzi. Room service provided by the award-winning Grand Café.
🔲🅿️📶📺♿🛗✂️➡️📶

Westin Saint Francis
335 Powell Street
Tel. 415 397 7000
Fax 415 774 0124
westin.com
The Westin is to San Francisco what the Plaza is to New York: opulent, old-fashioned and just as grand. The 1189 rooms of this skyscraper overlooking Union Square all have the famous Westin 'Heavenly Beds'. Stores, business center, fitness centers and gyms. Afternoon tea is a popular ritual, as are the martinis and caviar served in the Compass Rose restaurant.
🔲🅿️📶🗄️📺📶♿✂️➡️
♣️🛗

York Hotel
940 Sutter Street
Tel. 415 885 6800
Fax 415 885 6990
yorkhotel.com
The York had an illegal bar during Prohibition and was chosen by Alfred Hitchcock as a setting for Vertigo
● 91. *It has 96 single*

rooms, with dressing rooms and minibars. The Plush Room is one of the last remaining cabarets in San Francisco.
🔲🅿️📶📺♿🛗♣️

→RESTAURANTS

Farallon
450 Post Street
Tel. 415 956 6969
Open Tue.–Sat. lunch and evenings, Sun.–Mon. evenings. Closed public holidays.
Modern Californian cuisine which gives pride of place to fish and seafood. An award-winning decor with wall lamps in the shape of jellyfish and motifs evoking seaweed. Impeccable service.
🔲📶📺📶

Postrio
545 Post Street
Tel. 415 776 7825
Open daily, lunch and evenings.
Since it was opened by the famous chef, Wolfgang Puck, the Postrio has been a huge success. A monumental staircase leads to a glittering dining room decorated with landscaped gardens. The menu is brim-full with dishes inspired by a blend of Eastern and Western cuisine, while the pastry cook, Susan Brinkley, is one of the best in the city.
🔲📶📺📶♣️

VAN NESS
◆ E B6 TO A1

→HOTELS

Most of the standard – and often most inexpensive – motels are to be found on Van Ness Avenue.

→RESTAURANT

Venture Frogs
1000 Van Ness Ave
Tel. 415 409 2550
vfrogs.com

Open daily, lunch and evenings.
The Venture Frogs company served as a springboard for a dozen or so start-up companies. Since its employees never had time to go out for lunch, it opened a restaurant in the company building (1921). Its culinary creations are named after the great icons of the new economy: Cisco Chinese chicken salad, Priceline pot-stickers, ICQ Indonesian beef, eBay eggplant. The bar – a mixture of microchips, original ceramics and African burr walnut – symbolizes the alliance between 1920's style and high-technology.
● P 🏊 ▤ Ⅲ ⚇ 🌂

AROUND SAN FRANCISCO

BERKELEY
◆ **A** B6
→**RESTAURANT**
✪ Chez Panisse
1517 Shattuck Ave
Tel. 510 548 5525
Fax 510 548 0140
chezpanisse.com
Open Mon.–Sat. lunch and evenings.
An absolute must if you want a taste of Californian gourmet cuisine. Alice Waters ● 58 is a perfectionist who keeps an eye on everything: the choice of seasonal produce, the kitchens, the renewal and creativity of the menus and her good-humored staff. Downstairs, a dining room whose clean lines are set off by a touch of wood paneling; upstairs, a less formal café favored by the 'regulars'. Advance booking essential (up to 1 month in advance.)
🔲⚇▤Ⅲ⚇🌂

LARKSPUR
◆ **A** F1
→**RESTAURANT**
Lark Creek Inn
234 Magnolia Ave
Tel. 415 924 7766
larkcreek.com
Open Mon.–Fri. and Sun. lunch and evenings; Sat. evening; Sunday brunch.
The restaurant, which occupies a yellow-brick house (1888) in a peaceful village, only buys produce from small local growers. Try

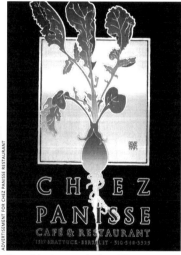

ADVERTISEMENT FOR CHEZ PANISSE RESTAURANT

the wild salmon and Caesar salad. For dessert: Valrhona chocolate and custard soufflés. House cognac. A romantic setting for Sunday brunch.
🔲⚇▤Ⅲ⚇🌂🎵

MOUNTAIN VIEW
◆ **B** A1
→**HOTEL-RESTAURANT**
Hotel Avante
860 El Camino Real
Tel. 650 940 1000
Fax 650 968 7870
hotelavante.com
A luxury hotel in the heart of Silicon Valley. Its 91 rooms are designed to stimulate creativity – they all have high-powered Internet access and boxes

containing yo-yos and Rubik's cubes! Pool, Jacuzzis and night-time snacks – all courtesy of the management.
🔲P▤Ⅲ⚇🗙→🌂🌂

REDWOOD CITY
◆ **B** A1
→**HOTEL-RESTAURANT**
Hotel Sofitel
223 Twin Dolphin Drive
Tel. 650 598 9000
Fax 650 598 0459
sofitel.com
The hotel has its own lagoon on the

bay. 419 rooms on eight floors, all with Internet connection. Pool, tennis court, thalassotherapy, gyms, free newspapers and shuttles to San Francisco airport. Ask for a room with a view of the lagoon so you're not overlooking one of the business parks typical of Silicon Valley.
🔲P🏊▤Ⅲ⚇🗙→🌂🌂

SAUSALITO
◆ **A** F1
→**HOTEL-RESTAURANT**
The Inn Above Tide
30 El Portal
Tel. 415 332 9535
Fax 415 332 6714

innabovetide.
citysearch.com
As its name suggests, the hotel stands above the ocean. Bright rooms with a fireplace and terrace overlooking the bay, seals and fishing boats.
🔲P🏊▤⚇🌂🌂

TIBURON
◆ **A** F1
→**RESTAURANT**
Sam's Anchor Café
27 Main Street
Tel. 415 435 4527
Open daily, lunch and evenings. Weekend brunch.
Sam's is situated on the shores of the bay opposite San Francisco. It is invaded on Saturday and Sunday mornings by a crowd of stylish trendies who come to eat brunch and sip Bloody Marys. There is a ferry link from San Francisco.
🔲▤🌂🌂

WINE COUNTRY

CALISTOGA
◆ **A** B5
→**HOTEL-RESTAURANT**
Calistoga Inn & Restaurant
1250 Lincoln Avenue
Tel. 707 942 4101
Fax 707 942 4914
The inn (1882) has 18 rooms and a 'Far West' restaurant with a terrace. Its varied menu ranges from chilli to smoked, unfilleted breast of chicken. It also has the liveliest bar in the Napa Valley, specializing in regional beers: Calistoga Beer and Napa Valley Brewing.
🔲▤🌂🌂

NAPA
◆ **A** B6
→**RESTAURANTS**
Cole's Chop House
1122 Main Street
Tel. 707 224 6328
coleschop.citysearch.com
Open evenings only.

◆ HOTELS AND RESTAURANTS

Closed July 4, Dec. 24, Jan. 1.
Stone walls and high, beamed ceilings, a glossy club-style bar and a dining room decorated with French art posters. The chef, Greg Cole, serves steaks, fish and seafood and truly amazing martinis. A fine selection of Merlots, Cabernets and Zinfandels.
⊡P⊡□⊡⊡⊡⊡

Mustard's Grill
7399 St. Helena Highway
Tel. 707 944 2424
Fax 707 944 0828
Open daily, lunch and evenings.
Closed Thanksgiving and Christmas.
This busy grill is typical of the stylish and relaxed atmosphere of the region and the attention paid to good food and wine. First-class roast chicken, smoked Peking duck and fried onion rings. The hamburgers are also delicious.
⊡P⊡□⊡⊡⊡⊡

RUTHERFORD
◆ A B6
→HOTEL-RESTAURANT
Auberge du Soleil
180 Rutherford Hill Road
Tel. 707 963 1211
Fax 707 963 8764
aubergedusoleil. com
The Auberge du Soleil, nestling in the heart of an olive grove, was originally a restaurant. It proved so successful that the owner added luxury accommodation rooms and now offers thermal treatment. An idyllic setting with a magnificent view of the vineyards.
⊡P⊡□⊡⊡⊡⊡⊡⊡
⊡⊡

SONOMA
◆ A B6
→HOTEL-RESTAURANT
Sonoma Mission Inn & Spa
18140 Sonoma Hwy
Tel. 707 938 9000
Fax 707 938 4246
sonomamissioninn. com
The hot springs – pumped from a depth of over 1100 feet – offer guests an ideal way to relax. In the 1980s, thalassotherapy facilities were added to the 1927 Mission-style building. There is a choice of restaurants, from the simplest to the

National Exchange Hotel, Nevada City.

Nevada City CALIFORNIA

most stylish. Superb professional-class golf course.
⊡P⊡⊡□⊡⊡⊡⊡⊡⊡
⊡ ⊡⊡

YOUNTVILLE
◆ A B6
→RESTAURANTS
Bistro Jeanty
6510 Washington St
Tel. 707 944 0103
Open daily, lunch and evenings.
Situated on a minor road just off the main Napa Valley highway. Philippe Jeanty pays tribute to the wine-growing and gastronomic heritage of France

with his coq au vin, cassoulet and snails. Individual tables or a communal table for a more convivial meal.
⊡P⊡□⊡⊡⊡

French Laundry
6640 Washington Street
Tel. 707 944 2380
Open Mon.–Thu. evenings, Fri.–Sun. lunch and evenings.
Closed Thanksgiving and Christmas.
You'll need patience if you want to eat here – you have to book more than two months in advance! But there is no

shortage of praise for the modern American cuisine of Thomas Keller who runs one of the best restaurants in the United States. Rustic setting.
⊡P⊡□⊡⊡

NORTH COAST
EUREKA
◆ A A2
→HOTEL-RESTAURANT
Carter House Inns
▲ 154
301 L Street
Tel. 800 404 1390
Fax 707 444 8067
carterhouse.com
This hotel-restaurant occupies

four Victorian houses on the shores of Humboldt Bay. It offers a range of different types of accommodation with prices to match. Some rooms have a marble fireplace and whirlpool bathtub. Restaurant 301 is one of the best in North California. Extensive menus for lovers of good wines and gastronomic experiences.
⊡⊡⊡P⊡⊡⊡⊡⊡⊡

LITTLE RIVER
◆ A A4
→HOTEL-RESTAURANT
○ **Heritage House Inn**
5200 N Highway 1
Tel. 707 937 5885
Fax 707 937 0318
heritagehouseinn. com
This romantic hotel occupies a spectacular location on the rugged coast of Mendocino. It comprises a main building and several cottages in the heart of a vast estate. The 66 rooms are so comfortable that you could almost be at home. Three restaurants.
⊡P⊡⊡□⊡⊡⊡

POINT ARENA
◆ A A5
→HOTEL
Coast Guard House Historic Inn
695 Arena Cove
Tel. 707 882 2442
Fax 707 882 3233
coastguardhouse.com
This former signal station has stood on the cliffs since 1901. The decor of its cozy rooms is inspired by the Arts and Crafts style. Unrivaled views of the Pacific. Truly delightful.
⊡P⊡□⊡⊡⊡

UKIAH
◆ A B5
→HOTEL-RESTAURANT
Vichy Springs Resort
2605 Vichy Springs Road

RESTAURANTS
- ▣ < $15
- ▣ $15–30
- ▣ > $30

Tel. 707 462 9515
Fax 707 462 9516
vichysprings.com
Since the 19th century, the springs – rich in carbonate and bubbles – have attracted visitors with their promise of 'champagne baths'. The thermal resort is still extremely popular with modern visitors who come to relax in the 140 year-old baths. A choice of 22 country-style rooms (with magnificent views of the mountains), private suites and cottages.
▣P▣▥▥▩▨▤

THE GOLD COUNTRY
→SHOPPING
Bargain hunters will be pleased to know that every town in the Gold Country has its own antique store!

GRASS VALLEY
◆ A D5
→HOTEL-RESTAURANT
The Holbrooke Hotel
212 West Main St
Tel. 530 273 1353
Fax 530 273 0434
holbrooke.com
Having welcomed such famous guests as Mark Twain and Teddy Roosevelt, this Victorian-style hotel (1862) prides itself on having the oldest bar in California. The restaurant serves very good American cuisine. Continental breakfast included.
▣P▥▣▥▩▨

GROVELAND
◆ B C1
→HOTEL-RESTAURANT
Groveland Hotel and Restaurant
18767 Main Street
Tel. 209 962 4000
Fax 209 962 6674
groveland.com
The hotel is less than 25 miles from the Yosemite National Park. In 1914, a Queen Anne building was added to the original inn, which dates from the time of the Gold Rush (1849). The 17 rooms are furnished with European period furniture. The saloon-style Victorian Room serves very good Californian cuisine. The wine list was awarded a prix d'excellence by the Wine Spectator magazine.
▣P▣▥▣▤

NEVADA CITY
◆ A D5
→HOTEL-RESTAURANT
✪ **National Hotel**
211 Broad Street
Tel. 530 265 4551
Fax 530 265 2445
This charming city-center hotel is a listed building (1854). It combines its original country style – meals are served in the Victorian dining room by the light of oil lamps – with concessions to modern living (pool).
▣P▣▥▥▩

SACRAMENTO
◆ A D6
→HOTEL
Delta King Hotel
1000 Front Street
Tel. 916 444 5464
Fax 916 447 5959
deltaking.com
This former steamship (1920) has 44 mahogany-paneled staterooms. Continental breakfast included. The Pilothouse restaurant gives pride of place to fish and seafood. The cabaret stages an interactive murder mystery.
▣▥▥▣▥▩▩▨

→RESTAURANT
Esquire Grill
13th and K Street
Tel. 916 448 8900
Open Mon.–Fri. lunch and evenings, Sat.–Sun. evenings. The brainchild of Randy Paragary, the famous Sacramento restaurateur. A menu rich in modern American-style cuisine and attentive service. Situated near the Convention Center, it is a popular rendezvous for politicians.
▣P▥▥▣▥▩▨▤

SUTTER CREEK
◆ A D6
→HOTEL
Foxes Bed & Breakfast
77 Main Street
Tel. 209 267 5882
Fax 209 267 0712
foxesinn.com
The inn, run by the same proprietors for the past twenty years, has a romantic charm. Original country-style rooms. For breakfast, Swedish pancakes served on a silver platter.
▣▣▥▣

TUOLUMNE
◆ B D1
→HOTEL-RESTAURANT
Slide Mountain Guest Ranch
19280 Mira Monte Road
Tel. 209 928 4287
slidemountain.com
A real ranch, where guests can have riding lessons or try their hand at the traditional mounted skills practised by cowboys. Camp fires and friendly atmosphere. The cost of a night in one of the rustic cabins is reasonable.
▣▣▣▤▥

LAKE TAHOE
SOUTH LAKE TAHOE
◆ A E6
→HOTEL
Tahoe Keys Resort
599 Tahoe Keys Blvd
Tel. 530 544 5397
Fax 530 544 2741
tahoe-resorts.com
A dozen or so different self-contained units and apartments. Ideal for sporting and open-air activities: volley-ball on the beach, body-building, mountain biking or swimming in the pool. Alternatively, you can relax on the beach which – like much of the access to Lake Tahoe – has the advantage of being private.
▣▣▥▣▥▩▨▤▥

→RESTAURANT
California Red Hut Waffle Shop
2749 US-50
Tel. 530 541 9024
Open daily, mornings and lunch. Traditional American diner with two long counters and small tables. The pancakes, waffles and omelettes are excellent. Very popular with skiers and other sports enthusiasts.
▣P

TAHOE CITY
◆ A E5
→HOTEL-RESTAURANT
Sunnyside Restaurant and Lodge
1850 W Lake Blvd
Tel. 530 583 7200
Fax 530 583 2551
sunnysideresort.com
The former country residence (23 rooms) of a lock magnate has been a tourist institution since the 1950s. The marina can harbor 25 boats. In summer, you can sip a beer and enjoy Hula pie on the largest terrace on the lake. A much sought-after venue.
▣P▣▥▣▥

CENTRAL VALLEY
BAKERSFIELD
◆ B D5
→RESTAURANT
Wool Growers
620 East 19th Street
Tel. 661 327 9584
Open Mon.–Sat. lunch and evenings. Bakersfield has the largest Basque community in the

◆ HOTELS AND RESTAURANTS

United States. This is why visitors have been able to enjoy roast lamb and other Basque specialties in this downtown restaurant since 1954.

MONTEREY AND SURROUNDINGS

BIG SUR
◆ B A3

→**HOTEL-RESTAURANTS**
Deetjen's Big Sur Inn
Highway 1 at Castro Canyons
Tel. 831 667 2377
One of the icons of Big Sur. This fairytale inn was built in the 1930s by Helmut Deetjen in his native Norwegian style. An association ensures that its authentic rusticity is preserved. No phones or TVs. Heated by wood-burning stoves.

Post Ranch Inn
Highway 1
Tel. 831 667 2200
Fax 831 667 2512
postranchinn.com
Guests are encouraged to explore every nook and cranny of this 100-acre domain. Activities include relaxation exercises, yoga, walking and astronomy. 30 rustic rooms with views of the ocean or the mountains. They don't have TVs, but they do have CD players and a satellite radio system.

→**RESTAURANT**
✪ **Nepenthe**
Highway 1, Big Sur
Tel. 831 667 2345
Fax 831 667 2394
Open daily, lunch and evenings.
This former 'Mecca' of the hippie community has stood on the peaceful slopes of the Santa Lucia

Mountains since 1949. Customers can sample the famous Ambrosia burgers and house desserts on a terrace with an unrivaled view of Big Sur. A more eclectic menu in the Café Kevah and New Age nicknacks in the Phoenix Shop.

CARMEL
◆ B A2

→**HOTEL-RESTAURANT**
Quail Lodge Resort and Golf Club
205 Valley Greens Drive
Carmel-by-the-Sea
Tel. 831 624 2888
Fax 831 624 3726
quail-lodge-resort.com
A vast estate with 100 luxury suites, cottages and villas. Magnificent golf course with 10 lakes. The Covey (one of the hotel's three restaurants) serves top-quality European-Californian cuisine. Organized visits to the vineyards and picnic baskets for lunch.

→**RESTAURANTS**
Anton & Michel
Mission & 7th Street
Tel. 831 624 2406
Open daily, lunch and evenings.
Seafood specialties (fish from Monterey Bay and farmed abalone) served in the pastel tones of an elegant and romantic setting. Impeccable service.

Flying Fish Grill
Carmel Plaza
Tel. 831 625 1962
Open Wed.–Mon. evenings.
Closed Thanksgiving and Christmas.
The grill, which is more like a Japanese country inn, serves the best

modern fish and seafood dishes in Carmel. Traditional Japanese dishes include yosenabe and shabu-shabu, a sort of fondue.

MONTEREY
◆ B A2

→**HOTELS**
Lone Oak Lodge
2221 North Fremont Street
Tel. 831 372 4924
Fax 831 372 4985
loneoakmotel.com
Each of the 46 rooms has fresh flowers and a Kona coffee-maker. Some are suites, others have a fireplace and Jacuzzi. Fitness center with sauna and body-building facilities. Diving equipment available.

Hotel Pacific
300 Pacific Street
Tel. 831 373 5700
Fax 831 373 6921
innsofmonterey.com
The Pacific pays tribute to the Spanish Colonial Revival style. Its 105 vast rooms, decorated with original works of art, have a fireplace, bar and French windows opening onto a private balcony or the patio.

→**HOTEL-RESTAURANT**
Monterey Plaza Hotel and Spa
400 Cannery Row
Tel. 831 646 1700
Fax 831 646 5937
montereyplazahotel.com
A first-class luxury hotel on the waterfront, only a stone's throw from Monterey Bay Aquarium. The rooms are decorated in Biedermeier style and have huge marble baths. Fitness center and award-

winning restaurants: the Schooners and Duck Club.

→**RESTAURANT**
Fresh Cream
99 Pacific Street
Tel. 831 375 9798
freshcream.com
Open evenings only.
Closed Christmas.
An award-winning restaurant serving French gourmet cuisine. More than 180 vintages on the wine list. Magnificent view of Monterey Harbor.

MOSS LANDING
◆ B A2

→**RESTAURANT**
Phil's Fish Market
7600 Sandholdt Rd
Tel. 831 633 2152
Fax 831 633 8611
philsfishmarket.com
Open daily, lunch and evenings.
Phil DiGirolamo certainly knows how to give his grilled, smoked, fried and skewered fish an Italian flavor. Try the ciopino, the house specialty. Live music at weekends when the population of this fishing village suddenly increases. The restaurant's website has recipes and practical hints on shelling crab!

PEBBLE BEACH
◆ B A2

→**HOTEL-RESTAURANT**
Lodge at Pebble Beach
17-Mile Drive
Tel. 831 624 3811
The hotel has four international-class golf courses, 161 luxury rooms (including 6 suites) with a view of the Pacific, ultra-modern fitness centers and a choice of restaurants: snack bar, sophisticated French cuisine or a busy American grill.

RESTAURANTS

- ◧ < $15
- ◧ $15–30
- ◧ > $30

The Casa Palmero, a separate building with 24 rooms, is only a stone's throw from the first golf course.
◧P☆▤◧♡ᴕ✕➤⌕
▨☒

SANTA BARBARA AND SURROUNDINGS

CAMBRIA
◆ **B** B4

→HOTEL
The Pickford House Bed and Breakfast
2555 MacLeod Way
Tel. 805 927 8619
This small hotel (8 rooms) stands on a hillside, with a view of the mountains, near the center of Cambria and Hearst Castle. It is dedicated to the film star Mary Pickford, whose portraits decorate the walls. The delicious, copious breakfast includes Danish pancakes and fresh fruit. Excellent service.
◧P▤◧♔

GOLETA
◆ **B** C6

→HOTEL-RESTAURANT
Bacara Resort & Spa
8301 Hollister Ave
Tel. 805 968 0100
bacararesort.com
The Bacara stands on 75 acres, less than 2 miles from a white, sandy beach. It has 360 rooms and suites (225 with a fireplace), 24-hour room service, 36 fitness rooms (including massage) and one-to-one training. Guests who prefer outdoor pursuits can play golf, sail a catamaran, visit the vineyards or enjoy a wine-growers dinner.
◧P☆▤◧♡ᴕ✕▨☒♔
▨➤

LOS OLIVOS
◆ **B** B5

→HOTEL-RESTAURANT
Fess Parker's Wine Country Inn & Spa
2860 Grand Avenue
Tel. 800 446 2455

fessparker.com
A good reason for visiting the delightful village of Los Olivos. The hotel is run by a family of wine-growers. Elegant country-style rooms. In 2000, the Vintage Room restaurant received an award from the Wine Spectator magazine.
◧P▤Ⅲ▨♔♫▨≋➤

OJAI
◆ **B** C6

→HOTEL
Lindley Retreat Krishnamurti Foundation
1130 McAndrew Rd
Tel. 805 646 3967
This peaceful, isolated retreat is an ideal place to study the philosophy of Jiddu Krishnamurti. Rustic comfort.
◧♫

→RESTAURANT
Ranch House
South Lomita Road
Tel. 805 646 2360
theranchhouse.com
Open Wed.–Sat. evenings, Sun. lunch and evenings. Closed Christmas, Jan. 1, July 4.
An idyllic setting with an aromatic herb garden and

delightful stream. Quality Californian cuisine (chicken with citronella from the garden, ice cream with wild strawberries). Well worth the detour for Sunday brunch.
◧P▤◧♔♫▨♪

SAN LUIS OBISPO
◆ **B** B4

→HOTEL-RESTAURANT
✪ **Madonna Inn**
100 Madonna Road
Tel. 805 543 3000
madonnainn.com
Showy and incredibly kitsch with its overdone decor – from the acid stripes of the restaurant to the different decorative styles (prehistoric to science fiction!) of the 109 rooms. Fantastic or horrifying, depending on your taste. The name of the inn has nothing to do with the singer.
◧P▤◧Ⅲ♔▨

→RESTAURANT
Buona Tavola
1037 Monterey Street
Tel. 805 545 8000
Open Mon.–Fri. lunch and evenings, Sat.–Sun. evenings.

This downtown restaurant, owned by the famous chef Antonio Varia, is one of the most popular in San Luis Obispo. Potato and pumpkin gnocchi in a creamy gorgonzola and walnut sauce, prawn ravioli and timballo di Parma, home-made pasta, fish and seafood.
◧▤◧Ⅲ♔♫

SANTA BARBARA
◆ **B** C6

→NIGHTLIFE
State Street
A host of cafés, restaurants, theaters and discotheques on the main street of Santa Barbara.

→RESTAURANTS
Cold Spring Tavern
5995 Stagecoach Road
Tel. 805 967 0066
Open daily, mornings, lunch and evenings. Weekend brunch.
This former post restaurant, dating from the stagecoach era, serves excellent modern American cuisine (game and strong cocktails) in a country setting. A mixed clientele from the Hollywood smart set and the local farming community.
◧P▤◧▨♫♪

La Super-Rica
622 N Milpas Street
Tel. 805 963 4940
Open daily, lunch and evenings.
Mexican cuisine using fresh produce and amazing sauces. Don't be deceived by its roadside-café appearance (you order at the counter).
◧Ⅲ

Soujourner Café
134 E Canon Perdido
Tel. 805 965 7922
Open daily, lunch

MADONNA INN

◆ HOTELS AND RESTAURANTS

HOTELS
⬚ < $100
⬛ $100–200
⬛ > $200

and evenings.
Brunch Sat.–Sun.
*The town's oldest
vegetarian
restaurant (1977)
serves salads with
amazing dressings,
crunchy tofu with
onions and
energizing soups.
Dishes are inspired
by Mexican, Indian
and African cuisine.
Turkey and fish
burgers for
unrepentant meat-
eaters.*
⬛⬛⬚⬛⬛

SOLVANG
◆ B B5
→HOTEL-RESTAURANT
**Alisal Guest Ranch
and Resort**
1054 Alisal Road
Tel. 805 688 6411
Fax 805 688 2510
alisal.com
*An ideal family
ranch located in the
heart of Santa Inez
Valley, a horse-
breeding region
since the eighteenth
century. Its 73
cottages have no
phone or TV, but
they do have a
fridge, radio-alarm
and a fireplace.
Attractions include
morning horseback
or buggy rides,
breakfast with
cowboys singing or
reciting poetry,
children's activities,
golf or tennis for
the adults and
good food.*
⬛⬛⬚⬛⬛⬛⬛⬛⬛

LOS ANGELES
→SHOPPING
**Abbot Kinney
Boulevard**
Art galleries,
antique stores,
fashion boutiques
and restaurants to
suit every taste!
**Fashion District
Downtown**
A bargain hunter's
paradise. Don't miss
the huge Santee
Alley market where
you can pick up
quality accessories
and clothing at
knockdown prices.

Melrose Avenue
◆ G B4
A high
concentration of
trendy fashion
boutiques between
La Brea and Fairfax
Avenue. For those
who can't afford to
shop on Rodeo
Drive.
**Montana Avenue
Santa Monica**
10 blocks of antique
stores, art galleries,
fashion boutiques,
cafés and
restaurants. Trendy
and stylish.
Rodeo Drive
The most famous
avenue in Beverly
Hills. Julia Roberts
did her shopping
here in *Pretty
Woman*. Sheer
luxury.

→NIGHTLIFE
**3rd Street
Promenade
Santa Monica**
This pedestrianized
street is particularly
busy at weekends.
Street musicians,
movie theaters,
restaurants, cafés
and stores open in
the evening.
**Sunset Strip
Santa Monica Blvd.**
The 'Mecca' of jazz
clubs. Stylish
restaurants and
hotels.
**Universal City Walk
Burbank** ◆ G D1
A very commercial,
pedestrianized
street leading to
Universal Studios.
Very popular with
Angelinos.

BEL AIR
◆ I A1
→HOTEL-RESTAURANT
Hotel Bel Air ▲ 202
701 Stone Canyon Rd
Tel. 310 472 1211
hotelbelair.com
*Here, at the end of
the canyon, guests
can relax in gardens
planted with fig
trees, where swans
dip and splash on
the water, and
forget they are in
LA. The impression*

*created by the 1946
building is enhanced
by the French-style
decor which
reinforces the
feeling of
disorientation.
Excellent restaurant
and impeccable
service.*
⬛⬛⬛⬛⬛⬛⬛⬛⬛⬛
⬛⬛⬛⬛

BEVERLY / FAIRFAX
◆ G A4
→RESTAURANTS
Canter's
419 N Fairfax Ave
Tel. 323 651 2030
Open daily, 24 hours.
*The best Jewish deli
in the city. Soup
with matzo balls,
pickles and
enormous pastrami
sandwiches. In the
evening, live music
and dancing in the
dynamic atmosphere
of the Kibbutz
Room cocktail bar.
Pleasant waitresses.
Wide choice of
breads. Takeaway
dishes.*
⬚ ⬛ ⬛ ⬛ ⬛ ⬛ ⬛ ⬛ ⬛

El Coyote
7312 Beverly Blvd
Tel. 323 939 2255
Open daily, lunch
and evenings.
*Opinions vary on
the cuisine, but
after a few
margaritas, you can
understand why El
Coyote has been
popular with
students, gays from
West Hollywood and
other Angelinos for
generations.
Inexpensive dishes,
pleasant waitresses,
kitsch painted-wood
toucans and booths
with red leatherette
benches.*
⬛⬛⬛⬛⬛⬛⬛

BEVERLY HILLS
◆ F C2-C3, I
→HOTEL-RESTAURANTS
Raffles l'Ermitage
9291 Burton Way
Tel. 310 278 3344
Fax 310 278 8247
lermitagehotel.com
*An ascetic, Asian-
style decor. The beds*

*seem to hang in
mid-air, supported
by a pale-colored
trellis of English
sycamore. The
rooms have mobile
phones that operate
within a 40-mile
radius of the hotel.*
⬛⬛⬛⬛⬛⬛

**Regent Beverly
Wilshire Hotel**
9500 Wilshire Blvd
Tel. 310 275 5200
Fax 310 275 5986
fourseasons.com
*The hotel has been
world famous since
it featured in* Pretty
Woman. *The subtle
gilt decor of the
rooms is enhanced
by walnut,
shimmering silk
hangings and
marble bathrooms.
Chef Fabriceio
Schenardi
introduces daring
ideas into the
venerable Dining
Room.*
⬛⬛⬛⬛⬛⬛⬛⬛⬛

→RESTAURANTS
Locanda Veneta
8638 W Third Street
Tel. 310 274 1893
Open Mon.–Fri.
lunch and evenings,
Sat.–Sun. evenings.
*An intimate and
friendly restaurant
popular with the
rich and famous.
Venetian dishes:
carpaccio served
with olive oil,
risotto, escalopes de
veau in garlic and
rosemary, lobster
ravioli.*
⬛⬛⬛⬛⬛

Spago Beverly Hills
176 N Canon Drive
Tel. 310 385 0880
wolfgangpuck.com
Open Mon.–Sat.
lunch and evenings,
Sun. evenings.
*One of the most
sought-after
restaurants in
California. Delicious
creations using a
blend of Eastern
and Western cuisine
by the famous chef*

HOTELS AND RESTAURANTS ◆

RESTAURANTS
- ▧ < $15
- ▧ $15–30
- ▧ > $30

Wolfgang Puck. His specialties can also be found at Chinois on Main (Santa Monica), Granita (Malibu), in the Puck Cafés – and the frozen pizza section in supermarkets. Lavish interior decor by his wife, Barbara Lazaroff.
▧▧▧▧▧▧▧

The Grill on the Alley
9560 Dayton Way
Tel. 310 276 0615
Open Mon.–Sat. lunch and evenings, Sun. evening.
An American restaurant nestling between the world's most sought-after fashion boutiques and casting agencies, which says everything about its high-profile clientele. White linen tablecloths, wood paneling and dark leather. On the menu: steak, chops and salads. Quieter in the evening.
▧▧▧▧▧

CHINATOWN
◆ **G** E4
→**RESTAURANT**
Phillippe the Original
1001 N Alameda St
Tel. 213 628 3781
phillippes.com
Open daily, lunch and evenings.
A deep, cavernous interior, sawdust-covered floor and jars of pink, pickled eggs on the counter. This historic sandwich restaurant (1908) is reminiscent of the age of Philip Marlowe, when men wore trench coats and broad-brimmed trilbies and women had that 'tapered' look. House specialty: the French dip sandwich (the inside of the bread is dipped in the cooking juices before being filled with meat). Very reasonably priced.
▧▧▧▧▧

DOWNTOWN
◆ **G** E5
→**HOTEL-RESTAURANT**
Westin Bonaventure Hotel
404 S Figueroa St
Tel. 213 624 1000
Fax 213 612 4800
westin.com
Featured in True Lies, Line of Fire *and* Forget Paris. *The epitome of LA with its 1300 seventies-style rooms, numerous boutiques and restaurants, and glass elevators offering amazing views. A real maze where you can easily get lost without a map.*
▧▧▧▧▧▧▧▧▧
▧▧

→**RESTAURANT**
Ciudad
445 S Figueroa St
Tel. 213 486 5171
Open Mon.–Fri. lunch and evenings, Sat.–Sun. evenings.
Chefs Mary Sue Milliken and Susan Feniger also star in TV cookery programs. Their Latin-American nouvelle cuisine is a subtle blend of culinary styles from north and south of the border. Avant-garde decor in a whirl of pastel colors. Cuchifritos in the afternoon, a sort of tapas happy hour.
▧▧▧▧▧▧▧▧▧▧

ENCINO
◆ **F** B2
→**RESTAURANT**
Versailles
17410 Ventura Blvd
Tel. 818 906 0756
1415 S La Cienega Blvd
Tel. 310 289 0392
10319 Venice Blvd
Tel. 310 558 3168
1000 North Sepulveda Blvd, Manhattan Beach
Tel. 310 937 6829
Open daily, lunch and evenings.
A mini-chain of Cuban restaurants serving ropa viejas (roast pork), arroz con pollo (chicken with rice) and garlic specialties. Excellent value for money, especially at lunch.
▧

HOLLYWOOD
◆ **G** B3-C3
→**HOTEL-RESTAURANT**
Hollywood Roosevelt Hotel
7000 Hollywood Blvd
Tel. 323 466 7000
Fax 323 462 8056
hollywoodroosevelt.com
The hotel, built in 1927, hosted the first Academy Awards ceremony with its attendant following of stars – it has an exhibition on the early years of Hollywood. Huge Spanish-style lobby and rooms decorated in fantastic colors. Singers perform regularly in the Cinegrill Cabaret Lounge.
▧▧▧▧▧▧▧

→**RESTAURANTS**
Bouchon
7661 Melrose Ave
Tel. 323 852 9400
Open daily, evenings only.
The bistro deserves its name. Lyonnais atmosphere and cuisine: flank of beef and steak au poivre served at dark wood tables. Very competitive prices. A touch of Hollywood on Friday evenings when the bar serves flavored martinis.
▧▧▧▧▧▧▧

Musso & Frank Grill
6667 Hollywood Blvd
Tel. 323 467 7788
Tue.–Sat. lunch and evenings.
Since 1919, this has been the favourite rendezvous of the movie and literary sets. However, it is more popular for its outdated atmosphere than its cuisine: steaks, chops, chicken casserole, fish and seafood. The bar is renowned for its martinis and Bloody Marys.
▧▧▧▧

Palms Thai Restaurant
5273 Hollywood Blvd
Tel. 323 462 5073
Open daily, lunch and evenings.
Atmosphere guaranteed – a Thai 'Elvis Presley' sings most evenings to a karaoke backup! Excellent cuisine: sautéed beef with curries, flavored rice. If you prefer somewhere quieter, the district – hailed as the first Thai town in the United States – has no end of restaurants serving similar cuisine.
▧▧▧▧

Patina
5955 Melrose Ave
Tel. 323 467 1108
Open Sat.–Thu. evenings, Fri. lunch and evening.
The flagship restaurant of Joachim Splichal who creates an extremely innovative Californian cuisine. Splendid wood paneling, European silverware and delicate porcelain. The chef also demonstrates his skill at the Pinot, Patinette at MOCA and Nick & Stef's Steakhouse (downtown) restaurants.
▧▧▧▧▧▧

KOREATOWN
◆ **G** C3
→**RESTAURANT**
Chung Ki Wa
3545 W Olympic Blvd
Tel. 323 737 0809
Open daily, lunch and evenings.

A favorite venue among the Korean community. Very varied menu: japchae sautéed noodles, bibimpap (rice and vegetables served on a warm metal dish) and a range of barbecue dishes for customers to cook at their table. Country atmosphere, thick wood paneling and Korean paintings.
⊡⊡▥▥

LONG BEACH
◆ **K** A3
→**HOTEL**
Queen Mary
▲ *212*
1126 Queens Hwy
Tel. 562 435 3511
Fax 562 437 4531
queenmary.com
Today, the famous ocean-going liner (1929) is a hotel whose 375 staterooms still have their original decor and furniture. Bar, boutiques and restaurants on board. A Sunday buffet-brunch is served in the high-ceilinged dining room.
⊡⊡🅿▥▥⊡▥⊡⊡⊡
⊡⊡⊡⊡

MARINA DEL REY
◆ **J** C3
→**RESTAURANT**
C&O Trattoria
31 Washington Blvd
Tel. 310 823 9491
Open daily, mornings, lunch and evenings.
Excellent, unpretentious cuisine from southern Italy. Convivial – sometimes musical – evenings. Here, the wine flows freely and customers are trusted to keep track of and pay for the amount of wine they consume (the 'honor system'). Garlic bread and huge plates of pasta. Tables on the patio are at a

premium for Saturday and Sunday brunch.
⊡⊡⊡⊡▥⊡

MONTEREY PARK
◆ **F** F3
→**RESTAURANT**
Ocean Star Seafood Restaurant
145 N Atlantic Blvd
Tel. 626 308 2128
Open daily, lunch and evenings.
Chinese specialties: dim sum (steamed appetizers), shark's-fin soup, prawn fritters, mango pudding. Get there by 11am if you want to avoid lines at lunch. Round off your meal with a stroll in Monterey Park, which claims to be the Asian equivalent of Beverly Hills.
⊡⊡🅿▥

PASADENA
◆ **H** B3
→**RESTAURANT**
Café Bizou
91 N Raymond Ave
Tel. 626 792 9923
cafebizou.com
2450 Colorado Ave
Santa Monica
Tel. 310 582 8203
14016 Ventura Blvd
Sherman Oaks
Tel. (818) 788 3536
Open daily, lunch and evenings. Brunch at weekends. Closed Christmas and New Years Day. Affordable, top-quality French-Californian cuisine. Stuffed mushrooms, salmon topped with a potato chiffonnade, chocolate tart made without flour. Friendly atmosphere. Customers can bring their own wine ($2 corkage).
⊡⊡▥⊡▥▥

SANTA MONICA
◆ **J**
→**HOTELS**
❍ **Cal Mar Hotel and Suites**

220 California Avenue
Tel. 310 395 5555
Fax 310 451 1111
A converted apartment building, a block away from the ocean, with an all-Californian atmosphere. The suites, which have their own kitchenettes, overlook a pool in the central courtyard. There's no restaurant, but the hotel is near Third Street Promenade. Alternatively, guests may prefer to cook their own meals in the apartments.
⊡⊡🅿⊡▥⊡▥⊡⊡

Hotel Casa Del Mar
1910 Ocean Front Walk
Tel. 310 581 5533
Fax 310 581 5503
hotelcasadelmar.com
One of the most luxurious hotels in Santa Monica, built in 1926 in 18th-century style. It has a sumptuous lobby, with a mosaic and wood-paneled decor, overlooking the Pacific. All rooms have a view and are renowned for their comfortable beds. Bathrooms with Jacuzzis.
⊡⊡🅿▥⊡⊡▥⊡⊡⊡⊡

Santa Monica International Youth Hostel
1436 2nd Street
Tel. 310 393 9913
Fax 310 393 1769
This brick building – the oldest in Santa Monica – is only a stone's throw from the ocean and the town's nightlife. You don't have to belong to the Youth Hostel Association to stay here or enjoy lectures, films and excursions at reduced rates. Extensive overnight accommodation,

from dormitories to double rooms.
⊡⊡⊡⊡⊡

→**RESTAURANTS**
Back on the Beach
445 Pacific Coast Highway
Tel. 310 393 8282
Open daily, mornings and lunch (Oct.–Feb.), lunch (Mar.–Sep.).
An ideal place to sit and watch the skaters, cyclists and walkers on the waterfront – which doesn't stop you eating your breakfast, sandwiches or pasta with your feet in the sand. The largest sandpit in the world keeps children amused. You can also eat inside.
⊡⊡⊡

La Serenata de Garibaldi
1416 4th Street
Tel. 310 656 7017
1842 E 1st Street
Tel. 323 265 2887
East Los Angeles
10924 W Pico Boulevard
West Los Angeles
Tel. 310 441 9667
Open Mon.–Fri. lunch and evenings; Sat.–Sun. mornings, lunch and evenings.
Expensive for Mexican restaurants, but they serve exceptional fish accompanied by amazing sauces. A more informal atmosphere at the Pico Boulevard restaurant.
⊡

TOPANGA
◆ **F** B2
→**RESTAURANT**
Froggy's Topanga Fish Market
1105 North Topanga Canyon Boulevard
Tel. 310 455 1728
Open evenings only. Closed 1 week at Christmas.
Hidden deep in the heart of the forest where frogs provide

HOTELS AND RESTAURANTS ◆

RESTAURANTS
- ◧ < $15
- ◧ $15–30
- ◧ > $30

the background music! An ideal place to end a day spent in the surrounding parks or discover the bohemian atmosphere of Topanga. The day's fresh fish is on display. You can choose how you want it cooked: pan fried, grilled Cajun style, etc. Delicious, crunchy coleslaw.
◧P◨◧▨

VENICE
◆ J B3
→HOTEL
Venice Beach House
15 30th Avenue
Tel. 310 823 1966
Fax 310 823 1842
Right next to the beach and the nightlife of Washington Blvd, this Arts and Crafts-style B&B is both quiet and charming. One suite per floor.
◧P◨→▨

→RESTAURANTS
Hama Sushi
213 Windward Ave
Tel. 310 396 8783
Open Mon.–Fri. lunch and evenings, Sat.–Sun. evenings. Closed public holidays.
Sushi is given pride of place in this restaurant in the heart of Venice. The music is loud, the bar futuristic, the alcohol strong, the chefs dynamic and the fish delicious. An ideal place to enjoy food and meet people.
◧P◨◧

Joe's
1023 Abbot Kinney Boulevard
Tel. 310 399 5811
Open Tue.–Sun. lunch and evenings. Brunch at weekends.
With luck, you'll be welcomed by chef Joe Miller who creates the restaurant's original

Californian cuisine: tuna with foie gras, crème brûlée with hazelnuts. Subdued atmosphere and friendly service. Choose a table on the covered patio rather than in the long, narrow dining room. Better value for money at lunch.
◧P◨◧▨◧◧

WEST HOLLYWOOD
◆ G A3
→HOTEL-RESTAURANT
The Standard
8300 Sunset Blvd
Tel. 323 650 9090
Fax 323 650 2820
standardhotel.com
Like the live dummy in the front window, this 1960's 'Mod' hotel is deliberately eccentric: inflatable armchairs, carpet on the floor, walls and ceiling of the main lobby, and no end of electric fans. The artificial lawn surrounding the pool is cobalt blue! A very fashionable restaurant.
◧◨◧◨◧▨◧→

→RESTAURANT
House of Blues
8430 Sunset Blvd
Tel. 323 848 5100
Open Mon.–Sat. evenings, Sun. brunch.
It may be part of a chain, but the 'soul' cuisine is excellent, as is the live music in the evenings. A honky-tonk style building, typical of the Mississippi Delta. Gospel brunch on Sundays.
◧P◨◧▨◧

WEST LOS ANGELES
◆ G A3
→RESTAURANTS
Hamasaku
11043 Santa Monica Boulevard
Open Mon.–Fri. lunch and evenings, Sat. evenings. Closed public holidays.
Tel. 310 479 7636
Subdued, quiet

interior. Delicious sushi, marinated fish and other meats. A popular venue with the Hollywood smart set – and ordinary mortals.
◧P◨◧◧◧

WESTWOOD
◆ F C2
→RESTAURANT
Shahrezad/The Flame
1442 Westwood Blvd
Tel. 310 470 9131
Open daily, lunch and evenings.
Situated in a predominately Iranian district. Good-quality Persian cuisine served in an elegant setting with live piano music. Very varied menu: kebabs, pilaffs, fessenjan (étouffée of pomegranates and walnuts). Extremely generous helpings.
◧P◨◧

ORANGE COUNTY
→SHOPPING
Orange County is renowned for its shopping malls.
South Coast Plaza
3333 Bristol Street (Route 405)
This vast shopping mall is a real city within a city, with hotel-restaurants, theaters, stores and top luxury boutiques.
Fashion Island
Newport Center Drive at Pacific Coast Highway
A beautiful mall where you can eat round a fountain. Farmers' market in the interior courtyard.
Block at Orange County
A trendy mall with a high-tech decor.

→NIGHTLIFE
Downtown Laguna Beach
The most visited resort in Orange

County. A host of boutiques, bars, cafés and restaurants in the commercial center of the town, which is very popular with artists.

GARDEN GROVE
◆ C B4
→RESTAURANT
PHO 79
9941 Hazard Avenue
Tel. 714 531 2490
9200 Bolsa Avenue
Tel. 714 893 1883
Open lunch and evenings.
In the heart – and style – of Little Saigon. Grilled or braised meats, spring rolls with spicy sauce and, of course, pho (soup with noodles and basil), the Vietnamese national dish. Prices are so reasonable that you could be forgiven for thinking the waiter has made a mistake!
◧P◧

HUNTINGTON BEACH
◆ C B4
→RESTAURANT
Chimayo at the Beach
315 Pacific Coast Hwy
Tel. 714 374 7273
culinaryadventures.com
Open daily, lunch and evenings.
Enjoy David Wilhem's Southwest Californian cuisine – lobster tacos, seafood, pizzas cooked over a wood fire – in the atmosphere of a waterfront villa with a Mexican flavor and a view of the famous Huntington Beach pier. The same chef presides at the Chimayo Grill, in the Fashion Island mall, and at the French 75 – a French-style, 1940s bistro – at 75, Laguna Beach.
◧P◧◨◧▨◧▨

307

◆ HOTELS AND RESTAURANTS

- ⬚ < $100
- ⬚ $100–200
- ⬚ > $200

LAGUNA BEACH
◆ **C** B5

→HOTEL-RESTAURANTS
Coast Inn
1401 S. Coast Hwy
Tel. 949 494 7588
Fax 949 494 1735
boomboomroom.
com
*The most popular
gay bar in a town
with one of the
largest gay
populations in
Orange County. On
the second floor,
tables with a view
of the ocean and a
more subdued
atmosphere. A
funky decor
throughout in
rooms that look like
beach huts.*

⬚⬚⬚⬚⬚⬚⬚⬚

✪ Surf & Sand Hotel
1555 S Coast Hwy
Tel. 949 497 4477
Fax 949 497 4037
surfandsand.com
*The hotel occupies
several buildings.
Rooms with pale
wood shutters and
traceried windows
have a view of the
Pacific. Restaurant
on the beach.
Thalassotherapy.*

⬚⬚⬚⬚⬚⬚⬚⬚⬚

→RESTAURANT
✪ Five Feet
328 Glenneyre St
Tel. 949 497 4955
Open evenings only.
*A temple of
innovative Chinese
cuisine: chicken
kung pao and
braised catfish
accompanied by a
range of different
sauces. Industrial-
design decor set off
by brilliant colors.*

⬚⬚⬚⬚

NEWPORT BEACH
◆ **C** B4

→RESTAURANT
Aubergine
508 29th Street
Tel. 949 723 4150
Open Tue.–Sun.
evenings. Closed
public holidays.
*A renovated beach
house. The chef,
Tim Goodell, is*

*renowned for his
Californian creations
and the restaurant is
often fully booked.
But there's always
the Troquet,
another – simpler
more relaxed –
Goodell restaurant
in the South Coast
Plaza mall. First-rate
desserts.*

⬚⬚⬚⬚⬚⬚

SAN DIEGO
JULIAN
◆ **C** C5

→HOTEL-RESTAURANT
**Angels Landing
Country Inn
& Resort**
2323 Farmer Road
Tel. 760 765 2578
Fax 760 765 2571
angelresort.com
*Set in a 50-acre
park, a favorite
resort among San
Diegans and visitors
who want a quiet
retreat where they
can recharge their
batteries. Ten
country-style rooms
with no telephone
or TV, to encourage
guests to make the
most of the outdoor
activities: walking,
visiting the gold
mines, mountain
biking and
canoeing. Families
and small groups
welcome. The Pie in*

the Sky restaurant is
decorated in 1950s
style.

⬚⬚⬚⬚⬚⬚⬚

LA JOLLA
◆ **C** B6

→HOTEL-RESTAURANT
Hotel Parisi
1111 Prospect Street
Tel. 858 454 1511
Fax 858 454 1531
hotelparisi.com
*Its 20 peaceful
and beautifully
decorated rooms
have a view of the
ocean or overlook a
quiet street. They
are equipped with
stereo systems, VCRs
and remote alarm
clocks. Mother-Earth
style is the order of
the day: terracotta
tiles and natural-
fiber sheets. The
hotel has its own
psychologist,
acupuncturist, yoga
instructor and
masseur.*

⬚⬚⬚⬚⬚⬚⬚⬚

→RESTAURANTS
**✪ George's at the
Cove**
1250 Prospect Street
Tel. 858 454 4244
Open daily, lunch
and evenings.
*The innovative
cuisine of chef Trey
Foshee makes this
one of the best*

restaurants in the
region. Melon soup,
fillet of free-range
Barbary duck and a
wide variety of fish
and seafood. View
of the Pacific.

⬚⬚⬚⬚⬚⬚⬚

Roppongi
875 Prospect Street
Tel. 858 551 5252
rappongiusa.com
Open daily, lunch
and evenings.
*Named after Tokyo's
busiest district.
Tapas-style dishes
with a blend of
Asiatic flavors
(curry-flavored
hummous toasts,
Korean-style spare
ribs, crab
brochettes). A decor
of exotic wood
paneling, exposed
stonework and, in
accordance with the
principles of Feng
Shui, the presence
fire, water and
earth.*

⬚⬚⬚⬚

Trattoria Acqua
1298 Prospect Street
Tel. 858 454 0709
trattoriaacqua.com
Open daily, lunch
and evenings.
*Innovative Italian
cuisine: pasta
orecchiette with
prawns, ham and
asparagus, roast
lamb with grape
and olive 'stew'. A
number of dining
rooms and quiet,
smaller rooms.
Romantic decor with
a view of the Pacific.*

⬚⬚⬚⬚⬚⬚

RANCHO BERNARDO
◆ **C** C5

→HOTEL-RESTAURANT
**Rancho Bernardo
Inn**
17550 Bernardo
Oaks Drive
Tel. 858 675 8500
Fax 858 675 8501
ranchobernardoinn.
com
*This Mission-style
hotel is situated in a
peaceful suburb
north of San Diego.
Rustic rooms with
exposed beams.*

FIVE FEET

GEORGE'S AT THE COVE

RESTAURANTS
▪ < $15
▪ $15–30
▪ > $30

Pool and world-famous golf course. Excellent modern French cuisine in the El Bizcocho restaurant.
▯▯▯▯▯▯▯▯▯▯
▯▯▯

SAN DIEGO
◆P-Q-R
→SHOPPING
Horton Plaza
◆Q B2
A multi-level mall in Mediterranean colors.

→NIGHTLIFE
Gaslamp Quarter
◆Q C2
This working-class quarter has a lively nightlife. Restaurants, bars and theaters.
Hillcrest ◆P C3
A popular meeting place among San Diego's gay community, and one of the city's busiest districts.

→HOTEL-RESTAURANTS
Courtyard by Marriott – Gaslamp
530 Broadway
Tel. 619 446 3000
Fax 619-446-3010
courtyard.com/sancd
The luxurious Courtyard by Marriott occupies a former bank (1928) only a stone's throw from the busy Gaslamp Quarter. The lobby has vaulted ceilings in neo-Romanesque style and the original marble and brass counters. Guests can visit the former shooting room, where bank employees were trained to defend themselves against gangsters!
▯▯▯▯▯▯▯▯▯▯

☺ **Hotel del Coronado**
1500 Orange Ave
Coronado Island
Tel. 619 435 6611
Fax 619 522 8262
hoteldel.com
A Victorian 'jewel' opened in 1888

▲ 225. Its most famous guests include the Duke and Duchess of Windsor, the Reagan family, Frank Sinatra, and Marilyn Monroe, Jack Lemmon and Tony Curtis in Some Like it Hot ● 90. Wood-paneled interiors, smart pool and views of the Pacific.
▯▯▯▯▯▯▯▯▯▯
▯▯▯▯

→RESTAURANTS
Cafe 222
222 Island Avenue
Tel. 619 236 9902
cafe222.com
Open Mon.–Fri. mornings and lunch, Sat.–Sun. mornings.
A cozy, modern restaurant near the Convention Center. Creative Californian breakfasts (pumpkin and sweetcorn pancakes) and lunches flavored with herbs.
▯▯▯▯▯▯

Candelas
416 Third Avenue
Tel. 619 702 4467
Open daily, lunch and evenings.
Top-quality Mexican cuisine. Excellent fish and seafood, delicious sauces made with cream and tequila, a truly memorable pea soup and a very respectable wine list. Subdued and elegant decor of ceramics and wood paneling. Friendly, professional service.
▯▯▯▯▯▯▯▯

Kemo Sabe
3958 Fifth Avenue
Tel. 619 220 6802
Open evenings only. Closed Thanksgiving.
A successful blend of Far Eastern and Southwest Californian cuisine in the trendy district of Hillcrest. The interior seems to have been placed

under the aegis of Navajo dolls and Samurai art. Smoked chicken, Indonesian lamb, skirts on fire (flank of beef on a bed of vegetables).
▯▯▯▯▯▯

Parallel 33
741 W Washington Street
Tel. 619 260 0033
Open Mon.–Sat. evenings. Closed public holidays.
Enjoy a world tour along the 33rd Parallel with flavors from Morocco, Lebanon, India, China, Japan and San Diego. Ahi tuna poke with Asian pears and mango, spicy wasabi sauce, crackling and chocolate chai crème brûlée. A decor of saffron tones, maple wood, goatskin and red lacquer.
▯▯▯▯▯▯

The Prado House of Hospitality
El Prado
Balboa Park
Tel. 619 557 9441
Open Mon. lunch, Tue.–Sun. lunch and evenings.
The restaurant occupies a beautiful Spanish Colonial Revival-style building in the heart of Balboa Park. Latin-American inspired cuisine and cocktails (Cuban mojitos) served in a lavish and colorful setting. Magnificent terrace and solarium. Cookery courses organized by the restaurant.
▯▯▯▯▯▯

PALM SPRINGS AND JOSHUA TREE
DESERT HOT SPRINGS
◆C D4
→HOTEL-RESTAURANT
Hope Springs
68075 Club Circle Drive
Tel. 760 329 4003

Fax 760 329 4223
hopespringsresort.com
Minimalism is the order of the day: furniture by Saarinen and Eames, futons and polished concrete floors. Magnificent view of Coachella Valley and Palm Springs from the pool fed by a natural spring. Be warned: the sign (Cactus Springs) is a red herring to prevent people finding one of the favorite venues of Hollywood celebrities and fashionable photographers!
▯▯▯▯▯▯

LA QUINTA
◆C D5
→HOTEL-RESTAURANT
Quinta Resort & Club
49–499 Eisenhower Drive
Tel. 760 564 4111
Fax 760 564 5718
laquintaresort.com
A vast complex devoted to golf (72 holes), tennis (23 courts) and swimming (39 pools) – as well as thermal treatments, excursions and shopping – in the middle of the desert. Later additions have not spoiled the charm of the original 1926 building in Spanish Colonial Revival style. Holiday bookings.
▯▯▯▯▯▯▯▯▯▯
▯▯▯▯

PALM SPRINGS
◆C D4
→NIGHTLIFE
Palm Canyon Drive
A number of clubs, theaters, gay bars and nightclubs, including the famous Palm Springs Follies (n° 128) and Muriel's Supper Club (n° 210).

HOTELS
- *< $100*
- *$100–200*
- *> $200*

Indian Canyon Drive
For its Spa Resort Casino (n° 100).

→HOTEL
✪ Ballantine's Hotel
1420 N Indian Canyon Drive
Tel. 760 320 1178
Fax 760 320 5308
ballantineshotels.com
Guests at Ballantine's and its sister hotel, Ballantine's Movie Colony Inn (726, North Indian Canyon Drive), receive a warm English welcome. The superb Modernist architecture is in complete harmony with the clean lines of the rooms and the furniture by Eames, Miller and Knoll. The 1950s Hollywood atmosphere is reminiscent of an era when the hotel welcomed such stars as Marilyn Monroe, Gloria Swanson and Hugh O'Brien.
summer winter

→RESTAURANTS
Johannes Cosmopolitan Cuisine
196 South Indian Canyon Drive
Tel. 760 778 0017
johannesrestaurant.com
Tue.–Sun. evenings. Closed Thanksgiving.
Restrained and elegant, this is one of the most sought-after restaurants in Palm Springs. A relaxed, stylish atmosphere and original cuisine: mahi mahi on sauerkraut with potato strudel, Thai chicken sausage with mango and passion-fruit mustard. Wine list with more than 120 vintages.

Melvyn's, Ingleside Inn
200 W Ramon Road
Tel. 760 325 2323
Open daily, lunch and evenings.
Former film stars love this restaurant with its chandeliers, silverware, white tablecloths, mirrors and waiters in tails. A good excuse to dress up for dinner, although in Palm Springs stylish casual is also fine. Don't miss the succulent veal cutlets.

✪ St James at the Vineyard
265 South Palm Canyon Drive
Tel. 760 320 8041
st-james@msn.com
Open Mon.–Sun. evenings. Closed Mon. June–Aug.
A whirl of blended and experimental dishes: Burmese bouillabaisse, New Zealand mussels with coriander and coconut milk. An exception in Palm Springs where chefs rarely take risks. Decor inspired by Africa and Asia.

The Falls Prime Steakhouse & Martini Bar
155 S Palm Canyon Drive
Tel. 760 416 8664
thefallsprimesteakhouse.com
Open evenings only.
Two waterfalls freshen the atmosphere in this unusual grill where quality beef ribsteaks are cut at the table and the barmen prepare the most outlandish martinis. All this and an art gallery too.

PIONEERTOWN
◆ **C** D4
→RESTAURANT
✪ Pappy & Harriet's Pioneertown Palace
Mane Street
Tel. 760 365 5956
Open Thu. evening, Fri.–Sun. lunch and evenings.
A saloon dating from the time when westerns were filmed here. This dance-hall restaurant is extremely popular for its Old-West style, cowboy cuisine (grilled steaks and chicken) and country concerts. The stars, in particular, like the isolated location.

BALLANTINE'S HOTEL

TWENTYNINE PALMS
◆ **C** D4
→HOTEL-RESTAURANT
Twentynine Palms Inn
73950 Inn Avenue
Tel. 760 367 3505
Fax 760 367 4425
29palmsinn.com
Near the North entrance to Joshua Tree National Park. The inn covers an area of several acres with its early-20th-century cottages and tastefully decorated suites. Owner Jane Smith is a mine of information on the region. During the high season, guests can eat beside the pool and enjoy dishes made with vegetables from the kitchen garden.
off season
high season

NATIONAL PARKS
CROWLEY LAKE
Crowley Lake
◆ **B** E2
→HOTEL
Rainbow Tarns Bed & Breakfast
HC 79, Box 1053
Tel. 760 935 4556
rainbowtarns.com
The tarns after which the B&B is named are small glacial lakes situated at an altitudes of over 6500 ft in the High Sierra. 3 rooms only. Nearby: fishing, footpaths, ski slopes on Mammoth Mountain, cross-country skiing and hot springs. Warm, friendly welcome.

DEATH VALLEY NATIONAL PARK
◆ **O** B2
→HOTEL-RESTAURANT
Furnace Creek Inn and Furnace Creek Ranch

Tel. 760 786 2345
furnacecreek.com
The two hotels, only a few hundred yards apart, have tennis courts and a pool fed by a natural spring. Furnace Creek Inn is the more luxurious establishment, with 66 rooms decorated in different styles and a terrace planted with palm trees. The Ranch, which has 274 rooms and a sports pitch, is ideal for families with children. Golf course.
Inn ▣
Ranch ▣
▣P◻▥㿿♿🍴♨↯

→HOTEL-RESTAURANT
Stovepipe Wells
Highway 190
Tel. 760 786 2387
Fax 760 786 2389
It may not be very stylish, but this 83-room motel is a welcome sight in this isolated region. The typically American menu – steaks, chicken and fish – is of surprisingly good quality.
▣P◻▥㿿→♨▥

◼◼◼ **LASSEN VOLCANIC**
◼◼◼ **NATIONAL PARK**
◆ A D3
→HOTEL-RESTAURANT
Drakesbad Guest Ranch
End of Warner Valley Road
Chester
Tel. 530 529 1512
Fax 530 529 4511
drakesbad.com
Open first Fri. in June until second Sun. in Oct.
This wooden, cottage-like guest ranch is more than 100 years old. The pool is fed by hot springs. An ideal place to immerse yourself in nature for a few days. Full board only.
▣P◻㿿♿♨▥

◼◼◼ **LAVA BEDS NATIONAL**
◼◼◼ **MONUMENT**
◆ A D1
→HOTEL
Sis-Q-Inn Motel
1825 Shastina Drive
Tel. 530 938 4194
Fax 530 938 3304
An excellent base for exploring the Lava Beds National Monument. The motel is situated on the shady terrain of the small town of Weed, which has the added bonus of looking onto Mount Shasta. 22 large family rooms with continental breakfast included. Picnic tables and covered whirlpool. Shopping.
▣◻P▥㿿

◼◼◼ **MAMMOTH LAKE**
◆ A D2
→HOTEL
RESERVATIONS
Mammoth Reservations
PO Box 3006
Mammoth Lakes
Tel. 800 223 3032
mammoth reservations.com
This reservation agency has a wide range of accommodation on its books. Its inclusive ski packages in the Mammoth region attract winter-sports enthusiasts from Los Angeles.

◼◼◼ **MOUNT SHASTA**
◆ A C2
→HOTEL
Mount Shasta Ranch Bed & Breakfast
1008 W A Barr Rd
Tel. 530 926 3870
Fax 530 926 6882
stayinshasta.com
Mount Shasta Ranch may be rural and restful but it certainly doesn't compromise on elegance. It has 10 different types of rooms, with a copious Far West breakfast included, a huge lounge with a stone fireplace

and a games room with table-tennis and billiards tables. An ideal hotel for groups and families.
▣P◻▥♿▥

◼◼◼ **REDWOOD NATIONAL**
◼◼◼ **AND STATE PARKS**
◆ L B2
→HOTEL
Hosteling International
14480 Highway 101
North Klamath
Tel. 707 482 8265,
norcalhostels.org
The hotel, a simple pioneers' cabin built in 1908, has all the conviviality of a family home. Guests can gather in the friendly atmosphere of the living room and exchange information on the region. 30 beds, one private room, a kitchen and self-service laundromat. Unbeatable prices.
▣P

◼◼◼ **SEQUOIA AND KINGS**
◼◼◼ **CANYON NATIONAL**
◼◼◼ **PARK**
◆ N
→HOTEL-RESTAURANTS
Cedar Grove Lodge
Tel. 559 335 5500
Fax 559 335 5507
Open May-Oct.
A group of rustic cabins on the banks of the Kings River offering simplicity, peace and isolation (no TV). Counter service in the restaurant.
▣P◻▥♿▥

Grant Grove
Tel. 559 335 5500
Fax 559 335 5507
A complex of 56 bungalows with or without bathrooms, electricity and carpets – and even with or without a solid roof! Some are open all year. The restaurant is good, but guests who have the appropriate equipment can cook out of doors. The

nearby John Muir Lodge has 30 motel-type rooms and suites.
Bungalows ▣
Lodge ▣
▣P◻㿿♿▥

Winnedumah Hotel
PO Box 147
211 North Edwards
(Route 395)
Independence
Tel. 760 878 2040
Fax 760 878 2833
winnedumah.com
This comfortable inn has 24 peaceful rooms and enjoys magnificent views of the Sierra Nevada. Ideal for outdoor pursuits and exploring Owens Valley (a number of westerns were filmed nearby at Lone Pine). Weekend courses in art, walking, etc. NB: this is a non-smoking hotel and some rooms don't have a bathroom.
▣P㿿♿▥

◼◼◼ **YOSEMITE**
◼◼◼ **NATIONAL PARK**
◆ M B2
→HOTEL-RESTAURANT
Ahwanee Hotel
Tel. 559 252 4848
yosemitepark.com
This 1927 hotel, classified as an historic monument, stands in the heart of the Yosemite Valley. It has 123 luxury rooms and offers guests the opportunity to go fishing, walking, play tennis and practise winter sports. The rooms, decorated with Indian motifs, combine rustic charm and modern comfort: TV, fridge and bathroom. It served as the model for the Colorado Lounge in Stanley Kubrick's The Shining ▲ 255.
▣P♿㿿▥㿿♿☎▥
▥→

Appendices

◆ BIBLIOGRAPHY

HISTORY & CULTURE

◆ BOORSTIN (D): *American Civilization*, Thames and Hudson, 1972
◆ DOWNIE, WILLIAM: *Hunting for Gold*, California Publishing Company, 1893
◆ DUMAS, ALEXANDRE: *A gil blas in California*, trans. M E Wilbur, Hammond & Hammond, 1947
◆ GREENBLATT, STEPHEN: *Marvelous Possessions; The Wonder of the New World*, Clarendon Press, 1991
◆ HILL, MARY: *Gold – The California Story*, University of California Press, 1999
◆ HOLLIDAY, J S: *The World Rushed In: the Californian Gold Rush Experience*, Gollancz, 1983
◆ MILLS, BARRY: *Jack Kerouac, King of the Beats*, Virgin, 1998
◆ SLATTA, RICHARD: *Cowboys of the Americas*, Yale 1990
◆ STANNARD, DAVID E: *American Holocaust: Columbus and the Conquest of the New World*, Oxford University Press, 1992
◆ STURVENANT, WILLIAM C: *Handbook of North American Indians*, Smithsonian Institution, 1978
◆ VARLEY, JAMES: *Lola Montez*, Arthur H Clark, 1996

TRAVELERS

◆ HARTE BRET: *The Luck of Roaring Camp and Other Sketches*, 1870
◆ MUIR, JOHN: *Our National Parks*, 1901
◆ STEINBECK, JOHN: *Travels with Charley*, 1962
◆ TOCQUEVILLE, A DE: *Democracy in America*, University of Chicago Press, 2000
◆ WILDE, OSCAR: *Impressions of America*, 1882

ART, ARCHITECTURE

◆ BOUTELLE, SARA HOLMES: *Julia Morgan; Architect*, Abbeville, 1988
◆ GEBHARD, DAVID: *'Romanza': the Californian Architecture of Frank Lloyd Wright*, Chronicle Books, 1988

◆ J PAUL GETTY MUSEUM: *Masterpieces from the J Paul Getty Museum*, volume 4, *Decorative Arts*, Thames and Hudson, 1997
◆ J PAUL GETTY MUSEUM: *Masterpieces from the J Paul Getty Museum*, Volume 6, *European Sculpture*, Thames and Hudson, 1998
◆ J PAUL GETTY MUSEUM: *Masterpieces from the J Paul Getty Museum*, volume 7, *Photography*, Thames and Hudson, 1999
◆ J PAUL GETTY MUSEUM: *Masterpieces from the J Paul Getty Museum*, volume 1, *Paintings*, Thames and Hudson, 1997

CINEMA

◆ BUKOWSKI, CHARLES: *Hollywood*, Black Sparrow Press, 1989
◆ DARDIS, TOM: *Some Time in the Sun*, Deutsch, 1976
◆ DUNAWAY, DAVID KING: *Huxley In Hollywood*, Bloomsbury, 1989
◆ FADIMAN, WILLIAM: *Hollywood Now*, Thames and Hudson, 1973
◆ GABLER, NEAL: *An Empire of Their Own: How the Jews Invented Hollywood*, Crown, 1988
◆ GOLDMAN, WILLIAM: *Adventures in the Screen Trade*, Abacus, 1996
◆ HAMILTON, IAN: *Writer in Hollywood, 1915–51*, Heinemann, 1990
◆ KOBAL, JOHN: *Hollywood: The Years of Innocence*, Thames and Hudson, 1985
◆ MAZON, MAURIACIO: *The Zoot-Suit Riots*, University of Texas Press, 1984
◆ NORMAN, BARRY: *Taking Pictures*, Hodder and Stoughton, 1987
◆ PALMER, CHRISTOPHER: *The Composer in Hollywood*, Marion Boyars, 1990
◆ PHILLIPS, JULIA: *You'll Never Eat Lunch in This Town Again*, Heinemann, 1991
◆ SHERWIN, DAVID: *Going Mad in Hollywood*, Deutsch, 1996
◆ THOMSON, DAVID: *Beneath Mulholland: Thoughts on Hollywood and its*

Ghosts, Little, Brown, 1998
◆ WOOD, ROBIN: *Hollywood from Vietnam to Reagan*, Columbia University Press, 1986

WINE

◆ BROOK, STEPHEN: *The Wines of California*, Faber and Faber, 1999
◆ PINNEY, THOMAS: *A History of Wine in California*, University of California, 1989
◆ JANCIS ROBINSON (editor): *The Oxford Companion to the Wines of North America*, Oxford University Press, 2000

FICTION

◆ KEROUAC, JACK: *Big Sur*, Farrar, Straus and Cudaly, 1962
◆ MAUPIN, ARMISTEAD: *Tales of the City*, Black Swan, 1989
◆ PYNCHON, THOMAS: *Vineland*, Secker and Warburg, 1990
◆ STEINBECK, JOHN: *Cannery Row*, Heinemann, 1945
◆ STEINBECK, JOHN: *The Grapes of Wrath*, New York: Literary Classics of the United States, 1996

FILMS

◆ *1941*, Steven Spielberg, 1979
◆ *East of Eden*, Elia Kazan, 1955
◆ *American Graffiti*, George Lucas, 1973
◆ *Annie Hall*, Woody Allen, 1977
◆ *Bamba (La)*, Luis Valdez, 1986
◆ *Barton Fink*, Joel Coen, 1991
◆ *Blade Runner*, Ridley Scott, 1982
◆ *Bullitt*, Peter Yates, 1968
◆ *Some like It Hot*, Billy Wilder, 1959
◆ *Singing in the Rain*, Stanley Donen, Gene Kelly, 1952
◆ *Chinatown*, Roman Polanski, 1974
◆ *Citizen Kane*, Orson Welles, 1941
◆ *Silent Movie*, Mel Brooks, 1976
◆ *Easy Rider*, Dennis Hopper, 1969
◆ *The Bad and the Beautiful*, Vincente Minnelli, 1952
◆ *Fat City*, John Huston, 1972
◆ *The Big Sleep*, Howard Hawks, 1946
◆ *Hammett*, Wim Wenders, 1981

◆ *Hellzapoppin*, H C Potter, 1941
◆ *Kalifornia*, Dominic Sena, 1993
◆ *LA Confidential*, Curtis Hanson, 1997
◆ *The Graduate*, Mike Nichols, 1967
◆ *Murder in Hollywood*, Blake Edwards, 1988
◆ *The Birds*, Alfred Hitchcock, 1963
◆ *Player (The)*, Robert Altman, 1992
◆ *The Grapes of Wrath*, John Ford, 1940
◆ *The Gold Rush*, Charles Chaplin, 1925
◆ *Sunset Boulevard*, Billy Wilder, 1950
◆ *Natural Born Killers*, Oliver Stone, 1994
◆ *Shortcuts*, Robert Altman, 1993
◆ *A Star is Born*, George Cukor, 1954
◆ *Winchester 73*, Anthony Mann, 1970
◆ *Zabriskie Point*, Michelangelo Antonioni, 1970
◆ *The Last Tycoon*, Elia Kazan, 1976
◆ *Follow the Fleet*, Mark Sandrich, 1935
◆ *Safety Last*, Fred Newmayer, 1923

RECORDS

◆ The Beach Boys, *California Girls*
◆ The Eagles, *Hotel California*
◆ Lightnin' Hopkins, *My California*
◆ The Mamas & The Papas, *California Dreamin'*
◆ Joni Mitchell, *California*
◆ New Riders of the Purple Sage, *California Day*
◆ Grateful Dead, *Wharf Rat*
◆ Chris Isaak, *San Francisco Days*
◆ John Lee Hooker, *Frisco Blues*
◆ Scott McKenzie, *San Francisco (Be Sure to Wear Some Flowers in Your Hair)*
◆ Frank Sinatra, *I Left my Heart in San Francisco*
◆ Hot Tuna, *San Francisco Bay Blues*
◆ Mike Wilhelm, *The Nob Hillbillies*
◆ Jimmy Witherspoon, *Mean Ol' Frisco*
◆ Country Joe & the Fish, *Rock Coast Blues*
◆ David Crosby, *Tamalpais High*
◆ Doug Sahm (Sir Douglas Quintet), *Mendocino*
◆ The Doors, *LA Woman*

◆ LIST OF ILLUSTRATIONS

LIST OF ILLUSTRATIONS ◆

◆ LIST OF ILLUSTRATIONS

LIST OF ILLUSTRATIONS ◆

◆ LIST OF ILLUSTRATIONS

LIST OF ILLUSTRATIONS ◆

ACKNOWLEDGEMENTS

We would like to thank the following publishers or copyright-holders for permission to reproduce the quotations on pages 94–106.

◆ PENGUIN BOOKS LTD: Excerpt from *The High Window* by Raymond Chandler, copyright © 1943 by Raymond Chandler. Reprinted by permission of Penguin Books Ltd. Excerpt from *Travels with Charley* by John Steinbeck, copyright © 1962 by John Steinbeck. Reprinted by permission of Penguin Books Ltd.

◆ BLACK SPARROW PRESS: Excerpt from *Hollywood* by Charles Bukowski, copyright © 1989 by Charles Bukowski. Reprinted by permission of Black Sparrow Press.

We have been unable to locate the copyright holders and authors of certain documents before going to print. We will, however, acknowledge these sources in the next editions and an account is being held open for them in our offices.

◆ INDEX

◆ INDEX

◆ INDEX

◆ INDEX

◆ INDEX

◆ NOTES

◆ NOTES

Map section

Key

▤	Freeway or highway
▤	Main road
▤	Secondary roads
▢	Other roads
▦	State boundary
▦	Railroad
■	Urban area
◉	Main town or city
○	Secondary town
▣	Tourist attraction
Ⓜ	Subway station
▲	Summit

A

A B | B | C

PORTLAND

Medford

OREGON

JEDEDIAH SMITH STATE PARK

SISKIYOU MOUNTAINS

POINT ST. GEORGE
Crescent City

7310 ft

Yreka

REDWOOD NATIONAL AND STATE PARKS

Klamath

KLAMATH

SCOTT

SHASTA

1

PRAIRIE CREEK REDWOOD S.P.

Orick

C O A S T

KLAMATH MOUNTS

SALMON

14,16 MT SHAS

Mount Shasta

McClou

McKinleyville

Arcata

HUMBOLDT BAY

Eureka

Fortuna

CASTLE CRAGS STATE PARK

C L A I R E N G L E L A K E

TRINITY

MCCLOUD

Ferndale

Scotia

MAD

2

S H A S T A L A K E

SHASTA CAVERNS

Weaverville

299

Petrolia

CAPE MENDOCINO

EEL

254

S. FORK TRINITY

Redding

Honeydew

Gaberville

Anderson

BATTLE C

Shelter Cove

HUMBOLDT REDWOODS S.P.

8091 ft MT LINN

Red Bluff

36

3

S. FORK EEL

T R A N G E S

W. FORK EEL

Leggett

THOMES

DEER CR

BLACK BUTTE LAKE

Orland

Chico

P A C I F I C

Fort Bragg

JUGHANDLE STATE RESERVE

Willits

101

Caspar

LAKE PILLSBURRY

Willows

SACRAMENTO

Mendocino

Little River

EAST PARK RESERVOIR

Thermalit

4

O C E A N

Ukiah

20

S A C R A M E N T O V A L L E Y

Colusa

FEATHER

POINT ARENA

Lakeport

C L E A R L A K E

Marysvil

Yuba City

Point Arena

Clearlake

20

Linda

Olivehurs

Cloverdale

CACHE CR.

Geyserville

RUSSIAN

Fort Ross

Healdsburg

Calistoga

NAPA VALLEY

LAKE BERRYESSA

Woodland

5

Windsor

PETRIFIED FOREST

Santa Rosa

St. Helena

Rutherford

Roseville

N. Highlands

Jenner

Sebastopol

Rohnert Pak

Oakville

Davis

West Sacramento

BODEGA BAY

Glen Ellen

Yountville

SONOMA VALLEY

Dixon

Tomales

Cotati

Sonoma

Napa

Vacaville

Inverness

TOMALES BAY

Carneros

Fairfield

Galt

POINT REYES NATIONAL SEASHORE

Petaluma

Point Reyes

SAN PABLO BAY

Vallejo

Lod

N

Bolinas

San Rafael

YERBA BEVENA I.

Martinez

0   25   50 km

San Francisco

BAY BRIDGE

Berkeley

Richmond

Pittsburg

Antioch

Walnut Creek

Stockto

6

0   15.5   31 miles

A B | B | C

MARIN HEADLANDS

Oakland

Brentwood

LOS ANGELES

FRESNO

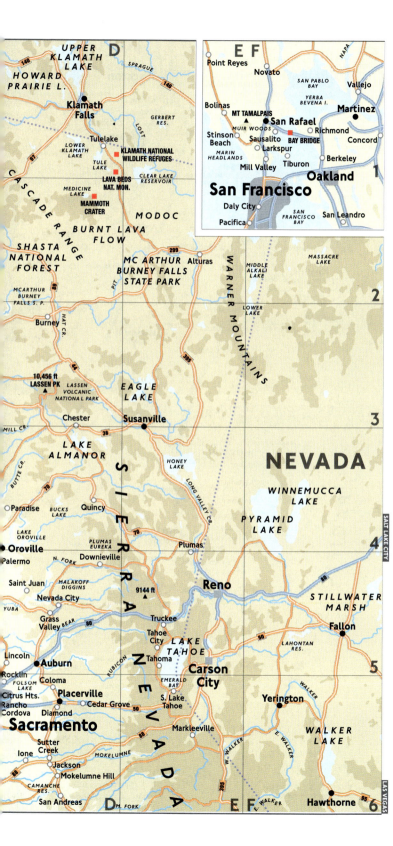

B

SANTA ROSA SACRAMENTO

A B C

San Francisco
San Oakland
Richmond
Walnut Creek
Antioch
Brentwood
Lodi
San Andreas
CAMANCHE RES.
M. FORK

Daly City
San Ramon
Danville
Stockton
Columbia
Tuolumne
S. FORK
NEW MELONES LAKE

Pacifica
San Leandro
Hayward
Livermore
Lathrop
Manteca
Sonora
DON PEDRO RES.

SAN FRANCISCO BAY
PILLAR POINT
Half Moon Bay
San Mateo
Pleasanton Tracy
Ripon
Oakdale
STANISLAUS

Redwood City
Fremont
205
Riverbank
L. MCCLURE

Stanford university
Palo Alto
Milpitas
Modesto
MERCED

San Gregorio
Mountain View
Santa Clara
Patterson
Ceres

La Honda
Cupertino
San Jose
Turlock
Merced

PIGEON POINT
Saratoga
MT HAMILTON 4261 ft
Livingston
Mariposa

Pescadero
Los Gatos
Atwater
Winton

ANO NUEVO STATE RESERVE
MONTEREY BAY NATIONAL MARINE SANCTUARY
Scotts Valley
Morgan Hill
SAN LUIS RES.
Los Banos
Chowchilla

Santa Cruz
Aptos
Gilroy
Firebaugh
Madera

Capitola
Moss Landing
152
Kerman
Fresno

MONTEREY BAY
Castroville
San Juan Bautista
Hollister
SAN JOAQUIN VALLEY

Marina
Salinas
Soledad
SAN BENITO MT 5240 ft
Selma

Monterey
Seaside
Greenfield
KINGS
Hanford

17-Mile Drive
Carmel
DIABLO RANGE
Lemoore
Huron

POINT LOBOS STATE RESERVE
BIG SUR S.P.
POINT SUR
King City
Coalinga

JULIA PFEIFFER N.P.
5843 ft
Avenal
Corcoran

Big Sur
SANTA LUCIA RANGE
L. SAN ANTONIO
SALINAS
ALLENSWORTH NATIONAL PARK

LOPEZ POINT
CAPE SAN MARTIN
TEMBLOR RANGE
Wasco

RAGGED POINT
L. NACIMIENTO
Paso Robles
46

HEARST CASTLE
San Simeon
Atascadero

Cambria
POINT ESTERO
Morro Bay
Los Osos
San Luis Obispo

POINT BUCHON
Pismo Beach
Arroyo Grande
Taft

PACIFIC OCEAN
Grover Beach
Oceano
Nipomo
TWITCHELL RES.

Guadalupe
POINT SAL
Santa Maria
Orcutt
SAN RAFAEL MTS

LA PURISIMA MISSION S.P.
Surf
Lompoc
Los Olivos
SISQUOC

POINT ARGUELLO
Santa Inez
Solvang
6880 ft
L. CACHUMA

POINT CONCEPTION
Goleta
SESPE CR.

Santa Barbara
Ojai

SANTA BARBARA CHANNEL
Ventura
Santa Paula

N
CHANNEL ISLANDS
SAN MIGUEL I.
SANTA ROSA I.
ANACAPA I.
Oxnard

0 25 50 km
0 15.5 31 miles
SANTA CRUZ I.
CHANNEL ISLAND NATIONAL PARK

A B C

1 2 3 4 5 6

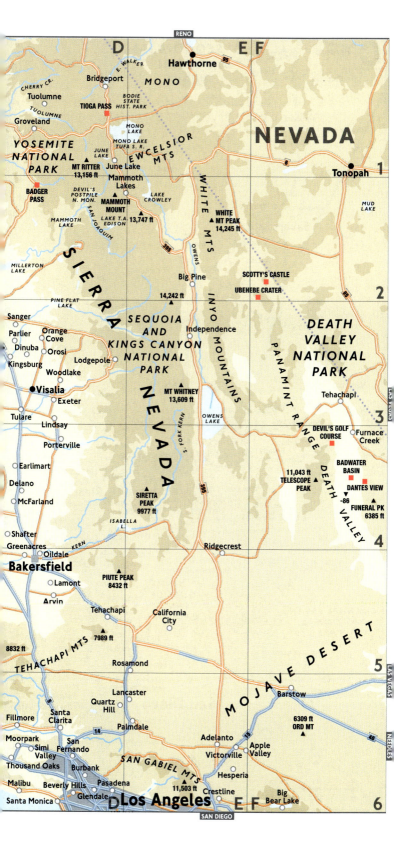

◆ SOUTHERN CALIFORNIA

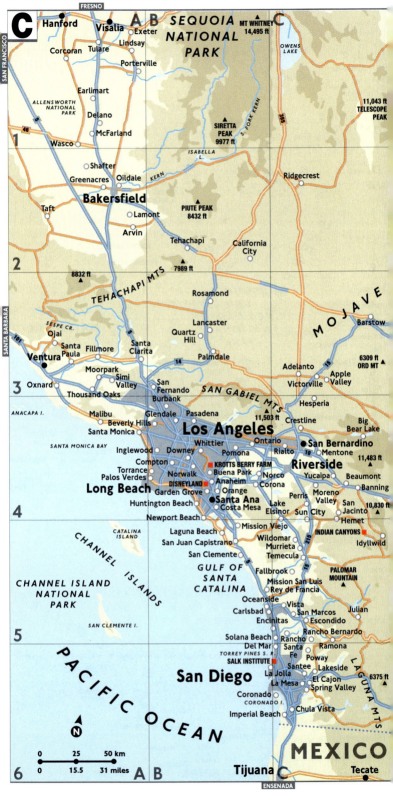

C

FRESNO

Hanford · Visalia · Exeter · Lindsay
Corcoran · Tulare · Porterville

SEQUOIA
NATIONAL
PARK

MT WHITNEY
14,495 ft

OWENS
LAKE

Earlimart

ALLENSWORTH
NATIONAL
PARK

Delano
McFarland

Wasco

SIRETTA
PEAK
9977 ft

S. FORK KERN

11,043 ft
TELESCOPE
PEAK

385

Shafter
Greenacres · Oildale
Bakersfield

ISABELLA
L.

KERN

Ridgecrest

Taft · Lamont

PIUTE PEAK
8432 ft

Arvin

Tehachapi

California
City

8832 ft

TEHACHAPI MTS

7989 ft

Rosamond

MOJAVE

SESPE CR.
Ojai
Santa · Fillmore
Paula
Ventura
Oxnard

Lancaster
Quartz
Hill
Santa
Clarita

14

Palmdale

Adelanto
Victorville

Barstow

6309 ft
ORD MT

Moorpark
Simi
Valley
Thousand Oaks

5

San
Fernando
Burbank

SAN GABIEL MTS

Hesperia

Apple
Valley

ANACAPA I.

Malibu
Beverly Hills
Santa Monica

Glendale · Pasadena

Los Angeles

11,503 ft

Crestline

Big
Bear Lake

SANTA MONICA BAY

Inglewood · Downey
Compton
Torrance
Palos Verdes
Long Beach

Whittier
Pomona
KROTTS BERRY FARM
Buena Park
Norwalk
DISNEYLAND · Anaheim
Garden Grove · Orange
Huntington Beach · **Santa Ana**
Costa Mesa

Ontario
Rialto
Norco
Corona

San Bernardino
Mentone

Riverside

11,483 ft

Yucaipa
Moreno
Valley

Beaumont
Banning

Perris
Lake
Elsinor · Sun City

San
Jacinto

10,830 ft

Newport Beach

CATALINA
ISLAND

Laguna Beach
San Juan Capistrano
San Clemente

Mission Viejo
Wildomar
Murrieta
Temecula

INDIAN CANYONS
Hemet

Idyllwild

CHANNEL ISLANDS

GULF OF
SANTA
CATALINA

Fallbrook

PALOMAR
MOUNTAIN

Mission San Luis
Rey de Francia

CHANNEL ISLAND
NATIONAL
PARK

SAN CLEMENTE I.

Oceanside

Carlsbad
Encinitas

Vista
San Marcos · Julian
Escondido
Rancho Bernardo

Solana Beach
Del Mar
TORREY PINES S. R.
SALK INSTITUTE

Rancho
Santa
Fe
Poway

Ramona

LAGUNA MTS

Santee · Lakeside
6375 ft

San Diego

La Jolla
La Mesa

El Cajon
Spring Valley

Coronado
CORONADO I.

Imperial Beach

Chula Vista

N

0   25   50 km
0   15.5   31 miles

MEXICO

Tijuana

Tecate

ENSENADA

PACIFIC OCEAN

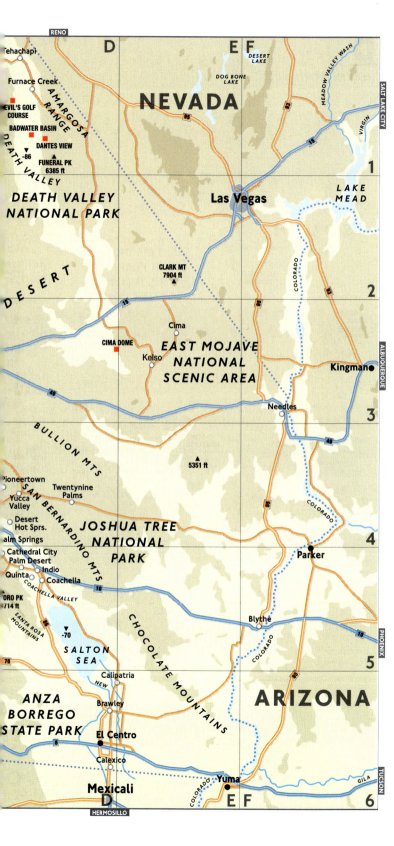

D   E   F

Tehachapi

Furnace Creek

EVIL'S GOLF
COURSE

BADWATER BASIN

DANTES VIEW

▼ -86

FUNERAL PK
6385 ft

NEVADA

DESERT
LAKE

DOG BONE
LAKE

MEADOW VALLEY WASH

95

93

15

VIRGIN

1

AMARGOSA RANGE

DEATH VALLEY

**DEATH VALLEY
NATIONAL PARK**

Las Vegas

LAKE
MEAD

D E S E R T

CLARK MT
7904 ft ▲

CIMA DOME

Kelso

Cima

**EAST MOJAVE
NATIONAL
SCENIC AREA**

COLORADO

Kingman

ALBUQUERQUE

15

40

95

15

40

93

2

Needles

3

BULLION MTS

Pioneertown

Twentynine
Palms

Yucca
Valley

Desert
Hot Sprs.

Palm Springs

Cathedral City

Palm Desert

Quinta

Indio

Coachella

ORO PK
/14 ft

70

SAN BERNARDINO MTS

**JOSHUA TREE
NATIONAL
PARK**

5351 ft ▲

COACHELLA VALLEY

SANTA ROSA
MOUNTAINS

▼ -70

**SALTON
SEA**

C H O C O L A T E   M O U N T A I N S

COLORADO

Parker

95

40

10

Blythe

10

COLORADO

PHOENIX

4

5

78

Calipatria

NEW

Brawley

**ANZA
BORREGO
STATE PARK**

El Centro

8

Calexico

Mexicali

ARIZONA

95

8

Yuma

COLORADO

GILA

TUCSON

6

D

SAN RAFAEL–SANTA ROSA

A B C

MARIN PENINSULA

GOLDEN GATE BRIDGE (TOLL)

1

FORT POINT

MARINE DRIVE

YACHT HARBOR

MARINA BLVD BEACH

RICHARDSON AV. MARINA DISTRICT

PALACE OF FINE ARTS

LINCOLN BLVD.

LOMBARD

PACIFIC HEIGHTS

FLOO MANSIO

SOUTH BAY

BAKER BEACH

PRESIDIO OF SAN FRANCISCO US MILITARY RESERVATION

TUNNEL

DIVISADERO ST.

BROADWAY

WEST COAST MEMORIAL

LINCOLN BLVD.

2

LANDS END

CALIFORNIA PALACE OF THE LEGION OF HONOR

CHINA BEACH

WEST PACIFIC AVENUE

Alta Plaza

WESTERN ADDITION

SEA CLIFF

EL CAMINO DEL MAR

WASHINGTON STREET

HAMILTON PLG

LINCOLN PARK

LAKE STREET

CALIFORNIA STREET

LAKE STREET

CALIFORNIA

GEARY

KIMBEL PLGD

CALIFORNIA

GEARY BLVD.

HAYES VALLEY

CLEMENT STREET

MASONIC

ARAVAL

ALAM SQUAR

25 TH

BOULEVARD

STREET

RICHMOND

GEARY

PARK PRESIDIO BLVD.

15TH. AVENUE

STREET

OAK

3

BALBOA STREET

AVENUE

FULTON

STREET

HAIGHT-ASHBURY

HAIGHT WALLE

CABRILLO STREET

JAPANESE TEA GARDEN

CONSERVATORY OF FLOWERS

FELL STREET

FULTON STREET

M.H. DE YOUNG MUS.

BUENA VISTA PARK

DUBOCE

BUFFALO PADDOCK

GOLDEN GATE PARK

MUSIC CONCOURSE

JF KENNEDY DRIVE

SHAKESPEARE GARDEN

MIDDLE LAKE

STRAWBERRY HILL

METSON LAKE

ELK GLEN LAKE

STOW LAKE

STRYBING ARBORETUM

FREDERICK STREET

MARTIN LUTHER KING JR DRIVE

MALLARD LAKE

LINCOLN WAY

CALIFORNIA ACADEMY OF SCIENCES

PARNASSUS STREET

IRVING STREET

IRVING STREET

JUDAH STREET

24 TH AVENUE

KIRKHAM STREET

7 Th. AV.

9 TH AVENUE

BUENA VISTA

17 TH STREET

Harvey Milk Plaza

EUREKA VALLEY

DIAMOND

CASTRO STREET

45 Th. AVENUE

41 Th. AVENUE

4

SUNSET

MORAGA STREET

19 TH

GRAND VIEW PARK

LAGUNA HONDA

TWIN PEAKS

CLARENDON AVENUE

NORIEGA STREET

BOULEY

33 TH. AVENUE

NORIEGA STREET

17 TH. AVENUE

WOODS SIDE AV.

TWIN PEAKS

DIAMOND HEIGHTS

ELISABET

ORTEGA STREET

ORTEGA STREET

BOULEVARD

DIAM

PACHECO STREET

43 Th. AVENUE

RIVERA STREET

FOREST HILL

O'SHAUG

GLEN CANYON PARK

DIAMOND HEIGHTS BL

VALLE

SANTIAGO STREET

MIRALOMA PARK

25

SUNSET

TARAVAL STREET

TARAVAL STREET

WAWONA

DRIVE

NESS Y. BD

ULLOA STREET

PARKSIDE

VICENTE STREET

WEST PORTOLA PARK

MOUNT DAVIDSON PARK

STREET

VICENTE STREET

SIGMUND STERN GROVE

PORTAL

5

WAWONA STREET

PINE LAKE PARK

19 TH

BUENA VISTA

MANGELS AVENUE

CHENERY

BOSWORT

SLOAT BOULEVARD

ST. FRANCIS

MONT

GLEN PARK

GREAT HIGHWAY

OCEAN AVENUE

WOOD

DARIEN

BOULEVARD

FLOO

FREEW

ZOO ROAD

EUCALYPTUS DRIVE

WAY

OCEAN

AVENUE

CITY COLLEGE OF SAN FRANCISCO

AVENUE

SAN JOSE

CAYUGA AVENUE

OCEAN BEACH

LAKE

HARDING

SAN FRANCISCO STATE UNIVERSITY

OCEAN

WESTWOOD PARK

BALBOA PARK

MISSIO STREE

SKYLINE

ROAD

HARDING PARK GOLF COURSE

URBANO AVENUE

SAN

SOUTHERN

OCEA ER

OCEAN BEACH

MERCED BOULEVARD

WEST OF TWIN PEAKS

FONT BLVD

JUNIPERO SERRA BOULEVARD

GARFIELD STREE

SHIELDS STREET

OCEAN VIEW

GRAFTON AVENUE

ALEMANY

MISSION

6

FORT FUNSTON

SARGENT STREET

OCEAN VIEW PLGD.

A B C

SALINAS–LOS ANGELES

◆ DOWNTOWN SAN FRANCISCO

E

A B C

PIER 45   PIER 41

HYDE STREET
PIER   PIER 39

FISHERMAN'S
WHARF

AQUATIC
PARK   EMBARCADERO

MUSEUM OF THE CITY
OF SAN FRANCISCO

MARITIME
MUSEUM

GHIRARDELLI   THE CANNERY   JEFFERSON   BEACH   STREE

SQUARE   JONES   TAYLOR   POWELL   NORTH   PO

1 GOLDEN GATE   BEACH   STREET   STREET

RECREATION AREA

NORTH POINT STREET   STREET

BAY   BAY

OCTAVIA FRANCISCO STREET   RUSSIAN   SAN FRANCISCO   FRANCISCO   STREET

HILL PARK   ART INSTITUTE   CHESTNUT   STOCKTON

CHESTNUT   CHESTNUT   LOMBARD   RUSSIAN   STREE

POLK   LOMBARD   LEAVENWORTH   HILL   GREENWICH

FRANKLIN   STREET   TAYLOR   FILBERT

LOMBARD STREET   LARKIN   WASHINGTON

2 GREENWICH   FILBERT   JONES   STREET   SQUARE

GOUGH   STREET   UNION   NORTH BEACH

FILBERT   STREET   GREEN   STREE

STREET   UNION   GREEN   LARKIN   VALLEJO

PACIFIC   HOLY'S TRINITY'S   STREET   FLORENCE   INA   VALLEJO

HEIGHTS   CATHEDRALE   STREET   COOLBRITH   BROADWAY

VALLEJO   STREET   BROADWAY TUNNEL   PARK

VALLEJO   BERNARD ST.   PACIFIC

BROADWAY   AVENUE   CABLE-CAR

LAGUNA   PACIFIC   AVENUE   STREET   BARN

3 PACIFIC   JACKSON   STREET

JACKSON ST.   HAAS LILIENTHAL   POLK   WASHINGTON   CLAY   STREET

SPRECHELS   HOUSE   GRACE   HUNTINGTON

MANSION   GOUGH   STREET   CLAY   STREET   SACRAMENTO CATHEDRAL PARK   POWELL

WASHINGTON   STREET   MASONIC TEMPLE

LAFAYETTE   CALIFORNIA   STREET   STREET AND MUSEUM

PARK   SACRAMENTO   STREET   BUSH

CALIFORNIA   STR   CALIFORNIA   PINE   STREET

WESTERN   FRANKLIN   STREET   HYDE   BUSH   STREET

4 ADDITION   AUSTIN STREET   FERN   BUSH   STREET   SUTTER

LAGUNA   BUSH   VAN   STREET   POST

SUTTER   STREET   HEMLOCK ST.   STREET   TAYLOR   UNIO

POST   STREET   POST   STREET   GEAR   LEAVENWORTH   MASON SQUAR

JAPANTOWN   MYRTLE STREE   GEAR   STREET   O'FARR   STREE

POST   STREET   O'FARRELL   STREET

PEACE PAGODA   GEARY   BOULEVARD   OLIVE   STREET   LARKIN   ELLIS   JONES   STREE

FILLMORE   STREET   WILLOW   POLK   TURK   EDDY   MARKE

ELLIS   STREET   LARKIN   CIVIC CENTER

LAGUNA   EDDY   STREET   TURK

5 JEFFERSON   STREET   AVENUE

SQUARE   ELM STREET   FEDERAL   AVENUE   STEVENSON

TURK   GOLDEN GATE   BUILDING

GOLDEN GATE   AVENUE   REDWOOD ST.   STATE BUILDING   OLD FEDERAL   MISSION

GOUGH   ASIAN ART   MAC ALLISTER STREET   BUILDING   STREET

MAC ALLISTER   VETERAN'S   MUSEUM   Civic   PUBLIC   GREYHOUND   MINNA

BUILDING   CITY HALL   Center   LIBRARY   BUS DEPOT   NATOMA

FULTON   STREET   WAR MEMORIAL   Plaza   MISSION   HOWARD   STR

GROVE   OPERA HOUSE   GROVE   BILL GRAHAM

IVY   STREET   LOUISE M. DAVIES   STREET   CIVIC AUDITORIUM   MINNA

HAYES   STREET   SYMPHONY HALL   HAYES STREET   NATOMA   FOLSOM STREET

LINDEN   STREET   FELL   STREET   9TH STREET   HOWARD

6 HICKORY STREET   HICKORY   OAK STREET   MARKET 10 TH ST.   STR

A B C

SAN JOSE-SALINAS-MONTEREY

POINT LOBOS

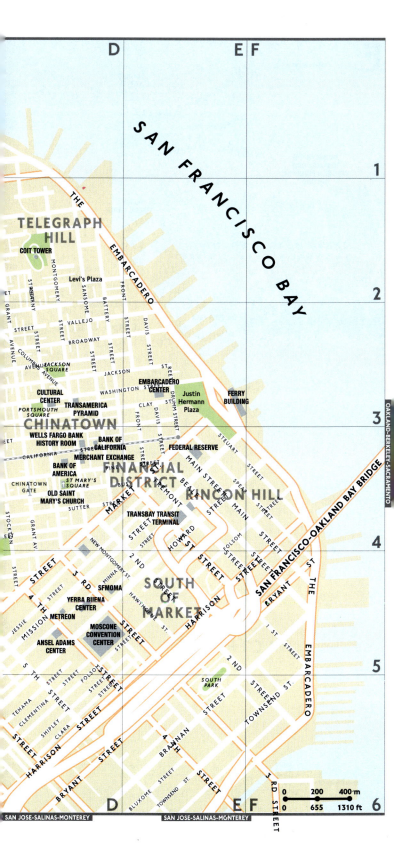

◆ LOS ANGELES

F

A **B** **C**

CHATSWORTH
RES.

VAN NUYS
AIRPORT ✈

HOLLYWOOD

SAN FERNANDO VALLEY

TUJUNGA WASH

SHOUP AV

LOS ANGELES RIVER

SAN DIEGO FREEWAY

SAN FRANCISCO

1

MOTION PICTURE
TELEVISION FUND-
HOSPITAL & RESIDENTIAL
SERVICES

VENTURA FREEWAY

ENCINO

VENTURA

SHERMAN
OAKS

SKIRBALL
CULTURAL CENTER

GLENVIEW

STONE
CANYON
RES.

WESTWOOD BD

WESTWOOD
VILLAGE

CITY
HALL

SANTA MONICA MOUNTAINS
NATIONAL RECREATION AREA

TOPANGA

THE UNIVERSITY
OF CALIFORNIA
AT LOS ANGELES

SUNSET BLVD

MONICA

2

TOPANGA STATE
PARK

GETTY
CENTER

BEVERLY
HILLS

MUSEUM
OF TELEVISION
& RADIO

MALIBU

THE GETTY VILLA

UCLA HAMMER
MUSEUM

WEST
LOS ANGELES

WESTWOOD
MEMORIAL PARK

MUSEUM OF
TOLERANCE

PACIFIC COAST HIGHWAY

SUNSET BD

PALISADES
PARK

WILSHIRE BLVD

SANTA MONICA BLVD

SAN DIEGO FREEWAY

MGM/
SONY PICTURES

MALIBU LAGOON
STATE BEACH

PACIFIC
PALISADES

SANTA
MONICA

SANTA

MUS. OF JURASSIC
TECHNOLOGY

3

LINCOLN BLVD

VENICE

MARINA
DEL REY

SANTA MONICA BAY

PLAYA
DEL REY

✈
LAX
LOS ANGELES
INTERNATIONAL
AIRPORT

4

MANHATTAN
BEACH

SOUTH
BAY

PACIFIC COAST

PACIFIC

REDONDO
BEACH

5

OCEAN

PALOS VERDES
POINT

RANCHO
PALOS VERDES

ABALONE
COVE BEACH

0   3   6 km
0   1.9   3.8 miles

6 **A** **B** **C**

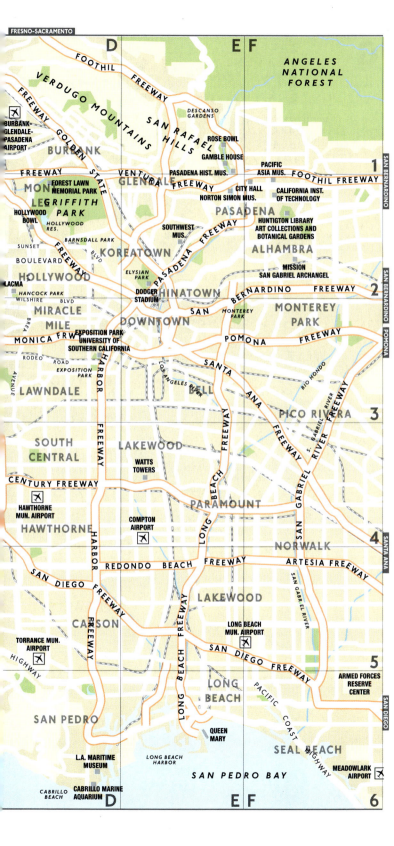

G

SAN FRANCISCO

A B   **C**   L O S

CAMARILLO   AV.

N. HOLLYWOOD

VENTURA

ALAMEDA AV.

RIVERSIDE DR.

FREEWAY

WALT DISNEY
STUDIOS
NBC
STUDIOS TOUR

RIVERSIDE DR.

MOORPARK ST.

NORTH HOLLYWOOD

WARNER BROS
VIP TOUR

FOREST LAWN DR.

TRAVEL TOWN
MUSEUM

COLFAX AV.

LANKERSHIM BLVD

TUJUNGA AV.

VINELAND AV.

CAHUENGA BD

OLIVE

BARHAM BLVD

LAKESIDE
GOLF
CLUB

FOREST LAWN
MEMORIAL PARK
(HOLLYWOOD HILLS)

WEDDINGTON
PARK

HOLLYWOOD BLVD

UNIVERSAL
STUDIOS TOUR

VENTURA

UNIVERSAL CITY

1   UNIVERSAL
CITY

HOLLYWOOD
SIGN

LAUREL

HOLLYWOOD FREEWAY

CANYON DR.

MULHOLLAND

WOODROW

WILSON DR.

HOLLYWOOD
RES.

LAUREL
CANYON
PARK

WOODROW

DRIVE

MOUNT

GRIFFITH OBSERVATORY,
PLANETARIUM, THEATRE
AND LASERIUM

BOULEVARD

WATTLES
PARK

HOLLYWOOD BOWL

GOWER DR.

2

HOLLYWOOD /
HIGHLAND

MANN'S
CHINESE
THEATER

HOLLYWOOD
STUDIO
MUSEUM

HOLLYWOOD
VINE

HOLLYWOOD / WESTERN

ENTERTAINMENT MUS.

HOLLYWOOD WAX
MUSEUM

CAPITOL
RECORDS
TOWER

SUNSET PLAZA

HOLLYWOOD (WALK

HIGHLAND

HOLLYWOOD ROOSEVELT
HOTEL

OF FAME)

BOULEVARD

KOREATOWN

BD

EL
CAPITAN
THEATER

CELEBRITY LINGERIE
HALL OF FAME

VINE ST.

HOLLYWOOD

WEST
HOLLYWOOD

W. SUNSET BD

EGYPTIAN
THEATER

W. SUNSET

SUNSET

CURSON

FOUNTAIN

AVENUE

AVENUE

SANTA   MONICA   BOULEVARD

3

SUNSET STRIP

SCHINDLER
HOUSE

SAN

LA BLVD

FAIRFAX

AV.

FULLER AV.

LA BREA AV.

HOLLYWOOD FOREVER
MEMORIAL PARK

PARAMOUNT
STUDIOS

WESTERN AV.

NORMANDIE

MELROSE

LA CIENEGA

NORTH KINGS ROAD

JOLLA

HEIGHTS

AV.

MELROSE

VAN NESS

WILTON PK

SANTA MONICA

DR.

SAN VICENTE

BEVERLY

WILSHIRE
COUNTRY
CLUB

BEVERLY

BD

DOHENY

ROBERTSONS

CRESCENT

AV.

BOULEVARD

CBS TELEVISION CITY

W. 3RD ST.

FARMERS MARKET

ROSSMORE AVENUE

W. 3RD ST.

WILSHIRE /
NORMANDIE

4

BLVD

HANCOCK PARK

LACMA

WILSHIRE

PETERSEN AUTOMOTIVE
MUSEUM

GEORGE C. PAGE MUSEUM
OF LA BREA DISCOVERIES

CRAFT AND FOLK
ART MUSEUM

WILSHIRE BD

RD

SOUTH

WILSHIRE /
WESTERN

WEST 8TH

WEST

BD

W. PICO BLVD

AV.

FAIRFAX

CURSON AV.

COCHRAN AV.

MUIRFIELD RD

OLYMPIC BOULEV

MIRACLE
MILE

W. PICO BLVD

WESTERN

VENICE

AIRDROME

ST.

BOULEVARD

BD

5

CADILLAC

AV.

VENICE

BLVD

VINEYARD AV.

W. WASHINGTON BOULEVARD

NORMANDIE

SANTA   MONICA   FREEWAY

W. WASHINGTON

ADAMS

BOULEVARD

ADAMS

AVENUE

SANTA MONICA

NATIONAL BD

LA BREA

W. JEFFERSON BLVD

CRENSHAW

W. JEFFERSON BLVD

BD

HIGUERA ST.

BD

RODEO

ROAD

HEPBURN

ARLINGTON

AV.

JEFFERSON

CULVER
CITY
PARK

KENNETH
HAHN
STATE
PARK

COLISEUM ST

MARTIN LUTHER KING JR

SOUTH
CENTRAL

6   **A B**   **C**

BOULEVARD

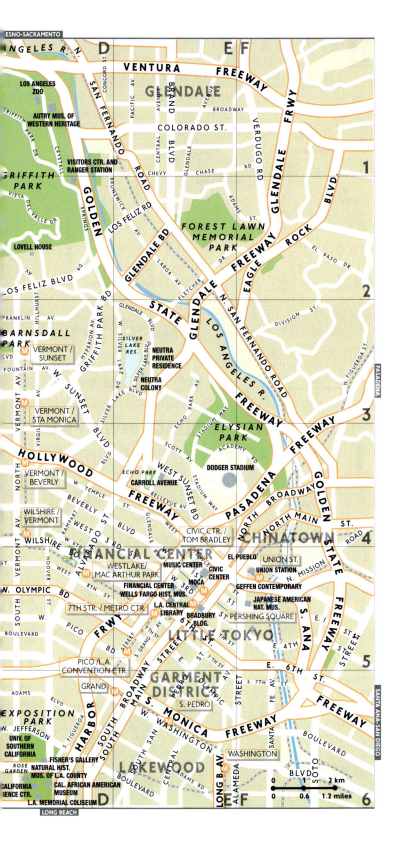

◆ PASADENA

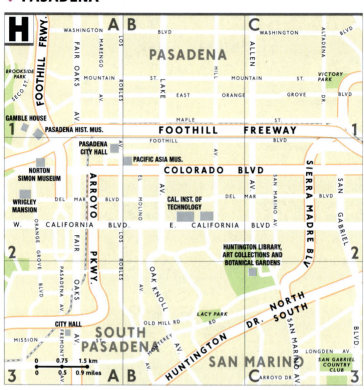

H

WASHINGTON | A | B | BLVD | C | WASHINGTON | ALTADENA | BLVD

FOOTHILL FRWY.

FAIR OAKS | MARENGO | LOS ROBLES | AV.

PASADENA

BROOKSIDE PARK

SECO ST.

MOUNTAIN | AV.

ST. | LAKE

HILL

MOUNTAIN | ST. | GROVE | DR. | **VICTORY PARK**

ALLEN

EAST | ORANGE | BLVD

GAMBLE HOUSE

MAPLE | ST.

1   **PASADENA HIST. MUS.**   **FOOTHILL**   **FREEWAY**   **1**

PASADENA CITY HALL

FOOTHILL | AV. | BLVD

PACIFIC ASIA MUS.

NORTON SIMON MUSEUM

ARROYO

COLORADO BLVD

AV. | AV. | SAN MARINO AV.

SIERRA MADRE BLV

SAN GABRIEL

EL MOLINO

DEL MAR

CAL. INST. OF TECHNOLOGY

WRIGLEY MANSION

DEL MAR | BLVD.

W. | ORANGE GROVE BLVD | CALIFORNIA | BLVD. | E. | CALIFORNIA | BLVD

FAIR OAKS | PKWY. | LOS ROBLES

2   **HUNTINGTON LIBRARY, ART COLLECTIONS AND BOTANICAL GARDENS**   **2**

PASADENA AV.

OAK KNOLL AV.

LACY PARK RD

NORTH SOUTH

CITY HALL

OLD MILL RD

HUNTINGTON DR.

SAN MARINO AV.

BLVD.

MISSION | ST. | FREMONT | **SOUTH PASADENA**

MONTEREY | AV.

LONGDEN AV.

0   0.75   1.5 km

SAN MARINO

SAN GABRIEL COUNTRY CLUB

0   0.5   0.9 miles   **A**   **B**   HUNTINGTON   **C** Arroyo Dr.   **3**

◆ BEL AIR, WESTWOOD VILLAGE, BEVERLY HILLS

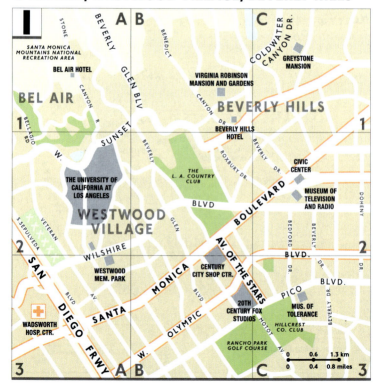

I

STONE | A | BEVERLY | B | BENEDICT | C | COLDWATER CANYON DR.

SANTA MONICA MOUNTAINS NATIONAL RECREATION AREA

GLEN BLV

GREYSTONE MANSION

BEL AIR HOTEL

CANYON R

VIRGINIA ROBINSON MANSION AND GARDENS

BEL AIR

BELLAGIO RD

CANYON DR

BEVERLY HILLS

1   **BEVERLY HILLS HOTEL**   **1**

W.

SUNSET

BEVERLY

ROXBURY DR.

BEVERLY DR.

CIVIC CENTER

THE UNIVERSITY OF CALIFORNIA AT LOS ANGELES

THE L. A. COUNTRY CLUB

BLVD.

BOULEVARD

MUSEUM OF TELEVISION AND RADIO

DOHENY

VETERAN

S. SEPULVEDA

WESTWOOD VILLAGE

GLEN

BEDFORD

BEVERLY

2   WILSHIRE   AV. OF THE STARS   BLVD.   **2**

SAN

WESTWOOD MEM. PARK

MONICA

CENTURY CITY SHOP CTR.

DIEGO

SANTA

BLVD

PICO

BEVERLY DR.

DR.

BLVD.

FRWY

W.

OLYMPIC

MOTOR

20TH CENTURY FOX STUDIOS

MUS. OF TOLERANCE

WADSWORTH HOSP. CTR.

HILLCREST CO. CLUB

RANCHO PARK GOLF COURSE

0   0.6   1.3 km

0   0.4   0.8 miles

3   **A**   **B**   **C**   **3**

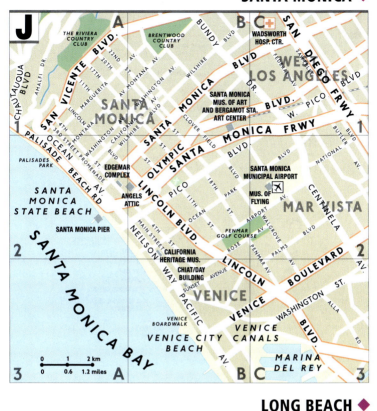

SANTA MONICA ◆

J

THE RIVIERA COUNTRY CLUB

BRENTWOOD COUNTRY CLUB

WADSWORTH HOSP. CTR.

BUNDY BLVD.

SAN DIEGO FRWY

WEST LOS ANGELES

CHAUTAUQUA BLVD

AMALFI DR.

SAN VICENTE BLVD.

22ND 20TH 17TH 11TH

MARGUERITA AV.

MONTANA AV.

WASHINGTON AV.

CALIFORNIA AV.

WILSHIRE

SANTA MONICA

SANTA MONICA BLVD.

SANTA MONICA MUS. OF ART AND BERGAMOT STA. ART CENTER

W. PICO BLVD.

FEDERAL

NATIONAL AV.

BUTLER BLVD.

1

PALISADES PARK

OCEAN

PALISADE BEACH RD.

LINCOLN BLVD.

4TH 3RD

OLYMPIC

CLOVER FIELD

SANTA MONICA FRWY

BLVD.

EDGEMAR COMPLEX

SANTA MONICA STATE BEACH

SANTA MONICA PIER

ANGELS ATTIC

ST.

LINCOLN BLVD.

PICO

11TH ST.

OCEAN ST.

18TH

PARK ST.

AIRPORT

SANTA MONICA MUNICIPAL AIRPORT

MUS. OF FLYING ✈

WALGROVE AV.

CENTINELA AV.

MAR VISTA

2

SANTA MONICA BAY

NEILSON WAY

4TH ST.

MAIN STREET

CALIFORNIA HERITAGE MUS.

CHIAT/DAY BUILDING

PACIFIC

AVENUE

PENMAR GOLF COURSE

ROSE AV.

PENMAR AV.

PALMS

LINCOLN

VENICE

BOULEVARD

ST.

ALLA RD.

SUNSET

VENICE BOARDWALK

VENICE CITY BEACH

VENICE

VENICE CANALS

WASHINGTON BLVD.

MARINA DEL REY

3

0 1 2 km
0 0.6 1.2 miles

A　　**B** **C**

LONG BEACH ◆

K

LONG BEACH FRWY.

WILLOW ST.

WILLOW ST.

SIGNAL HILL

STEARNS PARK

SANTA FE AV.

SAN FRANCISCO AV.

LOS ANGELES AV.

HILL

PACIFIC

LONG BEACH BLVD.

ATLANTIC AV.

CALIFORNIA AV.

ORANGE

CHERRY AV.

JUNIPERO

HILL ST.

REDONDO

Los Alamitos Circle

PACIFIC COAST HWY

1

LONG BEACH RIVER

PACIFIC

COAST

PACIFIC COAST HWY Ⓜ

HIGHWAY

XIMENO

ANAHEIM

AV.

ANAHEIM ST.

Ⓜ ANAHEIM

ANAHEIM ST.

MAGNOLIA

10TH

7TH 6TH

PACIFIC

Ⓜ
CIVIC CENTER

Ⓜ
TRANSIT MALL

5TH ST.

Ⓜ 1ST ST.

ST.

2ND ST.

7TH ST.

4TH ST.

2ND ST.

ST.

AV.

LONG BEACH

4TH ST.

7TH ST.

NAPLES

APPIAN WAY

2

HARBOR SCENIC DR.

L.B. AQUARIUM OF THE PACIFIC

QUEEN MARY

L.B. MUSEUM OF ART

E. OCEAN

BROADWAY

BELMONT PIER

BOULEVARD

LIVINGSTON DR.

GETAWAY GONDOLA

PANORAMA DR.

HARBOR SCENIC DR.

LONG BEACH HARBOR

WHITE ISLAND

FREEMAN ISLAND

CHAFFEE ISLAND

3

SAN PEDRO BAY

0 1 2 km
0 0.6 1.2 miles

A　　**B** **C**

◆ REDWOOD NATIONAL AND STATE PARKS

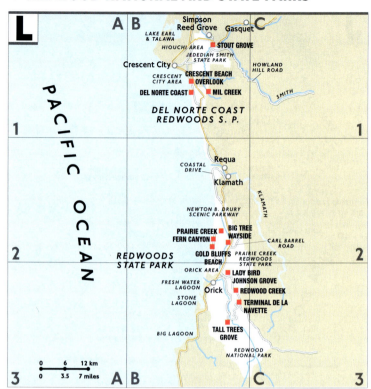

◆ YOSEMITE NATIONAL PARK

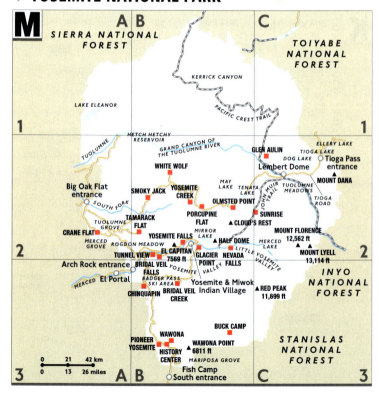

SEQUOIA AND KINGS CANYON NATIONAL PARKS ◆

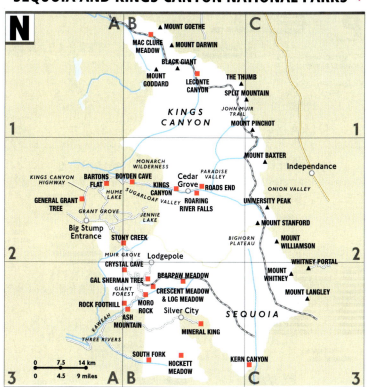

N

A B   C

▲ MOUNT GOETHE

MAC CLURE
MEADOW

▲ MOUNT DARWIN

BLACK GIANT
▲

MOUNT
GODDARD

LECONTE
CANYON

THE THUMB

SPLIT MOUNTAIN

*KINGS
CANYON*

*JOHN MUIR
TRAIL*

MOUNT PINCHOT

1   1

MOUNT BAXTER ▲

*MONARCH
WILDERNESS*

*PARADISE
VALLEY*

Cedar
Grove

Independence ○

*KINGS CANYON
HIGHWAY*

BARTONS
FLAT

BOYDEN CAVE

KINGS
CANYON

ROADS END

ONION VALLEY

*HUME
LAKE*

SUGARLOAF VALLEY

ROARING
RIVER FALLS

UNIVERSITY PEAK

GENERAL GRANT
TREE

GRANT GROVE

*JENNIE
LAKE*

▲ MOUNT STANFORD

Big Stump
Entrance

STONY CREEK

*BIGHORN
PLATEAU*

MOUNT
WILLIAMSON ▲

2   2

MUIR GROVE

Lodgepole

CRYSTAL CAVE

WHITNEY PORTAL

GAL SHERMAN TREE

BEARPAW MEADOW

MOUNT
WHITNEY ▲

*GIANT
FOREST*

CRESCENT MEADOW
& LOG MEADOW

MOUNT LANGLEY ▲

ROCK FOOTHILL

MORO
ROCK

Silver City ○

SEQUOIA

ASH
MOUNTAIN

KAWEAH

MINERAL KING

THREE RIVERS

SOUTH FORK

HOCKETT
MEADOW

KERN CANYON

0	7.5	14 km
0	4.5	9 miles

3   A   B   C   3

DEATH VALLEY NATIONAL PARK ◆

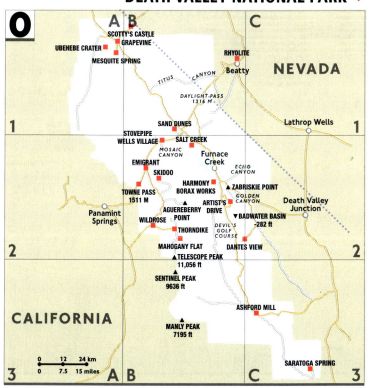

O

A B   C

SCOTTY'S CASTLE
GRAPEVINE

UBEHEBE CRATER

RHYOLITE

MESQUITE SPRING

Beatty ○

NEVADA

TITUS   CANYON

*DAYLIGHT PASS
1316 M.*

1   1

SAND DUNES

Lathrop Wells ○

STOVEPIPE
WELLS VILLAGE

SALT CREEK

*MOSAIC
CANYON*

Furnace
Creek

EMIGRANT

*ECHO
CANYON*

SKIDOO

HARMONY
BORAX WORKS

▼ ZABRISKIE POINT

TOWNE PASS
1511 M

ARTIST'S
DRIVE

*GOLDEN
CANYON*

Death Valley
Junction ○

Panamint
Springs ○

AGUEREBERRY
POINT

WILDROSE

▼ BADWATER BASIN
-282 ft

THORNDIKE

*DEVIL'S
GOLF
COURSE*

MAHOGANY FLAT

DANTES VIEW

2   2

▲ TELESCOPE PEAK
11,056 ft

▲ SENTINEL PEAK
9636 ft

ASHFORD MILL

CALIFORNIA

▲ MANLY PEAK
7195 ft

0	12	24 km
0	7.5	15 miles

SARATOGA SPRING

3   A   B   C   3

◆ SAN DIEGO

P

A B C

UNIVERSITY OF CALIFORNIA-SAN DIEGO
V. A. MEDICAL CEN.

STEPHEN BIRCH AQUARIUM MUSEUM

UNIVERSITY TOWNE CENTRE

TERRA SANTA

LA JOLLA

PROSPECT

SOLEDAD PARK

GOVERNOR DR.

MARION BEAR PARK

GILMAN DR.

JACOB DEKEMA FREEWAY

CABRILLO FREEWAY

SANTO BLVD

MISSION TRAILS REG. PARK

LAKESIDE

LA JOLLA

CLAIREMONT

MESA

CLAIREMONT MESA

AVENUE

1

SESSIONS MEMORIAL PARK

BALBOA

MISSION VILLAGE

MISSION SAN DIEGO DE ALCALÁ

EL CAJON

PACIFIC BEACH

MISSION BAY PARK

GRAND AVENUE

MISSION BOULEVARD

MISSION BAY PARK

SEA WORLD

UNIVERSITY OF SAN DIEGO

FASHION VALLEY MALL

MISSION VALLEY

FRIARS ROAD

JACK MURPHY STADIUM

MISSION VALLEY FRWY SHOP. CEN.

KAISER FOUND. HOSPITAL

YUMA

2

MISSION BAY

OLD TOWN

JUNIPERO SERRA MUS.

PRESIDIO PARK
OLD TOWN ST. HIST. PARK

UCSD MEDICAL CENTER

NORTH PARK

EL CAJON BLVD

UNIVERSITY AV.

SOUTH PARK

JACOB DEKEMA

OCEAN BEACH

SPORTS ARENA

LE BAZAR DEL MUNDO

PACIFIC HIGHWAY

LINDBERGH FIELD

6TH AVENUE

FREEWAY

ZOO

MUSEUM

BALBOA PARK

SPRING VALLEY

POINT LOMA NAZARENE COLL.

LA PLAYA

SHELTER ISLAND

LOMA PORTAL

HARBOR DR.

CENTRAL

C. DE CITY

Horton Plaza

30TH STREET

GOLDEN HILL

JR FREEWAY

VILLA MONTEZUMA

3

SEAPORT VILLAGE

M. L. KING

STOCKTON

FORT ROSECRANS NATIONAL CEMETERY

CARRILLO MEMORIAL BLVD

POINT LOMA

CABRILLO NATIONAL MONUMENT

CORONADO

HOTEL DEL CORONADO

ORANGE AV.

CORONADO BAY BRIDGE

HARBOR DR.

CONV. CEN.

IMPERIAL AVENUE

NATIONAL AV.

WABASH BOULEVARD

EUCLID AVENUE

HIGHLAND

TIJUANA

NATIONAL CITY

4

SAN DIEGO BAY

SILVER STRAND

CHULA VISTA NATURE INTERPRETIVE CENTER

CHULA VISTA CEN.

CHULA VISTA

18TH ST.

H ST.

BROADWAY

BAYER BLVD.

FREEWAY

SILVER STRAND STATE BEACH

IMPERIAL BEACH

5

PALM AVENUE

CRONADO AVENUE

TIJUANA RIVER NAT'L. ESTUARINE RESEARCH RESERVE

MONUMENT ROAD

TIJUANA

0   2   4 km
0   1   2 miles

6   A   B   C   6

Q

LOS ANGELES

A | **B** | **C**

BALBOA PARK

COUNTY ADMINISTRATION CENTER

CO. CEN. / CEDAR ST.

CALIF. WESTERN SCHOOL OF LAW

AEROSPACE HALL OF FAME

BALBOA STADIUM

MARITIME MUSEUM & STAR OF INDIA

STATE BUILDING

ASH

COPLEY SYMPHONY HALL

RUSS BOULEVARD

BROADWAY ST–PIER

AMERICA PLAZA TRANSFER STATION

MUSEUM OF CONT. ART

Emerald Plaza

America Plaza

SAN DIEGO CONCOURSE

U.S. GRANT HOTEL

SAN DIEGO CITY COLLEGE

POLICE HEADQUARTERS

BROADWAY PIER

SANTA FE RAILWAY DEPOT

WYNDHAM HOTEL

U.S. CT. HOUSE

BROADWAY

NAVY PIER

CRUISE SHIP TERMINAL

METRO. CORR. CEN.

THE PALADION

INT'L VISITORS INFORMATIONS CENTER

Horton Plaza

GASLAMP QUARTER HISTORIC DISTRICT

MARKET

US GRANT HOTEL

CHILDREN'S MUSEUM

DAVIS HOUSE

GASLAMP QUARTER

ISLAND AVENUE

SEAPORT VILLAGE

HARBOR

SAN DIEGO CONV. CEN.

IMPERIAL AVENUE

EMBARCADERO MARINA

CONVENTION WAY

GULL STREET

0 — 300 — 600 m
0 — 985 — 1970 ft

A | **B** | **C**

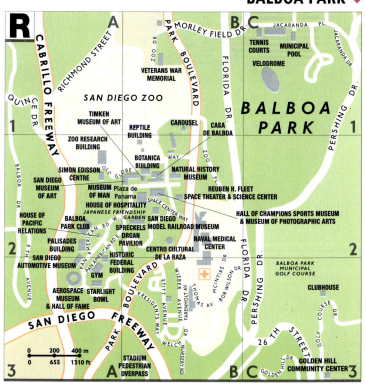

R

A | **B** | **C**

CABRILLO FREEWAY

MORLEY FIELD DR.

JACARANDA PL.

RICHMOND STREET

PARK BOULEVARD

VETERANS WAR MEMORIAL

TENNIS COURTS

MUNICIPAL POOL

VELODROME

SAN DIEGO ZOO

BALBOA PARK

TIMKEN MUSEUM OF ART

ZOO RESEARCH BUILDING

REPTILE BUILDING

CAROUSEL

CASA DE BALBOA

BOTANICA BUILDING

NATURAL HISTORY MUSEUM

SIMON EDISSON CENTRE

SAN DIEGO MUSEUM OF ART

MUSEUM OF MAN

Plaza de Panama

REUBEN H. FLEET SPACE THEATER & SCIENCE CENTER

HOUSE OF PACIFIC RELATIONS

HOUSE OF HOSPITALITY

JAPANESE FRIENDSHIP GARDEN

SAN DIEGO MODEL RAILROAD MUSEUM

HALL OF CHAMPIONS SPORTS MUSEUM & MUSEUM OF PHOTOGRAPHIC ARTS

BALBOA PARK CLUB

SPRECKELS ORGAN PAVILION

NAVAL MEDICAL CENTER

PALISADES BUILDING

CENTRO CULTURAL DE LA RAZA

SAN DIEGO AUTOMOTIVE MUSEUM

HISTORIC FEDERAL BUILDING

GYM

BALBOA PARK MUNICIPAL GOLF COURSE

CLUBHOUSE

AEROSPACE MUSEUM & HALL OF FAME

STARLIGHT BOWL

SAN DIEGO FREEWAY

PARK BOULEVARD

26 TH STREET

GOLDEN HILL COMMUNITY CENTER

0 — 200 — 400 m
0 — 655 — 1310 ft

STADIUM PEDESTRIAN OVERPASS

A | **B** | **C**

◆ SAN FRANCISCO PUBLIC TRANSPORT

◆ LOS ANGELES PUBLIC TRANSPORT

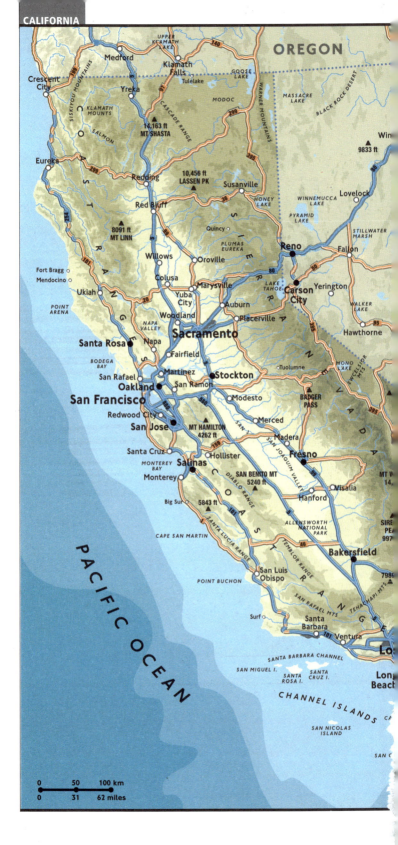